MODERN JEWISH HISTORY

Robert Mandel, series editor

Unwanted Legacies

Sharing the Burden of
Post-Genocide Generations

Gottfried Wagner
and
Abraham J. Peck

Forewords by Michael Berenbaum and
Steven Leonard Jacobs

Translation of Gottfried Wagner's manuscript
by Ivan Fehrenbach

Texas Tech University Press

This book is typeset in Minion. The paper used in this book meets the minimum requirements of ANSI/NISO Z39.48-1992 (R1997). ∞

Designed by Jouve North America

Cover design by Ashley Beck

Cover photographs courtesy of Gottfried Wagner and Abraham Peck

Library of Congress Cataloging-in-Publication Data

Wagner, Gottfried, author.
    Unwanted legacies : sharing the burden of post-genocide generations / Gottfried Wagner and Abraham J. Peck ; forewords by Michael Berenbaum and Steven Leonard Jacobs.
        pages cm.—(Modern Jewish history) Includes bibliographical references and index.
    ISBN 978-0-89672-834-9 (hardback)—ISBN 978-0-89672-835-6 (paperback)—ISBN 978-0-89672-836-3 (e-book) 1. Holocaust, Jewish (1939–1945)—Influence. 2. Holocaust, Jewish (1939-1945)—Moral and ethical aspects. 3. Wagner family. 4. Wagner, Gottfried—Biography. 5. Peck family. 6. Peck, Abraham J.—Biography. 7. Reconciliation—Social aspects. 8. Germany—Ethnic relations. I. Peck, Abraham J., author. II. Title.
    D804.7.M67.W34 2014
    940.53'180922—dc23

                                                                                    2013036234

14 15 16 17 18 19 20 21 22 / 9 8 7 6 5 4 3 2 1

Texas Tech University Press
Box 41037
Lubbock, Texas 79409-1037 USA
800.832.4042
ttup@ttu.edu
www.ttupress.org

I dedicate my part of this book with Abraham J. Peck to my courageous, beloved, and always loyal mother-in-law, Antonietta Malacrida (February 16, 1921–March 20, 2006).

Gottfried Wagner

I dedicate my portion of this book to the memory of my parents, Shalom and Anna (Kolton) Peck, z"l and to the memory of my murdered grandfather, uncles, aunts, and extended families. May their memory be for a blessing and may their suffering be a source of redemption for our world and for all those who continue to suffer.

I also dedicate this portion of the book to my wife, Jean Marcus Peck, and my children, Abby and Joel. They have shared the journey to this publication with love, understanding, and support. I am forever grateful.

Abraham J. Peck

Contents

I

The Shadows of Richard Wagner as a German Myth   1
Gottfried Wagner

Ilustrations

Three generations of the Drexel family with their African relatives
Eugenio, Teresina, Gottfried, and Stella

Plates following page 250

Zwolen synagogue, destroyed by the Nazis in 1939–1940
Synagogue in Linshits/Łęczyca, Poland
Yankel, Chaskel, and Asher Zelig
Documents from the Buchenwald concentration camp
Document ordering the transfer of prisoners
List of prisoners being transported from Stutthof to Dresden
Abe in the arms of his father at the Landsberg Jewish DP camp (1947)
The *USS General C. H. Muir*
A Jewish New Year's card: Abraham, his mother, and his father
Part of the *USS General Muir* passenger list
Partial list of immigrants sailing on the *USS General Muir*
Peck in conversation in Linshits/Łęczyca
56 Franciszkanska Street
Plaque commemorating the April 1945 death march
Ulica Zydowksa (Jews' Street)
Sitting with Stephan Kwapisiencz
Father Zbigniew Luczak, Łęczyca priest
Site of Jewish cemetery in Zwolen
Stone quarry (Steinbruch)
Schandauer Strasse 68, the cigarette factory in Dresden
Hans Biebow, German administrator of the Łódź ghetto
Plaque commemorating Jewish slave laborers
Abraham and proud parents shortly after his birth (1946)
Abby and Joel Peck
Abraham and wife Jean
Major Irving Heymont and Dr. Samuel Gringauz

Foreword

Rabbi Irving "Yitz" Greenberg once remarked that it is a paradox of the Holocaust that "the innocent feel guilty and the guilty innocent."

No generation is more innocent than those Germans who were born after the war, who never marched in Nazi parades, never cheered Hitler, never wore a Wehrmacht uniform, never joined the SS, never served in the *Einsatzgruppen* or in the death camps, and never participated directly or indirectly in the killing process. They have shed no blood and yet they are the descendents of those who did. This legacy has been haunting to the best of them.

There is much psychological research into survivor guilt, many discussions about the guilt of the perpetrator by psychiatrists and sociologists, historians and theologians, ethicists and jurists, but there are few perpetrators who have confessed to their own guilt, who were haunted by their past deeds. Their memoirs are few; their visits to mental health professionals rare.

Some eighteen years ago Daniel Jonah Goldhagen's controversial book *Hitler's Willing Executioners* provoked strong feelings among Holocaust scholars who felt uncomfortable, perhaps even angered, by his sweeping generalization. Yet even as his work was provoking stinging criticism at home, he traveled to Germany and held extensive dialogues with German students who had rejected the working assumptions of the first generation of post-Holocaust Germans who made peace with their past—and their parents—by distinguishing between Nazis and Germans, and who shaped a "preferred narrative," the all too comfortable story that many Germans had opposed Hitler's regime. The first generation after were prepared if not to minimize the crime of their parents, then at least to limit the scope of Nazi domination. A decade earlier Helmut Kohl had sought to close the chapter on the Holocaust for Germans by having President Ronald Reagan visit

Bitburg and differentiate between the "bad Nazis" and the good German soldiers. His efforts were unsuccessful not only because of domestic opposition to Reagan's visit within the United States but because in the coming decade German youth were prepared to confront the past.

Thus university students—grandchildren of the perpetrators—sat with Goldhagen well into the night as he spoke of the central role of anti-Semitism in the Nazi enterprise and told them that that it was "ordinary Germans," not Professor Christopher Browning's "ordinary men," who had perpetrated the genocide now known as the Holocaust. Their grandparents, Goldhagen argued, moved easily—all too easily—from the "eliminationist" anti-Semitism that had characterized the early years of the Nazi regime to "exterminationist" anti-Semitism as it progressed from mobile killing units to stationary mobile gas vans and found its ultimate expression in the death camps— systematic killing centers, termed "extermination centers" by their creators, where industrialized killing became routine. The then youngest generation of Germans was prepared to ask the tough question and unwilling to accept a simple solution.

Unwanted Legacies is the story of a friendship, an unlikely friendship, between two men of the same generation, one whose last name is virtually synonymous with Nazi ideology and anti-Semitism and the other who is the descendant of ordinary Jews who suffered brutally at the hand of the perpetrators.

Gottfried Wagner is the great grandson of Richard Wagner, a musical genius and a notorious anti-Semite, whose ideology and talent were exploited posthumously in the service of the Reich. His family was an intimate of Hitler, and Gottfried has become the enfant terrible of that family for confronting its legacy and telling the uncomfortable truths of the Nazi era and its cover-up. Estranged from his father and his grandmother, denounced by others in his family who wanted to continue the legacy of Bayreuth, their key to wealth and significance, and to cleanse it, he chose to live in Italy and convert to Catholicism—his family legacy was so deeply Protestant—as he confronted the past he had to reject. Yet he never changed his name for to do so would rid him of the past all too easily; something he refused to do.

Even given his family's past and the difficulties of the Wagner name, it must be stressed that Gottfried Wagner has built a successful and professional life in the world of music and theater, supported by his Italian family. His important and perceptive analyses of his family's past, his great-grandfather's own anti-Semitism and work, and his family's direct links to National Socialism have been welcomed in many circles, and his family heritage in no way diminishes his own important work as a successful musicologist.

His partner in dialogue, his unlikely friend, is Professor Abraham J. Peck who, despite his academic and intellectual achievements, grew up with the wounds of the children of survivors. His parents were not "Holocaust royalty" but working-class, simple Jews, who struggled to make a living in the United States and to adjust to their new surroundings. They acted with honor and decency and gave all that they could of their limited resources and unlimited love to their beloved son.

Before friendship could blossom two requirements had to be met. Both men had to tell the truth of their origins, and both had to stress the ties that bind rather than the divisions that could not be bridged.

Gottfried Wagner's narrative is deeply rich. A musical historian, he has written a history of German music and German politics from the days of Richard Wagner forward. It examines the legacy of Wagner and Bayreuth, not only for its scion but for the German people and the West. He is brutally honest but also scrupulously fair. He airs his family laundry in public rather than pretend otherwise and only thus purges himself of that stain.

Abraham Peck's story is not German but American. His is not the legacy of world renowned figures but of the time and place in which he was raised, post-war America and its Jewish community that welcomed the future and not the past and that received the survivors conditionally and embraced them halfheartedly. One must, however, honor his decision to engage his personal history in his scholarship and in his many writings and to uncover in archives and in historical works the past that was shared with him in anecdotes and poignant instructions. He lived in Germany, he traveled to Poland, a land of dread to his parents, and he surrounded himself with the documents that bore witness to the crime that so few had lived to tell. He did so with integrity and tenacity, with talent and creativity, and through his archival work he enabled others to encounter this past. Though the world he traversed, which consisted of scholars and rabbis, of Germans, Poles, and Jews was so distant from the more basic world of his parents, there is no distance between father and son. He tells of the evening after the burial of his mother when his father refused to sleep in the marital bed so father and son slept on the floor *together*—echoing the Hebrew word for together—as one.

Permit me a personal word: I am neither the child of Holocaust survivors nor of refugees. My parents were both born in Europe, but they came to the United States as very young children when in the second decade of the twentieth century their parents decided to immigrate for safety, security, and economic opportunity. My parents were immigrants' kids who were raised in Yiddish and saw it as their task to "Americanize," to speak unaccented English and to "make it in America." My grandparents harbored no nostalgia for Europe, and no matter how tortured their English, they cherished the freedom of America, which was a land of opportunity for them and above all for their children. I grew up in a traditional world. My teachers at yeshiva were either survivors or refugees; the synagogue we attended religiously was comprised of German-Jewish refugees with portable wealth who had escaped Nazi Germany or nearby Belgium or France while there was still time and tried to recreate the lost Orthodox world of Frankfurt or Antwerp on American soil. I was surrounded by the children of survivors, many like my friend Abe Peck. If truth be told, we were conscious not of their parents' survival but of their immigrant status.

Reading this book came at an opportune moment, it seemed almost *bashert*. I was cognizant of the story of Germans who confronted their past and asked unwanted questions and were thus forced into exile. Some two decades ago I saw the film *The Nasty Girl*, the story of a young girl who set out to tell of the heroism of her townspeople, who had opposed Nazism and offered a haven to Jews, only to discover that the opposite had been the case and that the entire postwar story had been fabricated. When she wrote her high school term paper, she scandalized the entire town, Passau in Bavaria, which soon could no longer be her home. Shortly thereafter, I got to know the formidable Anna Rosmus—in exile from Germany—and to work with her at the United States Holocaust Memorial Museum. I understood her choice of exile, her integrity, and her courage.

Last year the Los Angeles Opera performed the *Ring Cycle*, Richard Wagner's great operatic masterwork. The LA Opera invited all the cultural institutions, museums and universities, schools and theaters in Los Angeles to join them in celebration of Wagner. Naturally, at the Sigi Ziering Institute, which explores the ethical and religious implications of the Holocaust at the American Jewish University, we could not celebrate Wagner but had to confront the legacy of Richard Wagner's anti-Semitism, and so we convened a day-long symposium just as the *Ring Cycle* was opening. We invited Gottfried Wagner and then began to hear all the stories of how he had betrayed his family and his legacy. The more he was attacked, the more comfortable I felt in the invitation that we had tendered. Gottfried Wagner did not disappoint. His presentation was insightful and informative, powerful and passionate, deeply reflective of what you will read in this book.

And in the spring of 2012, I was invited to Mexico to speak on the Holocaust. I was told that my partner in the lecture series would be a Himmler, as in the family of Heinrich. I was taken aback. So I began to read Katrin Himmler's work *The Himmler Brothers,* which reexamined the role of her family in the history of the Holocaust. Heinrich Himmler's role could not be denied, but he was only one of three brothers; the other two, she was told, were not Nazis but ordinary patriotic Germans who, of course, would not do what the black sheep of the family did. Katrin never knew her grandfather Ernst, who had died well before she was born, but she did know and love her grandmother Paula and was shocked to learn of her role both during and after the Holocaust. She too had to confront her past. Like Gottfried, she too had allies in her family, willing to speak and thus to purge themselves of family secrets, and like Gottfried, she could not discover the truth without paying the ultimate price—distance, alienation, and shunning.

Unwanted Legacies reaches its most poignant moment when the two friends, Gottfried and Abe, joined by Gottfried's son and nephew, go together as pilgrims to Germany and Poland, and most especially to Auschwitz. *Lech Lecha,* "journey forth from your land, the land of your birth, the house of your father" was the first call to the first patriarch of the Jewish people, Abram. The Hebrew is more complex: *Lech Lecha,* can also mean "go unto yourself." Every pilgrimage has an internal and external dimension. Every journey forth is also a journey within. Gottfried and Abe, German and Jew, journeyed forth and journeyed within together.

A word about the title of this book: *Unwanted Legacies: Sharing the Burden of Post-Genocide Generations.* I have been uncomfortable with the move to speak about genocide and not the Holocaust. Part of this movement has been a discomfort with the singularity of the Holocaust and also with its Judeo-centricity, and part of it arises from the distance that has now developed between the human-rights community and the pro-Israel community. But in this joint memoir between Wagner and Peck, the title is all important and entirely appropriate. If German and Jew of the next generation can speak as friends and explore the unwanted legacies of their past, so can Hutu and Tutsi, Serbian and Bosnian, Armenian and Turk, and others in the succeeding generations—the children of survivors of genocide.

We the readers are joined with their individual story and their collective journey. If within one generation Germans and Jews, not by forgetting the past but by embracing it, can be soul mates then, with courage and integrity, healing is possible. We can overcome. It is a lesson that may be essential to twenty-first-century humanity.

Michael Berenbaum, director of the Sigi Ziering Center for the Study of the Holocaust and Ethics, and Professor of Jewish Studies, American Jewish University
Los Angeles, California, May 2012

The Curse of Gurs: Way Station to Auschwitz (with Werner Frank, 2012)
Not Your Father's Antisemitism: Hatred of the Jews in the Twenty-First Century (2008)
The World Must Know: The History of the Holocaust as Told in the United States Holocaust Memorial Museum (2005)
The Holocaust and History: The Known, the Unknown, the Disputed, and the Reexamined (with Abraham J. Peck, 2002)

Foreword

I have had the great and good fortune to know both Gottfried Wagner and Abraham Peck for now more than two decades and have been continually inspired and motivated not only by their friendship but by their ongoing efforts in conversing across the boundaries of the German-Jewish divide resulting from the tragedies and horrors of the Second World War and, especially, the Holocaust/Shoah. This text now placed before its readers is the latest fruit of their labors and tells their own stories as only they themselves could share them. Even in print, supplemented by photographic memories, it remains part and parcel of their conversation, and we who are sitting at their table, albeit a bit silently perhaps, can only benefit by observing and learning from their interaction.

Personally, as the child of a Holocaust/Shoah survivor, now deceased, who lost more than 150 members of his own rather large and extended family between the years 1939-1945 (only eight of whom survived—including my Father Ralph Albert Jacobs [1921-1981]), I am slightly bemused by those who are startled (shocked?) to learn that I have German friends today, Gottfried included. Such a reaction recalls an incident my Father shared with me after a presentation on "The Evils of National Socialism" (i.e. Nazism) when he was asked "Don't you hate the Germans?" To which he told me he responded, "No, I am a German by birth and do not reject that aspect of my identity, though it was stolen from me. To the degree to which any hatred exists within me, it remains towards those who perpetrated these deeds for which they must pay for their crimes, not only against Jews but against humanity as well." Though Gottfried's legacy is a painful one as is transparently clear, not only from this text but his earlier writings as well, born after the end of World War II, he is most assuredly in no way responsible for the sins and crimes of the previous generations who continue to reject the imputation of their own guilt. That Abraham Peck—born in a DP camp to survivors after the war as well, and whose pain is that of one who has inherited a different though connected pain—has committed himself to this conversation and dialogue is itself an important response to all those, Jews included, who would allow the past to rob them of both the present and the future. (It is today, somewhat ironic, that the fastest growing European Jewish community is that of Germany, and Israel's strongest ally on that same continent is Germany itself, most especially under the astute and committed leadership of its Prime Minister Angela Merkel.) Thus, Gottfried's and Abraham's intertwined stories and conversations demonstrate boldly and loudly that the past is never to be ignored but can serve as both a foundation and a bridge to move in new, important, and different directions.

That they have done, most particularly by their creation of the "Post-Holocaust Dialogue Group," in which both the composer/conductor Michael Shapiro and I were involved from its earliest inception and beginnings. Their vision of the children and grandchildren of the perpetrators in conversation with the children and grandchildren of the victims was and remains a bold venture, and one which has been duplicated and replicated in both the US and Europe, though, of late, it, too, like so much else of importance, has fallen victim to changing circumstances and times.

Yet both Gottfried and Abraham are not content to let the past remain the past, but this initial work inspired them, and others as well, to move forward into the arena of an equally-painful contemporary reality, that of genocide *after* the Holocaust/Shoah. As one who studies, teachers, writes, and lectures on historical and contemporary genocides in addition to the Holocaust/Shoah, I am encouraged by their own moral and ethical commitments that challenge both scholars and activists as well as larger communities, Jewish and other, not only to learn the past but to learn *from* the past (which we have seemingly not done well, if at all) to address fully this ongoing scourge of humankind. Post-World War II, we have allowed genocides to occur in Cambodia, Bosnia, Iraq, Rwanda, Darfur, the Congo, and other places now on the African continent, even as I write these words, with the apparent indifference and/or impotence of the international community to step across nation-state boundary lines and either prevent or intervene in genocides once they have begun. Tragically, therefore, one must perversely applaud the unknown cynic who quipped, "History teaches us that history teaches us nothing!"

On an even larger playing field, *Unwanted Legacies* forces us to address a question which all-too-many would rather not raise nor answer: *Why study the Holocaust/Shoah at all, and its effects on those who survived and those who came after them, if not learn from it and construct systems and institutions which have at their core methodologies to prevent future occurrences and repetitions?* Scholarship for its own sake is a valued commodity contributing to the storehouse of human knowledge and a central Jewish value, the Hebrew phrase for which is *Torah lishmah*. But one must also make the argument that this knowledge is somehow different because it directly intrudes into the lives of human beings at the very center of their own existences, too often preventing them, their families, and their communities from realizing their own goals, ambitions, and dreams. Genocide is murder on a grand scale; those who commit genocides are murderers without exception and unworthy recipients of the best legal-punishment systems we human beings are able to construct. The International Military Tribunal held at Nuremberg in the aftermath of World War II to try, punish, and execute those guilty of their crimes was a beginning, not an ending. Internationally, we have benefited from it and its legacies: the United Nations Convention on the Punishment and Prevention of the Crime of Genocide (1948); the United Nations Universal Declaration of Human Rights (1948); the International Criminal Court (2002); the International Criminal Court for [the former] Yugoslavia (1993); and the International Criminal Court for Rwanda (1994), as well as the various Geneva Conventions on the treatment of both war prisoners and civilians already begun prior to the First World War.

Yet genocide remains a very real option in-country for any nation-state where those in control continue to regard any minority as a threat to regime power. Indeed, since the 1648 Treaty of Westphalia, the nations of the world continue to regard as sacrosanct their own borders and boundaries at the expense of their own vulnerable populations, and thus permit genocides to occur. The United Nations, both in its General Assembly and its Security Council, continues to lack the courage to address both the implications and the consequences of this orientation, most particularly in the matter of genocide, preferring to allow the creativity of its organization and member-states to address intervention task forces, especially on the African continent once genocides have already begun, and/or creating a Special Rapporteur answerable directly to the Secretary-General to issue reports and studies on genocides and concrete suggestions for both prevention and intervention but which, more often than not, are not implemented. This, too, is something of an irony in that, in the aftermath of World War II and building upon the failed League of Nations during World War I, much of the impetus for this new beginning was, in point of fact, prevention of repetition and mechanisms of intervention.

Finally, as both a writer and a reader, my hope is that this conversation in print between Gottfried Wagner and Abraham Peck will achieve a wide audience and that they will have multiple opportunities to share their story in live, public venues, especially to audiences of young people. It is one thing to read about such a unique journey between two unique individuals; it is another to interact with them as living witnesses and living inheritors to the painful legacies which they have embraced. To engage with the two of them, mindfully and respectfully in their presence, is to point all of us forward to possibilities for both future conversations and future activisms. My own repeated trope has long been that the past is no guarantor of either the present or the future, but can serve as a catalyst for us to redirect our energies in ways which we cannot foresee. *Unwanted Legacies* invites all of us to share in their burden and challenges us to move into as yet uncharted territories. In an age of genocide after a century of genocide, one can only hope humankind will, ultimately, prove worthy of the challenge.

Steven Leonard Jacobs, Aaron Aronov Endowed Chair of Judaic Studies,
University of Alabama
Tuscaloosa, Alabama
1 November 2013

Lemkin on Genocide (Lanham: Lexington Books, 2013)
Fifty Key Thinkers on the Holocaust and Genocide (London and New York: Routledge, 2011; with Paul R. Bartrop)
Confronting Genocide: Judaism, Christianity, Islam (Lanham: Lexington Books, 2010)

Authors' Acknowledgments

I thank Ivan Fehrenbach for his first translation into English of the orginal of my German text. I am especially grateful for the help of Annegret Ehmann in publishing this book. Martin Rooney, Christina Whitelaw, and Dr. Alan Poland supported me as friends with the thoroughly revised translation and corrections of my new afterword for this USA edition. Without the help of Annegret Ehmann, Oscar Fabbro, Ralph Tatu, Prof. Dr. Dr. hc. Utz-Hellmuth Felcht, former president of Degussa Corp. and the Degussa Foundation, as well as Dr. Eberhard Posner, former director of the communication center of Siemens AG, Munich, and my Italian family in Cerro Maggiore, this book would not have been possible.

The Wagner scholar Philip Maxwell provided important advice on the history of the Wagner Festival in Bayreuth. To all, my warm thanks. The Steegmann-Foundation Liechtenstein sponsored parts of the translation into German for the German edition of a similar volume in 2006.

Gottfried Wagner
Cerro Maggiore, Italy

August 1, 2012

Without the financial support of the Harry and Ursula Guterman Foundation and Joe Brodecki, among others, the publication of this book would have been much more difficult. I am grateful to Ivan Fehrenbach, a true Renaissance man, for his skillful translation of the greater part of Gottfried Wagner's manuscript from the German. I am also grateful to Dr. Michael Berenbaum for his continued support of my work and to Charles Dibner and Peter Murray, Esq. for their many years of support. My thanks also go to Morgen Van Vorst, a truly skilled editor, for her many helpful suggestions with the manuscript and to Bonnie Fetterman, an equally skilled editor, for her advice.

Finally, my gratitude to my old friend and colleague, Robert Mandel, the director of the Texas Tech University Press, for renewing our decades-long relationship at a crucial time in the preparation of this book and for seeing it through to completion. My thanks also go to Jada von Tungeln Rankin of the Press for her thoroughness and efficiency, to Juanjuan Chen Henderson for her skillful initial preparation of the text, to Joanna Conrad for her editorial supervision, and to my copyeditor, Aimee Anderson, distinguished in both a legal and editorial career, for the eye of a lawyer and the heart of an editor, and to the anonymous readers of the manuscript for their comments and suggestions.

Abraham J. Peck
Saint Leo University, Saint Leo, Florida
November, 2012

Introduction

Gottfried Wagner

This book, co-authored by Abraham Peck and me, is based on a previous German edition titled *Unsere Stunde Null—Deutsche und Juden nach 1945. Familiengeschichte, Holocaust und Neubeginn—Historische Memoiren* ["Our Zero Hour"—Germans and Jews after 1945. Family History, Holocaust, and New Beginnings—Historical Memoirs]. It was published in 2006 by Böhlau Publishing House (Vienna and Cologne) on my behest and after a lengthy process of negotiation about content and personal compromises between both authors and the publisher.

After the German edition appeared in print, Abraham Peck tried to find an American publisher. He, however, seemed to be primarily interested in documenting the meetings between us as post-Shoah dialogue partners since 1991. This became problematic for me, since an evolution toward a truly open, unprejudiced discussion between us, which I had hoped for, had not taken shape in the course of all those years.

In fact, during the past five years the personal communication between Abraham Peck and me had come to a standstill, last but not least because of growing differences of opinion on various issues. In these years, without much mutual communication or growth toward common ground, I became aware that the original structure, and even the old title and subtitle of the 2006 German edition, would no longer comply with the current standard of research and post-Shoah discourse, and even more so, with my very personal development since then. Moreover, I felt, the title could be misunderstood by an American public. Proposed alternative titles labeled Abraham Peck as a "son of Holocaust survivors" versus me as a "son of Nazi perpetrators." I refused to accept this because I felt it to be a violation of how I see myself and thought it could well promote resentment: those who will read impartially my parts of the book may understand why I do not accept being reduced to belonging to the "Nazi–Wagner–Hitler clan."

My decision to critically reappraise the history of my family in the context of the German past did not provide any material benefits for me, and in fact it weakened my professional career as a music historian. I was sustained in my work, however, by the solidarity and support of my Italian wife, Teresina Rossetti, and her family.

I hold the belief that the Nazi genocide of the European Jews will remain a fundamental historical event to be remembered and to be studied by those in the generation born after 1945 and those to come, regardless of their respective national, ethnic, religious, or cultural descent. I further strongly believe that the discourse of the aftermath will best be understood as relevant if equal respect is paid to *all* victims of Nazi mass murder, avoiding a hierarchical valuing of suffering.

The American historian and Holocaust survivor Henry Friedlander convincingly proved with the research for his book *The Origins of Genocide: From Euthanasia to the Final Solution*, published in1995, that Nazi genocide was targeted nearly identically against three biologically determined groups—the mentally and physically disabled, the Sinti and Roma, and the Jews. They were all murdered for what they were. It also needs to be emphasized that the Nazi extermination policy in Eastern Europe during World War II went far beyond the genocide of the Jews.

Those were *my* reasons for the new title, *Unwanted Legacies: Sharing the Burden of Post Genocide Generations.* The structure of the old German edition, however, also needed to be profoundly revised, the text shortened and updated. Instead of interrelating parts of the narratives of the two families as before, the authors now present their parts complete and juxtaposed. In my opinion this new arrangement underlines the two different perspectives on an equal level. It will also make comprehension easier for readers less familiar with this specific period of history. Thus, the much restructured American edition now sees the light due to an offer in 2011 by the director of the Texas Tech University Press, Dr. Robert Mandel, and also due to a new initiative by Abraham Peck.

In the hope that readers of the book will judge me by what I did with my life up to now, and by my political and moral convictions, I present my very personal story to people of the USA to whom I will always remain grateful for the wonderful human encounters and open acceptance I experienced there, when few in Europe wanted to hear my voice.

German *and* Jewish—German *or* Jewish? Since 1945 the following questions, among others, have divided Germans from Jews:

How much did the non-Jewish, average German know before 1945 about the fate of European Jewry under the Nazi regime? To what extent are the Germans of today still responsible for the crimes of the past? What lessons can we learn from the history of the Holocaust?[1]

This polarization of Germans and Jews can only be understood within a historical context. The historian Christoph Schulte's interpretation helps one comprehend the problem. In his view, it is crucial to name the exact times and conditions under which German-speaking Jews (Hannah Arendt) began the discussion about Germanness and Jewishness.

Only after breaking with orthodox Talmudic tradition could Jews attempt on a larger level to define "Jewishness" in clear, abstract terms, in terms that were not exclusively religious. In addition to the break with religious tradition, the second condition for opening the discussion about Germanness and Jewishness was the civil emancipation of Prussian Jewry in 1812.[2]

Schulte explains further:

After the appearance of Theodor Herzl's *The Jewish State* in 1896 and the origin of Zionism, a split developed among Jews discussing Germanness and Jewishness. Suddenly, not only anti-Semites proposed the alternative of Jew *or* German instead of combining the two groups, but so did the Zionists, and between 1896 and the beginning of the First World War, the Zionists were the most insistent Jewish voices on the topics of Germanness and Jewishness and whether the two could be merged. Nonetheless, many Jews volunteered for the First World War with great national enthusiasm. After the war, and given the number of Jews in the German army even in 1916, the statements turned more cautious and more discerning: even if the convergence of German and Jew remained an ideal of the Kaiser Wilhelm Reich. This ideal would be supplanted by the Weimar Republic's focus on the indivisible duality of Germans and Jews. After the Shoah, the polarity between Germans and Jews was magnified.[3]

Even with the knowledge of these historical facts, the *and* and its alternative *or* are challenging for post-Shoah generations, especially in the context of collective classifications and generalizations. Who are "the" Germans, and who are "the" Jews whose shared German history makes it seem impossible to understand the twelve years from 1933 to 1945, even today?

Is the German historian Christian Meier correct when he says of the German-Jewish past:

> It rises into our lives with an undiminished vitality. It seems to want to plague us, even down to the third and fourth generations. When we discuss the destruction of the Jews, even our enlightened, prominent contemporaries make innumerable mistakes, leave things out, and speak with caution and prudence. Some arguments resemble the stupid smiles children make when they are caught in the act, when they don't want to show their embarrassment. . . . Imagine what a real language critic could discover from the style of debate about Auschwitz, what he could find in unambiguous testimony that proves how deep memory sits within us! Even claiming that we wouldn't have had anything to do with it betrays how much it still concerns us.[4]

As part of this discussion about Germans and Jews after 1945, Auschwitz survivor Renate Harpprecht's comments take on a special meaning. She writes:

> We cannot choose our people. Many times back then, I wished that I weren't a Jew, but then I became one in a very conscious way. Young Germans must accept that they are Germans, that they cannot avoid their fate.[5]

Does Renate Happrecht's challenge apply to the current situation of young Germans? Has the time not come to examine more critically the polarity of Germans and Jews? Starting from the trauma of Auschwitz, Christoph Schulte demonstates an important alternative:

> It is one-sided and misleading to regard German-Jewish history as if Auschwitz were the inevitable result. In view of the Shoah, we can and will judge German-Jewish history differently, but we, not "history,"

make this judgment. . . . Some would like to regard German-Jewish history as a finished period of history, but the history of Jews in Germany goes on.[6]

He continues:

> The discussion over Germanness and Jewishness before Auschwitz is for those who only deal partly with modern German and Jewish history, the hermeneutic, a priori result of all such judgments. . . . Even those born afterwards cannot understand the postwar debate without considering the other side, which has shaped the attitude and behavior of German Jews from the emancipation era up until the time of National Socialism: Germanness and Jewishness.[7]

Even though I know that all historical discussion of Germans and Jews is connected to the discussion of Germanness and Jewishness, the talk should limit itself to German and Jew, individual and individual, to avoid those fatal constraints on discourse that arise when we debate according to a generalized scheme of the collective terms: Germanness and Jewishness. Such terms force individuals into stereotypes, which, because of mental laziness and stupidity, can then be used against the individual. In any case, only individuals can actually enter into a discussion not collectives and certainly not collective terms. The discussion of Gershom Scholem's polemic *Against the Myth of a German-Jewish Conversation* (1962) reminds us of this reality. Scholem disputes that

> there has been a German-Jewish conversation in a collective sense or as a historical phenomenon: a conversation that should not be conducted as a Jewish monologue under implied expectation of Jewish self-abnegation. And any claim of a German-Jewish conversation in a collective sense or even of a German-Jewish symbiosis should be expelled to the realm of mythology: for as long as these two beings have lived together, the allegedly indestructible, spiritual connection between the German being and the Jewish being has existed solely in the chorus of Jewish voices and was, on the level of historical reality, never anything more than fiction, a dream which, if you will permit me to say, came at too high a price.

But Scholem's argument, which arose from a Zionistic perspective, provoked a philosophical discussion that was ideological from its very beginning. It suffered from the distorted alternative of two claims: "There is a German-Jewish conversation" and "the German-Jewish conversation is a fiction." This alternative seems to be an erroneous way of approaching the problem. Conversations take place only between individuals, and not between collectives like "the Germans" or "the Jews." Collectives can shout and bellow, but they cannot conduct a conversation as a crowd. Conversations (necessarily a plural) exist only between individuals.[8]

The argumentative writer, diplomat, and Israeli expert Jörg von Uthmann, stresses the common German-Jewish history:

Jews have had a closer relationship with Germans than with any other people. German culture is indebted to them for their contributions to German international reputation—one only needs to think of Marx and Freud, two patriarchs of Eastern and Western doctrines of salvation. Beginning with the salons of Rachel Varnhagen and Fanny Arnstein, the Jewish bourgeoisie has exhibited a particular devotion towards the cultivation and advancement of German literature, music, and philosophy, and it has distinguished itself with a striking, confident aesthetic.[9]

Uthmann continues:

But what is it that binds Germans and Jews so closely? Is it the almost feverish business intelligence that has made them both so unpopular throughout the world? Or their admiration for the printed word, the Jews as the people of the Book, and the Germans as poets and thinkers? Is it perhaps their shared belief in the absolute, the obsession to push every good thing so far that it becomes bad? Or is it that inimitable combination of tactlessness and sensitivity, of arrogance and subservience, of being a chosen people and yet feeling self-contempt, that distinguishes both peoples? Certainly some of it all.[10]

The German-Jewish relationship becomes even more strained when one introduces historical parallels as does Uthmann:

For Jews and Germans, political history and the history of salvation have always been connected to one another. Both peoples have developed a specific theology of history. Signs of this theology are the chiliastic hope for the return of the first (Solomonian, Hohenstaufen) Reich, which has become an idealized myth—which represents, or has represented for a long time, the embodiment of national wishful thinking. The second and third Reichs were incompetent attempts to make this myth a reality. In this respect, German Romanticism and Zionism are comparable phenomena. Communism, too, has its roots in this chiliastic impulse.[11]

From a contemporary point of view, Uthmann's explanation of German-Jewish affinity seems to have gone too far when he includes Hitler as an especially "competent witness," who confessed to the chairman of the Danzig senate, Hermann Rauschning, that:

> All Jews without exception are the exact opposite of Germans, and yet are also related to them as only brothers could be. There cannot be two chosen people. We are the people of God; does that not say everything?[12]

Edgar Allan Poe's novella *William Wilson* summarizes the tragic dilemma of the German Jew, whom his fellow citizens treat with more and more hostility the more he resembles them. At the end of the novella, the *Doppelgänger*, dying, declares that Wilson has killed the best in himself.[13] Is it true that with spiritual affinity grows the sharpness of contradiction? Or is Sigmund Freud's claim true about "the narcissism of minor differences" when he writes that people are strangely more intolerant of minor differences than they are of fundamental differences?[14]

The relationship of Germans and Jews to their history remains conflicting and, in some ways, dichotomous. Weimar and Bayreuth symbolize this split for the Germans. Both are cities of German classicism and romanticism, the places where Goethe, Schiller, and Wagner worked; they are impressive examples of far-spreading provincial culture. But Weimar is also the home of Ettersberg and Buchenwald, and Bayreuth was also home to a branch camp of the Flossenbürg concentration camp.

In addition to its contributions to German cultural history, Jewish history includes the catastrophe of the Shoah, the Yad Vashem memorial in Israel, and the relationship to the Palestinians—even that cannot be understood without German-Jewish history. We understand that there are particular problems with the word *Erinnerungskultur*, or culture of memory, as it pertains to Germans and Jews. In a candid exchange that touches on dark chapters of our own history, Abraham Peck and I try to remain sensitive in this book when we make comparisons between Germans and Jews.

This book is, first of all, about our individual struggles to deal with familiar German and Jewish history, without the constraints of abstract, collective terms, in opposition to mental laziness and the dangerous nonsense surrounding the topic of "Germans *and* Jews." Not until after years of working together in the post-Shoah/Holocaust dialogue group that we cofounded, and after further development of our own monologues toward a fragile dialogue, did the decision finally ripen to venture into the current book.[15] The title we have chosen for the book, *Unwanted Legacies: Sharing the Burden of Post-Genocide Generations* shows that we, by being painfully aware of the past, also live our lives here and now and want to create future visions that integrate without any hierarchy other post-genocide generations. Otherwise, we risk having learned nothing from history.

Introduction

Abraham J. Peck

On December 9, 1948, the United Nations approved its first human rights document, "The Convention on the Prevention and Punishment of the Crime of Genocide," an effort to eliminate the evil that Winston Churchill had earlier called "a crime without a name." Now it had a name—genocide—and reporters searched not only for the man who was single-handedly responsible for the convention's passage but the individual who had created the term to describe the destruction of a people.

But that man, Raphael Lemkin,[1] a Polish-Jewish lawyer who had lost dozens of family members during the murderous years of the Holocaust, was nowhere to be found. Only much later did reporters find him sitting in the darkened UN assembly hall quietly sobbing, exhausted from the years of fighting for the passage of this historic legislation. The convention, Lemkin told them, was an epitaph for his mother, to prove that her death at the hands of the Nazis was not in vain.

If only. For over two decades, Gottfried Wagner and I have been involved in an effort to understand why that epitaph for Raphael Lemkin's mother's death seems to have been in vain as were the deaths of millions of Jews, Sinti and Roma, Jehovah's witnesses, gay men, the victims of Nazi euthanasia, and so many others.

We have carried on a dialogue on the German-Jewish encounter in an effort to understand why. That dialogue has focused on our family histories and the myths and realities of the relationship between Germans and Jews since the beginning of the nineteenth century and the process of reshaping that relationship for those generations, German and Jews born after 1945, and giving it new meaning.

We understand the importance of that epitaph and we, too, have mourned, not only for the losses of family members from the Jewish side but for the still-present shadows that hang over Germans and Germany for creating those losses and so many more. We have mourned, too, for the millions of non-Jews who have lost their lives after 1945, victims of an empty slogan and promise about the end of genocide, "Never again," that has occurred again and again and again. Genocide, we have learned with bitter reality, makes no distinction in race, religion, gender, or geography.

Our family histories are a part of the great tragedy that befell European Jewry during the years of the Holocaust and the consequences that it has created for Germans, Germany, and a great many Jews since 1945. We have looked at our family histories, one the history of a Polish-Jewish family centered in the life of that community for centuries and the other a family that formed one of the foundations of German cultural history, although in a perverse way, in a very real, direct and critical manner.

This book is the result of that dialogue and our critical approach to German and Jewish history before, during, and after the Holocaust, and our need to understand who we are because of the legacies we have inherited, and our efforts to create a new legacy for ourselves and our children. We have traveled a road filled with the land mines of guilt, shame, hatred, mistrust, and fear that have marked the way in which Germans and Jews have seen each other for over six decades.

Yet, could it have been different? Could Germans and Jews, one the people of the "land of poets and thinkers," the other the "people of the Book," have had a different kind of relationship, a dual drama crafted with a different ending?

After all, since 1945 Jews and Germans have shared a "special relationship" that, in the words of the German author Sabine Reichel, "is like an historical umbilical cord that can't be cut off and that pulls at the most unlikely moments."[2]

Why is it that this historical umbilical cord has found its most negative representation in Dan Diner's seminal description of Jewish life in Germany after 1945 as a kind of "negative symbiosis,"[3] what he sees as a continuation of the great scholar Gershom Sholem's dismissal of the pre-Holocaust German-Jewish symbiosis as a "myth" that makes Jews "aware of and forced to deal with their own difference from the Germans."[4] Why could not these two extraordinary peoples, gifted in so many ways, shapers of European and, indeed, world culture, have participated in a "special relationship" that would not leave both mired in more than six decades of hate, guilt, and mistrust? Did one people's victimhood seemingly stand in the way of another's efforts at achieving a similar status to go along with its place as history's premier perpetrator?

It was not as though German Jewry did not try. As Paul Mendes-Flohr, perhaps their most important spiritual interpreter, believes, German Jews "were no longer simply or unambiguously Jewish. Their identity and cultural loyalties were fractured, and they were consequently obliged to confront the challenge of living with plural identities and cultural affiliation." In short, German Jewry was possessed of a "bifurcated soul," perhaps more than any other Jewish community in history.[5]

Entering a new century, Germans and Jews, only a few decades removed from the Holocaust, seem unable to achieve a "normal" relationship. Indeed, in the eyes of many North American Jews, at least, such a normalcy seems an almost impossible aim.

Writing in 1945, the Swiss theologian Karl Barth, an important inspiration for the founding of the anti-Nazi Protestant community, the Confessing Church, in 1934, addressed the question of German guilt during the Nazi years and its awareness of that guilt for the long-term:[6]

> We have to reckon with the possibility that the great majority of Germans even now scarcely realize in what collective madness they have lived so long, with what deep-seeded and justifiable consternation Germany is regarded, what a responsibility they assumed when they supported first Bismarck, then Wilhelm II, and last of all, Adolf Hitler, and willingly and patiently did all they were told and that especially they have no inkling of the horror and loathing with which the German name has been surrounded in the last twelve years.

It seems that neither Germans nor Jews have truly understood the depths of their losses during those years. Jews have yet to understand that beyond unimaginable numbers of dead, they have lost a 1000-year-old civilization. Germans have yet to grasp just how deeply the Holocaust has affected their society as well as the manner in which they see themselves and are seen by others, but especially by Jews.

To understand just how little either side has learned, one need only look at the creation of the State of Israel in 1948 and the Federal Republic of Germany in 1949. The much-heralded "Stunde Null" (Zero Hour) concept,[7] seen by optimists in the spring of 1945 following the defeat of Nazi Germany as the opportunity for a new beginning for post-Holocaust Germans and Jews, lasted less than a half-decade. The events leading to the creation of both nations never allowed this new beginning to emerge from the shadows of Auschwitz.

Germany was intent on reentering the circle of civilized nations after its descent into barbarism. Eager to receive a collective *Persilschein* (absolution of involvement in Nazi crimes), the defeated nation was fortunate to become a focal point of the emerging Cold War struggle between the United States and the Soviet Union.

The Jewish people, still traumatized by the news coming from Central and Eastern Europe about the murder of two-thirds of its European population, faced the terrible reality of a tragedy unparalleled in Jewish or in human history. World Jewry also realized the need to redouble its efforts to create a Jewish homeland, a dream of two millennia that would stop the Jewish people from becoming a ghost nation, subject to the whims and madness of those intent upon its destruction.

According to the historian Michael Brenner, "while the political structures and ruling systems could change overnight, in day to day life and in the consciousness of those that were most affected [Germans and Jews] there was no 'Stunde Null.'"[8]

The idea of a Stunde Null was a good one. Germany was to undergo a radical reformulation of its political and economic systems. It was to be an effort to uproot the seeds of National Socialism and the development of ideas and actions that had led Germany to wage a war of unparalleled crimes against Europe's civilian populations, especially its Jews. Germany was also to undergo a change in the direction of its "humane orientation" (Ralph Giordano), rescuing itself from the nearly complete loss of its spiritual humanity through the creation of Goethe Societies, proposed by the venerable, liberal German historian Friedrich Meinecke in his book *Die deutsche Katastrophe* (1946) as a return to a kind of Goethean humanism.

The Legacy of *Bildung*

It has now been eight decades since Rabbi Leo Baeck concluded that "the end of German Jewry has arrived."[9] Baeck spoke those words not long after Adolf Hitler came to power at the beginning of 1933.

Perhaps his conclusion was premature, because the precise meaning of Leo Baeck's words was demonstrated to German Jewry with a furious and destructive finality more than five years later on the night and day of November 9–10, 1938, during a vicious national pogrom. The end of German-Jewish life had indeed arrived.

If German Jewry's physical presence had been all but eliminated, what about the spirit that defined more than a century of German-Jewish existence? Initially, of course, one must define that spirit. It is fair to say that German Jewry's faith in the ideals of the Enlightenment and its view of Germany as manifesting those ideals explains why so many Jews remained loyal to Germany even during the years before Leo Baeck's fatal pronouncement in 1933 and for a number of years thereafter.

In *German Jews: A Dual Identity*, Mendes-Flohr describes how the Enlightenment stimulated in Germany a faith in the notion of *Bildung*, a post-Emancipation idea with roots in the classical Greek notion of education, character formation, moral education, the primacy of culture, and a belief in the potential of humanity. It was and it was not the same as education. It went beyond to the ceaseless quest for the good, the true, and the beautiful.

Bildung was an important, perhaps the most important, secular concept that fueled the extraordinary transformation of German Jewry between the years 1780 to 1840 as it struggled for social and political emancipation.[10] German Jewry was not alone in those early years of effort. Enlightenment ideas, so appealing to Germany's Jews, were reflected in the writings of Germany's literary icons—Johann Wolfgang von Goethe, Wilhelm von Humboldt, Friedrich von Schiller, Gotthold Ephraim Lessing, and Immanuel Kant. The beauty in their works symbolized the ideal of a shared humanity, attainable by all individuals regardless of the accident of birth, nationality, or religion.

For German Jewry the aim and the mission of *Bildung* were to create a new German Jew, one who would be accepted by his or her Christian neighbors. This would be achieved by a process of reeducation—the acquisition of civility through improved manners and morals. Being too Jewish was evidently a bad thing. One could be that way in the synagogue, perhaps even in one's home, but never in the German street. But German Jewry had a second aim. It would use its notion of *Bildung* to secure a common ground with non-Jewish Germany. Above all, it would create an environment where the universal would be more important than the narrowly patriotic, where German history—which the Jew could not fully share with the German— would be less important than art, culture, or the humanistic ideal.[11]

In theory such aims might work. But reality in nineteenth-century Germany was another matter. In seeking, first of all, to maximize the process of political and civic emancipation on the path of assimilation into the mainstream of German culture, German Jewry created a clearly definable, if not yet visible, subculture.[12]

Second of all, even though the ideal of *Bildung*, channeled through the *Gebildeten*, the educated people, could be traced back to Martin Luther's universal view that all human beings were created in the image of God, German history, and indeed the later Luther himself, had changed that ideal beyond recognition. The nineteenth century gave rise in Germany to emotions that had little room for notions of the universal. Patriotism, romanticism, and pietism narrowed the German concept of *Bildung* and made it forever unacceptable to German Jewry.[13]

One can already see, from the very creation of the German nation-state in the 1870s, the growth of a hostile environment to the Jewish idea of *Bildung*. Indeed, the "Ideas of 1789," of the French Revolution and the Enlightenment, the foundations upon which the German-Jewish concept of *Bildung* were based, became a code word (along with anti-Semitism) for all that was thought to be in opposition to "true" German ideals.[14]

As one German nationalist wrote before the start of World War I, "The old terms have to be changed: instead of religion, [we need] language and artistic intuition; instead of humanity, [we need] the race."[15]

The outbreak of the First World War solidified the anti-1789 feelings into a coherent philosophy. The "Ideas of 1914," as this philosophy came to be known, was a direct rejection by the German nation of Jewish *Bildung*.[16] With one quick stroke, the "Ideas of 1914," would sever all alien influence from the German people. What the "Ideas of 1789," with their notions of humanity and democracy, had done to make Germany morally and intellectually impure, the new concept, with its uniquely "German" vision, would readily undo. The spirit of the Enlightenment and its legacy to German Jewry, *Bildung*, with its accompanying concepts of democracy and humanity, would finally be broken.

At the end of the war, German Jewry continued to believe in and advocate *Bildung* as an ideology that could become "the hyphen that joined and was eventually supposed to meld German-Jewish culture."[17] Despite the appearance of the Weimar Republic as a triumph of Jewish *Bildung*, a place where, on the surface, art and culture did indeed seem to prevail over the spirit of nationalism, where, in the words of Peter Gay, the "outsider" became the "insider,"[18] the illusion was soon played out. With few exceptions, Weimar culture, and the Republic itself, ended as a mostly inner-Jewish monologue.

The Nazi triumph in 1933 and the events of November 1938 finally destroyed the belief that *Bildung* could be used as a means of creating in Germany a more modern and democratic environment. Quite obviously the idea of *Bildung* as defined by the Nazis, linked as it was to racism, nationalism, and the German idea of truth, beauty, and culture, could not and would not have anything to do with an ideology created by Jews.[19]

After 1938 most German Jews found themselves leaving the Third Reich for places that would be more suitable environments for their particular ideas. Less than two months before the November pogrom, the leading German Zionist newspaper, the *Jüdische Rundschau*, paid tribute to those who had already left: "We are represented abroad by those who represent a people who cannot do anything else than institute the ideas of humanity and historical consciousness."[20]

In its transatlantic crossing from Europe to (primarily) America, the German-Jewish spirit, as represented by the notion of *Bildung*, became the German-Jewish legacy. [21]

Germans and Other Jews

For the great majority of Jews who had survived the Second World War and the Nazi Holocaust, there was no way to leave German soil. In the spring of 1945, as many as 100,000 Jewish survivors found themselves among the eight to ten million uprooted and homeless people wandering throughout Germany and Central Europe.[22] Many of the Displaced Persons (DPs) sought to return home to rebuild their lives and their nations.

Not so the Jews. As one survivor wrote:

The Jews suddenly faced themselves. Where now? Where to? For them things were not so simple. To go back to Poland? To Hungary? To streets empty of Jews? To wander in these lands, lonely, homeless, always with the tragedy before one's eyes . . . and to meet again a former

Gentile neighbor who would open his eyes wide and smile, remarking with a double meaning "What, Yankel! You're still alive!"[23]

After a tragic pogrom on July 4, 1946, in the Polish city of Kielce, in which at least forty Jews were killed, those Jews who had gone back fled to the American zone of occupied Germany from various nations in Eastern Europe. They numbered in the tens of thousands, perhaps as many as 150,000, and were channeled into the American zone by the clandestine rescue operation known as *Bricha* (Flight).[24]

Together, these Eastern European survivors formed the She'erith Hapletah (the Saved or Saving Remnant). The term was used as a description and a source of identity for those surviving the death camps, those who were partisans in the forests, and those who took refuge from the Nazis in the deepest reaches of Russian Siberia.

There was another group of Jews who had survived—German Jews who had been in Germany during the worst years of the Holocaust. In June of 1946, approximately 7,800 of them, the *Illegalen* (the Illegals), who had survived in hiding for the most part, were in the British zone of occupied Germany along with 12,000 Jews who had converted to Christianity. Most of these had married Christians and were grouped under the term "privileged mixed marriages" under the Nazi racial laws. These groups of German Jews were, in most cases, the direct opposite of the Eastern European survivors. They were older, usually more educated, less religious, and of course they had linguistic and historical ties to the German nation.

No doubt, some of them still believed in the notion of a German-Jewish symbiosis and the notion of *Bildung*. But the survivors of the concentration camps among the German Jews, like Philip Auerbach, knew otherwise. "We German Jews have become a museum piece," wrote Auerbach in April 1948.[25]

Gottfried Wagner and I were both born in this turbulent and historic time of Jewish destruction and German shame, guilt, and repression. One of us was born to two of those Eastern European survivors of the Holocaust, in a Jewish DP camp called Landsberg, located in the Bavarian town of Landsberg am Lech, where two decades earlier an inmate in its fortress-like prison, an Austrian veteran of the First World War and a revolutionary seeking to create a revolution, wrote a warning to the world about his vision for the destruction of Judaism and democracy. The other was born into a family of extraordinary cultural importance for Germany, whose great grandfather began a musical and political dynasty and whose grandmother delivered the materials to that same Landsberg prison so that that same Austrian war veteran could write the book called *Mein Kampf* (My Struggle). His name was Adolf Hitler.

The Holocaust continues to be a shadow that hangs over both Germans and Jews. The shadow is manifested by the ongoing image of Germans as perennial "Nazis," infected forever with a poisonous "eliminationist anti-Semitism" that may explain the huge sales success of the otherwise critically panned work *Hitler's Willing Executioners* written by Daniel Goldhagen.[26] To own a German car or to hum the music of Richard Wagner, a consummate nineteenth-century anti-Semite, is still considered by many American Jews as a *Schande* (shame), although the Wagner family history fascinates Jews and non-Jews alike.

Holocaust and Genocide

Imagine, then, that a son of Holocaust survivors and the great grandson of Richard Wagner would seek to break the cycle of hate, mistrust, shame, and guilt that has characterized the relationship between Jews and Germans for the past sixty years. What kinds of barriers did they have to cross, what kinds of family reactions did they face as they sought to create, perhaps for the first time in the history of both communities, a dialogue on their common histories, the legacies they inherited from the Holocaust as members of the second generation of perpetrators and victims, and a confrontation with the personal stops on both of their family histories, beginning in nineteenth-century Europe and ending with their chance meeting in 1991?

We ask ourselves what we can do with this terrible legacy that we have both inherited. Our answer is that we, and many more, especially our children and their children, need to confront the new ideologies of the world, and some of the old, that make a mockery of the term "Never again." We answer by creating an organization that is proactive against ongoing genocide, that does not deny the uniqueness of the Holocaust nor seek to hasten its end[27] as a defining failure of our civilization but understands its place in the broader issue of the struggle to eliminate for all time this most evil of human crimes, that seeks to create alliances between other generations of genocide, of which we are a part, and that pursues an active program of interreligious dialogue between Jews, Christians, and Muslims. As our esteemed colleague and the genocide scholar Professor Steven L. Jacobs has written, "Amen" to the comment of the Holocaust and genocide scholar and activist Professor Henry Huttenbach:

> Let this serve as an appeal that we, entrusted with the legacy of moral purposes emanating from the still warm ashes of Auschwitz, open our eyes and hearts to the genocide of this day, of today. Let us give purpose to our years of study by directing our energies toward the evil of the present, inspired by the evil of the past, before we find ourselves waking up when it will be too late. Only this time there will be no excuse for not having known. Let it not be said of us that we failed because of a myopic Holocaust fixation.[28]

To that we can also only reply "Amen." To stand among the generations of genocide from all parts of our world, from so many different religious groups, and from so many ethnic groups, as we have, is to understand Huttenbach's appeal in its truth and clarity. Indeed, the leading Holocaust institutions in America and Israel have accepted this truth and now pursue various antigenocide academic and proactive programs in addition to a continued focus on the Holocaust/Shoah.[29] As do we.

We do this because we believe that, despite the barriers of hatred, mistrust, and violence that shape our world, people everywhere will understand, will join us, and will ultimately act.

Unwanted Legacies

I

The Shadows of Richard Wagner as a German Myth

Gottfried Wagner

1

Family Trees: From the Founding of the Bayreuth Festival (1876) to the Collapse of the Third Reich (1945)

The Founder of an Enterprise

My late father, Wolfgang Wagner, was born on August 30, 1919, in Bayreuth to Siegfried (1869–1930) and Winifred Wagner (1897–1980), their second son and their third of four children. The most important part of my father's family history was undoubtedly the founding of the Bayreuth Festival, originally designed as a family enterprise.

The founder of the Bayreuth Festival was my great-grandfather, Richard Wagner (1813–1883). In 1876, with great national and international interest, he inaugurated the newly finished theater, the Bayreuth Festspielhaus, with his four-opera *Ring Cycle* (*Der Ring des Nibelungen*). Before he died he instructed his heirs and descendants exactly how to run this family enterprise in the future. He insisted that his own stage designs and productions, which were entirely in keeping with his ideas of *Gesamtkunstwerk*, or "synthesis of the arts," remain as he created them. Above all, he wanted his dramatic works to help advance his worldview, his *Weltanschauung*.

The essential themes of this *Weltanschauung* were man's redemption through a woman, humanity's deliverance from the curse of money, and the promulgation of an Aryan salvation myth as an alternative religion imbued with ascetic ideals. This religion included the purification of Aryan blood and the deliverance of humanity from the Jews. Although for Wagner humanity's deliverance from the Jews included a vision of a Germany free of Jews,[1] he was not averse to engaging in successful business and artistic relationships with them, including with his agent, Angelo Neumann, and with the conductor Hermann Levi, both of whom knew about his anti-Semitism and neither of whom found that cause to dissociate themselves from him.

These ideas of redemption were developed even in Wagner's early dramatic works, as well as in his theoretical writings and in his letters long before the founding of the Bayreuth Festival (1876). Following his move to Bayreuth in 1872—into the heart of the First German Reich only a year after its establishment—he was able to expound upon his ideas within the framework of the festival from his magnificent estate, Villa Wahnfried. In 1878 he began to advance those ideas in his journal, the *Bayreuther Blätter* [Bayreuth Pages]. Influenced by the French writer and racial theorist Joseph Arthur Comte de Gobineau (1816–1882), Wagner's regeneration essays represented particularly well his Bayreuth *Weltanschauung* and his Aryan, mythic religion.

Gobineau saw the Aryans as an "elite race" and predicted that the downfall of the white race would come from miscegenation. Wagner placed the historical figure of Jesus Christ in that context. In a letter on January 17, 1880, to his pupil Hans von Wolzogen (1848–1938), the editor of the *Bayreuther Blätter*, Wagner clarified the connection between the final words of his last opera, *Parsifal*, "Redemption to the Redeemer," and the Aryan Christianity growing out of his private Bayreuth cult:

> Which means and is for all the future, the truly recognized, the supreme, almighty redeemer, purified and delivered from all Alexandrian-Jewish-Roman despotic disfigurement: the historical figure of Jesus of Nazareth. [2]

Different theories have been offered to explain Wagner's pathological hatred of Jews. One is that his legal father, Friedrich Wagner (1770–1813), who died six months after Wagner's birth on May 22, 1813, of a typhoid epidemic following the Battle of Nations in Leipzig, was not his biological father. Coupled with this unsubstantiated claim is the conjecture that his actual biological father was his adoptive father, Ludwig Geyer (1779–1821). Geyer, a poet and successful portrait painter, married Wagner's mother, the widow Johanna Rosine Wagner (1774–1848), on August 28, 1814. Ultimately, the reason for speculation about Wagner's true ancestry is that Ludwig Geyer was purported to be Jewish.

Growing up in the fur-trading district of Brühl in Leipzig, Wagner went by the surname Geyer until he was fourteen. Since Geyer is a typical German-Jewish name and since, according to Christian, anti-Semitic stereotypes, Wagner looked Jewish, the theory developed that Wagner was a self-hating Jew. The question about his father's identity has never been resolved; the issue appears repeatedly in his autobiographical writings as well as in his dramatic works, and the uncertainty continued to shape Wagner's nationalistic and anti-Semitic attitude during his Bayreuth years.

The comments of the Wagnerian Arthur Seidl may illuminate how Wagner's *Weltanschauung* and his racist regeneration theories mirrored the radical right's thought and would influence future generations of Bayreuth pilgrims. In 1883 Seidl wrote about Richard Wagner's redemption opera *Parsifal* and its protagonists:

> Kundry appears . . . as the representative of Jewish . . . principles . . . ,
> and in contrast, Parsifal . . . is the Aryan-German figure of the Christian savior . . . In the mimetic scenes, Amfortas . . . wears the mask of
> the oriental-Semitic (black) Christ figure, while Parsifal displays the
> German (framed with blonde hair) Christ head in the final act. . . .
> That Klingsor, however, also wants to seize the grail for himself and
> stops at nothing to meet those ends . . . that pure Judaism everywhere
> usurps Christian German culture, wants to penetrate it and destroy it
> completely, is not only understandable to us but is a virtual commonplace, so that we hardly need to be reminded of it. [3]

Wagner knew of his political effect on the radical right, and they worshipped him as the founder of an Aryan religion of the future. Yet he also predicted what happened in the twentieth century, when he influenced the leftist, totalitarian political systems with his socialist ideas of redemption. One need only think of the commitment to these principles by Anatoly Lunacharsky (1875–1933), the close collaborator of Lenin and Stalin, one of the fathers of the leftist interpretation of Wagner—followed by those of Diebold and Bloch—in, of all years, 1933.

Cosima Wagner

My great-grandmother, Richard Wagner's second wife and in time his widow, Cosima Wagner (1837–1930), the second daughter of the composer and pianist Franz Liszt (1811–1886), worked to further her husband's *Weltanschauung*. As the director of the Bayreuth Festival from 1885 to 1906, she not only used her Bayreuth circle to prevent any deviation from the "Master's" *Weltanschauung*, she also radicalized the festival. In the spirit of Wagner, she regarded the Bayreuth Festival as a place of worship, as a union of art, religion, and an ideology with which she completely identified. She, too, had to confront the question of possible Jewish roots. Her grandmother was born into a family called Bethmann and belonged to that well-known Jewish banking family in Frankfurt. Even if that ethnic identification was speculative, as it was with Wagner, it is clear that both attempted to compensate for their problems of identity with an exaggerated nationalism and anti-Semitism. Though a militant anti-Semite, it is clear from her journals that Cosima followed her husband's dual strategy: she advocated the downfall of Judaism and yet simultaneously exploited Jews as sponsors of the festival.[4] She created the concept of "house-Jews," whom she tolerated because they were needed, even though she despised them deeply. Her house-Jew practice left its mark on the festival directors until 1945, and ironically, it later affected the concept of the philo-Semitic New Bayreuth as well. None of her actions prevented Jewish Wagnerians from making the pilgrimage to Bayreuth in order to be recognized by society.

Houston Stewart Chamberlain

While the festival was under the leadership of Cosima Wagner, the chief ideologist of the Bayreuth circle was the British-born cultural critic and race theorist Houston Stewart Chamberlain (1855–1927). He had worked for "Mistress Cosima" since 1882 and had married Eva Wagner (1867–1942), Cosima's second daughter from her marriage with Richard Wagner. Chamberlain was already one of Cosima's close confidants when *Parsifal* first premiered at Bayreuth and Richard Wagner was still alive (1882), a connection that must have proved helpful to Chamberlain's mission in Bayreuth and Germany. Chamberlain became well known from his writings about Richard Wagner but above all by his race theory, as expounded in his book, *The Foundations of the Nineteenth Century* (1899), which heavily influenced German nationalistic circles, the imperial family, and later, Hitler. With *The Foundations of the Nineteenth Century* he triggered a public debate among Wagnerians. The art historian Henry Thode, husband of Cosima's eldest daughter Daniela (from Cosima's first marriage, with the conductor Hans von Bülow), accused Chamberlain of taking the central ideas for his book from Richard Wagner without giving him credit. The dispute ended in reconciliation, but Thode stopped his justifiable accusations only because Chamberlain was married to Eva Wagner. The Bayreuth historian Karl Müssel points out that the fundamental ideas for Chamberlain's *Foundations* book did indeed originate with Wagner. In the book Chamberlain glorified Teutonicism and, according to his interpretation of Gobineau's teaching about racial inequality, wanted to award it the highest level among the races. Like Wagner, his concept of Christ was as a Nordic, Aryan man and nothing more. Chamberlain influenced the race teachings of the Third Reich with such ideas. Müssel wrote, "Alfred Rosenberg, the chief ideologist of National Socialism, processed Chamberlain's thoughts in the context of Hitler's ideology in his book, *The Myth of the 20th Century*."[5]

Siegfried Wagner

My grandfather, Siegfried Wagner, was born on June 6, 1869, in Tribschen, Switzerland. He was the third prenuptial child of Cosima and Richard Wagner, and Wagner's only son. As a weak but model son, he directed the festival from 1907 until 1930; he worked in the family enterprise as a conductor and a stage director and composed a few instrumental pieces as well as some insignificant fairy-tale operas, for which he also wrote the texts. He died of a heart condition during the festival in 1930, the same year as his mother. Siegfried was entirely convinced of the nationalistic, anti-Semitic *Weltanschauung* held by his overbearing parents, his sisters Isolde and Eva, and his stepsisters Daniela and Blandine von Bülow (daughters from Cosima's marriage with Hans von Bülow). He believed that he pleased his mother by continuing her strategy of duplicity in representing the Bayreuth *Weltanschauung*: privately he remained a radical anti-Semite, but when it served the interest of the family business, he, too, acted liberally towards Jewish Wagnerians and sponsors. This duplicity is clear from the writings of Rabbi Falk Salomon of Bayreuth, who in 1924 criticized the Wagner family's open support of Hitler, and also from a letter on February 25, 1925, which made it clear that Siegfried's business calculations led him to tolerate Jews, even employing Jewish singers to perform Wagner on the Festival Hill. Over time, as he maintained the "house-Jew politics" of his parents, and given his enthusiasm for Hitler, this apparently liberal sympathy seemed more and more preposterous.

Similar contradictions surrounded his homosexuality. On the one hand, his mother made a house (the original Siegfried Wagner house) available for him to act on his sexual preference, and on the other hand, continuing the family line required that he produce children from his marriage with my grandmother, Senta Klindworth, whose birth name was Winifred Williams.

Winifred Wagner

On June 23, 1897, my grandmother, Winifred Williams was born on the coast of the English Channel in Hastings. She was the daughter of the writer John Williams and the actress Emily Florence (Karop) Williams. She lost her father when she was two and her mother when she was three. After her mother died, Winifred stayed with English relatives, though when she reached school age she was sent off to the Margate Orphanage in East Grimstead—a difficult period that may make much of her later, domineering behavior more understandable. She never wanted to discuss that early experience.

At the age of ten, she fell extremely ill and recovered at the home of an English-Danish relative on her mother's side. That was Henriette Klindworth, the wife of Karl Klindworth (1830–1916), who had been a student of Franz Liszt, became a piano teacher, and was always an admirer of Wagner. During Winifred's stay there, her elderly relatives decided to accept her as a foster child. They provided her musical instruction and an education for a young lady, but she was not adopted by them until 1914, when she was sixteen years old.

The nationalistic, anti-Semitic, and Wagnerian Karl Klindworth, who composed one of the first piano arrangements of the *Ring Cycle*, educated Winifred entirely in keeping with the *Weltanschauung* of Richard Wagner. She proudly named herself Senta Klindworth when she was adopted, Senta in the sense of the women protagonists' self-sacrifice in Wagner's operas, in this case Senta from *Der fliegender Holländer* [The Flying Dutchman]. But her adoptive father's lessons about music not only included Richard's work but also the work of Siegfried Wagner. When Winifred met Siegfried in the summer of 1914, she was already a militant Wagnerian. Cosima, therefore, regarded Winifred as the perfect marriage candidate for guaranteeing the family enterprise through future generations of Wagners.

In the summer of 1914, Cosima invited the Klindworths and their adopted daughter Senta (that is, Winifred) to Bayreuth for the first time to see the festival's dress rehearsal. A year later, and following his mother's wishes, the forty-six-year-old, homosexual Siegfried married his bride in the family's Villa Wahnfried on September 22, 1915, during the First World War. Winifred, who was twenty-eight years younger, immediately (and for her own benefit) subordinated herself to Cosima's strictly organized schedule in the Villa Wahnfried.

Winifred followed her husband Siegfried's strategy of duplicity regarding Jews from the beginning of her marriage, and for the financial advantage of the Bayreuth Festival, she behaved as if she were impartial toward them. Even as she declared her support more and more openly for Hitler in 1923, she enhanced her dual strategy. On the one hand, she agreed with Richard Wagner's anti-Semitic, nationalistic *Weltanschauung*, which was essential to Hitler. But on the other hand, to advance the family business, she kept social connections with Jews when it was advantageous. Consequently, she was well prepared to become the director of the Bayreuth Festival after the death of her husband in 1930. As with her in-laws, the Bayreuth Festival for Winifred was, above all, about increasing power—her power.

Like her mother-in-law, her brother-in-law Houston Stewart Chamberlain, and her husband, she became a radical advocate of Germany's political and geographic aims during the First World War. She despised the 1919 Treaty of Versailles and the liberalism of the first German Republic, for which the Wagner family blamed the Jews. Those in the Villa Wahnfried hoped for a nationalistic dictator to free the country from "Jewish control." They became desperate when Wolfgang Kapp's radical right-wing coup failed in 1920, and they hoped for a redeemer to bring about prosperity for Germany, one who could also save the bankrupt family business from a difficult financial crisis.

In order to understand Winifred's Jewish politics as the festival director from 1930 to 1945, one must remember the intellectual influences that helped to form her worldview. A wild blend of unthinking, nationalistic, anti-Semitic, and racist ideas from Wagner, Chamberlain, and Hitler had one thing in common: the vision of a "Jew-free" Germany, a human race liberated from the Jewish people by an Aryan race, but, above all, by the Germans.

She authoritatively presented these ideological principles to her children and to those in her social sphere, always keeping in mind the great Wagner year of 1933 and particularly January 30, 1933, which for Winifred and the Wagner family meant much more than troublesome Reichstag elections.[6] She was convinced that despite her belief—shared with Hitler—that Jews were an inferior and threatening race, she and Hitler could come to terms about Jewish singers and Jewish Wagnerians for the health of the Bayreuth Festival. She also assumed that she would be able to convince Hitler about who was Jewish and who wasn't. Later, when she was forced to recognize that when Hitler spoke of the "Final Solution," he also meant those Jews who had repeatedly served her and the Bayreuth enterprise, she sought others to blame, not wanting to destroy her idealized vision of her friend "Wolf," her nickname for Hitler, as the savior of Germany with the Aryan Holy Grail—and thus as the savior of the festival. Hitler must have been horrified in 1931 by the Jewish singer who portrayed Wotan, Friedrich Schorr, and by the Jewish Wagnerian singers Henriette Gottlieb and Ottilie Metzger-Lattermann. As a consequence of the Final Solution, they were later murdered in Nazi death camps.

As both an entrepreneur needing to protect the family business and as an advocate for Hitler, Winifred pursued the duplicitous strategy of house-Jew politics until the end of the Holocaust and the Second World War. In contrast to her sons, she had a much more radical instinct for power as a business person; even when the tables turned after the Third Reich, she never ceased exploiting house-Jews. The mass murder of Jews and other Nazi victims did nothing to change her anti-Semitism (yet one of the last achievements of New Bayreuth was the manipulation of the Wagner archives in order to celebrate her as someone who rescued Jews). Her delusions led her to blame members of the "Nazi-mob" for executing the Final Solution, allegedly without Hitler's consent.[7] After 1945 she faulted Martin Bormann and others for carrying out the Final Solution in an attempt to gloss over and even falsify Hitler's role in history.[8] In Winifred's lifelong hatred of democracy, she saw people like Bormann, who was prepared to commit any crime for the good of the Nazi Party and of Germany, as useful, first and foremost. For her, the "party mob" would serve to help eliminate the hated Weimar Republic, and to help Hitler achieve victory after January 30, 1933, and to bring his illegitimate dictatorship to power. Yet one can scrutinize and compare the anti-Semitic writings and anti-Jewish remarks by Richard, Cosima, and Siegfried Wagner, Chamberlain, and Hitler, the people who formed Winifred's worldview, and find no significant ideological differences from the anti-Semitic writings and speeches by those in the "Nazi mob," such as General Kurt von Schleicher and Bormann. Perhaps the Wagners' plan for the future in Wahnfried was more refined, with mass psychological demagogy as part of their particular Jew-baiting (which necessarily contributed to the annihilation of the Jews in the Final Solution)—but they tolerated and promoted an outcome very similar to that promoted by the "Nazi mob."

In the run-up to this coming disaster, Winifred's four children were born in Bayreuth: my uncle Wieland on January 5, 1917; my aunt Friedelind on March 29, 1918; my father Wolfgang on August 30, 1919; and, a year later, his second sister, Verena. The Bayreuth city historian, Karl Müssel, described the conditions surrounding the First World War in which these Wagner children grew up:

> In the misery of the first post-war years, during which time great poverty reigned, the democratic forces had a very difficult time setting up a constructive local government in Bayreuth and winning the confidence of the population—despite obvious efforts and partial successes. Soon, there were also some people in Bayreuth who rejected the revolution of 1918 as a crime against the German people, and the treatment of Germany during the peace negotiations at Versailles strengthened nationalistic and anti-democratic forces. A "German National Defensive and Offensive League" [*Deutschvölkischer Schutz und Trutzbund*] with clear anti-Semitic tendencies formed in Bayreuth and held a solstice celebration on the Rodersberg crater in 1922. A local branch of the NSDAP was founded in November of 1922. When Julius Streicher spoke at a gathering in the Bayreuth *Sonnensaal* on March 18, 1923, the party already had three hundred members. Streicher was later built up as the "Frankonian Führer," widely known as a Jew-hater and publisher of *Der Stürmer*. After the event, the first large street battle between Hitler supporters and opponents took place in Bayreuth, which required a unit of one hundred policemen to clear the streets and restore peace and order.[9]

Hitler's First Pilgrimage and Visit to Bayreuth

In May of 1923, in the midst of this violent period, the thirty-four-year-old Hitler, then an unknown party leader, privately visited the Villa Wahnfried for the first time. From the time he was sixteen, Hitler had regarded both Richard Wagner and his work as his cultural-political model. He maintained this affection his entire life, as is recorded in a number of documents, including *Mein Kampf.* He closely and personally identified with the Bayreuth Festival. This intimate connection is shown by his love for the Wagner family, who called him "Uncle Wolf," by his remarkable financial support for the family enterprise, and even by his monopolization of the festival as a "War Festival" and part of the Nazi propaganda machinery after 1939. Much has been written on the subject, but especially impressive is the historian and publicist Sebastian Haffner's study of Hitler, *Germany: Jekyll & Hyde.* Recognizing Wagner's significance to Hitler, he commented on Hitler's goals of 1939:

1. To protect and broaden his personal power.
2. To take revenge on all persons and institutions whom he hates, and there are many of them.
3. To create scenes out of Wagner operas and paintings in the style of [Austrian painter Hans] Makart, in which Hitler is the primary hero.[10]

It was a crucial element of Hitler's Wagner cult that he identified with Wagner as both artist and politician, and above all with the desire for a Final Solution to destroy forever the cultural influence of Judaism.[11] Following Hitler's visit to Wagner's grave in Wahnfried Park, when he commented that "Wagner is my religion,"[12] my grandmother Winifred welcomed him into the Wagner household. She immediately and enthusiastically accepted him as a professed Wagnerian, a warm-hearted, modest man with beautiful blue eyes, a friend, and a liberator.

His first great political step came on September 30, 1923, the so-called German Day. In the old margravial indoor riding area, the historical predecessor to the current town hall, Hitler gave his first Bayreuth speech in which he warned of a "world catastrophe." A day later, praised for his speech, Hitler was welcomed again to Wahnfried. This first staged visit to the Wahnfried Villa was planned in detail. Hitler played both devoted Wagner pilgrim and friend, and he listened attentively to the explanation of the family's financial problems, which were caused by the discontinuation of royalties from *Parsifal*. He promised to help if he won his election. Then he took a walk to Richard Wagner's grave behind the Villa Wahnfried, and when he spoke of his putsch plans, he found support. Siegfried immediately told Hitler that he could address him with the informal "you" and was as enthusiastic as his wife: "When the Führer came to Bayreuth for the first time, as a real human being and a German Helferich, he won the hearts of everyone in Wahnfried."[13] This time Hitler also visited the elderly Cosima Wagner and met the deathly ill Houston Stewart Chamberlain, who lauded him with songs of praise, calling him the god-sent savior of the Germans.[14] And so Adolf Hitler entered Wagner family history.

Hitler and Siegfried Wagner

The following lines that my grandfather wrote to Rosa Eidam on Christmas Day of 1923 demonstrate his undiminished enthusiasm for Hitler. Only a few weeks after Hitler's unsuccessful November putsch in Munich, Siegfried rejoiced:

> We met the magnificent man (Hitler) on "German Day" this summer, and we will remain true to him if that means that we, too, have to go to prison. We have never been opportunists here in Wahnfried. [Alluding to the political unrest in the 1920s in Bavaria]. The conditions in Bavaria are indeed outrageous. The times of the Spanish Inquisition have returned. Perjury and treachery are considered sacred, and Jew and Jesuit walk arm in arm, trying to destroy Germanness. But perhaps Satan has miscalculated this time. Should Germanness really succumb, then I will believe in Jehovah, the god of revenge and hatred. My wife fights like a lion for Hitler! Splendid![15]

Hitler joined in Siegfried's jubilation with his words at the Landsberg prison on May 5, 1924, remembering his official "German Day" visit to Bayreuth on September 30, 1923. He was certain that the Wagner family would openly support him in any future election: "Proud joy seized me when I saw the nationalistic victory in the town where first the master [Richard Wagner] and then Chamberlain forged the spiritual sword we fight with today.[16]

Winifred Wagner and Hitler

On November 14, 1923, my grandmother wrote an open letter that was published in the Bayreuth newspaper, the *Oberfränkischen Zeitung*, that showed how closely connected she felt to Hitler. Its appearance came only six days after Hitler's failed putsch attempt in Munich on November 8 and 9. Among other things, the open letter stated:

> All of Bayreuth knows that we have a friendly relationship with Adolf Hitler. We were present during those disastrous days in Munich, and we were the first to return. Understandably, Hitler's supporters have turned to us to get the report from someone who was there. The extraordinary truth—that a woman in my position has done such a thing—has created stories and exaggerated rumors spread by enemies and even friends. We have followed the valuable work of Adolf Hitler for years, with great personal interest and approval. Filled with a passionate love for his fatherland, this German man sacrifices himself for his idea of a purified, united, nationalistic Greater Germany. He has accepted the perilous task of educating the labor class about the internal enemy, about Marxism and its consequences. And unlike anyone else, he has managed to bring people together in a spirit of harmony and reconciliation. He has learned how to bridge the almost unbridgeable class hatred. For thousands upon thousands of people in despair, he has restored the joyful hope and strong faith that a worthy fatherland will rise again. His personality has made a deep, moving impression on everyone he has met, and that includes us. We immediately understood how such a plain, physically fragile man is capable of exercising such power. His power is founded in his moral strength and purity. He supports and defends the ideas he recognizes as morally correct, and with the fervor and humility of divine determination, he attempts to make those ideas reality. Such a man, a man who stands up so unconditionally for all that is good, must thrill and inspire people. They must be moved by his self-sacrificing love and devotion. I freely admit that we, too, are under the spell of this man, that we stood with him during the fortunate days, and that we remain true to him during these days of difficulty.[17]

Winifred maintained such steadfast loyalty to Hitler her entire life. On December 6, 1923, she wrote her friend Helen Boy about her mission for Hitler while he was held in Landsberg "custody," and she described her "fantastic-package" that contained a jacket, wool blankets, socks, foodstuffs, and books.[18] During this period, sisters-in-law Daniela and Eva were also gripped by the Hitler hysteria. Before Christmas 1923, Winifred organized a collection point for "care-packages" to Landsberg.[19] It is widely known that Hitler did not want for anything during his prison term in Landsberg.

Therefore, even by 1923–24, Hitler had found complete social support from the Wagner family, and his adolescent dream of becoming a Bayreuth pilgrim had more than come true.[20] In her "care-packages," Winifred sent him the typewriter and the paper that Hitler used in his prison cell as he dictated his autobiography, *Mein Kampf*, to his secretary Rudolf Hess. Their relationship continued to grow. Hitler's marriage proposal to Winifred in the fall of 1930 (after Siegfried's death, according to the historian Robert Wistrich[21]) also strengthened that connection between Winnie and "Wolf." Yet because of her own cravings for power, and because she did not want to become only "Frau Hitler," she rejected his proposal.

The significance of my grandmother and Bayreuth to Hitler in 1923–24 is also clear in *Hitler's Table Talk at the Führer's Headquarters*. Henry Picker wrote the following from the night of February 28 to March 1, 1942:

I traveled through Bayreuth frequently, and I always stopped to visit. After all, Frau Wagner had brought Bayreuth and National Socialism together—that is her great contribution. Siegfried: he was a personal friend of mine, but politically he was passive. The Jews would have wrung his neck. That's just the way he was.[22]

The Jewish Issue: From Wagner's Great Solution to Uncle Wolf's Final Solution

Throughout my long struggle with the Third Reich and the history of my Wagner family, I have always been particularly interested in when and how the many personal abuses of power, which were the foundation of Richard Wagner's and Hitler's mania of Aryan self-promotion, began to affect my

Uncle Wieland, my father Wolfgang, and their plots to gain power. What follows are the significant events between 1931 and 1945.

1931: Hitler, Heil, and Punch and Judy Theater by the Wagner Children

Wieland was fourteen and my father was twelve in 1931. I should emphasize that the Wagner children were born into an anti-child, adult world full of power struggles. Children had a very short childhood—if it could be said that they had a childhood at all. Winifred's children even performed anti-Semitic Punch and Judy theater with a text by the writer of fairy tales, Karoline von Wolzogen.[23] An avid Nazi, Lieselotte Schmidt, was governess of Winifred's children and the lover of Hans Frank, later governor-general of German-occupied Poland. She gave an account of the theater, later recounted in a letter from Winifred:

> It was supposed to be "a Nazi-play as much as possible, in which a Jew appears," writes the [governess] Lieselotte [Schmidt]. Wolfgang had already gotten himself "a Jewish puppet with a beautiful hooked-nose." Wieland painted the backdrop and Verena played the "role of the woman," and Wolfgang took the lead. The play was called the *Princess Meatball* and, as Lieselotte writes, "There is a real Jew in it, and Punch is the Nazi." ... The contents [of the play]: "Punch keeps two ... [pushy] admirers, the rich farmer Protz and the perfumed traveler (Jew)" far away from the princess by hitting and kicking them, and for thanks, she gives him a kiss. In the closing rhyme, it reads, "it is truly a scandal / this Protz and perfumed man / in German land— we are ashamed of them / so we plunge the knife for noble purpose / the entire group is filth." "The play ends with ... [an outstretched Hitler salute by Punch]: Punch is silent with his own thoughts on the matter / and at the end calls only: Hitler Heil!"[24]

1934: Hitler's Intervention in the Wagner Children's War of Succession

Hitler visited the Wagners frequently in the fall, and as was his style, his visits were often a surprise. During one visit in October, he discussed Wahnfried's *Erbhof* (inheritance) status with Winifred. The Reich's *Erbhof* law would apply to the Wagner family: possessions of the family, both the festival and Wahnfried could then be declared indivisible and should only be handed over to one Aryan heir—Wieland.[25] Wolfgang and the sisters Friedelind and Verena were to receive no compensation.[26] That, however, would render invalid the last testament of Siegfried and Winifred, which they wrote together on March 8, 1929.[27] Naturally, the equally entitled heirs, Wolfgang, Friedelind, and Verena, were opposed to such an arrangement. So an open war of succession broke out among the Wagner children, and there was never true peace again. Discord, mistrust, and envy reigned among the siblings despite great efforts to conceal the conflict. Consequently, Hitler decided that they should follow Siegfried's last testament, for which Wolfi, as Hitler affectionately called Wolfgang from the time he was little, was always grateful. After 1945 my father concealed Wieland's and his connection to Hitler; otherwise neither he nor Wieland would have become the festival director. The fraternal feud that broke out later over the festival would affect the following generations of Wagners, and Winifred, as usual, continued to make things worse.

1937: The Festival and the Nuremberg Party Convention as Christmas

In 1937 Wieland, Wolfgang, and Verena became more active in Nazi propaganda, and the following episode demonstrates Hitler's relationship to the Bayreuth Festival. On August 15, 1937, he ordered all those participating in the festival to visit the Nuremberg party convention building. Everyone accepted the "invitation" and came in thirty buses. The Wagner children spent the night in the *Deutscher Hof,* the same hotel as Hitler, and convinced Uncle Wolf to return to the festival.[28] Hitler brought the chief Nazi ideologue, Alfred Rosenberg, to see *Götterdämmerung* [Twilight of the Gods] and converted him into a staunch Wagnerian.[29]

The festival had barely ended when the Wagners met Hitler at the Nuremberg party convention again; they again stayed in the *Deutscher Hof* hotel, this time as his guests of honor. Hitler wished to use Winifred in foreign affairs as a publicity figure to aid the future alliance of the Berlin-Tokyo axis—a role that Winifred happily fulfilled. At the time Winifred wrote, "Wolf is so thankful that he definitely wants to have Nickel [Verena] and me to the Mussolini reception in Munich on September 25."[30] Wolf, too, was very happy. Later, in 1942, Hitler still recalled enthusiastically these times at Bayreuth and Nuremberg:[31] "The day after the end of the festival and the first of the party convention at Nuremberg was sad for me like the Christmas decoration taken off of the tree after Christmas."

During Mussolini's state visit, Winifred attended this reception, where Hitler and Mussolini celebrated the pact that allowed Hitler to invade Austria in the winter of 1937–38. In the winter of 1937–38 Wieland was released from military service; the sensitive artist, the darling of the Führer, was doubtless helped by his connection to Hitler.

1938: The Wagners' Currency Trafficking and Hitler's Aid

On April 10, 1938, the "referendum" took place regarding the "annexation" of Austria to the "Greater German Reich." With almost 100 percent of voters turning out, Hitler won 99.73 percent of the vote. This political euphoria made Hitler feel especially generous toward the Wagners. With his help the children took week-long trips to Italy, and he also allowed the Wagner family to get away with trafficking currency. Under the guise of a 1930 donation to *Tannhäuser*, a donation that had been settled long before, the Wagners set up a secret account in Switzerland and invested a sum of about 800,000 Reichmarks.[32] With that money Winifred had been able to buy an estate on Lake Constance and to invest money in Switzerland since 1930—despite the strict foreign exchange regulations in place since 1933. In April of 1938, the customs investigation department brought criminal proceedings against the Wagners because of money-trafficking abroad.[33] They were saved by Hans Frank. Later they were made exempt from punishment because of the Karlsruhe publisher Albert Knittel's unsoundness of mind. Having made a lot of money as the Wahnfried property manager, he was now a convenient scapegoat. The money in Switzerland was transferred back into Germany, and thanks to Hitler's intervention, sufficient sums were released for the festival. And while all of this was happening in the spring of 1938, Wieland and Wolfgang took a week-long trip to Sicily in Wieland's new Mercedes—a present from the Führer. Uncle Wolf was negotiating with Mussolini at the same time, making a great show of his unity with *il Duce* by participating in large parades in Rome, and so with the Wagners' connection to Hitler, their special status increased in Italy as well.

In the midst of the Wagners' currency trafficking, Hitler ordered the construction of the Richard Wagner Research Establishment on May 22, 1938, Wagner's 125th birthday. Winifred had submitted a memorandum for the enterprise in March, which showed her efforts to infuse the festival with the spirit of Richard Wagner's *Weltanschauung*. As a result she could be certain of Hitler's support:

> In an era of liberalism, Wagner's writing "Judaism in Music" dared to throw down the gauntlet against a terrible power. He dared even to identify this power as the "plastic demon of mankind's fall."[34] Those who now ruthlessly turn the press against him have always been relentless in their hatred for him.[35]

Winifred's letter ends with a demand that there be a *Gleichschaltung*, a synchronization, in interpreting Wagner's work and life. She and Wagner generations to come would achieve this synchronization by repudiating all tendentious attacks against Wagner's work and against Wagner as an individual, by clarifying Wagner's pure Aryan heritage, by creating a complete critical edition of his writings, and by preparing a new biography of the master. [36]

So her plan included both the Aryanization of Wagner and a family monopoly on Wagner in the international opera business. Any doubts about Wagner's heritage from his adoptive, possibly Jewish father Geyer were supposed to be eliminated. With Hitler's protection, Winifred could exact revenge on her sisters-in-law, who had attempted to prevent her from presenting her racist, anti-Semitic image of Wagner within the context of National Socialist ideology. Meanwhile, during this period the Germans from the Sudetenland in Czechoslovakia marched into Bayreuth and demanded to be accepted back into the Reich, and in the Führer's annex of the Siegfried Wagner house, plans for the Westwall, or the Siegfried line, were presented secretly in a secured room.

On August 1, 1938, known as *Götterdämmerung* day, Wieland made his Uncle Wolf particularly happy by joining the Nazi Party. When several problems with the *Parsifal* decorations arose, Wieland chatted with Hitler about his intention to become a painter and pursue music. In keeping with the Wagners' privileged status (but which would have been remarkable in an ordinary family), Wieland received private painting instruction in Munich from Ferdinand Staeger, whom Hitler held in great esteem.[37] On December 7, 1938, the newspaper *Bayerischen Ostmark* reported that there would no longer be any Jewish businesses in Bayreuth.[38]

1939: Wagner Musical Scores for Hitler's Fiftieth Birthday, Winifred's Political Failures, and Problem Child Friedelind at the Beginning of World War II

On March 15, 1939, German troops marched into what remained of Czechoslovakia and made it the Protectorate of Bohemia and Moravia, thereby violating the Munich Agreement of September 30, 1938. My father was there as a soldier,[39] a fact he kept secret for years. Exempt from service, his brother Wieland made sick jokes: "Wolfie [my father] was there in Czechoslovakia and quashed the population. He's gained five pounds in the war from eating whipped cream."[40]

In the history of the Bayreuth Festival, however, 1939 marked a special gift from German industry to Hitler: the original scores that Richard Wagner had given to King Ludwig II of Bavaria. On the Führer's fiftieth birthday, with 800,000 Reichmarks quickly found for their purchase, Hitler became the owner of the original scores of *The Fairies*, *The Ban on Love*, and *Rienzi*; an orchestral sketch of the *Der fliegender Holländer*; the original scores of *Das Rheingold* [The Rhinegold] and *Die Walküre* [The Valkyries]; the original fair copy of the three-act orchestral sketch of *Siegfried*; and a copy of the orchestral sketch of *Götterdämmerung*.[41] Winifred asked Hitler to deposit these treasures in the Wahnfried archive, but Hitler wanted them to be with him always.[42]

Headlines of 1939 reported that ethnic Germans were apparently being deported to the Polish interior for forced labor.[43] The Siegfried Wagner house was secured as never before. Officers and government ministers came and went. My aunt Verena overheard the word "Lysagora," a town in Poland. Since my father's unit was stationed on the Polish border, these secretive comments frightened the family, but the family placed their hope in Hitler's protecting them again. Hitler attended all of the Bayreuth performances and savored the crowd's jubilation. On July 30, during an intermission of *Die*

Walküre, he awarded his Winnie a bronze "Cross of Honor for German Mothers,"[44] an award given to German mothers with "genetically healthy children of German blood." In the midst of these activities, on July 31, the German bombers' "world-best performance" was received proudly: 501 kilometers per hour averaged over two thousand kilometers.[45] During these days Hitler also met with the English newspaper czar, Lord Kemsley, in the Siegfried Wagner house. And while visiting Bayreuth, the Germany-friendly British ambassador Nevile Henderson hoped that he and Hitler could reach a cease-fire agreement for England, but Winifred's attempts to persuade Hitler to meet Henderson in the Siegfried house failed.[46]

On August 24 my father's company was transferred to Rosenberg in Upper Silesia. On August 26 headlines in the Nazi media covered alleged massacres at Bielitz and Łódź, which apparently included rewards for killing ethnic Germans.[47] With the invading Wehrmacht my father's unit entered Poland; meanwhile, Wieland was permitted to dedicate himself entirely to his painting. On October 7, 1939, during the first days of World War II, Winifred wrote Friedelind a letter about my father's deployment in Poland: "Four iron crosses have been given to Wolfgang's company. So far about six men have fallen."[48]

When my father was wounded, Hitler requested that his own doctor, Karl Brandt, keep Winifred updated regularly about his condition, and Brandt visited my father in the hospital. Reassured, Winifred could devote herself to Hitler's affairs again. Winifred had severe problems with her daughter Friedelind, who had blossomed into an anti-Nazi in Switzerland and was even denied reentry into Germany after the war broke out. Winifred wrote Friedelind on October 10:

> I very much regret that during these difficult, fateful times, you have decided to withdraw from your family and your nation. . . . Nothing that might happen compares to what we have already had to bear, and nothing changes that during these times, you belong in your family and at your mother's side.[49]

On Christmas, after a long delay, a letter came from Friedelind. Again Winifred demanded that her daughter obey her:

> I recognize that you are turning your back on your home and your fatherland. Yet out of consideration for your siblings, I ask that in the

New Year, you cultivate these family relationships at least, that you let us know more about your personal life and your well-being.[50]

For Winifred, this request did not at all derive from genuine, motherly concern. She simply wanted to know what the insubordinate daughter was doing. Friedelind's reputation with Hitler and the other important Nazi figures, however, could no longer be salvaged.

1940: The "Strength through Joy" Festival and Hitler's "Gift" from Occupied Paris

From 1940 until the end of the war, the Bayreuth Festival relied completely on Hitler and the Nazi Party.[51] That dependence, however, proved greatly advantageous to Winifred because ticket sales, recruiting, and advertisement were all done through the KdF (*Kraft durch Freude*), the "Strength through Joy" organization.[52]

But Winifred had other problems. Above all, Friedelind had become a great strain on Winifred's reputation with Hitler and others in the Third Reich. Severe tension developed between Friedelind and the rest of the family at the beginning of the year, when Friedelind wanted to emigrate from Switzerland to the United States to protest the persecution of Jews in Nazi Germany. In order to receive emigration papers for Friedelind, Winifred had to go to SS chief Heinrich Himmler's house in Berlin by herself. Himmler knew the details of the correspondence between the mother and daughter because the SS had intercepted the letters. Himmler commanded that Friedelind return to Germany.[53] So on February 9, 1940, Winifred met Friedelind at the Zürich hotel *Baur au Lac* where the two got into a heated argument. Winifred demanded that Friedelind immediately stop speaking publicly against Hitler. She then threatened her:

> If you do not consent, you will be taken by force to a secure location, and if you don't want to listen, the command will be issued for you to be destroyed and eliminated at the first opportunity.[54]

A year later, in March of 1941, Friedelind was able to emigrate to Buenos Aires with Winston Churchill's personal intervention. The conductor Arturo Toscanini helped by obtaining a visa for her. On July 23, 1940, the

Wagners were cheered by Hitler's attendance at a performance of *Götter-dämmerung*. During a morning conversation in the Wahnfried garden, they spoke about the black sheep, Friedelind. Before the performance "Uncle Wolf" came to Wahnfried for tea, but he did not stay there; the Friedelind fiasco was showing its first effects. They discussed building a bomb shelter, which Hitler believed was completely unnecessary. "The war is taking place hundreds of kilometers from Bayreuth," he pronounced optimistically.[55]

As a gift Hitler brought a Franz von Lehnbach painting from Paris, which Winifred gratefully hung in the music room of the Führer annex. It remained there until her death in 1980. The portrait doubtless came from among those German treasures that Alfred Rosenberg and his associates plundered from French museums and archives, objects that had been legally purchased by the French. Rosenberg also stole letters and autographs by Wagner, which Hitler was particularly interested in having for his own valuable Wagner collection. This visit is said to have been Hitler's last visit to the Wagners and Villa Wahnfried.

1942: The Wagner Descendants' New Order of Influence and Power in Bayreuth during the *Endsieg* (Final Victory)

It was now the Wagner children's time with Hitler, and Winifred was forced to play a subordinate role. When Hitler invited Wieland and Wolfgang to eat at the Osteria Bavaria restaurant in Munich on June 10, 1942, he showed the world the new order of influence and power among Wagner descendants. During lunch Hitler emphasized that he regarded them both as heirs of Bayreuth: he wanted Wieland to take care of the artistic side and Wolfgang the technical side.[56] Hitler's vision was not realized, however, until the reopening of the Bayreuth Festival in 1951.

In August, in another attempt to seize power, Wieland launched a coup against his mother. In a long letter to Hitler, he attempted to "make a clean sweep" by mounting a large-scale conspiracy against Emil Praetorius, the famous conservative stage-designer who had worked on large German stages before and during the Third Reich, in Berlin as well as Bayreuth.[57] Wieland wrote, "It was scandalous to offer the Führer 1934 Cubist and Expressionist drivel on the Bayreuth stage."[58] In so saying, Wieland adopted the vocabulary of the racists who spoke of "degenerate art" and music in the

Third Reich. His view was consistent with the ideology of Siegfried Wagner, who had spoken against "ultramodern designs in Bayreuth" in 1926.[59] The oil painting that Wieland created of his father, and which he gave to Hitler in 1940, demonstrates the type of art that Wieland advocated as a painter in the Third Reich: bourgeois, postcard kitsch—exactly what "Uncle Wolf" liked.

From 1942 on, Wieland's closeness to Hitler enabled him to engage in bold moves. He planned radio broadcasts and special recordings with the conductors Wilhelm Furtwängler and Richard Kraus and demanded that the Praetorius stage design and the Tietjen direction be replaced with his own.[60] As a result of Wieland's malicious campaign, Praetorius was banned from working. Then when his house was searched, the Nazis found correspondence between Praetorius and Jews in Holland. The Munich *Gauleiter* Paul Giesler declared him an enemy of the state.[61] But early in 1943 Hitler issued the astonishing order that Praetorius could continue working.[62] The reasons for that decision remain unknown. At any rate, Wieland's plot failed. The party press demanded "a certain restraint" regarding Praetorius, who was now subject entirely to the will of Goebbels. At this point Hitler preferred to accept the political unreliability of Tietjen instead of allowing the twenty-six-year-old, inexperienced Wieland to assume power at Bayreuth.[63]

1943: Wieland's *Ring* Project after the *Endsieg* or a Loss of Reality

Realizing that her sons Wieland and Wolfgang were influenced more and more by Hitler, and that they were maneuvering within the Nazi-elite world of plots and intrigues, Winifred's motivation grew stronger to devote herself elsewhere. She had an uncanny instinct for evaluating the political climate, and she sensed the necessity to leave herself a way out. That included helping the persecuted—just in case the worst of all possible outcomes came to pass, namely the fall of the Third Reich. In other words, in 1943 she developed a plan to survive if Hitler and the Nazi regime were to fall, though she never openly and honestly confessed as much. She believed that helping the persecuted would provide a means to save herself from the hangman's noose at a later time. The news from the front was growing worse, especially on the eastern front and in Stalingrad. It was devastating, and the bombardments on Germany, including Bayreuth, were growing heavier. In this desperate situation and in complete self-denial, she wrote to Hitler on March 8, 1943: "My dear friend and Führer, . . . I ask you to tell me your final decision in the matter [of the festival program]. . . . All of my thoughts and passionate hopes are with you and your enormous task! In eternal gratitude and admiration, your faithful, devoted, Winifred."[64]

During this phase of the worsening two-front war, Wieland, still free from military service—and equally free from reality as regards Germany and the international and political scenes—decided that he wanted to produce the entire *Ring Cycle* under his own direction, with his own stage set, and with his own costumes on Festival Hill after the "Final Victory." It is no surprise that this delusional project did not succeed. Remarkably, Goebbels gave Wieland a special grant of 120,000 Reichmarks, and Wieland was able to close the entire Altenburg theater for a week to prepare for his premiere of *Götterdämmerung*.[65] In the midst of all this, on April 11, 1943, my parents married in Wahnfried. Hitler sent them a large bouquet of roses with his congratulations.

My Mother's Family, the Drexels[66]

My grandfather on my mother's side was Adolf Heinrich Drexel, a wine merchant in Wiesbaden-Biebrich. He was born on July 23, 1887, in Vockenhausen and died on October 2, 1941, in Wiesbaden. He learned his vocation in Frankfurt am Main and then worked in Brighton (England) and Buenos Aires (Argentina). Drafted into the military in 1908, he ended up in the artillery like his brother Hans Christoph. Hans Christoph Drexel was a famous painter, a member of the Blue Rider German Expressionist painting group, and an anthroposophist. But since he was a declared anti-Nazi, he was forbidden to work.

After his stay abroad and his military service, Adolf Drexel ran a wine store in Wiesbaden-Biebrich. He enjoyed drinking quite a bit of wine himself, and he was a humorous, entertaining man always ready for a laugh. He married my grandmother on November 29, 1918, in Wismar. She was Thora Auguste Franziska Nissen, born on March 6, 1881, in Hamburg. She died of a drug overdose on October 22, 1953, in Wiesbaden, the result of her estrangement from her daughter, my mother. As a young woman, she was very pretty and well dressed. The Drexel relatives questioned her relationship with my grandfather, "What does our Adolf want with this chic woman?" She was never accepted by them. Modern and liberal, she could easily create a stir. Once, for example, she got into trouble for humming along with the music during a concert. Because of their different interests and attitudes, my grandparents' marriage was not a happy one. A business misfortune and a default on a bond forced my grandfather to give up his wine store, and that failure cast a dark shadow over their marriage and their family life. So grandmother Thora had to sustain the family alone as a teacher during the economically and politically unstable, difficult period of the Weimar Republic. On March 11, 1980, a friend of the Drexel family, Erika Vielhaber, wrote these revealing lines about my mother as a little girl and about my grandmother Thora:

> I can see her (Thora) very clearly in front of me, more clearly and more distinctly than most people whom we knew in Wiesbaden, when we lived on wonderful Walkmühlstrasse. She had a truly fashionable appearance; she was slender, very striking, fundamentally harsh, but always friendly to us. In my recollection she was an intriguing woman, not merely a "regular, middle-class" type, but a "working woman." I imagine she could have managed life fine without a husband, perhaps even with less sacrifice, even a somewhat easier, more comfortable life. Your parents were indeed very, very different. Your mother was certainly not the "housewife and mother" type; she was more like the woman journalists, doctors, and politicians of today. My mother liked and gradually grew to have great affection for this young, refined neighbor. Both my mother and we children very much liked your parents, and we got along very well with you children, but Ellen, you sure were a stubborn mule! I can picture you when you had your "attack" in the yard, when that lively, beautiful kid got mad and wanted to get her way with her parents, her siblings and the big girl next door, for whom you had been a living doll for a long time, before we got to know you as a person and someone to talk to.

In her autobiographical notes from 1981–82, my mother wrote:

> I don't believe my mother ever got over not working in theater. Her greatest dream had been to be an opera singer, yet that was not suitable in my grandparents' circles. So she became a teacher at a school for

young ladies in Hannover—until she married. As far as I can remember, she loved the job, and was also loved by the students. But she wanted me to do those things that she could not. She took care to see that I was a dancer, but I was not ambitious enough for her. That caused us both distress! My father loved me; I was his "Lala," his "so-so." That was my nickname in the family. Perhaps I was a little bit too slender, a little bit too undeveloped as a young girl—I was often compared to the actress Karin Hardt. . . . When I was twelve, I had to earn money to pay for dance lessons myself; I worked in the theater or danced in any organization I could. Together with my schooling, which therefore suffered, it was simply too much. From twelve to fourteen [1931–33] I was at the Children's School of Ballet at the Wiesbaden State Theater and then still two more years there as a student [1933–35], so four years altogether. Our ballet director was Arthur Sprankel from Frankfurt, and after Wiesbaden he took me with him to Breslau for a year [the season of 1935–36]. I was there at the great *Schauspielhaus*, which belonged to the opera and was purely for operetta theater. It was a frighteningly difficult, exhausting time because every fourteen days, the operetta changed, and there were double performances three times a week, and in the mornings we prepared for the next operetta. In Breslau, I had to take an extensive state examination and came out on top of the class. From 1936–1939 [that is, during the artistic seasons from 1936 to 1939], I went to Darmstadt and the regional theater. It was extremely busy, but I spent many blissful and happy hours there, too. . . . I remained close to my family, and my family's hardships, both emotional and financial, touched my heart and made me aspire to do something so that I could help them more. I applied to the Berlin State Opera. . . . I was asked for an audition in the winter of 1938–39, and I was hired. It even made the Darmstadt newspaper. I was tremendously happy about that, yet I wanted to improve even more, both professionally and educationally. Professionally by attending good ballet schools, and educationally by attending lectures at the university and taking private lessons. But the war thwarted my plans.

At the beginning of my contract [the season of 1939–40], World War II began, and very soon thereafter—I no longer remember exactly when, . . . they decided to lower the curtains—everyone turned his attention towards the war. At that point, everyone believed or hoped there would be a swift end, and yet it lasted six years. We found ourselves confronted with unspeakable horror and hardship. . . . In October of 1940, I met Wolfgang through two colleagues—Friedel Romanowski and Gertrud Reissinger—on the boulevard Unter den Linden in Berlin. It was a random meeting, and we were very reserved at first. We went to a restaurant somewhere on the boulevard. . . . From that point on we saw each other from time to time at the theater [Oper unter den Linden] at the rehearsals and the performances. . . . I continued to work as a ballet dancer, and he worked as an assistant stage director for the first year. The second year he worked as the assistant director, and the third year he was the director. . . . He invited me to Bayreuth. The rest of the family did not immediately welcome me— they viewed me with mistrust and envy—or whatever you want to call it—I came from an entirely different world.

I moved to Wahnfried in the fall of 1942, and I slowly came to know an immensely problematic and complicated family. Our lives, of course, were cast in the dark shadow of World War II, then three years old. Our wedding was set for April 11, 1943. An apartment was found for us on Leistikowstrasse near the radio tower. Wolfgang's bachelor days—and our secret place on Motzstrasse—were unfortunately at an end. But it was certainly a blessing because the house on Motzstrasse was destroyed by an air raid, and that could have been our end, too. . . . On April 11, 1943, we married in the Siegfried Wagner house in Bayreuth, but in 1942 I was already a part of the Wagner family, and therefore my life had already begun to grow more and more depressing.

I broke my contract [1942–43 season], ending my ballet position before the wedding. It was no great difficulty because my former director, Heinz Tietjen, was to be a witness at my marriage. However, on the day of our wedding, he was hospitalized in Berlin, and the current technical director of the Festspielhaus in Bayreuth, Paul Eberhard, took his place. The second witness was the painter Franz Stassen, among the best friends of my father-in-law Siegfried and a passionate admirer of Richard's and Siegfried's work.

Grandmother Thora criticized my parents' wedding because the Wagner family treated her like a poor, uninvited bystander. My mother's brother, my uncle Gustav Drexel, later told me that when the wedding witness Stassen noticed how she was being treated, he startled the guests by making a pointed toast to grandmother Thora.

On May 4, 1943, Uncle Gustav met my parents in Berlin and attended a performance of *Carmen* with them in Tietjen's box at the Oper unter den Linden. When Uncle Gustav, who was passing through on the way toward the Eastern Front and Russia, asked my father how he felt among the circles of the Nazi elite, my father said that everything is a matter of correctly assessing the balance of power. Uncle Gustav did not understand, and my father added that sometimes it is necessary to play one side against the other. My uncle did not agree at all. And so the estrangement began between the Wagner and Drexel families, and mother played her new role as a Wagner wife, as she was expected to do.

My mother's notes reveal that the break with the Drexel family did not always go according to plan. One entry from mother's diary reads, "In 1943, my dear younger brother Ernst, a nineteen-year-old sailor, was killed on a ship in the Black Sea. It affected me deeply."[67] In a letter from November 1943, Winifred wrote to her friend Helena Roesner of my mother's shock, "This completely sensible young woman became unpredictable from that point on."[68] My mother complained further that:

> My good, kind father didn't live to see it—he died in the fall of 1941. His death affected me profoundly. I recognized for the first time that I would never be able to say what I wanted to say to this good, dear man, and I would have given anything to have been more affectionate and understanding when he was alive. At the time, I resolved that something like that would never happen to me again. 1943 was my first Festival as Wolfgang's wife, and we suffered through my first miscarriage at the same time. Later I had an operation, and afterwards I had to make it through another miscarriage. The war brought along too much confusion. We wanted children more than anything, and then I was expecting again and spent all of my time in Wahnfried.

After the wedding Winifred went to Prague with my mother to buy furniture for the Berlin apartment. Winifred had heard that good bargains were available on Jewish-owned furniture and other Jewish-owned household objects, but she wouldn't say later whether she had actually taken advantage of them. At the time Winifred was also hoarding huge stocks of textiles in her stately home in Oberwarmensteinach. Sometime after the wedding Hitler hosted my parents in the Reich Chancellery for a full hour.

In the summer festival of 1943, Hitler insisted that the *Die Meistersinger von Nürnberg* [The Mastersingers of Nuremberg] be performed with Wieland's stage design in remembrance of the 1868 premiere. Tietjen was directing, and so Wieland had to work with the hated Tietjen for the first time. Furtwängler tolerated them and their plotting during the rehearsals. Hitler liked Wieland's stage designs because they were similar to the work of Reich stage-designer, Benno von Arndt. In order to transform the festival grounds into a Nazi mass demonstration at the end of the opera, Hitler gave his permission for the Hitler Youth (HJ), the League of German Girls (BDM), and men from the SS-Standard Wiking regiment to participate with the festival choir. To Hitler's joy Winifred crowned it all by making a connection in the program notes between *Die Meistersinger* and the Final Victory:

> In impressive form, the Mastersingers show the creative German man and his ethnically-conditioned creative will. . . . As the western civilized world struggles with the destructive spirit of the plutocratic-bolshevist world-conspiracy, this German man gives our soldiers insurmountable fighting strength and extreme confidence that our forces will achieve victory.[69]

With such phrases she displayed no doubts about the Final Victory. Moreover, nothing prevented Winifred from giving her usual reception for the artists. On July 10, though not intended for the public, she agreed to a long interview about the history of the Bayreuth Festival and the Wagner family. She proudly recounted, among other things, stories from the year 1923 and the failed putsch, and said:

> We were among those who steadfastly believed in the Führer, and who have stood by him through thick and thin. . . . No one has thanked us better and more nobly than the Führer himself.[70]

But between the lines it is apparent that she believed that everything was coming to an end. Then Mussolini's Italian dictatorship fell on July 25, greatly disrupting the spirit of the festival, especially because the Wagners particularly admired him.

In December 1943 my cousin Wolf-Siegfried was born—the first name Wolf was supposed to emphasize the family friendship with Hitler. After my uncle Bodo Lafferentz's divorce, he and my Aunt Verena hurried to marry on December 26, but documents were still missing. Two more witnesses were necessary in addition to the two who were there—Wieland and Wolfgang. To achieve the correct number of witnesses, Hitler and Himmler were registered in their absence.[71]

1944: Wieland's Deployment to the Branch Concentration Camp Bayreuth-Flossenbürg and Hitler's Vision of a Peace Festival in 1945

Even as the German anti-aircraft emplacements became more and more ineffective against the Allied bombings of Germany in 1944, Winifred was still able to complain about annoying trifles, for example, the telephone's going out in January because of the war. She also complained about the playing of the *Wesendonck-Lieder* [Songs] at the commemoration of Wagner's death on February 13. She had wanted to uphold the taboo that Cosima had imposed upon Wagner's lover, Mathilde Wesendonck, though if not for Wagner's relationship with Wesendonck, the *Tristan* opera would very possibly not exist.[72]

This year brought problems for Winifred from one as unlikely as the admiral of the French Marines, Trolley de Prévaux, whose first marriage was to the great-granddaughter of Franz Liszt, Blandine, one of my great aunts. Later, in 1939, he married Lotka Leitner, a Polish Jew who had emigrated to Paris. After the two of them joined the resistance and were arrested by the Germans on March 29, Blandine tried to intervene through Winifred and save her ex-husband.[73]

On Siegfried Wagner's seventy-fifth birthday (June 6), the Wagners were alarmed by the news of D-Day, the Allied invasion of Normandy. Despite the looming catastrophe, Hitler gave orders to prepare for the 1944 festival. The preparations included having Flemish war prisoners build trenches around the Festspielhaus.[74] At this point the majority of the Bayreuth population was against performing the Bayreuth Festival. Still far from any reality of war, Wieland demanded that he should finally take over the festival.

His insistence resulted in a compromise that he accepted halfheartedly: *Die Meistersinger*, for which he had created the stage design under Tietjen the year before, would be performed twelve times, but a new production without Tietjen would be planned for 1945. Otto Daube welcomed the Führer on his arrival at the Bayreuth Festival. His description is telling:

> On one track of the Bayreuth main train station, special cars arrived with Festival guests who were greeted by an orchestra, alternately from the Wehrmacht and the Labor Service, while on the other tracks, special cars crossed back and forth with refugees escaping nights of bombing in the large cities, pillars of smoke, and abandoned waste-lands of rubble.[75]

During the second intermission of *Die Meistersinger* on July 20, 1944, the rumor circulated that Hitler had been the victim of an assassination attempt. On July 21 the *Bayreuther Presse* reported, "His works are secure."[76] Even during the festival reports surfaced that the assassins, including Claus Schenk Graf von Stauffenberg, had been executed and that their families had been persecuted. Throughout her life Winifred remorselessly regarded Hit-ler's attempted assassins as traitors, and even my father found only scornful words for them, such as, "Dilettantes, not even capable of carrying out an assassination attempt."[77]

August 9 was the last performance of *Die Meistersinger* during the mobi-lization for "total war." The Wagner family found out a few days later that Trolley de Prévaux and his wife Lotka had been executed by Klaus Barbie, the Gestapo executioner from Lyon, a topic that became taboo after 1945. It didn't come up until 1999 in a book written by Aude Yung-de Prévaux, Jacques and Lotka's daughter. Winifred spoke with contempt for their "mixed marriage" and felt no sympathy whatsoever for their fate. But fate was soon reversed in France. When Paris was liberated on August 25, 1944, Germaine Lubin, the French Bayreuth-Wagner singer, supporter of Hitler and friend of Winifred, was locked up for ten months and banned from the stage for five years.[78] On October 16 Winifred publicly expressed her loyalty to Adolf Hitler and wrote:

> Today, after twenty years, after years of a passionate struggle for the German soul, after unimagined successes and profoundly emotional

disappointments—the Führer stands before us, faultless in character, as a shining model . . . he has grown into a hero figure, has been our Führer through darkness and light . . . and from a faithful heart, we pray that we, too, through our love, admiration, and loyalty to his God-ordained mission, have come to resemble, and will remain like him.[79]

In 1944 almost no young German male could escape participation in Goebbel's "total war." Thanks to brother-in-law Bodo Lafferentz, however, Wieland remained subject to different rules. After the German theater closed in August and he returned to Bayreuth, Wieland was able to dodge a draft notice for the *Volkssturm* by becoming the acting civilian leader of the branch concentration camp Bayreuth-Flossenbürg in the beginning of September.[80] He had every privilege there. He assigned himself workdays when he wanted, for which even his mother criticized him. Rather than writing a letter to the Führer, requesting that he be relieved of the bothersome concentration camp service, Wieland complained that his "Mother would rather he do the opposite."[81] Wieland believed that he could receive Hitler's help to take a trip abroad.[82] On December 21, 1944, following a Russian prisoner's escape from the branch concentration camp or the "institute," eighteen other prisoners were transferred to the concentration camp Flossenbürg, a place where only fifteen out of eighty-five prisoners survived because of tuberculosis and malnourishment.[83] Wieland remained at the "institute" until April 1945 and never mentioned it during the rest of his life. It all but disappeared from accounts; even the SS guards of the concentration camp were declared innocent in 1951 due to lack of evidence. Not until 1989 was the case uncovered by a Bayreuth high-school student, Karin Osiander.[84]

But in October 1944, Wieland planned a trip abroad, a subject he wanted to discuss with Hitler, and which infuriated his mother, who was ill at the time.[85] On December 2, Hitler congratulated his dear Verena on her birthday and discovered that Wieland and his wife Gertrud were also in Berlin. That night at two in the morning they dined in the Reich Chancellery, not in the secure bunker for the Führer.[86] Hitler tried to act normal to his youthful admirer, and he spoke of the good old times.[87] According to Gertrud Strobel's notes on what Wieland later told her about the meeting, Hitler talked about his serious injuries from the assassination attempt of July 20. Wieland also told Gertrud Strobel that Hitler resembled "paradoxically Frederick the

Great, but his eyes were larger, the lower lid bulging towards his nose and his body stooped."[88] Hitler took a great interest in Wieland's career and believed fervently that the Final Victory would come soon despite doubts on the part of my aunt Verena, doubts that Hitler would not entertain. He even had visions of a Peace Festival in 1945 and planned for it in rather strange ways; among other things, in anticipation of it, he had expensive costume and stage materials stored in the basement of the House of German Education in Bayreuth.[89]

Wieland saw that Hitler was ill and noted, "If it had been possible to be more confident, more affectionate, etc., then he would have been."[90] After this late meal, Hitler and Wieland went for a walk and spoke in length about the 1945 festival that Wieland would direct.[91] But when Lafferentz approached Goebbels on behalf of Wieland on December 19, attempting— despite the "total war"—to relieve Wieland of his service at the concentration camp for purposes of attending cultural events, Goebbels absolutely refused. Comforted and proud, Tietjen told Winifred on December 17:

> You will be amazed that I can answer "yes" to the Führer's question and say without reservation that, as far as the artistic and technical components are concerned, Bayreuth can be held in the summer of 1945. It would require no additional orders from the Führer.[92]

As the Third Reich collapsed during these months, Wieland wrote a letter to his mother on December 22, demanding that either he or Tietjen direct the 1945 Bayreuth Festival. My father, who was close to Tietjen, was supposed to convince him to withdraw. As an additional tactic he was to secure the collaboration of the conductor, Wilhelm Furtwängler, which didn't actually materialize until 1951.[93] The family spent the Christmas of 1944 in the Wahnfried basement amid an air-raid warning.

1945: "Even If We Live in a Lawless Time, We Can Still Look Out for Our Own Interests"

The year 1945 began with Wieland's usual plots against his mother and Tietjen. He gave his mother a seven-page letter—with a catalog of private and professional demands—on January 5, in which he said that Hitler supported his taking power as the 1945 festival director. First and foremost, he played Tietjen and Winifred against one another by justifying the next male generation's claim to power (by which he meant himself and my father): "It is bitter for us that this unflinching loyalty [to Tietjen] is more important to you than your duty to stand by our side and help us."[94] In the letter, Wieland related that he refused to work under Tietjen, whom he said he didn't trust, and who had been working for years "to split the family."[95] Wieland demanded that the sons take over the artistic direction, while Winifred would manage the organizational direction. The letter ended with a plea that she finally separate herself from Tietjen.[96]

Winifred, the politician of power, was fully cognizant of her secure legal position provided by her husband Siegfried's will—she could only lose her seat as festival director if she remarried—and she answered "I will think about everything and then decide . . . whether I can organize the Festival!"[97] Tietjen, also a master of plotting, drove Wieland mad by not reacting to his letter at all. Wieland stewed and connived to call Hitler, to play all his cards against Tietjen. Hitler's reaction was not at all clearly in favor of Wieland, especially since the last few months of war had brought him problems other than the power struggles of the Wagner family. It was my father's secret desire to take power with his brother, but he assisted Tietjen in Berlin and Tietjen trained him "diplomatically." My father worked just as an assistant stage-manager and then as assistant to the director, allowing his brother Wieland to contend with my mother and Tietjen, to whom my father offered his services at the decisive moment, breaking ranks with Wieland. He was brilliant in exploiting his position as the second son and boosting his own claims to power—without exposing himself. He understood how to win over my mother, Tietjen, his brother, and even Hitler at the right moments and to play them against one another.

Later these talents led him to unlimited power as the director of the Bayreuth Festival for life. His suggestions during the last months of the Third Reich reveal that he was the much more realistic of the heirs apparent; he prepared Wieland for events after the war, which he recognized would be lost. He suggested to his brother that they "wait" to take over power together until the war was over.[98] He obviously understood the importance of the right moment. During these months Winifred fought over the festival budget with Tietjen, who wanted to draw on unlimited resources as usual.[99]

The festival faced other problems at the time. In the last months of the Final Solution, the wife of the festival building contractor, Konrad Pöhner, and their children were in great danger because they fell under the Nuremberg race laws. Wolfgang Bayer, Frau Pöhner's cousin, had already been deported to Auschwitz-Birkenau. Winifred no longer had any influence on Hitler; nor were her sons any help since they were busy planning their seizure of power after the war. Wieland thought his job at the concentration camp was hindering his ability to plan for the future. Gertrud Strobel recorded something he said during this period, which shows how barbaric he had become: "Even if we live in a lawless time, we can still look out for our own interests."[100] After the brothers took over power in 1951, they used all means available to eliminate the statements of inconvenient witnesses. To that end, in his autobiography of 1994, my father continued his private war against Gertrud Strobel.

One of Wieland's last coups, an attempt to exploit the chaos during the last months of the war, was his letter of January 9 to Hitler. He asked him to have Cosima Wagner's diaries returned to the Wahnfried archive; Cosima's daughter, Eva, for dubious and manipulative reasons, had given them to the city of Bayreuth. Winifred supported Wieland's petition in a letter to Himmler,[101] yet in the interest of Bayreuth, its mayor, Kempfler, did not join the Wagners' game, and the Cosima diaries remained in the city's possession until their publication in 1976. Another of Wieland's attempts to raise money in these difficult times was his suggestion in January that a research institute should finance a reprinting of Wagner's collected scores, piano scores, and textbooks.[102]

On February 3 the Berlin Staatsoper unter den Linden, which had been rebuilt at great financial cost, was again destroyed by bombs, and my father and mother moved to Bayreuth. According to Gertrud Strobel, Hitler said to Wieland about the Bayreuth Festival, "I am unable to grant Bayreuth any special protection, but I can say this, if it makes it through the middle of February, then nothing more will happen!"[103] Many events of the time affected the Wagner family and its interests. The bombing of Dresden on February 13 and 14 so greatly shocked Winifred that she demanded Wieland and Verena move immediately to her safe home on Lake Constance. Meanwhile, my father had to remain on call for the *Volkssturm* (civilian defense force) in Bayreuth, and Wieland was working at the concentration camp. My mother was seven months pregnant with my sister Eva at the time. At the end of February 1945, Wieland, his brother-in-law Lafferentz, and their families, financed by the proceeds from the sale of *Parsifal* piano scores, began their escape to Switzerland,[104] supposedly a research trip to benefit the "institute" that is, the concentration camp. On March 12 the Vienna Staatsoper burned down, and Wieland's stage design for the *Ring*, which he had planned with Karl Böhm, burned with it. It was not until the 1960s that the two Nazi favorites collaborated successfully.

The destruction of Praetorius's and Tietjen's apartments in Berlin was just as significant, since many important documents from the history of the Wagner family and their connection to Hitler were destroyed, a loss that later helped the brothers take power. In March Winifred and my father were busy evacuating the most important and valuable objects and documents, including the extensive correspondence with Hitler, and storing them in the cellar of the Winifred Wagner Hospital.[105] On March 24, 1945, the end of the Third Reich began to become more and more apparent—even in Bayreuth. The Americans were already in Aschaffenburg, three days later in Coburg, and then in Bamberg.[106] Winifred, now completely void of reality, remained faithful to her Führer despite the approaching end. She wrote, "We hope that a turning point is still coming. I still firmly believe that the Führer has a trump card in his hand that none of us suspects!"[107]

On April 5, 1945, an especially heavy bombardment took place at Bayreuth, during which the Bayreuth Hofgarten and the Villa Wahnfried were both hit. As the chorister Friedrich Theiss wrote, the bombs "struck at an angle in the front of the garden. The hall is halfway destroyed; the 'children's hall' is completely shattered. The roof hangs down crooked."[108] At this point, my father was in the *Volkssturm* and Wieland still at the "institute."[109] My mother, Ellen, who sat in the Wahnfried cellar during the bombing, was never able to overcome that period of her life. The day after the bombing, the SS deployed the remaining prisoners to defuse bombs and clear the area.[110] On April 6 grandmother, mother, and the governess, Emma Bär, fled to the Fichtelgebirge mountains where they had a weekend home in Oberwarmensteinach.[111] My father began transferring the archives stored in the Winifred Wagner Hospital to Oberwarmensteinach, and as a result he gained control over all the documents, even those that could later implicate the Wagners.

Wieland and Lafferentz drove to Berlin during the night of April 6–7 to convince Hitler to return the Wagner scores that German industry had given him as a present on his fiftieth birthday.[112] Hitler instructed Bormann to tell them not to worry because the scores were in the most secure place imaginable, in the safe of the Führer's bunker in his private Chancellery on

Vossstrasse.[113] What really happened to the scores remains one of many secrets. Afterward, Wieland and Lafferentz cleared off to Lake Constance with other important documents; they wanted to take Winifred along with them. She refused and believed that by her presence she could protect the Wagner work entrusted to her—and therefore my father—from a disastrous end.[114] Her concern was not only for Wagner's work, however; she also wanted control over the incriminating documents after the fall of the Third Reich.

On April 11 thirty-five percent of Bayreuth was destroyed by bombs and the Bayreuth branch concentration camp was dissolved.[115] On April 12 *Gauleiter* Wächtler and his Nazi retinue, including a truck with stolen food, left destroyed Bayreuth despite the threat of capital punishment. The acting *Gauleiter*, Ludwig Ruckdeschel, immediately denounced his close enemy Wächtler to Hitler, and Wächtler was shot by an SS man in the Bavarian forest. On April 14 the Americans occupied Bayreuth, and the Bayreuth citizens quickly destroyed their party badges and pictures of Hitler, and to Winifred's horror, her friend Lis Becker burned the large portrait of Hitler.[116] During this chaotic time, my sister Eva was born in Oberwarmensteinach near Bayreuth.

Interestingly, the Americans swiftly confiscated the important technical documents regarding weaponry at the branch concentration camp.[117] It has never been clear what then happened to these documents. Though the Nazi period was over in Bayreuth, Oberwarmensteinach remained under constant artillery fire. Winifred wrote about this dramatic moment in the life of my mother and sister:

> Eva was born amid artillery fire—the flight formations buzzing overhead, the low-flying aircraft right next to us, etc. etc. I fled with the infant into the forest before it was even twenty-four hours old, and Ellen was transported into the so-called cellar on a ladder with a mattress, in case the wooden house caved in![118]

This version of heroic Winifred saving my mother and sister had little to do with what actually happened. Winifred ordered that Ellen be taken to the cellar, and my mother, weakened after just giving birth, could not defend herself against the order as Winifred ran with Eva into the forest. This episode led to a lifelong tension between the controlling mother-in-law and her daughter-in-law, and my mother's more credible version was never entertained.

On April 19 the Americans occupied Oberwarmensteinach, and with the Wagners absent, Bayreuth citizens and prisoners plundered Wahnfried and the Führer's annex. Even at the time, Winifred wrote Hitler on April 20, 1945, with greetings for his birthday, although it is unknown whether the letter ever arrived.[119] The Bechstein Villa was destroyed in the battle around Berlin on Hitler's birthday, and many more important documents were lost, including photos and letters from Hitler to the Wagner and Klindworth families.[120] Wieland's flight with his family and the Lafferentz family on April 22, 1945, with the intention of using the Wagner writings to build a new, opulent life for himself, failed.[121] Austria broke away from Germany on April 27 and declared its independence, the Austrian citizenry viewing themselves as the first victims of National Socialism. It was certainly no coincidence that after the suicide of Hitler and Eva Braun, who had married shortly before, the radio accompanied the report of his death with Wagner's funeral march from *Götterdämmerung*.

Winifred was supposed to have later remarked about the end of the war, "1945 was the absolute capitulation. Nothing else was possible!"[122] Winifred could now develop her theory that she was the victim of history, and the time had come for her sons to take over power.

2

*The Power Principle. German
History and Family History from 1945
to 1976: From "We Are Victims of World
History" to "One Hundred Years of
Self-Representation"*

From Conspiracies in the Third Reich
to "Neidhöhle," the Cavern of Envy,
in New Bayreuth: Business as Usual

After World War II the Wagners landed on their feet; it certainly helped that
Bayreuth and therefore the Bayreuth Festival lay in the American-occupied
zone of Bavaria. Many political events of the period, including the developing Cold War between Stalin's communist dictatorship and the Western
democracies, worked in favor of Winifred and her sons. On December 8,
1948, a triumphant Winifred Wagner received the final verdict of her trial:
she was classified as a *Minderbelastete*, or "a minimally incriminated person," and only had to pay the reparations fund six thousand marks. During a
two-and-a-half-year probation period, she was not permitted to run, super-
vise, control, or acquire any business, so she could no longer direct the festival, and her assets were frozen.[1] Nevertheless, despite these limitations, she
was able to live well.

Reading the court records from 1947 to 1949 closely, however, reveals the
lies that integrated this Hitler favorite with the elite keepers of the Wagner
Holy Grail: one of the most shameless assertions was that she—a lifelong
anti-Semite and admirer of Hitler—"was ultimately a woman who had
shown generous convictions and great humanity"[2] because she had saved

persecuted Jews. The truth is that traditional Wagnerian house-Jew politics always distinguished between useful Jews, often assimilated Jewish Wagnerians like Elsa Bernstein,[3] and Jews who were undesirable. Arbitrarily deciding who was an acceptable Jew and who was not did not make Winifred the Jews' saving angel during the Third Reich. The Wagners knew, for example, that the Jewish Wagner singers Henriette Gottlieb and Ottilde Metzger-Lattermann were murdered in Auschwitz. Everyone who knew Winifred knew that, until the day she died, she categorized Jews as full, half, and one-quarter Jewish, and she also derided them with racist epithets such as "poor mixed-breed," using the terminology from the Nuremberg Race Laws. Significantly, Karl Würzburger, a former Bayreuth Jew, spoke for Winifred during her trial on June 26, 1947, and it was also he who provided Wieland and Wolfgang their vital de-Nazification certifications, when they later took over the festival.

My father's earlier manipulations allowed Winifred to lie during the trial about Hitler's letters. In the dead of night during the last days of the war, he had taken all of the significant documents in the Wagner archive—most importantly, the extensive letters to and from Hitler—from my grandmother's house in Oberwarmensteinach, maintaining complete control over those documents. In September of 1946, neither Winifred nor my father gave the "Amis"—Colonel Floris and the CIC officer Lichtblau, the "Commander in Chief,"—the intimate letters from Winnie to Wolf and to Wieland and Wolfi, my father.[4] Immediately after the war ended, son and mother manipulated the most significant sources of information; they either withheld them or made them disappear. And as the years passed, nothing changed. After the scandal in 1975 about the Winifred Wagner documentary by Hans Jürgen Syberberg, all the crucial letters disappeared from the Munich home of my cousin Amelie Lafferentz Hohmann, the eldest daughter of my aunt Verena. It was not until 1987 that a Bayreuth schoolgirl stumbled upon some of Wieland Wagner's documents, which revealed his close relationship to the Führer, his membership in the Nazi Party from 1938 on, and his administrative position in the Bayreuth-Flossenbürg branch concentration camp. That late discovery shows just how long their manipulations were able to succeed.[5]

The court's ruling in Winifred's trial included other outrages. For example, Richard Wagner was cleared of any anti-Semitism though it was "recognized" that many Wagnerians had also been supporters of Hitler. The witnesses and trial spectators were also fraudulent. The witnesses were either afraid, like Lotte Warburg, or felt a false loyalty for Winifred, like Emil Praetorius. In the courtroom on June 25, Winifred's hired mouthpieces made unwelcome witnesses like Georg Spitzer, Gustav Kröninger, and the Bayreuth socialist Oswald Merz seem unreliable.[6]

Winifred and my father successfully undermined anyone who muddled their clean picture of the innocent family. They even had to undermine Winifred's own daughter and anti-Nazi, Friedelind, who attacked them with her autobiography, Nacht über Bayreuth [Night Over Bayreuth]. Winifred declared on November 9, 1947, "That book is full of inaccuracies."[7] She, my father, and Wieland used similar, malicious tactics to neutralize their unwelcome cousin, Franz Beidler, in March of 1947. In the end, such people were ignored during the investigation. But what actually happened before the signing of Winifred's official renunciation of power over Bayreuth, which did not occur until January 21, 1949?

In the spring of 1948, the Americans discontinued de-Nazification in Bavaria, which greatly helped the Wagner family and allowed them to recover their family possessions. The whitewashed de-Nazification certificates for Fritz Kempfler, lord mayor of Bayreuth during the Nazi period, for Hans Reisinger, Wieland's father-in-law, and for Otto Strobel, director of the Richard Wagner archive during the Nazi period, encouraged Winifred and her sons to hope that they, too, would be "spared." In keeping with their belief in male dominance, Wieland and Wolfgang worked to exclude their sisters in the draft agreement concerning the family's holdings. When Wieland's wife, Gertrud, claimed that she should become the "Mistress of Wahnfried," my father grew furious and spoke of "distributing spoils that were not yet theirs,"[8] when he wrote to Wieland in the middle of June, skillfully hiding his own desire for power: "the concept of a mistress is nonsense, because the notion implies that reasonable coexistence is impossible."[9]

In May a Wagner family friend, the Social Democrat (SPD) Hans Rollwagen, was elected lord mayor of Bayreuth. He made the Wagner family a pivotal feature of his campaign, for he recognized the family enterprise's financial significance to the otherwise unimportant, provincial town. The replacement of the Reichsmark by the Deutschmark in June 1948 was also significant to the Wagners because reconstruction could begin in the western zones. Winifred's meeting in August with the SPD lord mayor Hans Rollwagen helped assure her sons' securing power in what came to be known as New Bayreuth. Describing the meeting, Winifred wrote these revealing words to her friend Helena Roesener:

"The town is determined to forget the past [the last three years] and to rectify as best as possible the mistakes that were made. . . . I have always maintained that one day people would come and ask us to appear again—and now it seems as if we've arrived at that point."[10]

From that time on, the Wagners were in control again; the SPD became a part of the New Bayreuth lobby, which continues to this day to advocate for Wagner tourism in the summer. The family could not have wished for more: General Lucius Clay, head of the American occupational authority, stated that he wanted to resume the festival quickly, and the new lord mayor obediently followed the family's plans. Winifred's powerful, though indirect influence made clear that despite her official resignation as festival director, she was by no means prepared to relinquish her role as éminence grise. Until the foundation charter was completed with Wolfgang in 1973, Winifred actually had the final word.

Wieland's return from Lake Constance to Bayreuth in the middle of November 1948 intensified the two brothers' struggle. Meanwhile, Winifred calmly looked forward to the new appellate proceedings on December 1. The lord mayor and the Americans, who had been focused on the Cold War for some time, allowed her to appeal. No more witnesses were called, and Friedelind's autobiography was no longer taken as serious evidence. By this time the distribution of "de-Nazification certificates" had become a standard procedure in West German post-war politics. The struggle among Winifred, Wieland, and Wolfgang to become the Bayreuth Festival director could now begin. For Wolfgang the battle had actually began when he took control over the incriminating Wagner archive shortly before the end of the war. That control made Wieland extremely anxious, for both he and his mother were therefore dependent on Wolfgang, even subject to blackmail during the threatening de-Nazification trials.

Wieland cleverly avoided any punishment under the American de-Nazification laws by running off with his family to the French zone of Lake Constance. The de-Nazification provisions there were comparatively mild, and they focused almost exclusively on Nazis in important positions. Wieland also profited from lenient investigative commissions. As soon as there was no longer any danger of his being unmasked as a Nazi and a minion of the Führer, he presented himself to the world as an artist and waited for the right moment to take over power in Bayreuth. He and my father did everything possible to assure that no one anywhere spoke publicly about their close relationship to Hitler, about Wieland's party membership from 1938 on, and certainly not about Wieland's managerial position in the branch concentration camp of Bayreuth-Flossenbürg.

On May 6, 1946, Wieland wrote to his former teacher Overhoff about the issue: "I have serious reservations about going to the other zone before the Bayreuth thing is decided, before I have a guarantee I will be left undisturbed, and that no example will be made out of me."[11] Nor did he want to act either as a scapegoat or a representative for his mother "because she will have a hard time getting back on her feet in the future." He also feared others who knew about his friendship with Hitler. Emil Praetorius wrote in November 1946, "I know how much of Nazis these Wagner boys were, how proud they were to be in his graces, which they felt permitted their impertinence and intellectual-artistic presumptuousness."

Wieland's statements to Overhoff reveal an arrogant disdain:

Let any dear friend from Bayreuth or from Troublemaker Central, the Hirth house [i.e., a friend of Praetorius], go and make a report—it's completely irrelevant whether someone did something wrong or not.[12]

By "Troublemaker Central, the Hirth house," Wieland was referring to the Munich publisher Georg Hirth, who met with persecuted artists who had been considered "degenerate" during the Nazi period, including Praetorius. Wieland must have justifiably assumed that Praetorius would resist his takeover of Bayreuth, for Wieland had repeatedly denounced Praetorius to Hitler and other Nazi bigwigs in his earlier attempts to eliminate Heinz Tietjen as well. In plain language, Wieland was able to avoid imprisonment and manage what he had been unable to do during the Nazi period— eliminate his mother and finally come to power himself. But the price was high. Outwardly, at least, he had to share power with his brother Wolfgang, who was more clever and had apparently remained politically impartial, but who had otherwise and nevertheless enjoyed all the advantages of being a Wagner and chosen "son" of Uncle Wolf. But Wieland knew that his brother was fully aware of his and their mother's pasts.

Wieland anxiously spent his time on Lake Constance preparing plots to gain power, but he was also preparing the new company product post-Hitler. It was clear that in a democratic Germany, the Bayreuth Festival would fail if it remained tied to the style of its Nazi past. Above all, taking power meant making a decisive shift in dealing with Wagner's life, work, and anti-Semitism, as well as a need to conceal the Wagner family's friendship to Hitler and its role in the "Third Reich." Wieland's new strategy was to make these topics taboo, to falsify, suppress, and conceal information about them. Consequently, he created a new legend for his life; he wrote his friend Maria Dernburg in 1946: "I always distanced myself from the party and from its prominent anti-Wagner, inartistic figures. . . . As the grandson of Richard Wagner, a world separated me from those who yearned stubbornly for power. . . . You know that the question of Jews and anti-Semitism never existed for me or my parents."[13]

My father served up a similar lie in his 1994 autobiography, *Lebensakte* [Acts of Life]. In his seventh chapter, dubiously titled "From the End to the Beginning," he wrote:

Fortunately my brother had no reason, and I had just as little reason to dress myself in sackcloth and ashes and beat my breast in penance. Our past had been too short and too insignificant. We had done nothing criminal and did not need to seek justification for things we did or didn't do. We were much more interested in how we could be productive, creative, and effective.[14]

Other sections of his autobiography show my father's complete inability to regret and to mourn for the crimes of the Nazi regime and the murder of millions. For example, my father's affectionate descriptions of Uncle Wolf, that is Hitler, in the fourth chapter, titled "Opus Drei," and his descriptions of Hitler's official visits to the guesthouse of the Villa Wahnfried on the family estate between 1936 and 1939 show his inability to see Hitler for who he was. Hitler stayed in the Siegfried Wagner house in the so-called "Führer building," which had been set up specifically for him:

It was a given that Hitler would be there for each Festival, and his presence on the Wahnfried estate, thus right next to us, allowed him to invite us over and extend his bohemian-like friendliness to my siblings and me—especially during summer time when politically it was relatively calm (and still is). He always treated my mother with faultless manners, behaving like a gentleman from the old Austrian school. Reserved and courteous, he bowed and kissed her hand. He listened attentively and with an open mind to discussions, never interrupting anyone. In our presence, he avoided any uncontrolled flash of temper, and he never denigrated anything. One could, in fact had to get the impression that in our circle, he sought the harmony one expects in a family, but which he lacked. Perhaps he even found it with us. We children [my father is speaking of himself as a teenager between the ages of 17 and 19] were able to ask him candid questions without reservation, so our being together was uncomplicated and completely devoid of the cultish, awe-inspiring distance that elsewhere protected him, treating him like the ambassador of God for the honor and greatness of the common German. [15]

In addition to this insensitive, repressed German style of language, my father also made false statements about Richard Wagner's anti-Semitism, Richard Wagner's influence on Hitler, and whether Wagner was the son of Florian Geyer and whether Geyer or Cosima's grandmother Bethmann were Jewish. Those are topics for coming generations of historians to consider, one hopes without the typical fawning deference toward Bayreuth and the German Wagner cult. Only years after her sons' accession as festival directors did Winifred confess her true thoughts about Wieland and Wolfgang's takeover of power. In the context of my collaboration on the Hans Jürgen Syberberg film (1975), she said:

Wieland should have also been found guilty at a de-Nazification tribunal, etc. He was, for example, the regional cultural advisor here in Bayreuth and I know a lot more. He was released from a year of military service and his entire service at the front. Yes, dear God, if that is not profiteering. . . . He was never accused in front of the tribunal. . . . That Wieland made it through so smoothly . . . I mean, that is very good for Bayreuth . . . but fundamentally incomprehensible. And: if we want to be perfectly clear and frank: I took on everything . . . and I was the scapegoat . . . and in so doing I virtually cleared both of the boys.[16]

She would not have dared make such a statement when Wieland was alive. My father said nothing, worried only about clearing himself: Winifred and Wieland were guilty, and he was only the little innocent one. Their self-interest manifested itself repeatedly. For example, when my uncle Bodo Lafferentz was also classified as *Minderbelastet* and had to pay only a modest "expiatory sum," Winifred wrote a letter to her friend Gerdy Troost, complaining that the verdict was unfair, because Bodo had held a high position in the party and the SS.[17] But my father, now out of the woods, had good reason to defend his mother in his autobiography: Winifred, Wieland, and Wolfgang all knew too much about one another's guilt, and at any point they could blackmail each other. Their versions of history are, therefore, fundamentally suspect. Finally, on January 21, 1949, Wieland and Wolfgang convinced their mother to sign the text relinquishing her power, in effect her abdication, an achievement that they never could have realized during the Third Reich:

> I hereby solemnly swear that I will refrain from any involvement in the organization, administration or directorship of the Bayreuth Festival. In accordance with my intentions of some time, I will entrust my sons Wieland and Wolfgang with the designated tasks and grant them all necessary powers.[18]

What reads as a well-intentioned abdication is merely what her sentence by the courts (of December 8, 1948) forced her to do. Because Uncle Wolf (Hitler) convinced Wieland to renounce his sole claim to power in 1934, Wieland was compelled to share power with his brother. Later, the struggle between the brothers on Festival Hill had devastating consequences with Winifred, the éminence grise, constantly provoking them. She played the brothers against one another and even went so far as to include their families in her machinations. Their father, Siegfried, and their mother's mutual testament of March 8 was also ignored in the sons' power grab; the testament stated that all four children should inherit equal portions—but, in agreement with her sons, Winifred excluded the sisters. The sisters revolted. Nonetheless, so that the family's return to power was not endangered by internal quarrels, the sisters were mollified with vague promises.

Naturally, Winifred's abdication was also regarded as a muzzle for her—and if she did not follow the sons' vision, the sons knew how to pressure her:

by ignoring her until she capitulated to their wishes. They learned from her, Tietjen, Hitler, and other members of the Nazi elite in the Third Reich, how to pressure or eliminate unpleasant opponents and enemies. Yet in June 1949 Winifred wrote her friend Ilse Hess, the wife of Rudolf Hess, what she thought about her sons' new wealth of power:

> I remain completely in the background—but since the boys must use my property and my capital to perform the Festival, they are naturally accountable to me, and without my consent, nothing happens.[19]

Meanwhile, German society, which had long since reverted to subservience, accepted this new distribution of roles. Despite public reports about Wieland and Wolfgang's success, justifiable doubts also surfaced about the Wagner grandsons' qualifications. Praetorius wrote Tietjen in the middle of May 1949 with a correct assessment of the new Bayreuth "spirit":

> But the grotesque today is that Nazism, anti-Semitism etc. are no longer incriminating, that in fact the opposite is the case, that namely opposition towards them arouses suspicion. The entire thing is a pure fool's comedy.[20]

My father presented a detailed financial plan with the intention of opening the Bayreuth Festival under his and Wieland's leadership. It was a significant step, though he could not have created the plan without excellent advisors like Konrad Pöhner, who for a long time held the office of mayor and official cultural advisor. My father also timed the founding of the "Society of Friends of Bayreuth" perfectly with the help of the former right-wing Freikorps leader Gerhard Rossbach. With the aid of German industrialists and company leaders like Hans Bahlsen, Berthold Beitz, and Otto Springorum, the society returned the festival to solid financial ground. Winifred's confidant, Moritz Klönne, became the first president of the "Friends."[21]

Wieland withdrew entirely into Wagner's work and pondered how, after Hitler, Wagner's operas could be marketed as apolitical. Wolfgang managed money matters, and Wieland undertook the "new concept" for the festival product—"Wagner and Co." After the paralyzing years of de-Nazification, they were finally back in action.

As noted earlier, Dr. Karl Würzburger openly supported the new festival directors, who, he believed, promised success, and he provided Bayreuth with the right publicity, particularly facilitating the festival's assumption of its sparkling new name: "New Bayreuth."[22] And so the topic of Wagner and anti-Semitism had been cleared from the table. The brothers prohibited any public statements about Hitler or the Nazi period, and they forbade their mother to talk about either topic, which she seemed to manage, at least publicly. But among her old Nazi friends, she broke the prohibition repeatedly, especially in the Richard Wagner associations, where she was idolized as she had been during the "Führer" time. She remained faithful to her Wolf and lauded Hitler for having saved the Bayreuth Festival in 1933. Wieland later coined the cynical anti-Winifred slogan, "She continues to believe in 'The Final Victory.'" Consequently, laughing with him, people were distracted from his and Wolfgang's past.

During Pentecost Sunday 1950, at the first general assembly of the "Society of Friends of Bayreuth," Klönne announced that the Bayreuth Festival would be supported with 400,000 Deutschmarks, at that time an extraordinarily high amount of money. My father then announced that the Bayreuth Festival would be reopened on July 29, 1951.

1951: New Bayreuth's Refuge in Psychoanalysis and Abstraction

By the end of July 1951, the era of Wieland and Wolfgang Wagner and their New Bayreuth had begun. It was anything but new and hardly a beginning from zero. The slogan, "This is for art," which Siegfried had chosen for reopening the festival in 1924 after World War I, was even more dishonest after Hitler. With Wilhelm Furtwängler conducting Beethoven's Ninth Symphony at the reopening—an attempt to whitewash the past—Bayreuth in reality continued with the house politics of the Nazi period. Of all operas, the performances began with *Parsifal*. Wieland directed it and created the stage design. From the race myth he fashioned a psychoanalytic parable that could be interpreted in a number of ways—a brilliant tactic that created the myth of "Wagner and Freud" and prevented any political discussions about the "Wagner issue" before or during the Third Reich.

The production of *Die Meistersinger* by Rudolf Hartmann included a stage design by Wieland's father-in-law, Hans Reisinger, one of Hitler's architects, demonstrating that the New Bayreuth would not break from its aesthetic past. In the program distributed at the 1951 festival, the brothers heavily falsified their own pasts and the history of the Bayreuth Festival itself, particularly in the section covering the seventy-five-year history of the family enterprise. This manipulation is obvious in the shameless portrayal of the "Era of Winifred Wagner (1930 to 1944)."[23] All that is mentioned about the thirties and forties are golden voices and similar delights. Even the Wagners of the next generation, born shortly before or after 1945, became a part of the New Bayreuth marketing strategy—as clearly shown in that 1951 festival program.

My Early Life as an "Atypical" Wagner

The takeover of the Bayreuth Festival greatly affected both Wieland and Wolfgang's families, all of whom lived at Villa Wahnfried, so the events of that time greatly affected both my older sister Eva and me. The story of my childhood, of being in the "freezer," stuck among the second and third generations of Wagners, all of whom were obsessed with power, is one of constant questioning. As a child, I could never comprehend why I could not play with my cousins Iris, Nike, or Daphne, or with my cousin Wolf-Siegfried, whose godfather was Hitler and whom we all called Wummi. Other children, too, were not allowed to play on the family property. Why did American officers live in the Siegfried Wagner house on the Villa Wahnfried grounds, while we lived in the tiny gardener's house? Why did my grandmother speak scornfully about the wild "niggers" and their music, even though a friendly African American—despite orders to the contrary—always slipped me chocolate and oranges? Why did no one take any notice of my childish curiosity at the age of four? I received no answers to any of these questions. My first Wagner opera as a four-year-old child was *Parsifal*: death, blood, and endless suffering. My uncle Wieland's celebrated production of 1951 filled me with horror and fear. It was not until much later that I realized how right my instincts had been.

The person who kept me from becoming a "typical" Wagner was my mother, who suffered greatly from the constant family battles fostered by Winifred. In the beginning of the 1950s, my mother disappeared repeatedly to a psychiatric clinic; my father never explained these absences to us, and as a child, I unfortunately interpreted them as her lack of love for me. My older sister Eva and I were often sent to a children's home during Mother's periods of crisis or during particularly intense fights within the family.

I did not learn all the details until after the divorce of my parents in 1976. Only much later could I begin to understand my mother's deep depression at the time. Under pressure from my father, my mother had severed communication with her mother Thora in 1951. Highly educated but critical of the Wagners, Thora was not thought to be good enough for them. On October 22, 1953, she took her life in Wiesbaden by overdosing on sedatives. We never had an opportunity to know each other, and as my uncle Gustav told me much later, my grandmother Thora always spoke the following words to express the pain she felt from the estrangement: "Losing a child in life is more painful than losing a child to death."

Meeting my aunt Friedelind for the first time in 1954 was an important event in my life. My father's older sister had come to attend the *Lohengrin* performance in the Festspielhaus. I had heard strange stories about her from the family, stories that made me curious to meet her. My father made mostly derogatory remarks about her: she was a terrible, undisciplined child and simply ran away from home to America. I first met this "impudent American aunt," whom the family had nicknamed "Mouse," in the Festspielhaus, and I immediately had an entirely different impression of her. She resembled us, with her Wagner nose, and she impressed me with her exotic clothing and her casual, boisterous demeanor. She approached me with a smile and greeted me warmly. She was the only one in the family who asked about my interests and who knew how to treat a boy my age. She renounced the Bayreuth posturing and the Wagner cult that the rest of my family promoted with passion. My father prevented my having any further contact with her, which I found greatly disappointing. So I did not come to admire her until much later.

From Wahnfried to Festival Hill and the Daily School Routine in Bayreuth

In January 1955 we were able to leave the gardener's house and move into a villa on Festival Hill. The change from Wahnfried Park to Festival Hill was a profound break in my childhood. "We will finally be able to live in peace and quiet," said my mother, who was worried about my fragile health, but though

I now had my own, big room, my situation did not improve. Since our villa was only a few meters from the Festspielhaus and my father had now dedicated his time exclusively, day and night, to the Wagner enterprise, the last bit of family life quickly disappeared. Our new home had been transformed into a spacious annex of the Festspielhaus. My father focused on nothing but the cult and the Wagner legacy. He had the property enclosed by fences, bushes, and walls, so that I could only see out from a window on the third floor. In the summer, you could no longer see the Festspielhaus from the yard, so sometimes I felt as if I were in a prison. I missed the open yard, the proximity of the town to the Villa Wahnfried, and the forbidden games with the "Wieland children." Since we had moved to another part of the city, I had to attend the Graser School and found it difficult to make friends with the other children. There I succeeded only in music, especially singing.

The older I became, the more fascinated I became by the Festspielhaus, and more than anything I wanted to know what happened inside. As a result I witnessed firsthand the conflict between my uncle and my father, which was very painful at the time. In these stressful conditions, my father's production of *Der fliegender Holländer* was mounted. I was not aware of the Wagners' Dutchman history. I found the ghost ship frightening and could not understand how it related to Senta's suicide at the end of the opera, nor why the Dutchman should be "redeemed" because of it. In any case, my sister and I were sent away before this festival opened, this time to the children's home Reneé in Wyk on the island of Föhr. Saying goodbye to my parents and Bayreuth was easier than it had ever been. I didn't feel at home anywhere. That feeling didn't change after we returned to Bayreuth, where again I was frequently ill.

The Wagner Family's First Controversy with Its Nazi Past

My first painful encounter with my family's Third Reich history took place in 1956. I discovered pictures of National Socialism in newsreels, newspapers, and magazines. In an educational film at school, we saw excerpts from Nazi propaganda of the time, from the NSDAP's Nuremberg party convention and from the World War unleashed by Hitler: German soldiers marching in goose-step, hysteric mass celebrations for the Führer, war crimes of the Wehrmacht—and Richard Wagner's music accompanying it all. I was horrified by pictures from the concentration camp Buchenwald and its piles of corpses. Frightened, I told my father about the terrible films, and especially about the music in them. "You are too young to understand that," he answered. When that response did not satisfy me, he yelled that I should go out and play, or better yet, that I should do my homework instead of asking questions about things I could not understand. Since I knew that I would be beaten if I persisted, I kept quiet. But I was determined to learn more.

I then turned to my grandmother to see what she could tell me. When I asked her whether there had really been concentration camps in the Third Reich, she answered, "That is all propaganda from the New York Jews, who want to make us and the Germans look bad!" Then I better understood the meaning of the phrase "USA," which she often repeated during her celebrations on April 20, Hitler's birthday: Unser Seliger Adolf [Our Blessed Adolf]. I also began to understand why, when my grandmother reproached me for being restless and active at mealtimes, she said that I should not behave as if I was in a Jewish school. At the time, I thought that Italians were Jews because they were so full of life.

That fall of 1956 was a pleasant change because I began secretly to research my family history. As usual, my parents were on vacation after the festival, and so Gunda Lodes, who worked at the telephone switchboard for the festival administration, took care of my sister and me. Her warmhearted, affectionate manner made her a sort of honorary aunt, and I give thanks to her that my childhood years in Bayreuth were not a constant nightmare. Gunda's father, the kindhearted Hans Lodes, had been the Bayreuth Festival caretaker for decades.

Before my parents left for their vacation, my father strictly forbade me to play in the Festspielhaus. This prohibition felt like an invitation to find the master key, which Father had hidden away in a secret place. I found it, stuck it in my trouser pocket, and began my expedition into the Festspielhaus. With my heart thumping, I entered the room above the old painters' hall. There I found a large plaster model of the Festspielhaus, a painting with scenes from the *Ring Cycle*, tomes about different human races, festival guides from the years 1933–44, and photos of my grandmother, my Uncle Wieland, and my father with the Führer. I was horrified by an enormous oil painting that showed Hitler with a threatening German shepherd.

I particularly wanted to know more about the plaster model, and I deliberated over who best could answer my questions. I could not turn to Father since I had strolled down a forbidden path. In any case, his reaction to my questions about the Nazi-period films had shown his resistance to talking about these topics. Grandpa (Opa) Lodes—as I called him—eagerly gave me an answer:

> That is a plaster model of the Festspielhaus. The "Führer" wanted to cover the old Festspielhaus after the "Final Victory" and use it only on special occasions for very special guests. He wanted to build a new Festspielhaus next to the old one. The new one would be exactly the same, and it would be used for the performances.

"This Führer, was he here often?" I wanted to know. "The Führer loved Wagner and his family very much," he replied. Since Grandpa Lodes spoke so warmly about the Führer, I wanted to know where he was today. "He has been dead for a long time," Opa Lodes answered. But then he grabbed me vigorously by the hand and pulled me out of the storeroom. Silent and with a serious face, he shut the doors and said, "I don't want to see you here without your father anymore. Otherwise you can no longer come visit us." Much later I discovered that this plaster model was the Nazi architect Emil Rudolf Mewes's 1940 "monumentalization" of the Festspielhaus. When my parents returned, my family investigation was over, as was my carefree life with the Lodes family.

Our class at school got a new teacher named Popp, who enjoyed trying to make me more refined. He also enjoyed telling me about his experiences as a soldier in World War II. "If we Germans had only had a little more time, the Final Victory would have been certain. But "the whole world was against us," he complained.

In 1956 Grandmother Winifred's health led her to move from her house in the Fichtelgebirge mountain range to the Siegfried Wagner house, which had remained empty since the Americans' departure in 1954. Angered by his mother's move, Wieland built a four-meter high wall between the Villa Wahnfried and the Siegfried house, which Winifred continued audaciously— and to much applause—to call the "Führer's annex." She lived with complete nostalgia for Hitler, which heavily burdened her relationship to Wieland and his family, for Wieland understood that such a connection would tarnish his image in the West as a sublime artist.

Every now and then I visited her secretly. I usually found her on the ground floor in the antechamber to the dining hall, sitting at her writing table. She chain-smoked her nonfiltered North States cigarettes, wrote letters, or looked through the open window at Wahnfried Park. That way she could see who went in and out, usually making malicious remarks about the visitors. I also entertained myself in other ways. During the rehearsals of *Parsifal* in the Festspielhaus, for example, I was feeling particularly mischievous and wriggled the red lamp out of the grail. When Parsifal tried to light up the grail at the end of the opera, the trick did not work. Wieland was wild with rage. My young friends Werner, Helmut, and I laughed noiselessly: no redemption!

The more radical Wieland's productions became, the more Winifred began to lobby behind the scenes on behalf of my father. That damaged the brothers' relationship even further. What continued to bind them together, however, was anxiety about their mother: she still divulged too much in interviews, including compromising stories from the Nazi period, and they feared that she might attempt to terminate the family contract. Referring to Wieland's abstract, archetypical interpretation of *The Ring*, in which he increasingly dismissed his grandfather's German and Greek mythology, Winifred said, "Had the Third Reich not fallen, Wieland would never have worked in this style."[24] These problems between Winifred and her sons naturally affected her relationship with her grandchildren. We were isolated from our grandmother so that we would not discover anything else about the Nazi period or the family's close relationship to Hitler. This isolation pained her greatly. In exchange, she sought out friends from the golden days of the Führer, such as the Mitford family and the former English fascist leader Sir Oswald Mosley. Even in 1950 she continued proudly to proclaim:

> I have a very friendly relationship with him and his family, and, naturally, we also touch on the larger issue of England, Germany, and Europe. Mosley is certainly one of the more reasonable Englishmen, and he's found his feet again after he and his wife were imprisoned during the war.[25]

In 1957, when I was ten, I was so unhappy at home and school that I was finally sent off, supposedly for a worsening heart problem, to live for several months on Lake Schliersee with an older couple named Zankl. After my return to Bayreuth, my new teacher, Mrs. Moritz, tried to help me. She understood my situation and did her best to cheer me up. She explained why we children should not sing the first verse of the German national anthem: "Deutschland, Deutschland über Alles." She thought that it was too nationalistic. At the time, Grandmother said something like, "They're even distorting German history in school now. You poor children!"

In July 1958 I passed the entrance examination for the classical gymnasium, the advanced secondary school with a focus on Latin and Greek. I was extremely happy because until that point my schooling had seemed like one long nightmare, and now I could look forward to the gymnasium. But my optimism was soon dampened. I became ill, and again private instructors came to teach me in Bayreuth and Berchtesgaden, and I was not able to attend the gymnasium until April of 1959. I remember that while at Berchtesgaden my father liked to drive me up to Hitler's home in the mountains, a place called Berghof. At Bayreuth in August of 1958, because her sons repeatedly rejected her ideas, Winifred wanted to terminate their contract, which led to another one of our many family crises.

Wieland, the "Resistance Fighter" against the Nazis

In the fall of 1959, my father began to prepare his first production of the *Ring Cycle*, which he wanted to stage the following season. Even my mother had to serve the great Wagnerian cause by helping him. During these years Wieland used some sycophantic journalists to strengthen his legend as a resistance fighter against his mother and National Socialism. My father used the same journalists to create his own myth as a critical realist during the Nazi period. That resulted in a severe confrontation between Wieland and his teacher Kurt Overhoff, who was among a small group of people who recognized the falsifications in Wieland and my father's biographies. Overhoff believed that

> Wieland had only one idol and one guiding principle at that time [in the Third Reich], dear Uncle Wolf. And if anyone dared any criticism whatsoever of this idol, Wieland broke off discussion with that person and threatened him with "denunciation." That, and nothing else, is the full truth.[26]

Wieland defended himself against such attacks by repeating his slogan about his mother, that she continued to believe in the Final Victory. He told his children this distorted version of history, just as my father told Eva and me his own distorted version of history.

At the beginning of the 1960s, Wieland put his personal revolution on public display; he made no attempt to hide his romantic relationship with the singer Anja Silvia, an indiscretion that turned Winifred against him completely. As his financial needs multiplied, family life in Wieland's household began to spin out of control. Wieland even attempted to sell the score of *Tristan*, an act that Winifred worked adamantly to thwart. Later, in June of 1973, she told her friend Gerdy Troost that she regarded the failed transaction with the *Tristan* score as the "birth of the idea for a foundation."[27]

As the 1960 festival approached, I insisted on getting to know my Uncle Gustav Drexel, my mother's brother, and his family in Wiesbaden. I very much enjoyed the days I spent with him, his wife, Henny, and my small cousin Christa, and I was sad when I had to leave after only a week. Many questions remained unanswered; I particularly wanted to learn more about my grandmother Thora, but discussing her seemed to be a strain on Uncle Gustav, and he refused to speak about her sad end. Afterward, I was again sent to Berchtesgaden with my sister, this time to the fancy Hotel Geiger. At the festival that year, family peace was again threatened. My father was overextended and pressured by the constant competition with my uncle, and the family began to feel the effects.

1961: "Bayreuth Is Becoming a Bordello: Leftists, Jews, and Negroes"

The first time I openly confronted my father came in the summer of 1961, when I reproached him for repeatedly reprimanding my mother. I received a beating, and my parents argued violently. The quarrel had another consequence: I ended up at boarding school in Stein an der Traun. There I met my cousin Wummi, and we became dear friends. But when my father heard about it, I was immediately sent back to Bayreuth. This forced departure from Stein had, however, one advantage. I was permitted to watch Wieland's *Tannhäuser* rehearsals. The production created a great stir because the young, beautiful, African American singer, Grace Bumbry, sang the part of Venus, and Maurice Béjart choreographed a provocative and erotic Venusberg scene for the bacchanal in act one. Old Wagnerians were horrified and said, "Thank God that she doesn't sing the role of Elisabeth. That would be especially wrong, a negress singing the part of a Wagner heroine in Bayreuth."

But those were not the only reasons for turmoil that season. Opportunism had led Wieland to become involved with leftists, even though that summer the Walter Ulbricht regime in the German Democratic Republic, communist East Germany, had erected the wall in the middle of Berlin to prevent the communist state from "bleeding to death," due to a mass exodus of its citizens. The communist hysteria also gripped the "Society of the Friends of Bayreuth." They even spoke of war. Completely beside herself, my grandmother raged publicly, "How could Wieland get involved with the leftist, Jewish Ernst Bloch of all people? And then Bumbry! Bayreuth is becoming a bordello." My father sat there silently. At the time, I had only vague ideas about what "leftist," "Jew," and "Negroes" meant. But secretly sympathizing with Wieland, I became incensed by my grandmother's conspiracies and my father's silence.

1962: Confirmation and the Wagners as Pious Heathens

In April of 1962, I was confirmed by Mr. Flotow, a sharp and intelligent Protestant minister. In his meticulous and critical way he opened my eyes to the magnificence of the Bible as a book of history. I realized that my parents had not taught me any Christian values, nor had they been Christian examples for me. I enjoyed attending Sunday services, and I regretted that my family had no interest in them. Within the Wagner family I heard only about those "damn clerics" and "shitty churches." It is true that my parents sometimes spoke enthusiastically about Albert Schweitzer, but this was primarily because the man from Lambaréné had been acquainted with my grandfather Siegfried, and the relationship was good for the family image. My grandmother found Schweitzer's involvement in Lambaréné a "pointless commitment to Negroes" and was always openly against charity as a form of Christianity. My father called us Wagners "pious heathens" in the sense of Goethe, which I did not understand. I will always be grateful to Vicar Flotow for helping me develop an interest in ethical questions.

Gradually, step by step, I began to leave the well-worn family path. In time I found myself listening enthusiastically to Pablo Casal's version of

Bach's Brandenburg Concertos, and Mozart became my favorite composer, even as those around me accepted only Richard Wagner.

Discovering the Hitler Films

On February 13, 1963, the eightieth anniversary of Richard Wagner's death, Winifred decided to reenter the political stage. She believed that her subversive actions were in the interests of all Germany; she even invited East Germans to Wahnfried, including, in 1963, the director of the German Opera in East Berlin, Hans Pischner—all this two years after the construction of the Berlin Wall. Neither my father nor the Bayreuth lord mayor welcomed the delegation. Winifred invited them together with Friedelind and openly promoted reunification.[28] She also accepted invitations to visit other communist countries, like Romania. Officially, she regarded these actions as completely "apolitical," but she used them to promote her own ideology when the moment was right. She always thought a great deal of dictatorial forms of government, whereas she rejected Western democracies as decadent.

The summer of 1963 took place against the backdrop of Richard Wagner's 150th birthday. The theme was "A Life for the Theater." Wagner was again presented as an apolitical "European genius of theater"—entirely inconsistent with what was happening at Bayreuth, for Wieland's contact with the neo-Marxist philosopher Ernst Bloch (1885–1977) had made him turn more and more towards the left. The more that Wieland came to symbolize "parlor socialism," the more my father became a conservative. It only made sense, then, that Winifred regarded my father as the true heir to the Wagnerian legacy.

In the fall my sister was sent to a school of home economics for young ladies. That freed me from her constant supervision. I used this new freedom for my first "political action." A nationalistic, marble bust of Richard Wagner by the sculptor Arno Breker had stood in the festival park since 1955; I painted it red. I happily looked on as the fire department wiped the threatening monster clean. That same fall, when my parents were on vacation recovering from the strains of the festival, I discovered a woodshed near the garage. Father's powerful BMW motorcycle and sidecar were there. In the sidecar I found two cardboard boxes with numerous round aluminum canisters of various sizes. They were so rusted that I couldn't open them barehanded. I secretly moved them to my room, removed the rust, and carefully opened them with a screwdriver. Every canister contained a roll of film. I took one of the larger ones and stuck the strip of film underneath a magnifying glass. My discovery staggered me. There were my aunt, Uncle Wieland, and Grandmother Winifred together with Hitler, joking and promenading through Wahnfried Park. Hitler wore a fancy, double-breasted jacket. The happy Führer, the happy Wagner children, the happy Grandmother Winifred! Then I saw pictures of the Führer in the Festspielhaus. Everyone raised their right hand for the Heil Hitler salute. Wagner's art and the Führer's power. Strapping Herrenmenschen and smiling victors, the mood as the Final Victory was gaining ground. Uncle Wolf and the Wagners were bound together—that was the film's message. My father had turned it all around. With this discovery my father, Wieland, and the rest of the adult world began to terrify me, especially as I remembered the pictures from Buchenwald in the newsreel I had seen in 1956. It was clear to me, that I had to preserve these films, that I had to make sure my father did not hide them again—or even destroy them. I stored them in my closet. I smudged the empty canisters with dirt and returned them to the two cardboard boxes in the sidecar. I decided not to say anything about my discovery but to continue to question my father about Hitler.

My first opportunity came in December 1963. We were on winter vacation in the Swiss town of Arosa, and my parents, my sister, and I took many long walks. I did not want to make my father defensive for that would have ended the conversation quickly. So I emphasized—contrary to the truth—that I was interested in our family connection to the Führer for "purely" historical reasons. I asked him what kind of impression Hitler, as a person, had made on him. He did not try to hide his fascination for "Uncle Wolf." He described his encounters with him with restrained affection. He proudly told me—and he repeated this several times later—that the Führer had visited him in the Berlin Charité hospital, where the famous surgeon Ernst Ferdinand Sauerbruch had personally cared for my father after he had been wounded in the "Polish campaign." "Hitler released your uncle from military service, and only I had to serve the Fatherland," he added. With great enthusiasm he spoke on and on about his time in the labor service (*NS-Arbeitsdienst*) and about his military training, which he characterized as a period of wonderful camaraderie. He told me how the only friend of his life, Emil, was killed by "underhanded Polacks" in a small town, while the "more courageous German army" conquered Poland.

And always Hitler! After one production of *Götterdämmerung* in the Festspielhaus, Hitler invited my uncle and my father to the "Führer's annex" where they talked late into the night at the "Führer's fireside." They discussed the future of German art in the spirit of Richard Wagner, art as an expression of the world's renewal through National Socialism. It was difficult for me to comprehend my father's torrent of words, but I didn't ask any questions for fear he might stop talking. He went on:

We sat by the fireside, and Hitler sketched his vision of our future culture: "When we have finally purged the world of the Bolshevist, Jewish conspirators, then you, Wieland will direct the theater of the West, and you, Wolfgang, will direct the theater of the East."

Softly I asked him whom Hitler meant when he spoke of the "Bolshevist, Jewish conspirators." My question irritated him, and I feared that I had stifled the conversation. Instead, he began talking about German history. Everything had started, he said, with "the disgraceful Treaty of Versailles," for there was mass unemployment in the chaotic Weimar Republic that followed, full of incompetent leftists and "damned liberals." Thus he evoked "Hitler's great works before 1939." I wanted to know more about them, and my father explained:

Hitler overcame unemployment and returned the German economy to worldwide esteem. He freed our people from a moral crisis and united all the forces of good. We Wagners thanked him for rescuing the Bayreuth Festival.

"But what did that have to do with the Jews?" I asked. He replied:

There is a lot said about that, and the leftist intellectuals harass us Germans about the topic, about the number, etc. But that was the only real mistake that Hitler made. If he had won over the Jews, we would have won the war. After the war, the world would not have been as bad as the Allies' propaganda machine claims.

We strolled next to one another silently for the rest of the walk, until my mother began talking about Christmas presents.

1964: We Have Not Talked about Adolf Hitler since Auschwitz

After we returned from winter vacation in January 1964, I met Maria Kröll in Bayreuth. Because of her, I regularly drove to Creussen, thirteen kilometers south of Bayreuth. She lived there with her parents, Joachim and Ursula, and her younger sister, Dorle. Her father taught German, history, and geography at a German gymnasium, and because of his unconventional teaching methods, the students loved him. Joachim Kröll prompted me to read Heinrich Böll, Günter Grass, and other politically—and socially committed—writers, and he was the first person to tell me about the tragedy of German-Jewish history. After such discussions I found my parents' home, the business of the festival, and even the audience unbearable. My father could not prevent a critic from growing within me, and my interest in German history and politics grew. Soon I even dared to welcome the existence of the two German states. At the time my father regarded the conservative Bavarian politician Franz Josef Strauss as the only respectable German politician, and he was furious at my ideas. The discussion about the German Democratic Republic's right to exist ended as had many previous discussions: my father forbade me to say anything else and called Joachim Kröll a "lousy Socialist" who had a bad influence on me. At the end of April 1965, I was sent back to the boarding school at Stein an der Traun against my will to get me away from Kröll's influence.

The majority of my schoolmates there came from families that had benefited from the so-called West German economic miracle. Their parents had no time for them, or they were divorced, or their spoiled kids were lazy and so unskilled that they could never have passed the *Abitur* (the exam to qualify for university) at their normal school. Two students from the Bismarck family, relatives of Germany's first chancellor, were particularly arrogant. My constant battle with pretension increased my desire to read leftist literature. A schoolmate, Henry Hohenemser, son of the city of Munich's cultural advisor at the time, was the first person to discuss anti-Semitism with me. I began to read works by Ernst Bloch, Sigmund Freud, Theodor W. Adorno, Hannah Arendt, Max Horkheimer, and Bruno Bettelheim.

During the summer festival of 1964, a tough confrontation took place between Wieland Wagner and Hans Severus Ziegler. Ziegler in his book *Adolf Hitler. Aus dem Erleben Dargestellt* [Adolf Hitler: Presentations from His Life] expressed his unbroken admiration for Hitler and in this context praised Wieland's production of the *Ring* in Altenburg during the Nazi time, which he had supported. Wieland reacted harshly in a letter: "After Auschwitz there is no more discussion about Adolf Hitler. You damaged the reputation of my mother, the Bayreuth festival and the city of Bayreuth."[29]

1965: Wieland, Wolfgang, Bloch, and Mayer as Philo-Semitic Bayreuth Late Bloomers

During the summer holidays of 1965, I watched the rehearsals for Wieland's new *Ring Cycle*. I slowly recognized a discrepancy between the sponsors, the "Society of Friends of Bayreuth" and some festival guests, such as the Marxist philosopher Ernst Bloch or the self-centered leftist literary historian, Hans Mayer. Clearly opportunistic, my uncle maneuvered between the industrialists Krupp and Siemens on the one hand and Bloch and Mayer on the other, and my respect for him began to fade. Speculating that the culture industry was moving from the right toward the left, he pretended to be leftist.

After my holidays I returned to the Stein boarding school. At that time I was most interested in the early writings of Karl Marx, especially his essay "The Jewish Question." Later, when I talked to my father about my reading experiences, he resorted to his usual monologue. He began with the Nuremberg Race Laws of 1935, which, he stated, the Jews should blame on themselves because they were "the worst race in history." I countered that one should not confuse the Nuremberg Race Laws with the orthodox Jewish tradition. Furious, my father replied that the Jews themselves had clearly provided the impetus for the Nuremberg Race Laws. "Marx himself was an anti-Semite and wanted society emancipated from Judaism." "Yes, but hardly by the 'Final Solution,'" I answered, and the conversation ended there.

The End of Wieland Wagner's New Bayreuth

In 1966 Winifred openly disseminated propaganda for the neo-Nazi NPD, the National Democratic Party of Germany, which had emerged in West

Germany in the context of the public discussions around the Auschwitz trial at Frankfurt am Main (1963–65) and with the first economic recession after a long period of prosperity. A year before she had expressed sympathy for the movement in her letter to Ilsa Ernst: "The NPD will, one hopes, fulfill all our wishes and expectations. I am in the picture and was even invited to Hanover for the founding celebration."[30]

After further consideration, however, she did not participate in the festival. When in 1966 the NPD won 13.6 percent of the vote in Bayreuth, she was out of her mind with excitement. Her close friend Gerdy Troost recounted:

> Yes, the result of the elections was really surprising—one hopes that the representatives of the NPD will prove themselves. It is truly time for cleaning up the corruption.[31]

In the Bayreuth local elections of 1966, the neo-Nazis' election to three of the forty-two council seats reawakened my grandmother's "hope for the 'Final Victory.'" She slowly reshaped herself into the first lady of the radical right, and my aunt Friedelind was furious; Winifred welcomed political friends such as Edda Göring; Ilse Hess; the NPD chairman Adolf von Thadden; Gerdy Troost, the wife of Nazi architect and Hitler friend Paul Ludwig Troost; the fascist British leader Oswald Mosley; the Nazi film director and relative Karl Ritter; as well as the racist author and former Reich cultural senator Hans Severus Ziegler. At her invitation they could "finally" speak openly about the Führer again, for his name had been masked for years with the code word "USA" (*Unser Seliger Adolf,* or "Our blessed Adolf"). In a December 1967 interview with *Der Spiegel,* Friedelind correctly criticized the return of "the fascist demon."

Shortly before the festival in July, Wieland was admitted to the Kulmbach hospital, soon to be transferred to the Munich University clinic. My father did not tell me anything about my uncle's condition, but I suspected that it was serious, as did others. Open warfare broke out between the Wieland and Wolfgang camps as Wolfgang saw that his hour had come. The first rifts appeared when several people played with the idea of switching sides. My father happily welcomed the unexpected devotion from so many, and then, suddenly, he was the sole festival director. Even I was greeted kindly by people who had never paid any attention to me before. The Wolfgangs were "in," and the Wielands were "out." I found the new circumstances just as repugnant as the old. Bayreuth, Festival Hill, the family, and everything around them simply made me sick. I toyed with the idea of leaving Germany. But how without a job and without any money?

On October 17, while at a movie theater watching *The Spy Who Came in from the Cold*, I was informed that my uncle was dying. I immediately hitchhiked to Munich. There my father silently embraced me—for the first and the last time. Crying, my mother told me the news of Wieland's death. I will never forget Wieland's funeral service in the Festspielhaus on October 21, 1966. It was a giant hypocrisy. Winifred broke into tears for her poor Wolfgang, the poor "Wolf," who now had to bear full responsibility for the Bayreuth Festival, completely alone. All of a sudden, so-called fine society discovered their love for dead Wieland. In his speech Bloch paid tribute to Wieland as a leftist *anima candidissima*, the purest of souls—a glorification that is intolerable in the context of current knowledge. Cameras hummed and lights flashed as the long funeral procession moved toward the cemetery. Immediately afterward, a poker game began to decide the new balance of power. My father, my grandmother, and my sister Eva held the best cards.

My Escape from Bayreuth to Paris and London

On February 13, 1967, amid the normal familial disputes and constant financial problems, Winifred, in close collaboration with my father, wrote a three-page addendum to her will, sketching the covenant for a new Richard Wagner Foundation. The rest of the road was rocky, full of scandals and familial mudslinging. It finally ended in 1973 with the conclusive covenant for the foundation, which made my father the lifelong, absolute leader of the Bayreuth Festival. Under a lot of pressure from having the sole responsibility for the festival, he was unable to handle the normal battles on Festival Hill. These tensions did not help our relationship either, which was in danger of becoming even worse, so he allowed me to attend the school in Stein as a day student.

My friends Norbert Friedrich, Henry Hohenemser, and I were disturbed by the NPD functions in Upper Bavaria and decided to disrupt them. Henry and I made precise plans for escape routes, and then after dressing up as Charlie Chaplin's Great Dictator, I showed up at neo-Nazi gatherings. Running through the beer halls without a word was enough to rouse the rabble. I quickly sprinted down our escape route like a hunted rabbit and jumped into Henry's old VW Bug, which was waiting for me with the motor running.

It soon became clear that I no longer fit in at the Stein boarding school, which was rather liberal by Bavarian standards, so I left. In June Wilhelm Pitz, the choir director of the Bayreuth Festival, found me a position with Charles Spencer, the chairman of the prominent New Philharmonic Chorus in London. The Spencer family welcomed me warmly. I greatly enjoyed the season's offering of concerts and operas, and I attended a daily language school to improve my English. I was excited to live so close to the Beatles' studio.

Charles Spencer, a successful choir manager and businessman, was a passionate lover of music and a Wagner critic. This idyllic English stay was abruptly interrupted by an international event: the six-day war between Israel and the Arab countries in June of 1967. Never before was I so fiercely drawn to Jewish history. Full of dread, we sat in front of the television. Day and night we discussed what was happening with great intensity. During these discussions I learned that Charles's parents had been Viennese Jews. After the "annexation" of Austria to Germany in 1938, they had fallen victim to the Nazi terror, but Charles and his sister escaped. Charles's daughter Diana told me other, terrifying stories while we looked at family photos. So a family who had suffered horribly from the Nazi barbarity was allowing me, the child of perpetrators, to live with them, and they treated me like a son. Charles noticed my awkwardness and embarrassment. I confessed to him how oppressive I found the Bayreuth legacy with its anti-Semitism, and I told him about my grandmother's fanatical racism. He said, "Perhaps after the generation of perpetrators, there is hope for a new beginning between Germans and Jews, which might even allow for individual friendships between them. Do not feel guilty, but learn from your family's mistakes." Charles would become a powerful influence in my life, and this wise advice became a personal credo of mine. Similarly, when I was in Paris soon afterward, I met my aunt Blandine de Prevot, a great-granddaughter of Franz Liszt, and without reproach she told me that the Nazis had killed her husband, a resistance fighter. From that point on, ours was a relationship of honest and open conversation.

In the middle of July, Blandine's daughter Daniela invited me to Lessey in Normandy, where she lived in a mansion. There I met her daughter Blandine. She was my age, and her open opposition to the world of her parents fascinated me. After a brief exchange of pleasantries, we immediately recognized that we shared similar views on many significant topics and that in the few areas where we didn't agree, the differences were enriching. My cousin Blandine told me about her connection to the film director Jean-Luc Godard and the Maoist circles that she frequented at the time. She not only argued passionately but fought against social injustice, and for many a night we discussed how one might change our degenerating world society.

1968: The Vietnam War, First Doubts about the Leftist Scene, and Reminders of the Führer and Il Duce

The Vietnam war and the German students' rebellion, led in West Berlin by Rudi Dutschke and in Paris by Daniel Cohn-Bendit, dominated my discussions with Henry Hohenemser. In particular, the April 11, 1968, assassination attempt on Dutschke and the emergency laws of May 30 prompted me to get involved with politics. At home, to the horror of my father and my sister, I defended the students' position. My sister had discovered that sticking with the establishment was more profitable for her. I was so different that in the heated political summer of 1968, my grandmother introduced me to her "respectable circles" with the phrase: "This is Gottfried, friend of Bolsheviks and Jews." And then she would laugh her loud, masculine laugh.

Before the festival opened that year, a heavily armed contingent of police arrived, as if terrorists were threatening to blow up the Festspielhaus with its premiere guests. In reality, the police were there because a few harmless students arrived to protest against the West German industrialists among the guests. When I saw the policemen use force against the protestors, I berated the officers as "pigs." I was spared imprisonment only because I was the son of the boss. After the premiere the usual reception took place in the new castle where demonstrators had also assembled. Even though I was not particularly welcome at the reception, I sat at the table with Willy Brandt, at that time the German Socialist Party's (SPD) foreign minister and the vice chancellor of the largest coalition in Bonn. I regarded him as the sole credible German politician.

Leading figures of the Bayreuth SPD flattered Brandt, hoping for help with their careers. They became nervous when several members of the ballet demonstrated open sympathy for the protesting students. The anxiety grew as they began to ask Brandt uncomfortable questions about current world politics, about Vietnam and Rudi Dutschke, the head of the German Socialist Students' Alliance. Brandt handled the incident with masterly skill: he asked his opponents to his table, and to the horror of the Bayreuth establishment and the furious guests, he spoke with them. Many of the sponsors there were like my grandmother, who, within her narrow circles, referred to the SPD leader as a "Pig socialist" or "Willy Weinbrand." My father was silent, which I interpreted as agreement.

During this "Red" festival summer of 1968, Winifred was especially pleased that the NPD party chairman, Adolf von Thadden, attended a *Siegfried* performance with the Nazi combat pilot Hans Ulrich Rudel. Once again, Hitler seemed omnipresent. Mother's forty-ninth birthday, on August 20, 1968, was markedly in contrast, however: Warsaw Pact troops occupied Czechoslovakia. The clanging of the American tanks seemed ominous as they moved through Bayreuth toward the nearby border.

The following month, in September 1968, I drove to Italy with my exhausted parents for a week's vacation. We stayed at the elegant Astor Hotel in Bologna. During a taxi ride the driver noticed that we were Germans, and he turned around a picture frame that held a picture of Pope Paul VI. On the other side was a photo of Hitler with Mussolini. He called enthusiastically, "Berlino-Roma. Bravi, bravi, il Führer e il Duce!" Father then raved about his trip to Italy with Wieland in July 1938, during which Hitler and Mussolini helped them get their Mercedes going again. "How excited we were about Mussolini!" When I, however, called Hitler and Mussolini criminals, the vacation mood disappeared immediately. It made me even more disgruntled, when my father gave the fascist taxi driver a lavish tip.

My first doubts about the leftist student movement stemmed from watching the persecution of reform politicians after September 29 and from seeing the violent Berlin student demonstrations in the "Battle on Tegeler Way" on November 4. During these days my grandmother wrote her friend Troost, "The radio and the newspapers on November 9 glorify the November revolution in 1918 and deride our November 9, 1923—it drives you to despair."[32] Naturally she did not mention November 9, 1938.

At the time I was not yet mature enough to articulate my rebellion against the Wagner family's buried Nazi past, while distancing myself from the leftist propensity to violence. As a twenty-one-year-old student, I was still quite far from being able to understand Alexander and Margarete Mitscherlich and their 1967 bestseller *The Inability to Mourn*. Their ideas pertained to my complex familial situation, but also to the financial developments in Germany in 1968. Two years later I read Hannah Arendt's book *Power and Force*, which affected me deeply and helped me gain some distance from the radical leftist scene.

The year 1969 was also when I finally understood that the Abitur was my key to personal freedom, and I began to prepare myself extensively for the final examination. Above all, I was interested in the German-Jewish authors of the Weimar Republic. Therefore, to the astonishment of my German teacher Grütter, I chose to write about Arnold Zweig's novel *The Case of Sergeant Grischa*, and for my history course I chose Goebbels's propaganda speeches. With the background of the Vietnam War, I was interested in Zweig's antiwar themes and his claim that the structure of bourgeois capitalist society caused the war. Clearly intending to provoke her, I told my grandmother about my topics, and then I told my father. Grandmother was outraged, "Leftist, Jew—how can you do that to us?" Father, again, was meaningfully silent.

Around this time, I frequently heard about family meetings regarding the planned "Festspielhaus foundation covenant." I wanted to know more about it. Father repeatedly emphasized that everything was in my interest and would serve me in the future. He told me that a paragraph of the covenant saw to my succession, were I to prove qualified. I found this vague information unsettling, especially as I considered what kind of career I would pursue after the Abitur. First of all, I wanted to work in the theater as an assistant director, but my father had completely different plans for me: he wanted me to study law so that one day I could help the family enterprise as manager. My mother came to my Abitur celebration in Stein alone; my father believed that he was indispensable on Festival Hill. When I returned to Bayreuth, I found that much had changed. The throng of yes-men had grown. The 1968 rebellion had failed. The social-liberal coalition under Willy Brandt was imminent, soon to dare more democracy and devote itself to the neighbors in the East.

After Wieland's death my grandmother lost all restraint. I first realized this change as she spoke one evening about the American conductor, Lorin Maazel. Maazel had managed the musical portion of Wieland's *Ring Cycle* in 1968 and 1969 and was slated for my father's production of the *Ring Cycle* in

1970. During one of her receptions in the Siegfried Wagner house, my grandmother Winifred declared to the amusement of her guests, "Even though Maazel is Jewish, he seems quite gifted. So Wolf is going to take him next year anyway." I was sitting next to Lorin Maazel and his wife, and I was embarrassed to death. Maazel appeared not to have heard the comment, or perhaps he didn't want to hear it, but he canceled in 1970 "because of illness."

Since I didn't know exactly what I wanted to study, I bowed to my father's pressure and began studying law at the University of Munich in the fall. I also used the time, however, to attend lectures in the humanities, which interested me much more than law. When I visited my parents in Bayreuth during the semester break in October, I found them reading Albert Speer's *Memoirs*. Speer, Hitler's architect, had designed with the Führer grandiose buildings to be constructed after the Final Victory, and during the war, Hitler had appointed him the minister of armaments. In this function Speer made certain that Nazi Germany could prolong the war and therefore its system of terror. At the Nuremberg military tribunal Speer was sentenced to twenty years' imprisonment, which he served in Berlin-Spandau, using the time to write his book of self-justification.

Openly sympathetic to Albert Speer, my father's admiration for the former Nazi bigwigs including, of course, Hitler, was always apparent. This attitude provoked yet another quarrel between us, which we continued during the winter holiday in Arosa. I was astonished to find that Speer made only incidental references to the murder of European Jewry. As always when my father and I did not hold the same opinion, I was instructed to stop and listen—I was too immature to understand the tragic history of Germany, a history full of victims. The situation got even worse when I welcomed the change of government with Brandt becoming the chancellor, an unacceptable political event for my father. He suspected leftist conspiracies everywhere.

1970: Richard Wagner as Karl Marx's Comrade-in-Arms—a New Bayreuth Power Play

In any case, my father was in a good mood for *Götterdämmerung*. Critics of his 1970 *Ring Cycle* production were wearing at his nerves, as were discussions about the festival's future and the planned foundation. Meanwhile, my sister worked especially hard to win the favor of her idol "Omi," Winifred, and soon she was the darling of influential sponsors and industrialists. She agreed with our father that nothing I suggested was worth anything, and she joined in the festival enterprise wholeheartedly. Until 1975 those who didn't get along with her had a hard time on Festival Hill. My uncle Wieland's stated principle, "there will never again be a woman dictator after Cosima and Winifred," proved to be wrong.

At this point the only people tolerated on Festival Hill were those who subordinated themselves to my father's authoritarian rules, though publicly these rules were presented as liberal. The heyday of the fawning courtiers had begun. Those who praised the artist Wolfgang Wagner enjoyed privileges. With some astonishment I noticed that they were marketing the centennial celebration of Bayreuth, scheduled for 1976, with a leftist image. Responsible for this shift were Herbert Barth, the writer who promoted Cosima's diaries with publisher Dietrich Mack; Martin Gregor-Dellin, the Wagner admirer; Egon Voss, the later publisher of the new complete, critical edition of Richard Wagner; Dorothea Glatt-Behr; and later also Oswald Georg Bauer, today the secretary general of the Bavarian Academy of Fine Arts. Even Gudrun Mack, Barth's secretary and later my father's second wife, pretended to be leftist minded and saw new opportunities come her way. In the fall of 1970, I moved to Mainz and studied those things that really interested me: musicology, psychology, and German studies.

1971: My First Experiences with Totalitarian Leftist Students

At the end of March, I was horrified to read grandmother's interview with David Irving—a historian and Holocaust denier.[33] She raved about him when I spoke to her later. When I angrily exploded, she only laughed and made fun of me.

During the summer semester of 1971, I continued my studies in the Austrian town of Graz and then in the Bayreuth Festspielhaus with Maximilian Kojetinsky, the director of music studies for the festival, working on piano, counterpoint, and harmonics. While in Erlangen in the winter semester of 1971–72, I searched for positions as a director's assistant. During my studies in the theater department at the university there, I felt uncomfortable because I found many of the students were too narrow-minded ideologically—

latecomers to the generation of 1968. Anyone who was not as "progressive-Marxist" as they were was quickly identified as a reactionary.

Since Bertolt Brecht interested me at the time, I enrolled in a course about his theater, and so I temporarily fit in among the "progressive forces." But when the student guardians of the pure leftist doctrine discovered who I was, they didn't believe my interest in Brecht was genuine. How could the "reactionary Wagner" be reconciled with the "progressive Brecht"? So I became an outsider once again. I regarded Erlangen as a stopover; I just wanted to make enough money to continue my nomadic life somewhere else.

1972: My Father's Version of History and the *Tannhäuser* Scandal

In February of 1972, I began my first director's assistantship with Hans Peter Lehmann and continued to study in Erlangen. Since Erlangen is not far from Bayreuth, I visited my parents occasionally on the weekends. Peace between my father and me lasted for only short periods. If the discussion turned to Willy Brandt's policy toward the Eastern European countries, it was all over. I saw no alternative to Brandt's policy, whereas my father considered the policy of détente to be selling out German interests. During those weekends I also visited my grandmother to learn more about her and her years with the Führer. Even though she knew my "radical left" views, she generally answered my questions openly. She raved about Hitler's wonderful, light, hypnotic eyes, his kindness, his good manners, his charm, his love for my father and Wieland, his plans for those boys in the future, "better Germany," his extensive knowledge of Wagner's work, his love for nature and for humanity. I once interrupted her, asking how Hitler's love for humanity applied to the case of the Jews. She replied, "You don't know the Jews yet. You just wait. One day you will understand, and Hitler will occupy a different place in world history." That response was reminiscent of my father's when I asked him about Hitler.

Initially, during such discussions, I made the mistake of losing my temper after some of her more flagrant statements: "Enough! Could not six million Jews make you stop deluding yourself?" She persisted in defending herself: "Those are lies and aspersions cast by the American Jews!" When I was a child, I hadn't comprehended this attitude; I had uncritically accepted it, but at twenty-five, I wanted to know for certain what my family had done. I now recognized that my grandmother's anti-Semitism was brutal. I asked her about the fates of the Jewish singers who had appeared at Bayreuth before Nazi rule, those who later had to emigrate, or who were murdered in the concentration camps, singers such as Henriette Gottlieb, Ottilie Metzger-Lattermann, Margarethe Matzenauer, Hermann Weil, Alexander Kipnis, Eva Liebenberg, Friedrich Schorr, and Emanuel List. At such times, perhaps because she felt caught in her lifelong lies, she became particularly aggressive: "You cannot understand. That was not Hitler at all, but Schleicher, Bormann, and other criminals who betrayed National Socialism. I always tried to help those Jews who sang in Bayreuth!" she screamed tensely. "So," I replied, "you and the family knew about Auschwitz!" With that, the conversation ended.

I was no longer satisfied by such information, and so I changed my tactics. I controlled my feelings and acted as if I were a historian without any personal involvement. The trick worked. Grandmother answered my questions, and most important, she instructed her confidant, Gertrud Strobel, a militant anti-Semite, to give me historical materials without Father's knowledge. Astoundingly, Gertrud Strobel did not see through me and perceive my intentions. Rather, given my interest in the documents, she simply regarded me as the only "respectable" Wagner and provided me with masses of papers. She gave me all of the *Bayreuth Blätter*, festival guides, and other papers from the period between 1850 and 1944. I was especially absorbed by the correspondence between Hitler, my grandmother, Wieland, and my father. My horror grew as I read. I had not suspected the extent of my family's entanglement in the Nazi tyranny.

In the meantime my grandmother's unshakeable loyalty to my father prompted her to tell him about my interest in Bayreuth's political past, as well as about my numerous questions and notes on the topic. He was particularly irritable during these months if something arose about the festival, Hitler, and the Wagner family. He wanted to complete the covenant for the foundation and avoid any irritation that could detract from the larger business. So I had to proceed even more carefully with my investigations. Mrs. Strobel told me with dismay about the leftist musicologists of the Thyssen Foundation, who were inundating her with questions about the grand centennial planned for 1976. As I later found out, she was referring to Egon Voss, Dietrich Mack, Michael Karbaum, and Dieter Rexroth, with whom I had my own unpleasant experiences. The Thyssen Foundation sponsored these and other Marxist authors, who were working on the project "One Hundred Years of the Bayreuth Festival."

At the 1972 season premiere of the Bayreuth Festival, the epilogue at the end of *Tannhäuser*, which was directed by Götz Friedrich, opera and theater conductor and assistant to Walter Felsenstein at the Komische Oper in (East) Berlin, created a huge stir: with an unusual expression, the choir announced the joyful message that Tannhäuser was now redeemed. The majority of the spectators believed that final scene to be the East German director's tribute to the proletariat. They shouted out their hatred almost as fanatically as their predecessors several decades before had cheered the Führer. The reason for the hysterical, hostile behavior was clear: Friedrich had held a mirror up to those in the audience. Many of these fine, upstanding people from the land of the economic miracle had recognized themselves in the opera's depiction of Wartburg society as brutal and militaristic, including even a Nazi salute in the second act. The fascist behavior presented by the actors on the stage repeated itself in the auditorium after the premiere.

The atmosphere turned hostile. The president of the "Society of the Friends of Bayreuth," Ewald Hilger, and his followers were furious with Friedrich's production. Hilger had taken over his position from his father, an influential man in West German society and a promoter of Hitler's favorite sculptor Arno Breker. Hilger advised the festival management, and on this evening he lost control; he rebuked my father for having hired Friedrich. Father hardly defended himself. As Hilger's attacks became more and more severe, my mother and I intervened. Mother jumped up, pointed toward the exit and screamed so loudly that the hall turned quiet. "I've had just about enough! You stop insulting my husband. The 'Friends of Bayreuth' do not dictate my husband's opinions or anyone else's!" She remained there with her finger thrust out at Hilger, until he barged from the hall, greatly offended, but not without first issuing a threat: "This will have consequences!" It had no consequences. He and my father were soon the best of friends again.

I was impressed by my mother's action, but it remained icy around us, a foreshadowing of what my mother and I would frequently experience in the future. Even the "leftist vanguard" that surrounded Herbert Barth, the spokesman for the festival, cravenly deserted, and only a few people came to say any grateful words to my mother. My sister and my father were embarrassed and silent. My mother and I had seldom been as close as we were that evening.

Later, my father reached a hollow compromise with Friedrich and the "Friends." The age of the "leftist Richard Wagner" had dawned completely.

In the winter semester of 1972–73, I suddenly became the darling of the Erlangen theater department. The institute organized a seminar about Richard Wagner's music and theater, in which students conveniently and erroneously discovered that Wagner had been a pioneer of socialism in 1848. This inaccurate assessment of Wagner mirrored those by GDR musicologists, particularly Werner Wolf, although even he could not do without the old Wagnerian Gertrud Strobel in the Bayreuth archive. In the Erlangen seminar they indiscriminately counted authors such as Ernst Bloch, Martin Gregor-Dellin, Hans Mayer, and Walter Jens among the leftist Wagner interpreters. Eventually I even invited my professors and fellow students to the dress rehearsal of *Tannhäuser*.

During my brief visits to Bayreuth, I restrained myself from talking about my research into our family's Nazi past. Neither did I tell my father about my secret meetings with Gertrud Strobel. Under the pretext that I had to prepare myself for a Wagner seminar at the university, I intensified my investigations in the Siegfried Wagner house. I still remember perfectly that during one visit I heard my father complain that the "situation" with Gertrud Strobel could no longer be tolerated, since she was incessantly passing on materials concerning the family, which, especially now, right before the signing of the foundation charter, could not become public. Affecting ignorance, I asked him what materials he meant. "All the private letters between Hitler and Grandma, and other things that have nothing to do with politics or the family. If the leftists from the Thyssen Foundation find out about it, then all hell will break loose!" I replied calmly, though not very tactfully, "Everything should be on the table; otherwise there will never be a new beginning!" Father was enraged by what he considered my unreasonable suggestion. I was quiet because I feared he would remember the films from the Nazi period, which I had hidden. After that, I occasionally checked whether my father had taken the empty film containers from the motorcycle sidecar.

1973: The Wagner Foundation or my Father's Great Coup—Kurt Weill as My Balance

On April 24, 1973, Winifred finally signed the deed of assignment, which transferred the Villa Wahnfried, the Festspielhaus, and the archive from the seventy-five-year-old Winifred to the city of Bayreuth. She divided the money—12.4 million marks—equally among her heirs, a tax coup by which she saved 800,000 marks, as she proudly told Gerdy Troost.[34] In May I accepted a position in Amsterdam as the assistant director of Götz Friedrich's production of *Aida*. This appointment required me to combine practical theater work with my studies so that I did not have to postpone my final exam.

In the summer of 1973, I told my father that, as a result of my work on Brecht in Erlangen, I intended to write my doctoral dissertation on Kurt Weill and Bertolt Brecht's contemporary music theater. Brecht and Weill had been the most prominent opponents of Wagner and his Bayreuth shrine. When father realized that my decision was not for purely musicological reasons, his comments were scathing: "Couldn't you come up with anything other than this second-rate, honky-tonk music?" I reacted furiously, "I prefer the 'Pirate Jenny Song' a thousand times more than the lying, bourgeois, Wagnerian redemption shit!" That was a mistake; Father flew into one of his fits of raving madness and left the dinner table. With a certain enjoyment I also told my grandmother the bad news about my dissertation choice. She reacted calmly and unequivocally, just as I had expected. "So now you're doing business with the Jews, even with the leftists! I understand that in this current Jewish time, your father must work with them to some degree, but you? The clock of history will certainly turn back for us one day!" I interrupted her abruptly, "Perhaps Wieland was right: you do still believe in the 'Final Victory.'"

In May of 1973, the foundation charter for the Richard Wagner Foundation of Bayreuth was signed. My name appeared in the discussion of succession, but that role was not in any way related to my professional goals and was therefore completely meaningless. Nevertheless, it would significantly hinder me in establishing myself as a director and music journalist. Evidently, if one follows the letter of the foundation covenant—and assumes slavish obedience, a quality that I lack—a Wagner could never be anything but an advocate for Richard Wagner.

In the fall of 1973, I enrolled in the University of Vienna. There I found a doctoral supervisor in Professor Otmar Wessely and a dissertation advisor in Professor Gernot Gruber. I was happy to get some distance from the scheming figures in my Bayreuth surroundings. While in Vienna I was addressed according to the Austrian custom, so I was "Herr Dr. Wagner," which also lifted my spirits. The university library was a rich source for my studies, as well as for my research on Jewish history and the history of the Bayreuth Festival during the Nazi period. I often sat in the music publishing house, Universal Edition, where the reaction to my passionate interest in Weill and Brecht was puzzling to many. A discussion of Kurt Weill often revealed hidden anti-Semitism even though many Viennese wanted nothing to do with the Nazis, identifying Austrians as the first victims of National Socialism. Therefore, ingrained Nazi sympathy was not the issue, and there was nothing to "reprocess."

> But Herr Doctor, what are you poking around in the past for, and what about Weill? Wagner's music is much more beautiful!

That was some of the "helpful" advice I was given. During our winter break of 1973, Father spoke with me about the foundation charter. He said, "If you prove yourself according to the goals of the foundation covenant, you have a good chance of coming out on top." For him that meant: stay quiet about Hitler and the Wagner family. But then at Christmas time we got into an argument about the United Nations' acceptance of both the Federal Republic of Germany and East Germany. I believed that worldwide recognition of the GDR was the reasonable and logical continuation of Brandt's policy toward Eastern European countries. Referring to the UN's action, my father screamed, "That is the end of a unified Germany, and the communists are rewarded for the partitioning of Germany!" So much for my father's "leftist conviction."

1974: The Most Sensible *Parsifal*

After finishing the summer semester in Vienna in July, I returned to Bayreuth. Later, following my marriage to Beatrix Kraus, I met Ernst Bloch and his wife Karola in Tübingen. I found Bloch fascinating, especially his passion for culture. He gave me important advice for my doctoral work and connected me with several people, including the Austrian-American actress and singer Lotte Lenya.

At the beginning of December, Roland Aeschlimann, Gernot Gruber, Eberhard Wagner, and I held a meeting with my father in which we were to discuss a stage-set model designed by Aeschlimann for *Parsifal*. I made a great mistake by attempting to talk about the role of Kundry and Judaism, identifying her as "the female wandering Jew." My father replied irritably, "What does Kundry have to do with Judaism?" Since then, I no longer discussed Richard Wagner's art and his *Weltanschauung* with my father. In this area as well, he demanded absolute allegiance. The stage design that he finally used in 1975—not Aeschlimann's—prompted several critics to draw comparisons to the architecture of Albert Speer, Hitler's favorite architect.

1975: New Bayreuth's Association with the Nazi Period and Syberberg's Documentary

On January 20, 1975, my sister wrote that the film director Hans Jürgen Syberberg wanted my help creating a documentary about our grandmother. This fit perfectly with my interest in reappraising the Bayreuth Festival and the Wagner family's relationship with Hitler. I wanted to examine every document about Hitler and my family, in particular several documents that my grandmother had told me about or that I had found recorded in the archive catalog. My father, however, said that reading those documents would be out of the question. The documents included correspondence between Hitler, Winifred, Wieland, and my father from 1923 to 1945. What my father did not know was that my grandmother had given me some of the letters from the steel closet and allowed me to study them for a brief time; they revealed the intimacy between my grandmother, my uncle, my father, and Hitler, and they were full of statements demonstrating their belief in the Third Reich's Final Victory. My father simply changed the subject when I requested his and Wieland's correspondence with Hitler.

When I asked my father about Hitler's gifts to my grandmother and the family, for example, a copy of *Mein Kampf* with gold lettering on the cover and the 1924 dedication "From Wolf to Winnie," he was annoyed. Under no circumstances would he release such intimate family documents for the Syberberg film. He monitored the preparations skeptically, as he did the shooting later; he wanted to make certain that none of my grandmother's statements would damage the current, left-liberal image of the festival. In contrast, however, I wanted everything to be on the table. I believed that only when my family's entanglement with National Socialism was completely uncovered could we begin to deal with the guilt.

I showed Syberberg several films from the Nazi period that I had found in my father's sidecar. Imprudently, I allowed him to take a few of the reels to

Munich. He promised to preserve the film carefully and assured me that he would not use any of it without my consent. It is part of Syberberg's legend that he had already had an artistic vision for Bayreuth, or at least a concept for the film when he began. But he lacked two prerequisites for that vision: on the one hand, he lacked knowledge of the material, and on the other hand, he had no notion of my grandmother's character. She took command from the beginning. To be blunt: from the filming in the Siegfried Wagner house came a documentary by Winifred Wagner with Syberberg's assistance. She simply took control of the film. Her moment of truth had come, she believed, and she immediately seized the opportunity. Syberberg cooperated by acting like an enamored high-school student smitten with Winifred. Little by little, I came to understand what he was doing. When he described the filming later, he did not tell the entire truth. For instance, he never revealed that when my grandmother glorified her "Wolf" during the shooting, she was talking to me. By no means did I agree with her statements about Hitler, and I found it extremely difficult to restrain myself as the cameras rolled, but I was forced to do so because Syberberg specifically demanded that I make no comments. Nonetheless, during the breaks in the shooting, I spoke with my grandmother about her ludicrous vision of the Führer. Syberberg, however, sought only to let Winifred talk. He wanted no entangling arguments. His plan was simply to allow her to expose herself. Had I erupted at grandmother's preposterous stories, Syberberg would have immediately claimed that I was hindering his art. And so grandmother ended up saying things like the following, in the context of the "Jewish question":

> We [Hitler and Winifred Wagner] never discussed these things. . . . Honestly, I never felt competent enough; I am a completely apolitical person and I was astonished how in the de-Nazification tribunal [during the de-Nazification of 1947], I was repeatedly reproached for my politics. I said that I was not engaged in any politics. They all laughed. They said, naturally you were engaged in politics. I was not engaged in politics.[35]

The members of the de-Nazification tribunal were right to laugh: grandmother was, after all, an incredibly political woman. That also held true in what she described as private acts:

> For Christmas 1923, I made collections among the local National
> Socialists, who all brought their Christmas donations here, and I
> packed them in boxes and sent them to the director of Landsberg [the
> Landsberg prison where Hitler was incarcerated] . . . and requested
> that he distribute them. That happened, certainly. And yes, I asked
> what he needed, and yes, he said that writing paper would be impor-
> tant to him, and so I sent him large amounts of writing paper. Dear
> God, now people reproach me for having supplied him with the paper
> for *Mein Kampf*. Not true. But now I find that I am considered indi-
> rectly guilty for *Mein Kampf*. Whatever we do, we always end up under
> attack.[36]

During the summer semester of 1975, I went to Vienna to meet my cousin
Nike Wagner, the second daughter of my uncle Wieland. We began to meet
there regularly, and far from Bayreuth and the family intrigues, we were able
to have serious and intense conversations on a number of topics. Syberberg's
film about our grandmother played a special role in our discussions, and we
also came to discuss our fathers' roles during the Nazi period. The topic
proved to be delicate, for Nike did not want to speak about her father's privileged role during that time, and I spoke openly about him and my father.

I also told Nike about my mistrust of Syberberg, and at the end of June,
1975, Nike, my new wife, Beatrix, and I visited Syberberg in Munich. He
showed us several insignificant excerpts from his film. I asked him to show
us scenes with Hitler, to which he responded that it wasn't possible, that
those scenes were currently being edited. My mistrust grew. By chance, I
discovered that my father's film, which I had found in the BMW sidecar, was
projected onto a wall in another room with a camera in front of it. Obviously, Syberberg had not only photographed the film, but he had also made
complete copies. Furious, I demanded that he hand over both the original
and the copies. But he did not return those reels until fall, when I stored all
of my father's films with Beatrix's parents. They remained there until my
father's lawyer demanded they be returned in 1983. Later, while under my
sister Eva's watch, the films mysteriously disappeared. As a result of that
incident, my relationship with her grew worse. When I returned to Bayreuth
after Syberberg's documentary was released, criticism rained down from all
sides. Jewish Wagnerians suspected me of being a Nazi sympathizer. Right-
wing Wagnerians claimed that I was tainting the family, and the liberal left

public criticized me because I had allegedly deserted Syberberg for Winifred.

In July 1975, after an international press conference on the Winifred Wagner film, I visited my grandmother. When I opened the door, I looked with horror at her writing table: beside my father's picture was a photograph of Hitler with the dedication "from Wolf to his Winnie." When I asked her why she had put up the photo, she replied furiously,

> Wolf[gang] treats me the way Wieland did when he spread his rumor that I still believed in the Final Victory. Wolf was there during negotiations with Syberberg. Now he presents himself as a leftist resistance fighter.

About Hitler, Wieland, and my father, she said bitterly,

> They got along splendidly, even if he acts as if they had nothing to do with him. In 1945 I sacrificed myself for both of them.

The Syberberg film premiered in July 1975. My father asked Ewald Hilger, the chairman of the "Society of the Friends of Bayreuth," to attend the event. Hilger wrote me about it afterward. His letter of November 25 to my father stated, among other things, that he would not complain about Winifred's comments. The film had told the story of an honorable and fascinating life, which the public would understand. If people didn't want to hear about that life, then there wouldn't have been any need to approach Winifred. Hilger believed that the commotion about the film was unfounded, though he doubted that the filmed interview with Winifred should be published in book form, since it would convey an entirely different impression. He saw a distinction between hearing Winifred's "explosive statements" and reading them in print.

Hilger adopted a typical position for people with his convictions. He accepted without reservation that my grandmother regarded Hitler as a private individual—as if Auschwitz did not exist, nor *Mein Kampf*, in which Hitler described his plans for murdering Jews long before he made them a reality. I'm not sure what Hilger considered honorable about Winifred Wagner's stubborn refusal—thirty years after the war—to see her "Wolf" as a mass-murderer.

The problems with Syberberg, however, were not over. In December 1975, during our last Christmas vacation together in Arosa, my father showed me a letter from Ernst Bloch. The University of Tübingen philosopher had denied my father's request to contribute to a publication celebrating the festival's centennial. Bloch explained that as a Jew and anti-fascist he had no choice but to refuse. Obviously, Syberberg and Winifred had managed to revive the old relationship between the Nazis and Wagner's music, a connection that had been disavowed with Wieland and Wolfgang Wagner's de-Nazification. I regretted Bloch's refusal. However, I understood, for I have always held a critical opinion of the roles my father and Wieland played during the Third Reich. In my view, there is no logical way to speak about a de-Nazified New Bayreuth. With secret visits my father tried to change Bloch's mind, but as my mother told me, he was unsuccessful.

1976: One Hundred Years of the Bayreuth Festival—One Hundred Years of Self-Portrayal

Only once did I work as an assistant director to my father in Bayreuth. It was at the jubilee production of *Ring* in 1976, staged by Patrice Chéreau. To this day I look back with horror on the centennial celebrated on July 23, *Richard Wagner and the Germans*: so full of lies about Richard Wagner and his legacy! The highpoint was a public festival, after which the third act of *Die Meistersinger* was performed on the festival grounds, a production directed by my father with Karl Böhm conducting. The festivities nearly took over the upper Franconian province.

After the ceremony, I accepted my father's invitation to go to the Festspielhaus, but I didn't have a ticket and, like my colleagues, I was wearing casual clothes, so I suddenly found myself held by the police. I screamed at the two plainclothes officers, "I want to speak to my lawyer. This is not a police state!" An onlooker told the policeman that I was the "son of the festival boss." The word "boss" registered with the official, and he released me. Obsequiously he said, "Why didn't you tell me who you were? Please return with your invitation," something I couldn't do because I didn't have one. Since I had come to know Festival Hill like the back of my hand during childhood, I tried to enter the hall by a secret route. I had almost made it when two security officers caught me and began to lead me away. The publisher Klaus Piper, who sat at Martin Gregor-Dellin's table, witnessed the entire scene and hurried to help me. He reprimanded the policemen and invited me to his table. I looked around at the offended faces of the West German, high society guests, especially those from the "Society of the Friends of Bayreuth," and my father there surrounded by his chorus of uncritical admirers. I left the hall as quickly as I could and wished I could have left Bayreuth as well.

During the last days of July 1976, shortly after my parents got divorced, my father showed me the Cosima Wagner diaries, which were being edited by Martin Gregor-Dellin and Dietrich Mack. Shortly after that, I packed my bags to leave. The only person to whom it was difficult to say goodbye was Gunda, a woman I had called "aunt" since childhood. She broke into tears. To recover from the Bayreuth lunacy, my wife, Beatrix, and I went to Ireland, stopping over in London to visit Charles and Germaine Spencer. I could not, however, fully enjoy the days in Ireland; my experience in Bayreuth had shaken me too profoundly. Fortunately, rays of hope did appear in my professional life. I negotiated with the Bonn Theater for a production of *Fidelio* in the spring of 1977. In addition, I had an offer from Lys Symonette in New York to work in the Kurt Weill archive on the publication of Weill's writings and letters.

In the fall of 1976, I returned to my old Munich apartment on Wartburgplatz, and as I look back at that time, the role of the media surrounding the festival of that year 1976 becomes clear. Once again, my father had successfully promoted his version of history, of an alleged New Bayreuth supported not only by his servile followers, but by the majority of the international media as well. I see this in retrospect, but at the time my concerns had been focused elsewhere. I wanted to help my mother become settled and secure after her divorce, and I also had to prepare myself for the doctoral exam, following the acceptance of my thesis in May 1976.

Meanwhile, my father had discontinued his monthly payments. One of my guardian angels during this time was the hotelier Peter Kremslehner, who knew about my precarious situation and generously welcomed me as a guest to his Hotel Regina in Vienna. In December 1976, I passed my oral exam in musicology, German studies, and philosophy. Only my mother, my wife, Beatrix, and a few friends from Vienna came to my doctoral celebration.

3

In Search of a New Identity: Confronting the Shoah: 1977–1991

1977: On the Trail of Kurt Weill: Lotte Lenya in New York

In 1977 I directed my first *Fidelio* in Bonn. It was the center of my work that year and caused a great stir because of the radical interpretation.[1] But there was something more important than my work as a director: I met people who told me about their experiences as victims of National Socialism.

Among those people was Bettina Fehr, whom I had met in Bayreuth and befriended again in Bonn. She helped me through difficult moments of my life, becoming something like a family member to me, and she served as an example of social commitment. For a long time she worked as the business director of the Bonn Society for Christian-Jewish Collaboration, to which she had belonged since 1954. Much of her commitment centered on our mutual concern—the German-Jewish dialogue, which she fostered partly out of solidarity with her maternal Jewish grandfather. Through him she is distantly related to Heinrich Heine, and as of partly Jewish descent she was not allowed to attend university during the Nazi years even though she was the daughter of the Christian doctor, Arthur Lanke. So she became a book-seller, an occupation permitted her by the Nazis. After the war her marriage to Götz Fehr, for many years the director of *Inter Nationes,* helped her to convince people throughout the world to support her commitment to the German-Jewish dialogue. It does not surprise me that, despite her exten-sive work for people in need, and despite her own large family, Bettina has also been working in the Olga Havel Foundation for the disabled since 1992.[2]

In Bonn she put me in touch with the neurologist and psychiatrist

Johannes Meyer-Lindenberg, whom I had first met at the premiere of *Fidelio*. She told him about my difficult family situation, and I saw him frequently in the fall of 1977. He offered to help my mother, who was having a particularly hard time, and I was very grateful. But one of our primary topics was my conflict with my father. Because of his own past Johannes had a great sensitivity to difficult family situations. His father came from a Jewish family, and his aristocratic mother came from a Catholic family. Therefore, his parents had been forced to flee from the Nazis to Columbia, where Johannes had been born in 1938. He immediately understood that my family's Nazi past placed me in a difficult situation and that my ethical and cultural/political positions could not be reconciled with those of my father. Nevertheless, having recognized that I wanted to have a discussion with my father, Johannes offered to mediate. From the fall of 1977 until his early death in 1991 at the age of 53, he tried his best to convince my father to have an open dialogue with me. He visited Bayreuth and called him on numerous occasions. Shortly before his death we saw each other in Bonn for the last time, and he wanted to know everything about my son Eugenio and his adoption. He was delighted by the new lease on life that fatherhood had given me, and he said seriously:

> I very much regret that all of our efforts with your father were in vain. Concentrate on your son and build something beautiful! That seems to me the only way to resolve, finally, the broken relationship with your father. Unfortunately, his suppression of the past and his lies about the past have affected you. Look to the future!

In 1977, however, when I first met Johannes, I had to choose whether to define myself by accepting offers to direct Wagner operas or whether I should choose another, if less certain path. I chose the latter and accepted Lotte Lenya's offer to work as a director at the Kurt Weill Foundation for Music in New York. In November 1977 I departed for New York accompanied by my wife, Beatrix. During my visit I naturally wanted Lenya to tell me more about Weill. I listened enthusiastically to Lenya's stories about life in Berlin before March 1933, but soon she wanted to know everything about me. "There is not that much to tell," I responded, "and you can certainly imagine why I wrote my doctoral dissertation on Weill and Brecht."

1978: With Weill against the Wagner Cult and Voices from the Past

In January of 1978, I began to work systematically on the materials that Weill had completed after his flight from Nazi Germany, and I developed proposals for how his work could be promoted in Germany. While visiting the Metropolitan Opera, I came to know Malcolm and Yveta Graff, sponsors of that world-famous opera house; there had been a Wagner cult there even during the Nazi period. Discussions in the Graff house revolved around my opinion of Richard Wagner and his work, about my father's leadership style, and my personal relationship to him. Time and again such people wanted to know whether I would succeed my father as festival director. I found this turn of conversation unpleasant. On one occasion when I was asked why I had written my doctoral dissertation on Weill and Brecht of all people, the time for pleasantries had passed. I spoke plainly about Hitler, Bayreuth, and the Jews. Passionately I confessed that the fatal marriage of politics and culture in Bayreuth had left me no other choice. Many of the art sponsors present at that discussion were Bayreuth pilgrims and members of the arch-conservative Wagner Circle.

They were politely silent after my comments. After a few moments of silence, they began discussing whether Wagner was Jewish. If this presumption were true, their argument went, then it vindicated the Wagner family honor from my great-grandfather's known anti-Semitism and the family tradition culminating with Winifred Wagner. I was familiar with these theories from the Wagner biographer Robert Newman, who was condemned in Bayreuth. I pointed out that it was by no means clear whether Ludwig Heinrich Christian Geyer was Jewish or even whether he was Richard's biological father, though it could be proved that Geyer was Richard Wagner's adoptive father. At the time, however, I had no proof for my contrary position, but a few weeks later I found the answer in the New York Leo Baeck Institute, the leading research institution on German-speaking Jewry. The genealogical documents revealed that Ludwig Geyer was not Jewish.

At this time my financial situation became critical, and Lenya continued to delay the promised contract. She suggested that I write a biography of Weill. By March I finally had a contract in hand, which secured for me a modest existence. At an elegant lunch in the New York Metropolitan Club with Gert von Gontard, one of the most influencial sponsors of the New

York City Opera and the Bayreuth Festival, I met an unusual witness to Austrian Jewish history. John White was a former Viennese Jew who had fled from the Nazis to the United States and after that turbulent time in his life, became the successful administrative director of the New York City Opera. He immediately understood my situation, saying dryly,

> The great-grandson of the anti-Semite Wagner works on the leftist Jew Weill. That won't make you so popular in Germany. I won't even ask you about your family. You are following the anti-Nazi attitude of your aunt Friedelind!

We went straight to the heart of the issue. On one point I disagreed with White: "I do respect my aunt's attitude towards National Socialism, but I don't share her uncritical attitude towards Richard Wagner's anti-Semitism. Contrary to her, I see an ideological line from Wagner's 'Judaism and Music' to Hitler."

A few days later I met the well-known musicologist Eric Werner, whose significant works on Mendelssohn I knew, and that meeting was entirely different. He asked politely, but suspiciously, why I worked so intensively on Weill. Werner indeed found Weill intriguing but did not consider him important. Hardly had I expressed my interest in German-Jewish history when he began to lecture me—knowledgeably and with obvious distaste—on Wagner's anti-Semitism. More difficult for me was his general rejection of the Germans, which included my generation and me. He even identified me with the anti-Semitic tradition of my family, a view that I resolutely rejected. Later I found out that Werner had suffered an especially difficult fate as a Jew, an experience, however, that he did not speak about. That knowledge allowed me to judge his comments at our meeting more sympathetically.

During my search for people who had fled the National Socialist terror and come to America, another encounter affected me in particular. One day on the West Side, on Seventy-Third Street, I happened to see a name in English ornamental lettering on the bell plate of a ground-floor door. It was a name that evoked a very certain memory. There it was: Dr. Wolf, Kapellmeister (conductor). Hitler had jokingly used the name "Kapellmeister Wolf" when he spent the night in the hotel "Bubo" in Bad Berneck on the way from Berlin to Bayreuth in 1933 and phoned his "Winnie." My grandmother drove there immediately to bring the Führer to Bayreuth.

So who was this Kapellmeister Wolf on Seventy-Third Street? Curious to know, I boldly rang the bell. The door opened and a pleasant, friendly-looking man asked me with a heavy German accent, "What can I do for you?" I did not dare invade his house with the Hitler history, and instead I asked in German the unimaginative question, "Are you Kapellmeister Wolf?" He said yes, smiling. He opened his door and I discovered a wonderful old Steinway grand piano, which almost completely filled the small room. I also noticed a number of yellowed photos sitting on it. To the amusement of Kapellmeister Wolf, I began looking at the photographs more closely. To my excitement, I found a shot from 1927 that showed people on the stairs of the Baden Baden Spa concert hall. I read, "July 18, 1927, Baden Baden" and I didn't trust my eyes. I exclaimed enthusiastically, "That was the premiere of *Songspiel Mahagonny.*" Wolf found me amusing and said, "Yes, look at it closely." I recognized Kurt Weill, Bertolt Brecht, Lotte Lenya, Otto Klemperer, and Paul Hindemith. "I am on the left side there," Wolf said with unassuming pride. "What, you were there for the premiere?" I eagerly asked. "Yes, but tell me, since you are so interested, are you a descendant of Weill?" In all the excitement I had forgotten to introduce myself. I laughed and said, "I am sorry, I am only a Wagner." Wolf asked, "Like Richard?" I nodded, and he began to inspect my profile. Then he beamed, "A Wagner in my apartment!" With great emotion, we shook each other's hand.

With our sympathy growing for one another, we continued our discussion. I found out that he had not only been the *répétiteur* (rehearser for opera and ballet performances) for the *Songspiel* but also for the opera *The Eternal Road* [*Der Weg der Verheissung*], which was based on a novel by Franz Werfel with music by Kurt Weill. It had premiered in New York in 1937 under the direction of Max Reinhardt. We talked about the many good conductors during the Weimar years, and I told him that my favorites were Otto Klemperer and Bruno Walter. "Walter was my uncle," Wolf said, and we laughed warmly. But the gaiety came to an end when he told me about his emigration and his persecution by the Nazis. His vivid and detailed stories allowed me to travel, as if I were on a time machine, to the Berlin and New York of the twenties. When I left, we said goodbye like old friends.

At our second meeting in his apartment, I gingerly told Kapellmeister Wolf the memory that his bell plate had evoked. He found my story comical and generously said, "All things have two sides. Hitler brought us together here." I will never forget Kapellmeister Wolf; he kept me from feeling like a rotten German and a Wagner in New York. The city had accepted so many German Jews; nevertheless, many of them remained unable to speak to the children of the National Socialist perpetrators.

My collaboration with Lys Symonette, the soul of the Weill archive, was also an important part of my time in New York. She, too, had worked under Weill as a *répétiteur*. Her parents, who had come from Jewish families in Mainz, had left the organized Jewish community, so Lys was not raised in a religious environment. Still, in time, all of her family members had to flee Nazi Germany. She seldom talked about her dramatic escape from the Nazis, through Italy to New York. She also said that her father, Emil Holzinger, had a cousin connected to the Wagner family: Karl Zuckmayer, a well-known member of the Jewish community in Bayreuth. When the national financial crisis affected the festival after the First World War, my grandfather Siegfried asked Holzinger to convince rich Bayreuth Jews to support the festival, telling Holzinger not to take Richard Wagner's anti-Semitism too seriously. Embarrassed, I remained silent as Lys told her story. She was pleased by her relation to the émigré playwright and screenwriter Zuckmayer. She was a perceptive woman, and when she recognized that her life story moved me, she smiled and said:

> I must confess that when I heard that you, a Wagner from this Bayreuth family, had written your doctoral thesis about Weill, I thought to myself: he must really be a *meschuggener* [crazy] guy. Except for his aunt Friedelind, all the other generations of Wagners before him were Nazis and anti-Semites.

My search for Weill's trail did not end in New York. In April of 1978, I flew to Los Angeles. Paul Vambery's wife picked me up at the airport. Also persecuted by the Nazis, Vambery had written the musical political satire *Der Kuhhandel* [The Cattle Trade] with Kurt Weill in England in 1934.

I began to like the artificial America of Los Angeles when I spent a few days with the widow of Ernst Josef Aufricht, Margot. During the Weimar period, Aufricht was the most significant director of the Berlin Theater am Schiffbauerdamm. In order to prepare myself to meet with Margot Aufricht and Paul Vambery, who had been Aufricht's dramaturge, I read Aufricht's autobiography from 1966, *Erzähle, damit du dein Recht Erweist* [Tell, So That You May Prove Your Correctness]. I found the book intriguing, not only because it described how Brecht and Weill had collaborated on the *Dreigroschenoper* [Three Penny Opera] but also because of Aufricht's deeply unsettling story about his escape from the Nazis to America. Margot Aufricht spoke German with me to show that she did not reject all Germans, and certainly not my generation. During our discussions I thought of the strength she revealed for speaking to me without judgment: me, the grandson of Winifred Wagner, whose friend Adolf Hitler had driven the Aufricht family from Germany. As we discussed Nazi Bayreuth and New Bayreuth, she said kindly, "With its view of German history, your family has left you with a legacy to burden your entire life."

On April 13, during one of my visits to Margot Aufricht, I found that she had decorated the table with candles, and there was coffee and cake. It was my thirty-first birthday, and as a gift, she presented me with one of the last copies of her husband's book with a warm dedication. It will always be one of my favorite keepsakes. I was so touched that I could not keep back my tears, especially since I had received no birthday wishes from anyone in my family. At that moment I identified deeply with the German-Jewish generation of grandparents and parents.

The German-studies scholar Cornelius Schnauber, Fritz Lang's executor and an expert on Jewish exile literature, introduced me to several people, including Martha Feuchtwanger, the widow of the German-Jewish writer Lion Feuchtwanger; Ronald Schoenberg, a judge and a son from Arnold Schoenberg's second marriage; and his wife Barbara, the daughter of the Austrian composer Alexander von Zemlinsky. From Ronald, I wanted to know everything about his father and his Judaism, and the Wagnerian Ronald wanted to hear everything about Richard Wagner, but nothing about his anti-Semitism. We talked past one another.

On April 20 I flew through Chicago to Bloomington, Indiana, to meet with another witness: Hans Busch. He was the son of Fritz Busch, who had conducted *Die Meistersinger* in Bayreuth in 1924. Forced to leave Nazi Germany because of his liberal position, Fritz Busch was among the founders of the Glyndebourne Festival, something of a counter-Bayreuth. He had collaborated with Weill in 1923 and conducted the premiere of *The Protagonists* in Leipzig. His son Hans had also collaborated with Weill, directing the one-act "people's opera" *Down in the Valley*, which premiered in Bloomington in 1945, with a libretto by Arnold Sundgard.

Hans Busch spoke openly about his disgust for the conductor Karl Böhm, whom he called a Nazi favorite, and who drove his father away as conductor of the Dresden Opera in 1933. Even my grandmother detested Böhm. Busch's stories contained a great deal of pain and suffering related to the brutal expulsion of his family from Germany, for which I felt ashamed. As soon as I began talking of his period with Weill, however, his face began to beam. He spoke with warmth about the composer's great kindness and unpretentiousness.

Then Hans invited me to the dress rehearsal of the opera *Danton and Robespierre* by John Eaton, which made its successful premiere in Bloomington. During the dress rehearsal that evening, I wanted to leave the hall for a moment without letting in too much light. I pushed open one of the big swinging doors, stepped through, and tried to close it when I noticed a small form, which called out to me with an unmistakable German accent: "Attention, please." I held the door back and a woman, whom I couldn't see well in the lack of light, thanked me. I answered, "My pleasure!" and introduced myself. The woman asked curiously, "Like Richard Wagner?" Rather amused, I answered her, "Yes, but with mixed feelings. May I know with whom I'm speaking here in the dark?" A friendly, laughing voice said, "You may. My name is Busoni!" To which I responded just as curiously, "Like Ferruccio?" She said yes and suggested that we go to the foyer and talk in the light. Thus began one of my most important friendships—with Hannah Busoni.

So it was that in the summer of 1978 she took me into her apartment, her "Hansel and Gretel House" behind Carnegie Hall where, until 1994, I stayed when I came to New York. Whenever I felt as if I were drowning, Hannah helped me in her discreet, generous way. She told me a great deal about Busoni, Weill, her husband, the painter Raffaele Busoni, Lotte Lenya, the premiere of *The Three Penny Opera*, which she had attended as a girl in Berlin, and about her escape from Nazi Germany. She was born as Hannah Apfel, the daughter of an important Jewish lawyer in the Weimar Republic who escaped to France in 1933. With her parents divorced, she escaped to England only with her mother. An exceptionally alive intellect with a dry humor, Hannah had such a command of the German language that sometimes her expressions reminded me of my favorite German authors from the twenties. Indeed, if you lived with Hannah, it was as if you were in Berlin during the Weimar Republic. She stuck gratefully with New York, where she had struggled through life, taking all sorts of jobs until the Federal Republic of Germany finally awarded her the pension of a German judge as "reparations."

With great selflessness and social commitment, Hannah patronized young musicians and musicologists who were interested in her father-in-law, Ferruccio. In this musical world of Hannah, I found myself discussing the other intellectual legacy of my family for the first time in America—Franz Liszt, whom Busoni had admired. Many of her friends had suffered a similar German-Jewish fate and yet they all accepted me, the grandson of Winifred Wagner, as if I were their own grandson. One of those was Paul Falkenberg, who had been an important sound editor in Berlin until 1933. He found it both exciting and plausible when I told him that Weill had used sacred Jewish music in his songs with Brecht. He gave me my first Jewish prayer book.

When I questioned Hannah one day about her identity, she answered, "It's good to be Jewish," by which she meant sharing the community of fate with other persecuted German Jews, not being part of a religious community. Hannah was always with me, even if she never answered my letters— something none of her friends could make her do. But when I phoned her, she asked right away, "When are you coming? You can sleep up front in the salon!"

At Schuyler Chapin's apartment at the corner of Lexington Avenue and Sixty-Sixth Street, I met Leonard Bernstein for the first time in years, and memories returned of my difficult period in Bayreuth. Transfigured, he raved about Wieland and railed against my father, whom he called a Nazi in camouflage. When I asked how he had formed this opinion, he told me about meeting my father to discuss Bernstein's conducting *Tristan*, an arrangement that never came to fruition. "As long as he is festival director in Bayreuth, I will not conduct on Festival Hill," he declared angrily.

In contrast, like many Jewish artists, Bernstein had a great deal of sympathy for my aunt Friedelind. "You are indeed continuing the tradition of your aunt with your work on Weill," Bernstein said benevolently. "Friedelind," I replied, "still refuses to believe that Richard Wagner is guilty of anti-Semitism. But I don't!" Obviously, this topic moved Bernstein, who brooded for a minute and then said, "And how can it be that as a Jew, I so love the music of this revolting anti-Semite, above all his *Tristan*?" I replied, "As a great-grandson of Wagner, I really don't have any right to respond to that, but despite all of my aversions to the man Wagner, I see no anti-Semitism in *Tristan*, and you should take it up one day."

He did take up *Tristan* later in Munich and produced a video about his Wagner dilemma. In 1990 he gave me the unfinished film and asked me to review it. I found it unsuccessful, a criticism he cheerfully accepted during our last discussion in April, and he even asked me to work with him on the ending, but he died shortly thereafter.

After a short, disappointing visit in Germany, I turned all of my energy toward organizing a Weill biography. I moved twice during this hectic period. Finally I ended up subletting two small rooms in a house on the corner of Seventy-First Street and Lexington Avenue. My time there was depressing. A few neighbors did not like my living there, and so I was frequently called in the middle of the night and reviled in German: "Dirty German pig. Get out of our house. We don't want any Nazis here. Disappear, or we'll do you in." I had never encountered such aggression before. This vicious game repeated itself several times. Since all forms of hatred disgust me, I attempted to ignore the incidents. But I was not successful.

"Coming to Terms with the Past"— Back in Germany

In February 1979, since I could not earn enough money in the United States, I flew back to Germany. Without an agent I began looking for a job and wrote to all of the theaters in Germany. My search led me from pillar to post. I read an important article by Günther Anders about *Vergangenheitsbewälti-gung,* or "coming to terms with the past." He discussed the *Holocaust* television film in particular. Anders justifiably complained that

> the year 1978 is really the year 1945; the shock that should have come in 1945 has hit. Despite the abundance of events over the past 35 years, Germany has become ahistorical. What has happened, what has been prompted by film, is therefore the opposite of a psychoanalytical healing process: this change is just a slight disruption and not a state of distress. Distress is actually necessary for moral health.[3]

Because of my miserable financial situation in the summer of 1979, I accepted a position as assistant director at the Salzburg Festival. I worked with Dieter Dorn on his production of Richard Strauss's opera *Ariadne auf Naxos,* conducted by Karl Böhm. Meeting Böhm, I could not help but think about Hans Busch's stories of his father and Böhm. Similar to Bayreuth, Salzburg was a paradise for those who wished to suppress the Nazi period, and to my horror I repeatedly heard people say, "We Austrians were the first victims of National Socialism." After those unpleasant weeks in Salzburg, I accepted offers to work in Ankara, Turkey, Frankfurt am Main, Trier, and finally Wuppertal, but gradually I realized that I should not pursue a career in the German opera and theater scene.

1980: My Grandmother's Awkward Funeral as the Prelude to a New Power Struggle

On March 5, 1980, my grandmother died in an Überlingen hospital. I had seen her for the last time three weeks before, and I will always remember that encounter because she spoke of her approaching death with unusual honesty. My aunt Friedelind suffered greatly from my grandmother's death. The rest of the family was immediately preoccupied with distributing the inheritance and determining the new balance of power. More than ever, my father, who was relieved that his mother could now never reveal his Nazi past, was the center of attention. The solemn March 10 burial in Bayreuth was the only problem. My father and his second wife constructed a seating plan that distributed the family in a way that showed everyone whom they favored. A string quartet broke up the interminable, mendacious speeches. The speakers called my grandmother "Bayreuth's savior" and said nothing of the intimate friendship between "Winnie" and "Wolf." The Bayreuth mayor Wild was particularly adept at ignoring her National Socialist past.

And, of course, Bayreuth's professional PR men orchestrated an impressive media circus. Among the onlookers were representatives of the NPD (the neo-Nazi National Democratic Party) and my grandmother's old friends from the Nazi period, whose attempts to offer condolences I managed to dodge. My father, finally without his mother, was ubiquitous in his role as festival director and did not deem it necessary to welcome the family or the guests. Though most people in my family rejoiced that the oppressive shadow had finally been lifted, everyone feigned mourning. Soon we got to the most important activity: the distribution of the inheritance. I have never felt as relieved as when I finally left Bayreuth.

Much more difficult than my grandmother's death was my separation from my wife, Beatrix, which occurred later that year. During Christmas

1980 we realized that our "weekend" marriage could not last. Our separations had been too great a strain to sustain a relationship.

1981: Beginning My Own Life— Teresina and My Italian Family

In 1981, after years of attempts, my friend and psychological advisor Johannes Meyer-Lindenberg was finally able to convince my father to meet with me. Johannes and I drove to Bayreuth in February snow flurries and could only find a room on the second floor of the Hotel Goldener Anker, directly adjacent to number twenty-three, the room where Hitler had spent the night when he met my grandmother for the first time in 1923. I regarded this as an ill omen, but Johannes was quick to disabuse me of such superstitions.

Out of consideration for his wife and my half-sister Katharina, whom I didn't know, my father met us at the Festspielhaus. The atmosphere of the talks corresponded to the cold weather outside. Noticeably uncomfortable with the meeting, my father repeatedly stated that he didn't have much time and that he had many important obligations. Quite skillfully, Johannes explained that, should my father cease attacking me in public, we could finally begin a normal exchange. When Johannes proposed a new meeting between us, my father refused to set a date. Johannes grew exasperated and insisted on a meeting in Wuppertal.

In the end my father and I agreed to talk again, and he also agreed to refrain from making any more negative comments about me in public. Johannes left my father's office satisfied. The following month my father and his second wife, Gudrun, attended—for the first and last time—a production that I directed, Mozart's *Bastien and Bastienne*. I wanted to look my father in the eye when we said goodbye, but he avoided me, and I sensed that he would not keep his promise made at the February meeting.

Needing help to work through my divorce, I met with Johannes again in April. I began to talk, and after my half-hour monologue, Johannes responded with a kind smile, "You don't need psychoanalysis; you need a family and the right working environment, which you certainly don't have here." I stopped devoting all my energy to the theater and the careers of my superiors because I suddenly realized how meaningless my previous life had been. My life had to change. In July 1981 my friendly landlady Dodo Koch introduced me to Teresina Rossetti from Cerro Maggiore, a municipality in the province of Milan. I was fascinated by her well-developed sense of integrity, her varied analytical gifts, her pragmatism, and her beauty. Despite falling for one another immediately, previous bad experiences led us both to make clear, in no uncertain terms, what we regarded as a meaningful life. Indeed, the hurdles before us were anything but easy: they included my ongoing divorce, my difficult professional situation, her father's terminal illness, the geographic distance, and the great differences between our families.

On July 12, 1981, as I watched the train depart the Cologne station with Teresina heading toward Italy, I knew that with her I had a great opportunity for a meaningful and fulfilling life. Many of my problems that had seemed irreconcilable now appeared less important. I began to discover my true self, and through her, I finally began to feel as if I had a home. She became a loyal and dependable advocate of my work as a freelance author and director, even as I dealt with many uncomfortable topics, and she became the wonderful mother of our adopted son, Eugenio. In addition to all those responsibilities, she still managed professional independence by running her own business, and later she worked on the Cerro Maggiore local council in the Citizens' List political group *insieme* [together]. Living with her extended family taught me how meaningful a united family can be, something I came to value greatly.

With their help my negative experiences with the Wagner family began to slip into the background, and I finally embarked upon a new life with my Italian family. It was July 24, 1981, a day I will never forget. A new chapter in my life began: my integration into Teresina's family. It was, however, not without problems. Because of my own devastating family relationships, it was difficult for me to fit in with the Rossettis at first. In addition, since I only knew Italy as a tourist, I had to overcome several preconceptions, a process that led me to question my social and cultural education at Bayreuth. In the Rossetti house no one even thought of praising the alliance between Hitler and Mussolini. Her family had recognized the threat as early as 1943 when the *Lohengrin* overture from act three had been used to announce Nazi propaganda in Lombardy. By no means, therefore, was I—a Wagner— what they expected as their son-in-law. Moreover, I was uncertain how a Catholic family would react to the knowledge that my divorce had not been completed. And, as if those hurdles were not enough, my professional prospects were meager. Nevertheless, when Teresina glanced at me with her understanding smile, I began to feel at home.

When shortly afterward Teresina's father fell ill with cancer and died at the early age of fifty-nine, I realized what it meant for a family to come together. It also became painfully clear to me that one day our lives actually come to an end. So it is no surprise that I began to value life even more. During these difficult days, the priest, Father Giuliano, was an important friend to us. With a certain shame, I had to admit my ignorant preconceptions about priests and the Catholic Church. Giuliano was not only a warm-hearted, unpretentious man with a passionate vision of the Bible and Christianity, he also had an extensive education, and we began an interesting dialogue.

Back in Wuppertal in the fall, I decided to join the Catholic Church on Reformation day: October 31, 1981. In Bayreuth the news of my conversion to Roman Catholicism drew derisive remarks since the Wagners had built for themselves a Protestant façade. During these weeks my existence as a dramaturge and director in the Wuppertal opera house seemed absurd to me. I was waiting for the right moment to leave; I just needed another job. Feeling no regret at leaving the German stage, I worked from January 1981 to fall of 1983 as a trainee at Deutsche Bank, first in Munich and then in Milan. Teresina and I married in July, but I had to wait until the fall to move to Cerro Maggiore, where I continued my job at the Milan branch of Deutsche Bank until 1985.

1983: Dissonant Intermezzo in Bayreuth

Immediately following our wedding, Teresina, my mother-in-law, Mamma Antonietta, and I drove to Bayreuth to visit my mother. Since my father would not welcome us into his home, Aunt Friedelind invited us to dinner in the elegant hotel Schloss Tiergarten. When she realized that we didn't have tickets for any festival performances, she called my father against our will and demanded three tickets for *Tristan und Isolde*. As we headed for the stuffy family box, I gave Mamma Antonietta a brief summary of the opera's first act.

During the intermissions, we went to the festival restaurant, where several people made an obvious effort not to see us. I waited impatiently for the end of the performance; our quick visit with my father and his fawning courtiers had ruined Teresina's and my mood, especially because he had refused to greet Mamma Antonietta. I had hoped to prevent the two from getting an even worse impression of Bayreuth, and they were, at least, taken with the music and Ponnelle's production. After the performance, when I asked Mamma Antonietta what she thought of her stay in Bayreuth, she answered apprehensively, "The opera was beautiful, but I don't think that you can be happy in Bayreuth!" She said nothing about her cold reception as my mother-in-law, and that trip was her first and last to Bayreuth.

1985–1986: Return to the Cultural Sphere

After I gave notice at Deutsche Bank in the summer of 1985 and received a surprisingly positive leaving certificate, I sought to keep my head above water financially. Because of the problems with the official version of history in Bayreuth, and because I wanted to continue my German-Jewish studies, I began researching the nineteenth and twentieth centuries intensively. Working on a program commentary for Götz Friedrich's production of *Götterdämmerung*, I looked critically at Liszt, studying his ethics as contrasted with Wagner's. I took on this project out of necessity, for I saw it as an opportunity to work my way back into the world of culture.

It was not until the following year, however, that I truly discovered Liszt. Lectures and radio broadcasts in Switzerland, Italy, Belgium, France, and the United States provided many opportunities to exchange ideas with others. I was particularly interested in Liszt's position on the Jews. His 1859 work, *The Gypsies and Their Music*, and the significant chapter, "The Israelites," were certainly influenced by Wagner's racist and inflammatory 1850 essay "Judaism and Music." But Liszt did not conclude his work as Wagner did, with the "decline" or the "suicide" of the Jews. After an anti-Semitic analysis of the Jewish religion, he advised the Jews, whom he regarded as a nation, to recapture Palestine "by their own initiative and vigor."

1987: Renewed Analysis of Wagner, Bayreuth, and Hitler

In 1987 I produced radio broadcasts about Liszt and Wagner for parts of Germany and Switzerland, and the darker side of my ancestry became more and more apparent. The Bonn Theater offered me a contract as a freelance dramaturge for the 1987/1988 production of *Die Meistersinger von Nürnberg*, which required my presence in Germany during the spring of 1987. In particular, I had to spend time doing research in the Richard Wagner Museum in Bayreuth. It took me some time to get permission to look through the archive. The archive director knew his master's voice, and he followed my work with suspicion because I had not restrained my criticism of their exhibition "Wagner and the Jews" or of the equally horrifying 1985 catalog. Only after several severe confrontations was I allowed to read my own family's letters without having to provide a detailed reason every time. My anger over the bureaucratic chicanery prompted me to search even more extensively through the archive, and I began to study topics that were taboo in Bayreuth: anti-Semitism, Gobineau, Cosima Wagner, Houston Stewart Chamberlain, Winifred Wagner, and Hitler.

Disgusted by the pre-Nazi and Nazi readings in the *Bayreuther Blätter* and the festival programs from 1878 to 1943, I often needed a break to walk through Wahnfried park. That was my family's cultural foundation! I copied the materials at my disposal, knowing that in Bayreuth numerous sources are regularly withheld from critical researchers, sources that my father and his team of falsifiers would happily keep locked away forever. In retrospect that research became useful for a lecture I was asked to give in November 1987 at the Toscanini Symposium in Parma. Harvey Sachs, the internationally known Toscanini biographer, allowed me to pick my topic, and I decided to speak about "Toscanini's Conducting Style at Bayreuth."

In November I presented my lecture. Since the great Italian conductor's time on Festival Hill fell during the run-up to National Socialism, I discussed the political environment and the role of my grandmother, who had presented Hitler to the German bourgeoisie in 1923. It was under those circumstances that I reread my aunt Friedelind's 1944 autobiography, *Nacht über Bayreuth*, in which she wrote about the insurmountable abyss between her and my father.

1988: Karl Lubomirski and Ralph Giordano

Working on *Die Meistersinger* in the spring of 1988 and on the *Ring Cycle* in Orange, in the south of France, during the summer were opportunities for me to earn money. My single positive recollection of that time was the creation of my short, provocative video *The Ring Cycle or the Result of the*

Misuse of Power, which won first prize at the film festival in Biarritz. The collaboration in Bonn and Orange ended in a settlement after a legal dispute, which took place because my views on Wagner were irreconcilable with those of the theater and the festival. I then decided to end my work at established opera festivals, where I was repeatedly pigeonholed into the Wagner corner.

Much more important for me were two meetings that year: one with the poet Karl Lubomirski and the other with the journalist and author Ralph Giordano. I met the lyricist Lubomirski in Milan at the beginning of March. From the outset we became engaged in deep discussions and began to share one another's lives; just as I had made the irrevocable move from Bayreuth, Karl had left Innsbruck, Austria, behind him, but we remained—whether we wanted to or not—shaped by and dependent on German culture and language.

After my trip to Israel in 1990, Karl became a dependable ally, fighting for a German-Jewish dialogue during my struggle with the Wagner cult in Bayreuth. I will always feel bound to Karl because of his strength and integrity on humanitarian issues. He, too, was discriminated against by self-appointed popes in a seemingly leftist international cultural lobby, and in this regard we have similar stories.

Even from the beginning our friendship had a positive influence on me: I drove to Bonn where I first stayed with my old friend Bettina Fehr. Inspired by our conversations, she gave me some night reading that affected me greatly: Ralph Giordano's *The Second Guilt, or the Burden of Being German*. I didn't read the 363 pages of the book—I devoured them, because what I read was exactly what I was feeling. I was overwhelmed by Giordano's historical, political, and cultural analyses. It had been a long time since a German-speaking author had spoken to me. He and his Italian-Jewish family had suffered from persecution under the Nazis in his native Hamburg. This experience had made him into a humanist who argued courageously against a repressed German society. On March 15, Bettina phoned Giordano, and three days later we accepted an invitation to visit him in Cologne. We rang the bell and waited until the door opened to a beautifully decorated afternoon coffee table. Instead of being greeted by the host, we heard the overture to the first act of *Tristan und Isolde*. Then Giordano approached. Thoughtfully, he said to me, "This music is among my favorites of Wagner's compositions." I answered, "We cannot help but be fascinated by *Tristan und Isolde*, but we must also, unfortunately, live with the 'other Wagner.'" He agreed and gave me his hand.

I had meant to ask Giordano about his life and his work. But over the following three hours he instead asked a number of questions about my life. Feeling an unusual, immediate familiarity, I found myself opening up to him, speaking to him as I would to an old friend. When I told him about "Winnie" and "Wolf," he grabbed my arm and, interrupting me, asked me an irritating question, "Are you really Wolfgang Wagner's son?" I hardly reacted because I thought I misunderstood him. I continued talking about the correspondence between Hitler and my grandmother. With friendly persistence he repeated the question, "Are you really Wolfgang Wagner's son?" Finally it registered that he was actually asking me about my father. I laughed and asked, "Why do you want to know that?" He answered seriously, "I interviewed your father once in Bayreuth. I am sorry to say this, but I didn't believe a word he said. There is no humanity in that man." I answered, "You don't need to apologize to me. You are only saying what I have realized and known since childhood."

Giordano reached for his novel *The Bertinis,* based on the story of his family, and wrote a dedication, "For Gottfried Wagner, with sympathy at first sight." And then he said with emphasis, "Whether you want to or not, you must write your life story. You owe that to your generation and the generations of Germans to come." I did not agree and said, "Forty-one years old and write an autobiography about the decaying state of Bayreuth? Why? Who would find that interesting? So that I could isolate myself even more than before?" Giordano responded, "You have nothing to do with the Wagners' hypocritical Bayreuth, but you are a Wagner who is aware of his responsibility to humanity and to history. Write your life story. The work will help you personally, and one day it will also help your reintegration into Germany. I will support you." Moved, we left Ralph Giordano. I knew that the meeting would change my life.

In the middle of August, I gave a lecture about my thoughts on Nietzsche and Wagner under the auspices of the international youth festival in Bayreuth. Quoting from both "The Case of Wagner" and "Nietzsche against Wagner" created an icy atmosphere, and it was difficult for me to speak. By the time I ended the lecture with Nietzsche's praise for Bizet's *Carmen* and played a recording from the close of the opera, the atmosphere in the hall was what I had anticipated: angry and aggressive. The presentation of my prize-winning video clip on *The Ring* was not well received either. To my astonishment, however, the president of the West German Richard Wagner Association, Josef Lienhart, invited me to show *The Ring* video clip to his Freiburg association in the fall. Lienhart seemed to admire my critical analysis of the National Socialist past. He was particularly pleased by my intention to accept an invitation to Israel. He promised to support me in lectures to the association after my trip to Israel for he, too, seemed to think it was necessary that Wagner should be discussed in both Israel and Germany.

But I soon found out that he misunderstood my plans: he believed that despite all of my criticism of the Bayreuth Festival, I wanted to visit Israel as a propagandist for Wagner. That was obviously not my intention, and no presentations about my Israel trip took place at Lienhart's Richard Wagner Association meeting.

1989: Hitler and Wagner and Connections to Israel

The spring of 1989 was Hitler's one-hundredth birthday. Leo Haffner, one of the responsible cultural editors of the ORF Vorarlberg (regional Austrian radio) recorded a conversation between Karl Lubomirski and me about German culture, tradition, and politics; a conversation that could not ignore "Hitler and Bayreuth." Since Haffner was not one of those Austrians who made Hitler into a German, he asked me to give a lecture about Hitler and Wagner in the ORF regional studio at the beginning of April. As I prepared for the lecture, I became more and more conscious of the topic's relevance to me personally. I did not want to escape into the world of art, as did my father, uncle, and grandmother, a world in which Wagner the theater genius could be separated from Wagner the ideologue. This separation had led the Wagner generations before me to a disastrous repression and ultimately a denial of their individual responsibility.

The connection between Wagner and Hitler brought on a debilitating personal identity crisis, which I was only able to overcome with constant work. So, with deep reservations about my identity, I titled the lecture with a question, "Adolf Hitler and Richard Wagner?" The lecture was my first (though unsuccessful) attempt to derive some meaning from this relationship, but with the typical "New Bayreuth" tendency toward repression, I tried to separate Wagner's anti-Semitic writings from his work, particularly from *Parsifal*, which permits any number of interpretations. At the time I did not yet want to consider Richard Wagner responsible for the great "and" with Hitler. As I prepared for my lecture tour to Israel a year later and struggled with the topic again, I realized how completely wrong I had been. Today I must concede that I can no longer defend the conclusion of that lecture on the radio: "Wagner and Hitler? I hope that you find the 'and' troubling. . . . Wagner belongs to the world of art, Hitler to the world of criminals!"

In April 1989 I took my first lecture tour through Norway, Iceland, Denmark, and Sweden. Everywhere I went, I could sense animosity toward the topic of "Wagner and Nietzsche" as well as toward the *Ring Cycle*, which I introduced with the video clip, because everyone still associated Richard Wagner with Nazi aggression and German occupation during the Second World War. But when my listeners understood that I was not a *Herrenmensch* (a superior human being), that I had not come to sing the wondrous praises of Wagner, the ice began to melt. Gradually they and I were able to engage in open and honest discussions. For the most part I was accepted with great interest and warmth because I made it clear that I rejected not only the Wagner cult in Bayreuth from 1872 until 1945 but also "New Bayreuth's" repression of the Nazi era. The more unconventional the audience, the more open was the discussion about the cultural-political phenomenon of Wagner and the Nazi period. The media were also greatly interested. Aarhus and Stockholm were the only places where I met Wagnerians who, because of their hazy ideologies and their pilgrimages to Bayreuth, refused to criticize the "Master." On my flight back from Stockholm to Milan, I realized how much Wagner himself was still overshadowed by an unresolved Nazi past, even in Scandinavia.

In July 1989, while I was preparing for my Israel trip, Teresina and I drove to Bayreuth to see the premiere of my father's new *Parsifal* production. News of my invitation to give lectures in Israel had spread like wildfire on Festival Hill, and what before had been a chilly toleration of our presence had now turned to ice. After the premiere I was asked what I thought of my father's *Parsifal*. Recognizing that I was within earshot of tabloid journalists, I answered carefully. I referred to the opera's conclusion, "Redemption to the Redeemer," during which, according to Wagner's stage directions, Parsifal, a new, Aryan Christ figure, celebrates Holy Communion as a message of salvation to the world. But contrary to Wagner's directions, my father had allowed Kundry to survive in the masculine, Christian temple of the Knights of the Holy Grail. And contrary to all writings and stage directions by his grandfather, my father had made Parsifal disappear into the crowd of the Knights of the Holy Grail. This manipulative democratization meant that in the sphere of the Holy Grail, no single individual was responsible. Instead, the Knights held collective responsibility for salvation, a thought that shocked me. The questioner understood me and changed the topic. In 1994 I found out that my father had changed the ending again. As a female Messiah, Kundry offered the chalice as redemption to the Knights of the Holy Grail. In that action, "New Bayreuth's" repression reached its high point.

In July Teresina and I saw the *Ring* by Harry Kupfer and Daniel Barenboim, my father's close friend at the time, who supported "New Bayreuth's" veiling of Wagner's anti-Semitism. After *Götterdämmerung*, I saw him by chance in the restaurant Bürgerreuth, and he obviously awaited a compliment for his brilliant directing of the *Ring*. Instead I said, "I have never seen so much scenic nonsense." He acted interested in my opinion, and he promised to meet me the next day. I intended to confront him about some of his opportunistic statements regarding Wagner's anti-Semitism. Suspecting what I had in mind, he did not come to the planned meeting.

On August 3 in Zürich, I met Professor Herzl Shmueli from Tel Aviv, and the interaction was completely contrary to my last visit to Festival Hill! I had maintained a correspondence with this well-known musicologist since May 1988 but had never met him personally. As early as the 1970s, Herzl Shmueli had dared to give lectures in Israel about Wagner, and he had created great public interest in the process. Since the early Romantic period was a primary focus of his research, he could not ignore the "case of Wagner." He grew up in Istanbul in a traditional Jewish family, was educated in a German school there, and emigrated to Israel at the beginning of the 1930s. He studied mathematics and then musicology in Zürich. Why Zürich? Herzl explained, "Despite all my love for German culture, which had molded me in Istanbul, Hitler made it impossible for me to study in Germany." At our first meeting in August, he asked me about my plans. "Doctoral work on Kurt Weill in Vienna? That does not seem to be the typical development for a Wagner after Hitler." And thus began our critical, open dialogue that resulted in his inviting me to give four lectures in Israel in January 1990.

At the beginning of October, I suggested to Herzl Shmueli that I present the following at the University of Tel Aviv: the video clip *The Ring Cycle or the Result of the Misuse of Power,* "The Downfall of the Gods or Épatez le Bourgeois—anti-Wagnerian Musical Period Theater by Weill and Brecht," "The Cases of Nietzsche and Wagner," and finally "The Wagner I Mean—Approaching Wagner's Person and Work." I wrote as explanation, among other things:

> My intention remains to contribute what I can to a continuing dialogue on the topic "Wagner and German culture," a dialogue that can only proceed in small steps, and which requires calm and patience. I am fully aware of my responsibility and cannot understand why the West German institutions in Israel (Goethe Institute and the West German embassy) will not support my conciliatory work, which, after all, I have been pursuing for two decades.

Shai Burstyn, director of the University of Tel Aviv musicology department, became deeply involved and helped me. I told him the most significant details from my lectures, for I didn't want to offend my host country. During this correspondence I asked him the question I believed to be most important: "Would it be tactless to present a few short musical examples from Wagner's operas at the university?" He agreed that I could do so, even though he expected protests.

1990: Israel and Richard Wagner

Finally the day arrived: on January 2, 1990, Teresina and I flew to Tel Aviv. Even on the first afternoon and evening, discussions with our hosts were intense, and that intensity increased in the following days. My series of lectures didn't begin until January 7, yet as we visited a kibbutz, the town of Cesarea, and the Massada memorial, as well as Arab towns with our hosts Herzl Shmueli and Shai Burstyn, we discussed the topics I would soon be covering in my lectures. Herzl convinced me of the following—in Israel Richard Wagner is inextricably connected with Hitler and Nazi Germany. Nevertheless, this public sentiment did not prevent him from teaching seminars and giving lectures about this "erratic man" in the University of Tel Aviv music history department. I became aware that these discussions were changing me. In order to save the anti-Semite Richard Wagner, I had attempted to ascribe his guilt solely to the two generations after him. Now I recognized that this denial of reality could no longer defy the facts. I found myself in a quandary similar to that of my Jewish friends who are Wagnerians. And today I know that one cannot separate Wagner the brilliant composer from Wagner the chief ideologist: his *Weltanschauung* is inseparable from his work and his life. Unexpectedly, the discussion of Richard Wagner developed into a discussion of my life and my responsibility. In Israel I began to realize that I could no longer articulate my moral and political position indirectly, that I had to study German-Jewish culture more deeply. My time in the ivory tower of liberal left thought had come to an end. I challenged myself to achieve more credibility through deeds.

In Israel endless opportunities arose to take that challenge seriously. We repeatedly encountered people with sorrowful pasts, people who had been persecuted in Germany and elsewhere and had fled to Palestine from Nazi Germany. As my hosts, their friends, and people at my lectures explained their experiences to me, I became more and more open. From the dark, frightening, and yet vague, enormous shadow of six million victims emerged perceptible, individual life experiences—thanks to these conversations. I hoped that I would be able to take a clearer position on our mutual past and our shared responsibility in both the present and the future. I began to regard Israel as a central tile in my life's mosaic. Again I was reminded of my New York time in the Kurt Weill Foundation for Music. The connection between German history, the Wagner family chronicle, and my life's contrary path finally became more comprehensible. I wanted to make constructive use of the trust and understanding that had been shown me; I wanted to promote the German-Jewish dialogue in the future—even in Germany. My fear, uncertainty, and apprehension grew in the same measure as my understanding.

During our fourteen-day stay, I was interviewed by nearly all the important media outlets in Israel, and the effect could be sensed immediately. Complete strangers spoke to me. When I reacted with surprise to such an encounter in a Tel Aviv optician's shop, the owner said in accent-free German:

Mr. Wagner, did you not know how small our country is? In the morning we show our guests Israel, and in the afternoon we ask ourselves what we should do next. So don't be surprised that we saw you on television yesterday. Your coming here is not only important for the Yekkes—that is, the German Jews. Continue what you are doing!

I was not prepared for what occurred before my first lecture, which was scheduled to begin with my introducing the video clip *The Ring Cycle or the Result of the Misuse of Power*. One of the university workers told me that several fanatics had called to protest my visit. The university had therefore considered either giving me a bulletproof vest or protecting me behind safety glass. Despite Teresina's request that I do something for my security, I declined both. I explained that "I am not Eichmann who needs to sit in a glass booth. I trust my hosts." That hardly calmed Teresina, but she accepted my decision.

Instead of the expected eighty listeners, nearly four hundred people showed up in the medium-sized lecture hall. We had to move to a larger auditorium with heightened security measures: everyone was searched, and two young Israeli soldiers stood stationed with guns. The hall was larger but still overfilled, and yet the first row remained unoccupied. Given that I was a descendant of Wagner, I understood the reservations about me. Remembering a book titled *Who's Afraid of Richard Wagner?*, which had been given to me shortly before the lecture, I said, "There are still some places down here in the front. Who's afraid of Gottfried Wagner?" A hearty laugh broke out, and I laughed along. The laughter continued during the presentation of the video—and, indeed, my audience laughed at scenes only I had found amusing in the past, even though I had shown it on four continents! Shai's introduction in modern Hebrew had made sure of their understanding, for he introduced my text on the history of Wagner's tetralogy in exactly the sense I intended: as a history of the criminals Wotan and Alberich in a struggle for power.

The following day my lecture on Weill and Brecht also went smoothly. The room was filled because, even with my family background, I had the courage, the *chutzpa*, to appear at the largest university in Israel and speak about Weill's musical period theater as an opposing model to Wagner's *Gesamtkunstwerk*. An older woman from Berlin, who introduced herself only with her first name Isolde, asked me, "Mr. Wagner, why don't you lecture in our beautiful German language?" Somewhat confused, I answered, "Because the majority of people here in Israel understand English." Isolde responded quickly, saying, "You can imagine why I am named Isolde? Yes, my family loved Wagner's music, and I, too, love Wagner. I think often about the beautiful productions in the Kroll Opera House under Otto Klemperer's direction. And about Bruno Walter's *Valkyries.*"

Isolde turned out to be an educated Wagnerian, such as I had seldom met before. She beamed at me lovingly like a grandmother and finally said, "You cannot imagine what your visit means to us Berlin Jews." We embraced one another silently, fighting back our tears in vain. For me, the true test was my last lecture with the subjective title, "The Wagner I Mean." As with the other lectures, it was recorded. Following the advice of Herzl, I tried to clarify Wagner's significance for European music theaters and for music history. Since the lecture was not intended solely for experts, I decided to use slides and musical examples.

First I tried to focus on Wagner productions instead of reappraising my own past in Bayreuth. Today I think that lecture epitomized my uncertainty at the time, during which I did my best to analyze my family history apart from my inseparable personal development. I began to understand my own story better, but I continued to separate Wagner's life and his ideology from his theater. My lecture at the time no longer resembles my current opinion or level of understanding. Today, I am still surprised by the generosity and the benevolence of the audience at the time: a critical look at what I anxiously read from my manuscript shows that someone could have justifiably reproached me for giving short shrift to Wagner's anti-Semitism.

The trip to Israel prompted me to renew my study of Wagner's anti-Semitism. I wanted to understand its influence better, as well as its influence on the Bayreuth Festival. During the painful exploration of my history and my conscience, I not only began to distance myself from the basic beliefs of my youth but also from the interpretations of Jewish authors such as Ernst Bloch, Hans Mayer, and Claude Levi-Strauss, who had been misused in "New Bayreuth" to suppress and falsify the past and to deny the need to take responsibility.

Despite the events, interviews, and conversations with the listeners at my lectures, my wife and I did not want to miss visiting the Diaspora Museum in Tel Aviv. We were impressed by the material presented with writings, photos, and films about Jewish culture and history. One example made me realize how closely linked Jewish history is to German history and even to the Wagner family chronicle. Among other things, the Diaspora Museum has an extraordinarily precise and extensive database available to everyone who visits the museum. I looked up the keyword "Wagner" and received fascinating information, as I also did about the Jewish community in Bayreuth since the beginning of the thirteenth century.

The German media was suspicious during and after my stay in Israel. Most of them knew very little about Wagner's anti-Semitism, and consequently the coverage in Germany was limited. But the West German media in particular printed some sensational headlines. They presented me as Siegfried in a battle against Fafner. That did not help my effort to change the image of Wagner in Germany and Israel, nor did it help my reassessment of the Wagner family chronicle. The reports from Israel to Germany increased my isolation even more, though the Israeli media did strive to understand me in the context of my message.

At the end of January, I found out indirectly how my father had reacted to the Israeli visit. I spoke with the president of the Richard Wagner Association, Josef Lienhart, who told me that because of the many different West German newspaper articles about my trip to Israel and because of his authority as festival director, my father had demanded that the Richard Wagner Association revoke all authorized or existing invitations to me and issue no more in the future. If it didn't, he said, he would publicly distance himself from the Richard Wagner Association, all because of me and my statements in the newspapers.

I wrote to my father immediately and asked him to comment on the report. The official answer came two days later. He replied that he had told the Richard Wagner Association and its local committee that he would no longer participate in any of their events, if they still permitted me to give lectures, for his participation could be perceived as condoning my unacceptable views about the development and artistic nature of the Bayreuth Festival. One of his references was to an article of January 11, 1990, in *Die Welt*, in which I had explained that since Wieland's death the Bayreuth Festival had become a cross between an investment fund and a scrap-metal market. I had also emphasized that political and commercial elements dominated the festival to the detriment of the music, drama, and poetry. Naturally, he did not want his threat to the Richard Wagner Association to be understood as an "order." He had no legal basis for making such an order, but he believed that he was entitled to express clearly to Mr. Lienhart his "personal position." And my father maintained that none of this was at all related to my lecture trip to Israel.

Referring to my mention of the foundation charter's note on succession and the participation of the Wagner family in continuing the festival (in the *Süddeutsche Zeitung* on January 17, 1990), my father dismissed me by claiming I obviously lacked fundamental knowledge of the meaning and content of the charter. He also said that if I actually thought my grandmother was so horrible, as I had stated several times, then I should have refused my inheritance as "dirty money." At the end of the letter, mentioning his total responsibility for the Bayreuth Festival, he made a severe and absolute distinction between himself and me.

After receiving this letter, I attempted on numerous occasions to explain my position to my father, but all such attempts failed. I now see that I should have realized from my father's letter that he would never truly examine his own past, or his responsibility as festival director, or his responsibility as a father. What he cited from the newspapers was not always what I had said, and moreover, he took the statements completely out of context. They were incomplete and grouped together arbitrarily. But no one on Festival Hill, or among the Friends of Bayreuth, or even among the majority of the German and Austrian media, wanted to acknowledge that fact. An objective evaluation by the international press and Israeli academic experts resulted in an entirely different picture. After comparing the international reaction to my father's response and that of those around him, I recognized how pointless it had been to attempt an objective conversation with him. Despite all opposition, I had to continue following the path I had found in Israel. My father's boycotting me had both negative and positive consequences. In a positive sense I felt compelled to examine not only Wagner and Judaism but also the history of Christianity and Judaism. The resulting cultural and spiritual enrichment led to significant improvements in my personal and professional development.

The negative consequence of the break with Bayreuth was that my professional opportunities in Germany were severely diminished. News of the break traveled quickly, even to those places where I might have had an opportunity before. Anyone in the music world who considered offering me a position knew that doing so would make him an enemy of my father. Why ruin one's connection to Festival Hill? Nonetheless, some circles felt my father's behavior toward me was excessive and incomprehensible, and I found the generally negative international reaction to his autobiography (1994) encouraging.

Eugenio

In the first days of January, 1990, we read in the daily newspaper, *The Jerusalem Post*, that adoptions had become possible in Romania after the execution of the tyrannical dictator Ceausescu and his equally dreadful wife. Teresina and I immediately decided that when we returned from Israel in the middle of January, we would apply to adopt a child from Romania. After months of bureaucratic delays, we flew to Bucharest with the necessary documents. On June 6 we drove with the knowledgeable Romanian lawyer George Alexandru, whose name was provided to us by the Italian embassy, to a working-class district of Bucharest and to Orphanage No. 4. There, too, the Ceausescu regime had left behind complete despair. The orphanage was a prison, surrounded by high fences and barricades. Within the dark and dirty cement building it stank of urine and ammonia. Not a picture hung on the walls. Not a toy could be seen. Not a child's voice could be heard. The director's room was equally joyless; with her disdain for "her" orphans, she was a typical representative of the still omnipresent spirit of Ceausescu. She made it clear to us that only with a "little bonus" could we receive a child trouble free.

The door opened, and one after another, three children were presented to us. Elena, Christoph, and then Eugenio. Eugenio was in terrible condition. He was emaciated, and his stomach protruded distinctly. His skin was pale, sore, his musculature undeveloped, forcing him to sit down repeatedly, exhausted. But Eugenio smiled at me dimly, brightening up our first moment as father and son. Two days later, after an odyssey through a Bucharest court, we visited Eugenio as his parents. He suspected that something had happened. He called both Teresina and me "Mamma" since he had been raised only by women. He had no idea what a father was. We gave him a small plastic truck, and, beaming, he held it tight, fearing that someone would steal it from him. Finally, on August 30, 1990, a Bucharest court ruled that Eugenio was our son. That date was already significant to me, however: it was my father's birthday. So Eugenio became a Wagner on the birthday of his grandfather of all people.

In September 1990, just before our second trip to Romania to collect Eugenio, I interpreted the strange intersection of dates between the grandfather and the grandson as a starting point for a new period in my life. Because of my own childhood, I knew that I could never allow Ceausescu's shadow to overwhelm Eugenio the way Hitler's shadow had overwhelmed me. When we picked up Eugenio from the orphanage, he held our hands tightly and walked out with us, without saying anything to anyone or looking back for a moment. After Eugenio's baptism in December 1990, I sent my father a picture of him. It was returned without comment.

4

The Rocky Road to a Post-Shoah Discussion with Abraham J. Peck (1991–2005)

In the summer of 1990, I was invited to the twenty-first academic meeting of the annual Scholars Conference on the Holocaust and the German Church Struggle, scheduled for March 1991. I confirmed that I would come, for I was particularly interested in conversing with Jews of my generation. I suspected that my presence and my topic, "Wagner as I See Him," would meet resistance among the majority of conference participants. Dr. Jan Coljin, dean of general studies at Stockton College in New Jersey, allowed my invitation despite the objection of several groups within the conference committee and among the participants. He became one of my most valued friends and advisors, and not only in answering difficult questions about the Shoah's effect on generations born shortly before and after 1945.[1] The objections were due not only to Richard Wagner's anti-Semitism and his influence on Hitler but also because of my being a descendant of prominent Nazis, even though I had sought to engage in discussions about German history and family history with the descendants of Shoah survivors.

Preparing for the lecture began a year-long and difficult examination of my own ethical positions, which again revolved around topics such as guilt, shame, and mourning. Since I was aware that in Stockton I would be speaking to Jewish academics of my generation for the first time, I read the much-discussed book, *Children of the Holocaust: Conversations with Sons and Daughters of Survivors*, by the American-Jewish author Helen Epstein, born the same year as I, in 1947. The beginning of the book immediately sparked my interest:

For years it lay in an iron box buried so deep inside me that I was never sure just what it was. I knew I carried slippery, combustible things more secret than sex and more dangerous than any shadow or ghost. Ghosts had shapes and names. What lay inside my iron box had none. Whatever lived inside me was so potent that words crumbled before they could describe.

Sometimes I thought I carried a terrible bomb. I had caught glimpses of destruction. . . . Sometimes I felt my iron box contained a tomb.[2]

Disturbed, I searched for more literature about the second Jewish generation after 1945, and I came across two books by Peter Sichrovsky, *Wir Wissen Nicht, was Morgen Wird, Wir Wissen Wohl was Gestern War* (1985) [We Don't Know What Will Become of Tomorrow, But We Know What Happened Yesterday] and *Schuldig Geboren—Kinder auz Nazifamilien* (1987) [Born Guilty: Children from Nazi Families]. In the first book Sichrovsky—also born in 1947—tells about thirteen conversations he had with Jews who lived in West Germany and Austria. These conversations reveal the internal conflicts, the longing, the feelings of homelessness, and the fears felt by survivors' children. Sichrovsky's description of his own feelings reflects the same sentiments, as seen in the following passage:

My future is the past, and therefore it doesn't exist. Because Hitler and his people were victorious on one point at least. The Final Solution took place. In Austria, the Jewish question can be considered solved. We are not the remnants of a "sunken world" as one exhibition about Jews in Vienna is titled. We are the miserable remnants of a *scuttled* world.

After that I read the second Sichrovsky book, which particularly interested me because of the title *Schuldig Geboren—Kinder aus Nazifamilien*. Sichrovsky wrote:

Perhaps the most important discovery for me was that the post-war generation had never experienced their parents in the role of Nazi heroes. For them, too, that beaming, youthful hero in the SS uniform, believing in Hitler and the Final Victory, was just history. They knew him only from pictures and books. Born just before or after the end of the war, they had different memories of their parents. . . . Nevertheless, when the children of Nazis reached that certain age when they discovered their parents' true role during the war, they often became victims—victims of their parents. Many of those I interviewed presented themselves in this way: as victims of a mentality which, although the war was lost, perpetuated a fascist way of thinking in their own home. The external framework had changed. Germany and Austria had long been democratic states, yet the National Socialist ideas were deeply rooted in the minds of the perpetrators and their accessories, so that the generation after the war was confronted with a democratic environment on the one hand and a fascist family structure on the other.

Sichrovsky left many of my questions unanswered. For example, I had my doubts about such generalizations as the stigmatization "victims of their parents" for the descendants of Nazis. Nevertheless, reading the books by Epstein and Sichrovsky influenced my lecture in Stockton in March, 1991.

My Qualifications before My First Meeting with Abraham

Accepting this invitation was a risk. Academically, my only qualifications were my doctoral work on Weill and Brecht and a string of lectures that dealt with topics such as the Germans, Jews, and culture. Apart from that I was as unwelcome as former director of the Kurt Weill Foundation for Music in New York as I had been unwelcome as a guest speaker with some *chutzpah* at the University of Tel Aviv, lecturing about Wagner and Weill in January 1991. And those lectures had ultimately resulted in the end of my professional and private life in Germany.

Nonetheless, more important than the arduous search for my own ethical position were my often "uncomfortable friendships" with people who had suffered a Jewish fate. It was their warmhearted hospitality and help that influenced and molded me during decisive moments of my life: Charles and Germaine Spencer in London, Bettina Fehr and Johannes Meier-Linderberg in Bonn, Hannah Busoni in New York, and above all, Ralph Giordano. Later, after my first meeting with Abraham Peck, I also met Michael Wieck from

Stuttgart, Michael Shapiro from New York, Janice Hamer in Philadelphia (with whom I worked on the opera project *Lost Childhood*), Yehuda Nir in New York, David Faiman and his wife Ofra in Sde Boker, Israel, the Bruno Finzi family in Milan, Anna Flachova from Brno, and Helga Kinski from Vienna. Their life experiences, family histories, and views of the world helped me considerably, not only to accept my own fate, but also to venture down a new, untrodden path, crossing borders by confronting frank, existential questions. And always at the forefront was: how could the Shoah have happened, and why is it part of my German and familial history?

In the Stockton "Courtroom" on March 3, 1991

To set the stage for my first meeting with Abraham Peck, I should describe what preceded it. In order to avoid any general, abstract sentimentalism about the "good German," I tried to use factual research to connect my life experiences and my family history with anti-Semitism and the Wagner family entanglement during the Third Reich. As I drafted my lecture during the first weeks of 1991, I was particularly interested in the concept of reconciliation because I had not yet adequately grappled with its complexity and its implications for Christians and Jews after the Shoah. Since I had previously prepared for a discussion with a mostly Jewish audience in Israel by using an arrangement of autobiographical experiences and academic conclusions, I chose to connect my own childhood and youth, events from my first lecture trip to Israel, and my historical knowledge of Wagner and Hitler with a careful use of the term "reconciliation."

As I walked into the overfilled hall, I sensed that I was not at all welcomed by the majority of those present, mostly Jewish people spanning several generations. As in Israel, the atmosphere was tense, and given the strictly regimented allotment of time for my lecture, my anxiety grew. I began the lecture with my impressions of *Parsifal* and *Die Meistersinger* as a four-year-old child in the Bayreuth Festspielhaus, my experiences in the anti-children, Holy Grail world of Wagner theater, in the Wahnfried garden and in the Siegfried house, where Hitler had lived in the thirties and where the American officers' club had been until the mid-1950s. After a brief explanation of Wagner's historical significance in cultural and music history, I came to the most important issues: the historical connection of Wagner to Hitler, Hitler's relevance to my own family history as well as to my personal experiences after 1945.

My attempt to regard my contribution as part of a reconciliation between Christians and Jews provoked open objection. Every question after the lecture was first written down and given to the Shoah researcher Hubert Locke, the cofounder of the annual conference, and then passed to me. In that way Shoah researcher and historian Dr. Abraham Peck, born in 1946, rejected my thesis about reconciliation between Jews and Germans after the Shoah. He argued instead that from the Jewish perspective his generation needed a critical dialogue between Germans and Jews born after the Shoah. In his opinion reconciliation was only possible between the perpetrators and their victims directly, that is, those of the first generation. Aware that my understanding of this reconciliation was still inadequate, I searched for Abraham Peck after the lecture, hoping to talk with him about his criticism. We agreed to meet that evening. Rabbi Steven L. Jacobs joined our first, open, and personal discussion.

After telling me briefly about his position as director of the American Jewish Archives in Cincinnati, Abraham told me that his father, Shalom Peck, and his mother, Anna Kolton, had married in September 1943 in the Łódź, Poland, ghetto. They were separated after their marriage, and they met again in the Theresienstadt concentration camp in May 1945. His father was obsessed by his experiences during the Shoah: he lived in the Łódź ghetto from 1940 to 1944, then was imprisoned in camps like Skarżysko-Kamienna and Buchenwald and was finally liberated from Theresienstadt. His mother had survived Auschwitz, Stutthof, the bombing of Dresden, yet she never talked about her life there. Abraham's parents were his only family members to survive the Shoah; all the others had been murdered. On May 4, 1946, Abraham was born, one of the first in the Bavarian Jewish displaced persons camp in Landsberg am Lech. In this camp, he found a substitute for his lost extended Jewish family. His parents and he lived there until they emigrated to the United States in 1949. I felt ashamed, which Abraham did not fail to notice. He helped me through this difficult situation, making a joke about us "atypical Bavarians." He was born in Landsberg of all places, where my grandmother had delivered to Hitler the paper for *Mein Kampf*!

Rabbi Steven L. Jacobs's family history affected me just as powerfully. He was born in Baltimore on January 15, 1947, only three months before I was. His father Ralph (originally Rolf) Albert Jacobs was born in Rogowo, Poland, on May 1, 1921. He grew up in Zerbst, Saxony-Anhalt, and died on September 27, 1981, in Gaithersburg, Maryland. His mother, Ruth Buchler Fyman, was born on April 1, 1927, in New York. His father fled Nazi Germany and Nazi-occupied Europe and came to the United States in 1939, the only member of his family to do so. More than 150 members of his extended family were murdered by the Germans. Only seven family members were able to escape—five to Baltimore, Maryland, in 1933, one to Palestine in 1934, and another to Montevideo, Uruguay, at the beginning of the 1930s. So both Abraham's and Steve's family histories pointed toward Germany and therefore toward my family's past. That same night we resolved to found the Post-Holocaust/Shoah Dialogue Group.

These March days of 1991 were the beginning of special friendships: in addition to Abraham Peck and Steve Jacobs, I have had a number of ethical and Holocaust-related discussions with Jan G. Coljin, Henry Knight, then professor of religion at Tulsa University, and Leonard Grob. Apart from our intense conversations about the shadow of the past, these friendships also displayed the will—despite our mutual burdens—to enjoy life with similar intensity. At the conference I especially enjoyed the Jewish jokes. Some of the other participants were surprised by our loud laughing, or even disapproved of it, but we did not care. After our meeting in Stockton in March 1991, Abraham made the first, decisive step toward beginning our discussion, something I didn't dare to do, given the Wagner family's Nazi past. He wrote me on March 8, 1991:

> It was a pleasure and a joy to be with you at the Scholar's conference. Your sincerity, your sense of humanity, and your general desire to enter into serious dialogue convinced me that we must continue our discussion and our correspondence.

With the letter he enclosed his lecture, titled "*Trauerarbeit* and the Lost Legacy of the She'erith Hapletah," the reading of which became a turning point for me. By introducing me to both his familial and moral world, Abraham helped steer us together toward the same path.

What moved me most about Abraham's article was his conclusion:

Both survivors, their children, and the children of the oppressors need to mourn. Together? For the aging survivor generation that is a question that should not even be asked, an impossibility that should never be suggested. But for the children of the oppressors and for those of the oppressed that is not an unthinkable possibility.

Abraham ended with his vision and his hope for a dialogue:

> Perhaps the children of the survivors and their German counterparts, forced as they are to share the burden and the legacy of the Holocaust, can listen once more to the voice of the She'erith Hapletah and its prophetic message of the moral and social perfection of humanity. Such a lost legacy, recovered from the ashes of a "conspiracy of silence," would be for Jews and Germans a legacy worth finding.

Abraham won me over with these last sentences! For both him and me, our long and painful path from monologue to dialogue was full of crises, but we not only discussed complex, interdisciplinary analyses of the Shoah's effects on the generation after 1945, we also dared to follow a new, untrodden path. From the beginning we found it particularly important to connect our family histories to a general knowledge of Jewish and German history. Abraham always demanded with passion—which, as he said himself, bordered sometimes on obsession—that we keep alive the memory of German crimes against the Jews in the Shoah, a request with which I agreed entirely and even supported publicly. What I often objected to, however, was his generalized use of the word "Germans" since I disagreed with and still disagree with all generalizations employed about the Shoah. I repeatedly insisted on the distinction of Germans as perpetrators or accomplices, but I also insisted on clearly delineating both of those from the few persons who mounted resistance and as a result became victims—because there were some Germans with courage during the Nazi period, and they should not be left out of future generations' study of German history. We founded our Post-Holocaust/Shoah Dialogue Group in Seattle in 1992, and in general the group was met with suspicion: we were seen as black sheep—even though the critics seldom discussed the actual statutes, which were formulated with the help of Rabbi Steven Jacobs.

The Statutes of the Post Holocaust/Shoah Dialogue Group Founded by Abraham Peck and Gottfried Wagner in 1992

1. We, the children of the victims and the children of the victimizers, see the Shoah/Holocaust as a unique rift in Western and world civilization and the starting point of a new morality in terms of thoughts, feelings, and actions.

2. We stand opposed to the repressing and silencing of any and all discussion of the Shoah/Holocaust and the continuation of any and all prejudices and hatreds resulting from the activities of our parents and grandparents both now and in the future and directly attributable to the trauma of the Shoah/Holocaust.

3. We fully believe that the sharing of our own unique burden of this tragic past in a continuing present and future dialogue is of vital concern, independent of any religious, ideological, and/or political group. With our dialogue we give concrete evidence how our generation, and those after us, will confront the challenges presented by the Shoah and its ever present influence.

4. We begin our dialogue with tolerance, respect, and self-critical awareness as the children of the victims and the children of victimizers. Our mutual willingness to share our burden is coupled with our unhesitating commitment to overcome and to present to those who are open and receptive a model for present and future trust and understanding.

5. We see ourselves as an international activist organization whose avowed purpose is not only to inform others of the Holocaust but to fight both theoretically and practically against any kind of totalitarian dogmatism, religiously, politically, and ideologically. We stand for the adoption of human rights for all human beings, fully believing that we are responsible for our own actions, ever mindful of the different other.

6. We hope by our humanitarian actions and our scholarly work to influence governments and nation states, thus lessening fear of present or future repetitions of the Holocaust, striving at all times to realize our goal of a world living together in peaceful tolerance and appreciative of all diverse humanity.

These statutes must be understood as the result of our left liberal past and our political hopes. Abraham and I were molded by the liberal political developments at the end of the sixties. As members of the generation of '68, we held positions similar to those held by some of the Jewish intellectuals of the Frankfurt school, such as Max Horkheimer and Theodor W. Adorno, as well as Hannah Arendt. But the process of creating these statutes did not at all mean transfiguring our own years as students with nostalgia; it meant looking at ourselves critically as children of Nazi victims or Nazi perpetrators and setting new goals for responsible actions. During the course of this collaboration, it became clear that my idea of reconciliation between post-Shoah Germans and Jews did not stand up to reality, for reconciliation is only possible between perpetrators and victims directly. We children of the perpetrators cannot inherit any guilt, nor can we determine the conditions for reconciliation with the descendants of Shoah survivors.

Dan Bar-On

Among the many international, public events I attended over the past twenty years, my 1993 meeting with the Israeli psychologist and psychotherapist Dan Bar-On was of particular significance. His death in September of 2008 was a difficult loss for those involved in the German and Jewish, Israeli and Palestinian dialogues.

In 1989 Bar-On published *The Legacy of Silence: Encounters with Children of the Third Reich.*[3] In 1993 he asked us six questions about the Shoah's effect on our lives, questions something like the following: When and how were we confronted with the Holocaust? How do we cope with our rootlessness? How do we combat our social estrangement and "otherness"? Can we relate to the roles of victim and perpetrator? Do we live our lives without the shadow of the Holocaust? Through our knowledge of the Holocaust, have we found a middle path between the desire to die and to live?

Since these questions were too complex to answer at the conference, we wrote down our thoughts several months later. Abraham answered Dan Bar-On's questions by writing an article covering the general topics, whereas I answered the individual questions. Calling the exchange between Abraham and me a "microcosm of the German-Jewish dialogue," Dan Bar-On wrote:

Gottfried Wagner and Abraham Peck are brave people. Their parents would never have been able to talk with each other. Only fifty years have passed since the ancestors of one were deeply involved in the extremely atrocious act of attempting to annihilate the ancestors of the other. The survivors gave the solemn commandment to their descendants, never to forget and never to forgive. Why does Abraham try to break this commandment? Why does Gottfried try to break through the silence which came over the German people after the atrocities became public: a silence of a mixture of shame, the wish to shrink from the responsibility for the murder, to forget and to be forgiven? . . . For their own sakes they are looking for a dialogue which, though breaking their father's commandments, will help them address their internal quest for hope.

He then analyzed the effect of the Holocaust on our lives: having been uprooted from our surroundings during our childhoods, which created feelings of isolation and mistrust:

Gottfried found his emotional harbor in a family member who did not identify with the Nazis and his intellectual harbor in the post-war Jewish and gentile writers who tried to struggle, genuinely, with questions similar to his own about "Who is Wagner?" However, he had to pay a high price for his courage and was ostracized from his family, his homeland. He has a new personal harbor [Italy] which guards him from the storms waiting in the open sea. . . . After relating to their painful childhood memories which have shaped their [Abraham's and Gottfried's] life stories, they quickly disassociate themselves [from these memories]. . . . Abraham tells us that he believes the future will be good for the next generation, but his last sentences reveal that he cannot really believe whole-heartedly: "Can we ever free ourselves of the need to be watchful?" . . . We have to be watchful, to guard not to trust "yes" or "no," and if we do not succeed, what will happen to our children?

Bar-On continued: "Terrifying! There is still no real harbor in the world after Auschwitz." And then he proceeded to compare our dialogue with the construction of a house. At the end of his article, he perceptively said:

However, unlike bricklaying, there are so many participants in this process. All watchful eyes and ears of the living and the dead, all with such extreme and conflicting sensibilities that the possibility of failing is endless. The genuine discourse of yesterday may easily become the pseudo, as-if, discourse of tomorrow. How can we know? How can we find our ways?[4]

In retrospect, Dan Bar-On's warning was completely justifiable. That danger became especially clear after we looked critically at our theoretical knowledge and our personal experiences, deciding that we wanted to follow a different path from what was expected of us as "good Jews" and "good Germans" after the Shoah. Instead of being described as the son of Shoah survivors and the descendant of Richard Wagner and top Nazis, we finally became Abraham and Gottfried with our own identities, a change that resulted from our studying and confronting the Shoah.

Confronting My Own Experiences: Autobiographical Notes of 1997

In my autobiography, *Wer nicht mit dem Wolf heult* [He Who Does Not Howl with the Wolf], I described the path toward mutual responsibility. The book first appeared in Germany in 1997 and was published in English as *Twilight of the Wagners: The Unveiling of a Family's Legacy*. It depicts my years growing up in Bayreuth, the German edition ending with my first stay at the seminary in Auschwitz in 1995. As an epigraph to my autobiography, I chose the following passage according to Sanhedrin, 27b:

Are children responsible for the sins of their fathers? Yes, if they follow their fathers' disastrous path. But do not all suffer from the sins of others? We stumble unexpectedly over the sins of others. Does that mean that everyone should be responsible for everyone else? Yes, whenever someone has the power to protest and yet fails to do so.

I was primarily interested in conveying my personal experience as a descendant of active members of the Nazi elite between 1923 and 1945. These experiences were also important for the post-Shoah dialogue. I had to examine not only my family's unprocessed Nazi past, but also the role of the

Wagner family in the nineteenth century, especially in the context of National Socialism and anti-Semitism. For that reason I had to study my family's early history leading up to Hitler. Not only did I find a direct line from my great-grandfather Richard Wagner, Cosima Wagner, Houston Stewart Chamberlain, and my grandmother Winifred to Hitler, but I also discovered that the Wagnerian ideology in Bayreuth *contributed* to Hitler's racist madness and its consequences—all the way to Auschwitz. Many historians support this view. My analysis of the Wagner cult in Bayreuth after the Shoah demonstrated a phenomenon I call the "New Bayreuth" philo-Semitic pose, that is, the sublime form of conscious revisionism in conjunction with anti-Semitism, which despite the Bayreuth Festival's incantations to the contrary, appeared more and more after the Shoah. Remember that there were over fifty years of silence about the previous occupation of "New Bayreuth's" co-founder, Wieland Wagner. He had been a supervisor in the concentration camp Bayreuth-Flossenbürg from 1944 to the end of the Second World War. Therefore it is even more troublesome that some Jewish artists and intellectuals attempt to separate Richard Wagner the artist from Richard Wagner the ideologue and to diminish, in effect, his anti-Semitism, which—for non-Jews as well—ends up being a denial of Wagner's actual influence on Hitler's anti-Semitism.

Especially important to understanding the differences between our two family histories is Abraham's introduction to the American edition of my autobiography, for it demonstrates our development in the discussions we had about German, Jewish, and family histories in the previous years. He wrote:

I learned as a young boy that there was a reason for the absence of my uncles, aunts, and cousins. Indeed, because I had a father who was obsessed with his own experiences during the Holocaust years, from his time in the ghetto in Lodz, Poland, from 1940 to 1944 to his imprisonment at Buchenwald and Theresienstadt, I developed an unusual knowledge, at a very early age, of my father's tormentors.

In a way, this macabre cast of Nazi guards, commandants, and physicians became more real to me than the shadow figures who had been the murdered members of my family. All told, there were fourteen uncles and aunts, six on my father's side and eight on my mother's. But for most of my life they have remained only names. I cannot identify them by facial features, idiosyncrasies, or any other characteristics that make up the pleasures of the extended family.[5]

If you read these lines about the Peck family's fate and its effects on Abraham's life, and if you compare them to the Wagner family story in the context of history, it becomes clear what hurdles Abraham and I had to overcome to trust one another. As seen from Abraham's perspective in that introduction, the Peck family tragedy also shows me something else. It was not only for himself that Abraham spent the time to articulate his painful family history; he also did so as part of a process to develop trust with me in his examination of my fate. Given his experience with other, questionable post-Shoah dialogue meetings, Dan Bar-On had warned us that our conversations might develop into pseudo-dialogues—but they did not. Nor did we make it easy for ourselves, even having chosen topics such as "how does the Shoah influence our search for identity?"

Because of our constant struggle to make our dialogue a public debate, I became more and more able to lead my own life as an adult and a father. I increasingly viewed our events as a microcosm of the German-Jewish dialogue and as a macrocosm of our personal histories. Thus this book originated, and it put our friendship to a difficult test. During the arduous process, which we believe could be extrapolated from our individual experience and result in a general trust between Germans and Jews in the future, Abraham and I tried—independent of daily politics as transmitted by the media—to continue our path together as our contribution to the communication between the second and third post-Holocaust generations.

GOTTFRIED
WAGNER
Wer nicht mit dem Wolf heult

Autobiographische Aufzeichnungen
eines Wagner-Urenkels

Mit einem Vorwort von Ralph Giordano

Cover of autobiography of Gottfried Wagner (bottom), 5th updated German edition 2010, in front of the residence of the Wagner clan, Villa Wahnfried in 1940. From left: Wolf-Siegfried, Iris (the oldest), Nike, Daphne Wagner, Gottfried Wagner, and his sister. This picture of the fourth Wagner generation was taken in July 1951 for the promotion of the family enterprise. Inserted (top): Richard Wagner (right), founder of the family enterprise. Top from left: Winifred Wagner, Wolfgang Wagner, Hitler, and Wieland Wagner.

Friedelind Wagner, the rebellious anti-Nazi and Gottfried Wagner,
Wuppertal/Germany in 1980.

Cover of the second German edition of the autobiography of Friedelind Wagner in 1994. The autobiography was published first in English under the title "The Heritage of Fire" in 1944 and in Switzerland in 1945. It was used as part of the de-Nazification trial against Winifred Wagner. Courtesy of Eva Weissweiler.

Ellen and Franz Wilhelm Beidler, 1926. Franz, musicologist and grandson of Richard Wagner, had to escape from Nazi Germany for his socialist ideas and because his wife, Ellen, was Jewish. Courtesy of Dagny Beidler.

Franz Wilhelm Beidler

Cosima Wagner-Liszt
Der Weg zum Wagner-Mythos

Ausgewählte Schriften des ersten Wagner-Enkels
und sein unveröffentlichter Briefwechsel
mit Thomas Mann

Herausgegeben und mit einem Nachwort
versehen von Dieter Borchmeyer

PENDRAGON

Some of Franz Wilhelm Beidler's writings. From left: Franz as a little boy with his grandmother Cosima Wagner and his cousin Guido Count Gravina in Bayreuth in 1912. Courtesy of Dagny Beidler.

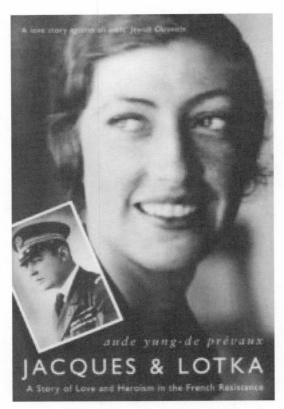

Jacques Trolley de Prévaux (left), related by his first marriage to the French branch of the Liszt family. The fashion model Lotka Leitner (middle), a Polish-Jewish woman married to Jacques, both murdered by Klaus Barbie in Lyon for their anti-Nazi activities in the French resistance. The author of the book is Aude Yung-de Prévaux, who works as a journalist for the French left daily newspaper Liberation and is the daughter of Jacques and Lotka. Courtesy of Aude Yung-de Préveaux and with the permission of Kiepenheuer & Witsch, Cologne.

Wieland Wagner und
Bodo Lafferentz im
»Institut für physikalische Forschung«

*In front of the main textile buildings of the New Cotton Factory in Bayreuth (below),
the small two-floor building used as the "Institute for Physical Research" which was
in reality the Bayreuth subcamp of the main concentration camp Flossenbürg,
where Wieland Wagner (top left) was the vice director from September 1944 to 1945,
assisted by his brother-in-law, Bodo Lafferentz (top right), co-operator with Porsche
Industries and assistant of Robert Ley, organizer of the Nazi "Strength through Joy"
organization. The Bayreuth Festival was part of the activities for the planned final
victory. Both were staunch followers of Hitler. Courtesy of Editor C.u.C. Rabenstein
Bayreuth.*

Blandine Jeanson, granddaughter of resistance fighter Jacques Count de Prévaux and cousin of Aude Blandine is a journalist and cofounder of Liberation.

Gottfried Wagner and his mother, Ellen Drexel, the former classic dance soloist in Bayreuth 1951.

Ellen's family: (from left) mother Thora, unnamed teacher, Ellen, her brothers Gus-tav and Ernst, and father, Adolf Drexel, a wine merchant. Courtesy of Renate Alberts.

Avant-garde painting, 1911, by Hans Christof Drexel, brother of Ellen's father, placed on the Nazi list as a "degenerate artist" who could not practice in the Third Reich after 1937. Courtesy of son Rainer Drexel.

Hans Christof Drexel, 1972. Courtesy of Rainer Drexel.

Gottfried at the golden wedding anniversary of Uncle Gustav Drexel and his wife in Wiesbaden, Germany, December 2001; (back row from left) their daughters Renate, Karin, and Christa. Courtesy of Renate Alberts.

Gottfried's Italian family in August 2003: Mamma Antonietta (front), the pillar of our families; second row (from left) brother-in-law Enzo Galli with dog Kitty; Teresina, Gottfried's wife; Silvia Galli and her mother Francesca; and Alberto Galli; back row: Gottfried and Eugenio Wagner. Courtesy of Janice Hamer.

Lotte Lenya and Gottfried Wagner after a concert dedicated to Kurt Weill's music in New York in March 1978.

Teresina and Gottfried Wagner in Massada, Israel, in front of the oldest synagogue in the world.

Abraham J. Peck, Harry Guterman, and Gottfried Wagner during a conference on the Holocaust in Tulsa, Oklahoma, in March 1992.

Gottfried Wagner before his lecture in the European parliament in Brussels on January 27, 1999.

Gottfried Wagner - Abraham Peck

UNSERE STUNDE NULL

Deutsche und Juden nach 1945:
Familiengeschichte, Holocaust und Neubeginn
Historische Memoiren

Böhlau

Cover of the original Austrian-German edition of the book by Wagner and Peck, 2006, which shows a composite of Abraham Peck as a child in Landsberg and Gottfried Wagner at the Wagner residence, Villa Wahnfried, in 1951. Courtesy of Silvia Galli.

The team of the opera Lost Childhood *in New York in March 2000. From left: Gottfried Wagner, Dr. Yehuda Nir, the poet and librettist Mary Azrael, and the composer Janice Hamer.*

Posters in New York of the opera Lost Childhood.

The Italian family branches Rossetti-Galli-Malacrida—Proverbio-Zullo at the marriage of Silvia and Alfredo on April 30, 2011. We are connected around the globe.

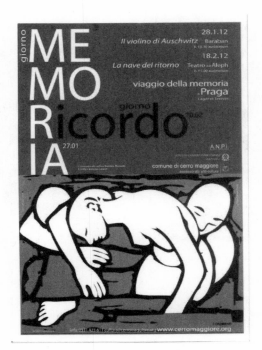

Poster of European Memory Day for the victims of National Socialism, Cerro Maggiore, 2012. Courtesy of Ivano Bollati.

Three generations of the Drexel family with African relatives and friends from Ghana at the marriage of Friedrike (with flowers in her hand and in her hair) and with her husband Bismark Oppong on May 4, 2012. Courtesy of Lena Ritschner.

From left: Eugenio, Teresina, Gottfried, and Stella in May 2010.

II

Running Toward and From the *Churbn*

Abraham J. Peck

5

The World of Our Yesterdays: The Families Pik and Kolton

We did not call it the Holocaust in my house. It had no name, except that my parents would refer to something called the *churbn*, which I later learned was the Yiddish word for destruction. *Churbn* was a generic term, applicable to a whole host of tragedies, destructions that marked the fractured timeline of Jewish history.

But in my house, the *churbn* of choice were the events that would forever be the leitmotif that defined my identity. I was a son of Holocaust survivors, and for the first three decades of my life that identity remained hidden beneath a host of other ways that I would identify myself: Jew, immigrant, stateless person, and outsider. My father, Shalom Wolf Peck (Pik), of blessed memory, was a small man, not much over five feet tall. But I never noticed this. His presence was always larger than life because of what he had to say and why. It more than made up for his lack of height. His voice was a voice of authenticity—he was a survivor of the Holocaust. It is not easy writing these words in the past tense. My father enjoyed the gift of a long, if tragic, life. He died on July 5, 2005 (28 Sivan, 5765 in the Jewish calendar), at the age of ninety-two and one-half. He died at home, with just a hospice nurse and me by his bedside.

As difficult as it was for me to bear the burden of his illness, a total collapse of his physical and mental systems that began in May, repeated trips that I took to hospitals and rehabilitation centers in Florida, and the round-the-clock vigil that I kept for over a week by his bedside as he slowly slipped away from life, I would have had it no other way.

When my mother, Anna (Anje) of blessed memory, died of a heart attack in her sleep on March 7, 1988 (18 Adar, 5748), at the condominium in Florida where they had lived since 1978, I received the news from my father via a telephone call at seven o'clock in the morning. There was no time to say goodbye or to make the promises that I know she would have wanted to hear: that I would provide for my family and my father; that I would always have a good and steady job; that I would be a good Jew and would always stay safe in a world that was inherently unsafe.

I vowed then and there that it would not be this way with my father. So many of his brothers and sisters, and my mother's brothers and sister, had died alone in unknown places and lay in unmarked graves in the great cemetery of Poland. They were murdered by the Germans, those "masters of death" as the German-Jewish writer Paul Celan (born Paul Antschel) called them. I kept my promise and I did not let him die alone. Near the end, my father struggled to tell me two things: "Abe, you were my whole life," and when I told him I was going on a journey to Poland to visit his and my mother's birthplaces and the ghetto and concentration camps where they suffered during the Holocaust, he whispered in Yiddish, "Don't go." But I did go. I went to experience for myself all the shadows that had been a part of my life for as far back as I could remember.

Poland was always the last frontier, the one place in my family history that was always waiting but never accessible. I could have traveled there on several occasions—to academic conferences, the March of the Living trips to Poland for Jewish young people, or as part of some American Jewish group. But I never did. The negative ways in which my parents described their feelings about Poles and Poland, before and during World War II, was enough to keep me away.

In the last year of my father's life, however, the need to go became great. The book that I was coauthoring with my colleague and friend Gottfried Wagner dealt with the family histories that had shaped so much of who we were. For nearly fifteen years we had engaged in a dialogue between a survivor's son and the son of a family that epitomized the loss of Germany's humanity. The need to see the places where that family history had taken place was a necessity for both of us personally as well as professionally. I had an even more important reason. I wanted so desperately to tell my father that I had seen his and my mother's birthplace and had stood in the earth of those places that had destroyed their families and created for me a world without family.

"The Two Saddest Nations on Earth": Poles, Jews, and Memory[1]

Jewish tradition asks us to remember. Jews are a people of memory. But what happens when that memory remains fixed on the most awful moment in the Jewish experience? What happens when Jews are so traumatized by the events of the Holocaust that there is no way to see beyond it? What happens when, unlike the efforts at a German-Jewish dialogue, the relationship between Jew and Pole has taken on, in the words of Eva Hoffman, "the form of a moral war and has proceeded in escalating rounds of accusation and counter-accusation, exaggeration and denial."

In Polish history it is uncertain who remains the "supervictim." Three million Polish Jews died during the Holocaust and three million non-Jewish Poles died during the Second World War. More than one million Jews died at the Auschwitz complex, but the first trainloads of prisoners to Auschwitz I, the so-called Stammlager, consisted of mostly Polish Catholics. Poles and Jews both claim a kind of "supervictim" status, a position much envied by post-Holocaust Germans. The Polish-Jewish poet Antoni Slonimski wrote in his epic poem, "Elegy for the Jewish Villages," the following:

> Gone now are those little towns where the shoemaker was a poet,
> The watchmaker a philosopher, the barber a troubadour,
> Gone now are those little towns where the wind
> Joined Biblical songs with Polish tunes and Slavic rue
> Where old Jews in orchards in the shade of cherry trees
> Lamented for the holy walls of Jerusalem.
> Gone now are those little towns, though the poetic mists,
> The moons, winds, ponds, and the stars above them
> Have recorded in the blood of centuries above the tragic tales,
> The histories of the two saddest nations on earth.

The two saddest nations on earth—one that lived through partition after partition, failed uprising after failed uprising, and saw itself as the crucified Jesus of Europe, and the other nation that saw itself as being a "light unto the nations," a holy community carrying the message of the one God, of moral and ethical values that would become a standard for the world.

And all that is left is a memory. All we have left is the knowledge that we cannot understand who we are and who we have become without understanding the other. Yet the paths of the two saddest nations on this earth have parted forever. How ironic. Poland gave its Jewish community the opportunity to be the largest and greatest Jewry the world had ever seen. Jews came to Poland a thousand years ago and continued to come because the Polish nobility, the *szlachta,* saw in the Jew something worth having. Jews saw in Poland a tolerance that they saw nowhere else in Europe, especially in the centuries where physical attacks and expulsions were the rule.

Jews created a legend about Poland. They named it *Polin* because in the sacred language of Hebrew, the *lashon hakodesh*, the two words *po* and *lin* mean "here shalt thou lodge," in the exile from the Land of Israel. Poland was a place where, as the great Polish-Jewish novelist Sholem Asch described it, "Satan has no power over the Jews and the Torah [the most sacred of Jewish texts] is spread over the whole country. There are synagogues and schools and rabbinical academies. God be thanked."

Not that everything was idyllic. When Jews fled the countries of Western Europe seeking shelter in Poland during the epidemics of the Black Death during the fourteenth century, they came in great numbers. They settled in Lwow/Lviv, Sandomierz, Kazimierz near Krakow, as well as in many cities in Great Poland, Little Poland Kuyavia, and Red Ruthenia.

In 1454 anti-Jewish riots flared up in Wroclaw and other Silesian cities. A papal envoy, the Franciscan friar called John of Capistrano, accused the Jews of profaning the Christian religion. In Silesia his words cut deeply, and Jews were banned from Lower Silesia. But when John of Capistrano sought to incite the Catholics of Kracow and other cities, he was less successful. By the end of the sixteenth century, there were 500,000 Jews living in Poland, not only the Ashkenazim from the German persecution, but Sephardic Jews who were driven away from Spain and Portugal during the Inquisition. The majority of Jews could not believe their good fortune. When they looked around at the rest of Europe and examined their lot in Poland, they understood that the words *Polin* meant something special. In many Polish towns— although not all—Jews were given complete freedom in carrying out trade and crafts. Even though Jewish economic activities were appreciated by the *szlachta* because Jews served as an alternative to a viable middle class that could rival the Polish nobility, Jews also joined in the first of many joint struggles with Polish burghers against often oppressive Polish gentry.

In a 1589 agreement with the municipal authorities in the town of Kamionka Strumiowa, the councilors of the town "accepted the Jews into their own laws and freedoms while the Jews undertook to carry the same burdens as the burghers." The latter promised that they would "defend those Jews as our real neighbors from intrusions and violence of both the gentry and the soldiers. We will prevent all harm done to them . . . since they are our neighbors." There was no parallel anywhere else on the face of the earth. Jews were allowed to govern themselves. In the sixteenth century the structure of Jewish self-government had no equal in all of Europe. The *Va'ad Arba Arazot,* the Diet of the Four Lands (in Hebrew), was called into existence by the Polish monarch, Stephen Bathory, in 1579. It was headed by a marshal general and included a rabbi general, scribe general, and treasurers general. This was a diet that represented all the Jews. It carried out negotiations with central and local Polish authorities through its liaison officials, called *shtadlanim,* who sought to influence the decisions concerning Jews taken by the *Sejm,* the Polish parliament, and the diets of the gentry.

There were times of common suffering as well. In 1648 the Cossack uprising led by the Ukranian hetman, Bohdan Khmelnitzky, was directed at both Poles and Jews. Neither group was strong enough to withstand the forces of partition. They lost what they knew as Poland to Russians, Austrians, and Prussians. In 1794, under the hero of the American Revolution, General Tadeuz Kosciuszko, Poland honored its Jews by creating a separate military unit composed of Jewish volunteers in the uprising against Czarist Russia. "Nothing can convince more the far away nations about the holiness of our cause and the justness of the present revolution," Kosciuszko wrote in the "Statement on the Formation of a Regiment of Jews," "than that though separated from us by their religion and customs, they sacrifice their own lives of their own free will in order to support the uprising." The Jewish regiment under Colonel Berek Josielewicz took part in the battle to save Warsaw. Josielewicz ultimately lost his life in a later battle.

If in the eighteenth century Jews in Poland were called comrades-in-arms, in the nineteenth century they were called "brother." The great Polish poet Adam Mickiewicz created Jankiel, the Jewish tavern keeper (a common Jewish occupation of the time) in his epic poem *Pan Tadeusz.* It was written in exile after the failure of the 1834 uprising against Russia. Jankiel is a dignified traditional Jew, who acts as a spy for the Polish landed gentry, who seek to exploit Napoleon's conflict with Russia to restore Poland's independence. Mickiewicz has Jankiel the Jew play the Dabrowski March ("Poland Has Not Yet Perished"), the tune that would later become the Polish national anthem.

And it is with Mickiewicz that the Jew in Poland was seen as the "older brother" of the Poles, a phrase that was repeated by the Polish Pope John Paul II when he, as a Polish Catholic, called Jews "our elder brothers." It was Mickiewicz's belief that only in alliance with its older brother could Poland, the new chosen nation, fulfill its divine mission to free European nations from the yoke of authoritarianism. "For your freedom and ours" became the battle cry of the Polish insurrectionists.

"I believe that a union of Poland and Israel," Mickiewicz wrote, "would be a source of spiritual and material strength to us. We would most efficiently prepare Poland's rebirth by removing the causes of its eclipse and reviving the union and brotherhood of all races and religions that regard our motherland as their home." There were Jews, Ukrainians, Germans, Belarusians, Armenians, and even Scots who were a part of the motherland and a part of a multicultural possibility.

By the beginning of the twentieth century, much of this thinking had changed. Other, more inward-looking forces sought to find different ways to create a free Poland, one that was Polish in a geographic but also in a linguistic and cultural sense. "Poland for the Polish Christian," said Roman Dmowski, the founder of the National Democratic Party, the Endecja. His Endeks did not see the Jew as an older brother but as an economic, religious, and cultural Other. Jews were no longer the *zydki*, the little Jews of Polish literature, who were crafty to be sure but also wise and often extraordinarily useful. Jews were now the epitome of the suspicious Other, who stood in the way of a true Polish national revival.

When a free Poland emerged from the shadow of the First World War, Jews were not seen as a partner in the creation. Indeed, in the interwar years more than three-quarters of Jews in Poland listed their nationality as Jewish, not Polish, and Yiddish as their mother tongue. Jews were seen as Jews in Poland but not of Poland, and often so believed themselves.

What had happened to the *Polin* of Jewish dreams that Poland helped nurture by saying to its Jews through poem and edict that you are different but you are our neighbor and we will defend you? In effect, Polish nationalism murdered the multicultural dream. Poles said that Jews were the Other, but they knew them well. Poles played with Jews, traded with them, shared the growing impoverishment of the Polish nation in the interwar years with them. By the mid-1930s, following the death of the benevolent dictator and protector of the Jews, Marshal Josef Pilsudski, a growing anti-Jewish sentiment concluded with a ban on the ability of Jews to work on Sunday, the Christian holy day of rest but not that of the Jews. Poland took away from its Jews the right to prepare their food in a religious manner by banning ritual slaughter. Poland barred most of its Jews from attending university as well as access to certain professions while claiming that Jews controlled Polish society and wished to create a Jewish nation within the Polish nation.

Łęczyca/Linshits

It was into this changing climate for Polish Jewry that my father was born on February 4, 1913, the sixth of seven children born to Isaac Nechemiah and Miriam Bracha (Berkovich) Pik, in the small town of Łęczyca, Poland. The Jews of Łęczyca called the town by its Yiddish name Linshits or Lintchits, but it had several other names as well, all within approximate spelling distance of Łęczyca or Linshits. Approximately thirty-eight kilometers northwest of Łódź, Poland's second-largest city and once the city of its second-largest Jewish population, Linshits was not really a shtetl in the mold of an Anatevka of *Fiddler on the Roof* fame. Among its more than 10,000 inhabitants were more than 4,000 Jews.

Jews had had a presence in Linshits as early as the year 970, although a Jewish community existed from the fifteenth century, as early as 1453. Not all of that Jewish history in Linshits was a good one. The great historian of Polish Jewry, Simon Dubnow, described the murder of two elders of the Linshits Jewish community after they were sentenced to death for killing a young Christian boy from a neighboring village. Neither man confessed to the then-common blood libel, but they were nevertheless put on the rack to die an agonizing death. Dubnow continued the story: "The bodies of the executed Jews were cut into pieces and hung on poles at the cross-roads. The Bernardine monks of Łęczyca turned the incident to good account by placing the remains of the supposedly martyred boy in their church and putting up a picture representing all the details of the murder."[2]

Years later Isaiah Taub, a guide for the Jewish Agricultural Society in pre-World War II Poland, was leading a group of Jewish tourists through Łęczyca. "Among the old remarkable buildings we visited," he wrote, "was an old church. Built into the walls on the inside of the church were coffins containing Catholic saints and martyrs. Among the latter we noticed in one niche, behind glass, the skeleton of a young child. The inscription, in gold letters, said: 'Here rest the remains of a Christian child whom the Jews killed for Passover and used his blood for baking matzos.'"[3]

The Pik family was a relatively new one in Linshits, having moved there from Czechoslovakia in the middle of the nineteenth century. The family name—Pik, or Pick in its Central and Western European spelling—is a *kinnui,* that is, a noun that appears in the Talmud. It means "by-name" or "substitute name." The *kinnui* was the way in which Jews in the Middle Ages made a distinction between a sacred first name and a secular one that had some relation to it. Pik is an adaptation of the Bohemian and Polish word *byk* or "bull," but it is not connected to the animal. Instead, it refers to the *kinnui* of the Hebrew name for Joseph. In the Bible Joseph is compared to a young bull.[4] Surrounded by his beloved parents, Isaac Nehemiah and Miriam Bracha, three older sisters, Rachel, Hinda Leah, and Rivka, as well as by two older brothers, Matthias and Chaim Leib, and a younger brother, Simcha Gershon, who died at the age of twelve in 1929, my father's life in Linshits was that of any typical small-town Polish Jew.

His education was limited to attendance in cheder, the Jewish elementary school, and a few years in a Polish school. By the age of sixteen, he was already apprenticed to a baker, a Polish Christian named Ignacy Solinski, who owned a small shop in Linshits. Solinski was the one Pole whom my father consistently referred to as a "decent and good Catholic" following the German invasion, a role model both in business and in his personal life. Ignacy Solinski was unusual. By the 1930s the growing anti-Semitism that was fueled by the National Democratic Party had come to my father's town. He especially remembered an incident as a teenager when on a warm summer day he and a group of Jewish friends had gone swimming. Moments after he entered the water, he heard the cry, "They are beating up Jews!" A horde of Endek youth had run down to the water and was attacking my father's friends as they came onto the shore. Never one to duck an encounter with anti-Semites, my father ran out of the water and punched the first Endek he saw. He apparently gave as good as he got.

After finishing his apprenticeship in the early 1930s, my father wanted more of a city life and moved to Łódź. Because of his talents as a baker and confectioner, he was able, with the help of Ignacy Solinski, to buy a partnership in a confectionary shop/bakery and begin life in the big city. My father's shop was a success. He produced marvelous cakes, pastries, and breads and was even given an award for his creations after an international competition in France. Yet the increasingly anti-Semitic atmosphere in Łódź and in Poland, fueled by the National Democratic Party, but not exclusively, was for my father a cause of great concern. Not only were physical attacks against Jews more and more commonplace, but a national economic boycott of Jewish businesses made profitability a very difficult issue.

One day in 1938 a young woman came into his shop to buy a challah, the ceremonial bread used on the Jewish Sabbath. When my father started up a conversation with her, he found out that she was twenty-three and had seven brothers. He was impressed with her self-assurance, her youthful good looks, and her sense of Jewish identity. He would not see her again for five years during a much darker time.

Zwolen/Zvolin

My mother's birthplace, Zwolen—or Zvolin as its Jews called the town—lay just beyond the large city of Radom, some thirty kilometers to the west. The first recorded mention of Jews in Zwolin was in 1554, a century after the town was founded, and by the outbreak of World War II, nearly 5,000 Jews lived there in a town of about 10,000 people. Zvolin was home to an influential Chassidic community, led by Rabbi Samuel-Elie Taub and his disciples, one that focused its Chassidism on the melodies that its rabbis composed to various prayers and on special occasions.[5] My mother was born on July 20, 1915, the youngest of nine children born to Abraham Joseph and Perle (Mandelman) Kolton. Her one sister was named Roza. Her seven brothers, each of whom she adored, were Yankel, Beryl, Yeheskiel, Pinchas, Asher Selig, Eli, and Schmuel.

The Kolton family owned a shoe repair and leather-goods store. My mother's father belonged to Zvolin's Chassidic community, and when part of the family, including my mother and her parents, moved to Łódź in the early 1930s to open a shop that produced prostheses for those who had lost legs, he became a follower of the Alexander Chassidic community, named for the village of Alexander, about twenty kilometers from Łódź.[6] But my mother was unhappy with Chassidism and ultra Orthodoxy. After a few years at the Orthodox Beis Yaakov (Beth Jacob) school, she left to work in the family business and sought to live a Jewish, if not Chassidic, life, much to the unhappiness of her parents.

The Łódź Ghetto—My Father

Łódź was the last of the great Polish cities to be founded and the first since the age of Jewish emancipation to create, under Nazi rule, a self-contained ghetto for its Jews. In the years between its beginnings and the end of its active existence as an autonomous Polish city, Łódź stood apart from the other great metropolitan centers of Poland. When the city received its official charter in 1820, Jews had already been a part of its development for over a quarter of a century. By 1939 nearly a quarter of a million Jews ran the city's newspapers, its commercial businesses, and its free professions. But in this "city of nationalities," another group besides the Jews played a vital role in its social and economic life. These were ethnic Germans, who had come to Łódź as early as 1820 to develop its manufacturing. By 1939 they numbered well over 60,000 individuals. Thus, in a city that counted over 700,000 inhabitants at the outbreak of World War II, more than 40 percent of the population was not Polish. Even more unusual was the sense of security felt by Łódź Jewry, despite the fact that Poland had a history of twentieth-century anti-Semitism. In this "most Jewish" city in Poland, Łódź Jewry had exerted a tremendous influence on the overall life of the city for over a century.[7]

Łódź was a working-class city similar to the northern English industrial center of Manchester. As the "Manchester of Poland," Łódź was an important textile center, but it was also a dirty, choking environment. Even the *Yizkor bukh* (memorial volume) of Łódź Jewry could not present a more romanticized image of the community. For its authors Łódź was a place where the "streets were narrow . . . not suitable for heavy traffic . . . no gardens, no attractive houses or boulevards. The gray smoke from the factory chimneys covered the sky. The factory whistles were the music of the city."[8]

Surface descriptions, however, could be deceptive. Łódź Jewry produced an exciting and impressive array of cultural, business, and political achievements, especially during the interwar years of 1918 to 1939. Julian Tuwim, perhaps Poland's greatest poet, was born in Łódź and wrote his first poems there. The pianist Artur Rubinstein and the artist Artur Szyk were natives. The interwar years produced writers such as Izchak Katzenelson, Israel

Rabon, and Moshe Broderson, as well as the brilliant comedy of Shimon Dzigan. The period also saw the development of a rich and diverse Jewish political life, with groups representing Łódź Jewry's affiliation to the left-wing socialism of the Bund, to the religiosity of the Agudath Israel, and, of course, to the enthusiasm of the numerous Zionist factions.

By the 1930s, however, the status of Łódź as Poland's most secure Jewish environment was increasingly in doubt. The rising nationalistic anti-Semitism of certain social classes was accompanied in Łódź by a growing anti-Jewish feeling among the Polish working class, which resented the non-Polish domination of the city's cultural and economic life. The ethnic German population, too, became increasingly anti-Semitic, taking its cue from the Nazi government in Berlin. During the 1930s it grew especially resentful of Jewish "domination" of the textile industry, an industry that the Germans had been developing for over a century.[9]

On September 8, 1939, the German army entered Łódź and began an occupation that would eventually put an end to more than 100 years of Jewish life in Poland's second-largest city.

September 1, 1939, at 5 a.m.: World War II was about to begin. My father was on guard duty, serving in the Polish army, somewhere between Łódź and Warsaw. He heard sirens wailing and ran to a bomb shelter. There he saw a woman standing outside the shelter with two small children. All three were crying. The woman asked my father if he was Jewish. At the same time the two civilian guards in front of the shelter repeated again and again, "This place is not for Jews."

My father knew that German bombers would be flying overhead at any moment. He took his rifle with a bayonet attached to it and held it against the throat of one of the guards. "Let them in," my fathered ordered. The guard was frightened and did so. Suddenly, my father heard a loudspeaker ordering all Polish soldiers "to Warsaw, to Warsaw." He mounted his horse-drawn cannon and rode off toward Poland's capital city. He entered Warsaw some days later. All around him Polish soldiers were looting jewelry stores. He saw a Polish officer running toward him. "The war is lost," the officer shouted. "I am lost as well." He ran to the side of a building, took out his revolver, and shot himself in the head.

By mid-October the six-week German blitzkrieg against Poland was nearing its end. My father was one of the many Polish troops who laid down their weapons in surrender. He was a corporal in the army, a rank that would have almost certainly become something higher if Poland had been victorious. He had disarmed an explosive within seconds of detonation, a device that would have killed and wounded numerous members of my father's company. His commanding officer told him that, although he was a Jew and almost all Jews were cowards, he, the officer, would turn in a glowing report about my father's actions and would recommend him for a medal and a higher rank.

Not long after my father watched the Polish officer commit suicide, a train full of soldiers approached. My father thought they were Poles, but they were Germans. The German soldiers told the Polish soldiers to empty their pockets. For any Polish soldier who did not give up all looted materials, ten of them would be shot. My father was arrested with the other Polish soldiers and put into a barbed-wire enclosure.

Another group of German soldiers arrived, in black uniforms with lightning bolts on their collars. They were SS, and they asked the prisoners of war just one question: "Which of you are Jews?" They then asked those who had identified themselves as Jews if any of them were ill. A number of Orthodox yeshiva students were among the captured Jewish soldiers. Many of them, gentle and afraid, had developed dysentery. The Germans took them away in trucks with the promise that they were going to a field hospital for treatment.

A few minutes later my father heard the sound of machine-gun fire. The Germans had shot these poor, ill, Jewish boys. It was the first time my father had come into contact with German deception. The Germans would deceive their Jewish victims, my father included, at every stage of their encounter. My father could not understand such behavior coming from such a good and kind people as the Germans. No one was more surprised than the Jews of Poland when Germany invaded Poland with a wish to destroy them. They had heard stories of how the Nazi government treated its German Jews and had heard that there would be sanctions, even expulsions.

Most Jews in Poland could only rely on folk memory, one that remembered how decent and kind the German Kaiser's troops were in the war years between 1914 and 1918. They stood in stark contrast to the hated Czarist Russian troops, who were "all anti-Semites." My father grew up with such a folk memory. During World War I the Germans had come into Linshits after driving out the Russians, and the Russians had come into the town after driving out the Germans. It had gone on this way for most of the war. His mother, my grandmother, told him about Willy and Hans, two German soldiers who had befriended her and became like members of the family. She remembered how kind they had been and how they had brought food and household items whenever they came to visit.

Much to my father's surprise, all the Polish soldiers, Jew and non-Jew alike, were freed and told to go home. My father took off his army uniform, unlike the Christian soldiers. He saw evidence of German brutalities against Jews on the trip back to Łódź. He wanted to give the Germans no reason to stop him and inquire again whether he was a Jew. Wearing a Polish uniform would be a reason. He immediately went to his confectionary shop to speak with his partner. But the partner was nowhere to be found. Instead, my father found the baked goods in the shop on fire. The next morning the partner's young daughter came to the shop, and my father asked her about his partner's whereabouts. She took my father to the Jewish cemetery. Apparently, two SS men had come into the shop and told her father to get away from the baking oven. They gave him five minutes. He thought it was a joke. They shot and killed him on the spot.

My father had no choice but to leave his shop and the neighborhood where he lived. He needed to get back to Linshits because in Łódź there was little food and thousands of SS. When he arrived in Linshits, he saw that his brother Chaim Leib had prepared food for him. Linshits was occupied by relatively few SS, mostly German Wehrmacht troops. It was easier to hide and not be discovered. But my father found out one of the sad truths of people *in extremis.* Survival overshadowed everything—loyalties, religion, and neighborliness. It became clear to my father that in a small place like Linshits the chance of being turned in by Polish informers was much greater than in a large metropolitan center like Łódź. Armed with a huge bag of foodstuffs, my father got a ride to the town of Ozorkow, near Łódź. From there he jumped on a trolley and to his dismay found that it was full of Germans. They grabbed my father and his food and took him into a building where he was beaten within an inch of his life. He could not breathe without pain for several days.

The Germans were not interested in my father's food but in the fact that he might be a Jew. Yet my father's facial features could not be classified as "Jewish." His Polish accent was very good, better than his Yiddish one. That was an important part of his survival during the Holocaust. Except for that one time on the Ozorkow trolley, he was able to pass for a Polish Christian in almost all cases where he still had his freedom.

When he returned to Łódź, my father saw posters that told all Jews that they had to be inside their homes by 5 p.m. Here it was after 6 p.m., and walking toward his apartment, my father was still carrying his many bags of food. By 7 p.m. he had almost reached his home. Suddenly, two German soldiers came toward my father. Miraculously, one of them stepped off the sidewalk to let my father pass. They thought he was a Polish Christian. At the end of October, my father decided to go back to Linshits to see his family. He found that his sister Hinda Leah and her children were no longer there. Apparently Hinda Leah had told a neighbor, a *Volksdeutsche*, an ethnic German woman, that Hitler would ultimately lose the war. The woman informed on her, and she and her family were taken away. My father decided on a course of action that would become his strategy for staying out of German hands until his deportation to several labor and concentration camps. He began hiding in the Jewish cemetery in Linshits, a place that he felt German soldiers would not enter to look for living Jews. His sister Rachel brought him food, and he made fires to keep warm. He also left the cemetery to visit Ignacy Solinski, who greeted him like a long-lost son. But Solinski's wife screamed that the Germans would kill her and her husband for harboring a Jew. She chased my father out of the shop with a rolling pin.

In December 1939 Linshits became one of the first Jewish ghettos established by the Germans in an attempt to segregate the town's Jews from its Polish Catholic population. The "Jews' Street," Ulica Zydowska, became the starting point of that effort. My father now felt that he had no choice except to go back again to Łódź. And again he began to hide, this time in the new Jewish cemetery on the outskirts of the Łódź suburb of Marysin. On May 1, 1940, the official date of the "closed" Łódź ghetto, more than 160,000 Jews became the total prisoners of their environment. Nearly 80,000 Łódź Jews had been resettled, had "escaped" to parts of Poland under Russian control, or had left the city in some other way.

The ghetto, like the rest of Łódź, had been renamed Litzmannstadt, in honor of the German General Karl Litzmann (1850–1936), who had captured the city in a 1915 battle. Litzmann later became a strong supporter of Adolf Hitler and joined the Nazi Party. Initially, my father had little choice but to become a part of the ghetto. He moved into an apartment at number 56 Franciszkanska Street, renamed Franzstrasse by the Germans. His roommate was Rabbi Boruch Leiserowski (later Baruch Leizerowski), whom my father had known in the pre-war years. Originally from Lithuania, Leiserowski was a gifted scholar of Torah who had married the daughter of a wealthy Jew who committed suicide at the outbreak of the war. The building in which my father lived had been owned by Rabbi Leiserowski's father-in-law, and the rabbi had managed it.[10]

It was quite clear that the fate of the Łódź ghetto and its inhabitants had been decided long before February 8, 1940, the day that more than 160,000 Jews were officially herded into the most neglected northern districts of the city, Stare Miasto (the Old Town) and the unbelievably squalid Baluty (Balut). The latter district was so poor that Jews living in central Łódź, out of shame, often maintained little or no contact with their poverty-stricken relations in Balut.[11] Within the official ghetto, whose circumference measured eleven kilometers, there were no sewers. Of the 31,000 apartments in the ghetto, only 725 had running water.[12]

At first my father did not work for any of the ghetto establishments that had been created to supposedly "help" the German military meet its demands for clothing, shoes, etc. He had already found a job in a ghetto bakery, but after a short while, with the creation of the ghetto, the Germans confiscated whatever flour the bakery had. Without a permanent position my father became the object of a search by the Germans. He did not want to become part of the ghetto labor force because, as a young and strong man, there was every possibility that he would be taken to do labor outside the ghetto, and he did not want to take that risk. Who knew what awaited him there? But to be caught as a nonworker in the ghetto was a certain death sentence. So he went back to his old hiding place, the Jewish cemetery. But this time he went as part of what was called in German the *Beerdigungsabteilung,* the division of cemetery burials. He reasoned that if he worked there, he would still be a part of the official ghetto work force, but he could also hide there if it became necessary to do so.

Łódź was unlike any other ghetto. It was a totally enclosed world where the Nazis' ability to deceive the Jew reached unparalleled heights. It was a "hermetically" sealed enclosure with very little news either coming in or going out. There was no chance for escape, none for armed resistance. No contact was made with a mostly hostile Polish underground, and the Jews faced the additional threat on the "Aryan" side of 150,000 hostile Germans now living in Poland's most Nazified and Germanized city. One ghetto resident called it a Nazi-made "fortress."[13]

From its very beginning, my father knew that the Łódź ghetto represented the end of Jewish life as he had known it. He saw Jews dying in great numbers from starvation. He knew this because he had to bury so many of them in the portion of the "new" Łódź Jewish cemetery that became known as the "Cemetery Fields," where at least 43,000 Jews and Sinti/Roma (Gypsies) from the Łódź ghetto were buried with no recognition or ceremony.

Except for one. My father remembered an evening in the cemetery. He had just finished his shift and wanted to go home because he was hungry and had some bread in his room. From out of the darkness, a German soldier ordered him to stop on threat of being shot. He asked my father whether he was a spy. My father replied that he was a part of the burial division and pointed to his hat and the patch on his coat that carried the division symbol.

The body of a high-ranking German general was then brought onto the cemetery grounds. Apparently it had been discovered that he had had a Jewish father and a Christian mother. This was not known at first, and he was an excellent officer. He had been fighting at the Russian front. When it was discovered that he was half-Jewish, Adolf Hitler had personally ordered him shot. The order was carried out, and he was brought to the Jewish cemetery in Łódź.

My father remembered it as an extraordinary sight. It was nearly midnight when the casket was brought in, accompanied by two rows of German soldiers. They buried him and placed grass on top of the grave so that there was no sign that the burial—or the general's existence—had ever taken place.

My father was the one who buried most of the Sinti and Roma who had been deported to Łódź, about 5,000 of them from the Austro-Hungarian border (Burgenland).[14] They were beaten mercilessly by the Germans, many to death, and starved as well.

My father had to deal with both Jewish and Roma/Sinti bodies. The rabbinic authorities in the ghetto, never before faced with non-Jewish burials in a Jewish cemetery, decided that each coffin was to be filled with one Sinto/Rom and two or three small Jewish children. The cemetery became for my father not only a place of employment and security, but a place where he pondered his fate and the fate of European Jewry. He often had conversations with the corpses awaiting burial. It was of course a monologue and revolved around only one question: why is this happening to us and doesn't the world and God care?

Sometime at the end of 1942, he finally received an answer to the question from an unlikely source. The Germans were scared to death of disease and infection. One evening a German SS officer came into the cemetery holding a handkerchief in front of his nose. My father had just cleaned and disinfected an entire group of graves, and the SS officer was impressed with my father's efforts. He complimented my father on the work and said he was doing a good job. My father had found several of the older German guards in the ghetto, some of them veterans of the First World War, to be "decent." But what Jew could ever feel comfortable with an SS man, especially an officer? For whatever reason, my father felt comfortable enough to ask the SS officer, who had just spoken to him in an almost human manner, a question that he had thought about for a very long time.

"Excuse me," my father asked, "but why do we deserve this as Jews? What did we do?" The German became agitated and began to shake. He took out his pistol and pointed it at my father. "Listen, you piece of Jewish crap," he screamed at my father. "I don't talk to Jewish vermin as a rule but I will tell you. If not for our Führer, Adolf Hitler, all of Europe and eventually the world would be in Jewish hands. You Jews are a people with no shame. You are forgotten by God and a superfluous people in the world."

At that point my father knew that the Jewish people were doomed to destruction. Because of the deception, because of the friendship of Willy and Hans in World War I, because of his own inability to believe what he experienced day after day, night after night, as he buried body after Jewish body, he had never thought such thoughts as he thought now. He was the prisoner listening to his own death sentence and the death sentence for every Jewish man, woman, and child who existed on the face of the earth.

The Łódź Ghetto—My Mother

In a sense the creation of the Łódź ghetto did not affect my mother as much as it did my father. When she and her parents moved to Łódź, they found an apartment in Baluty amidst the squalor of the poorest section of the city. But it was filled with Jews and Jewish life, and for small-town Jews like the Koltons, accustomed to a large family and an even larger extended family, the need for Jews was important. Yet, when the ghetto was created, my mother and her parents had to abandon their fairly large apartment and move into much smaller rooms at 36 Mlynarska Street, renamed Muehl Gasse. She was employed in the Strohschue Betrieb 86 located at Widok

Street 5, which the Nazis had renamed Rungestrasse. She made straw boots for German soldiers fighting on the German front and had a quota of six pairs per day. The work created terrible blisters on her hands.

The work that my mother had to do was exhausting. But far more terrible for my mother was the decimation of her family members. Her mother had died before the German invasion of Poland in 1939. Her father, employed as a shoemaker, was shot to death in 1941 by German soldiers who came into the shop looking for leather. He denied having any, and they shot him on the spot. A number of my mother's beloved brothers lived in the ghetto. The lack of food and the spread of disease began to take its toll on the residents within months of its creation. A picture of the conditions in the Łódź ghetto emerged clearly in the pages of the Łódź ghetto *Chronicle,* the secret but "official" publication that was produced in both Polish and German by a team of skilled authors and observers, Polish Jews and West European Jews who had been deported to Łódź in the autumn of 1941. The entry for April 22, 1944, reads:

> As you approach the area from Drukarska Street or from the court yards of Limanowska Street, a choking, pestilential stench assaults your nose. Only a truly God-forsaken ghetto could stink like this. . . . A swarm of boys, armed with spades and picks, bowls and small sticks . . . dig up the sand until they reach the garbage, and pull something out of the abominable filth. Horrified, I ask a boy: What are you doing, what are you looking for? We're digging for potatoes! I look at these potatoes in horror. Stinking, rotting remains from nearby kitchens. . . . And yet every tiny remnant is extracted with the fingers, carefully checked, and collected in a little sack or bowl. This is not simply hunger; this is the frenzy of degenerate animals, for the fruits of these hours of digging, the putrid, paltry dregs, will never compensate for the energy consumed. This is unbridled madness, a shame and a disgrace. This must not be; this cannot be.[15]

For my mother the unbelievable became the believable. Within a matter of months, three of her brothers died in her arms of starvation. At the beginning of 1943, my mother was living in the same building as my father. My father had developed a case of diarrhea, and he knocked on her door to see if she had any extra rice to help stop it. She reminded him of the time that they had met in his bakery in 1938. They thus became reacquainted and began to spend time together. They decided to get married in September 1943. Religious weddings were no longer allowed in the ghetto, so Mordechai Rumkowski, the notorious "eldest" of the Jewish Council, performed the ceremony. There were at least twenty or twenty-five other couples who were also married at the ceremony. Rumkowski told the couples that they needed nothing more than each other. Each couple was given a loaf of bread as a wedding gift. Fortunately for my parents, my father's roommate, Rabbi Leiserowski, secretly married them again in a religious ceremony. Thus, they began married life in the Łódź ghetto.

The head of the Jewish Council in the Vilna ghetto, Jacob Gens, told a young partisan in the ghetto that "the ghetto is a world alone, a special world. The ghetto is a death chamber which holds men, women and little children. The death sentence has already been pronounced but not yet carried out, and the final date is not known."[16]

Outside of Mordechai Rumkowski, who most likely knew of the killing grounds at Chelmno, to which Łódź Jewry was deported, the ghetto knew nothing of its fate. The *Chronicle* wrote uneasily on a number of occasions about certain mysterious events taking place in the ghetto: "Large shipments of baggage have been sent to the ghetto since May 25. The people of the ghetto are tremendously puzzled by the arrival of these shipments, which contain clothing of all sorts" (May 30–31, 1942). "Since the end of May the ghetto has been receiving colossal amounts of clothing" (July 21, 1942). Finally, on September 25, 1942, shortly after the great Nazi roundup and deportation, the *Chronicle* wrote in a frustrated tone that "absolutely nothing is known about the fate of any people resettled from this ghetto." Not until June 22, 1944, did the *Chronicle* begin to understand the fate of Łódź Jewry: "People generally suspect that a gradual liquidation of the ghetto is underway."[17] This lack of any information about Chelmno is extraordinary, especially when one considers that the Vilna ghetto was quite aware of the killing area in the Ponary forest, where its deported Jews were executed.[18] Even more astounding is the fact that the killing of the Łódź Jews in Chelmno was known in the Warsaw ghetto from the very beginning.

Six months after my parents' marriage, my father's luck ran out. In February 1944 he found out from one of my mother's surviving brothers that my father might be rounded up to go out on a work detail. A few days later, the Germans came for him, accompanied by two big German shepherd dogs. He asked to say goodbye to my mother. The German guards would not let him do so and threatened to shoot him if he said one word to her. She gave him some bread and his watch and watched him march out of the building. He was taken to the Czarnieckiego Street (Schneidergasse) Central Prison. My father knew that a terrible fate awaited him in this prison because it was the place from which prisoners were taken to the railway ramp at Radogoszcz (Radegast) where trains left for unknown destinations. After several beatings, my father escaped from the prison, but he had nowhere to hide. He went back voluntarily. My father was imprisoned in Czarnieckiego for an entire month. He did not see my mother at all during this time but received a visit from his sister Rachel's daughter at night and was able to talk to her briefly. She cried out to him, "Uncle Shalom, I hope we will see each other in the future." She, her sister, and her mother were driven into the sea from the concentration camp at Stutthof near the city of Danzig and drowned in late April 1945.

Finally, in March 1944, my father was taken to the labor camp at Czestochowa. My mother saw him just before he was sent away. She brought him a sweater and a piece of bread. He threw the bread back to her. After my father's deportation from the ghetto, my mother could only watch as the signs became clear that the Łódź ghetto was in the process of being liquidated. It was the last of the major Jewish ghettos in Poland that was still functioning. By the beginning of May 1944, the liquidation of the ghetto was ordered by SS Reichsführer Heinrich Himmler, and the following month more than 7,000 Jews were sent from Łódź to the death camp at Chelmno.

During August 1944—and throughout nearly the entire month—more than 65,000 ghetto residents, the remaining inhabitants of the camp (except for about 800 individuals), including Chaim Mordecai Rumkowski, were taken to the Radegast train station and deported from Łódź. My mother was among them. She had never heard of the place to which they were supposedly being sent. It had an unusual name. It was called Auschwitz.

Naked Among the Wolves— In the Concentration Camps: My Father

What my father did not know at the time of his deportation was the fact that he was part of a shipment of 1,500 Jews from the Łódź ghetto who were desperately needed to reinforce the slave labor operations of the Hugo Schneider Aktiengesellschaft-Metalwarenfabrik, commonly referred to as HASAG.

HASAG, which manufactured armaments, was the third largest of such companies, after I. G. Farben and the Herman Göring Werke. HASAG, whose main administrative offices were located in Leipzig, was given the rights to run the national munitions plants of Poland, located in the town of Skarżysko-Kamienna in the Radom district. The factories, spread over 3.5 million square meters, were divided into three sections, known as Werk A, B, and C. During 1942 an additional Jewish labor camp was added to each of the sections, and the whole complex became known as the Judenzwangsarbeitslager Hasag Skarżysko-Kamienna [Jewish Forced Labor Camp Skarżysko-Kamienna].[19]

My father did not know that with his transfer from Łódź to the HASAG complex, he was on a trajectory that had as its end result his ultimate destruction by any means possible. This becomes clear when one understands that the decision to turn the Łódź ghetto into a full-fledged work camp in the middle of 1942 was not based on any concern for the German war economy. It was simply the institution of a policy the Germans called Vernichtung durch Arbeit [destruction through work].[20] Ultimately, "overwork and semi-starvation" would "dispose of this labor force automatically, and the monetary aim of exploitation would converge upon the initial aim of annihilation. The two ends would meet in one."[21]

For its Jewish workers HASAG employed the same philosophy. It put little value on young, physically able workers like my father. More important were the older and potentially better-off Jews who might possess valuables. The younger workers were placed in Werk A and B, the older ones in Werk C. There the older workers were placed in highly poisonous chemical locations with no protective clothing. After three months of terrible working conditions, they were no longer seen as capable of working. They were then subject to "selections" and mass shootings. By the spring of 1944, a typhoid epidemic of massive proportions broke out in the HASAG-Skarżysko factory, killing hundreds of Jews. Replacements were desperately needed. Some of the 1,500 Jews from Łódź were taken directly to Skarżysko. Another group, my father among them, was taken to the HASAG company camp at Czestochowa.[22]

HASAG-Pelcery was the biggest forced-labor camp. By the end of June 1944, around 5,000 Jews from Łódź and Czestechowa worked there. Forty-eight people lived in a barrack, two to a bunk bed. Lice-infested straw was used for bedding. If a Jew was selected, he was taken to be placed among dead bodies and left to die. The sick were placed in a "hospital," which was previously a stable. In the hospital no one received treatment.

When my father arrived in Czestochowa, he met a prisoner named Pik who was a convert to Christianity. A native of Czestochowa, this Pik's father was a well-known member of the community. The younger Pik took my father under his protection on the assumption that they were somehow related. Although my father had gotten a job in a bakery, making baked goods for the camp, the Czestochowa Pik told him that it was better to be a member of the Jewish police force that patrolled the camp. But the head of the Jewish police was a terrible and vicious individual. Also a convert to Christianity, he was known as a sadist, even toward his own police. My father met a Jewish policeman, who, like my father, became a member of the force in order to escape a more dangerous job.

One evening the policeman fell asleep at his post. The head of the Jewish police discovered him and beat him within an inch of his life. My father was not interested in working for such a person. So, his new friend Pik from Czestochowa said, "Don't worry, we will make you a kapo." "What did that entail," my father asked? "Oh, just accompanying the Jewish workers to their jobs, or just making sure that they have their lights out at the appropriate time," he was told. For a few weeks my father walked to the workplace with the others. But he noted that many of the kapos were themselves sadists and seemed to enjoy beating fellow Jews for pleasure. My father had better food as a result of this position, but he would not become a sadist.

A chance to leave Czestochowa and return to Łódź nearly happened. An order signed by Rumkowski asked that a number of the former Łódź ghetto inhabitants be returned. My father worked furiously to get his name on the list of returnees so that he could see my mother, but he was not successful. He began to feel that he would never leave Czestochowa alive. His desperation turned to strategy. Where could he go where he would not be found? He decided that the best place to hide would be the shrine at Jasna Gora ("bright hill" in Polish), the home of Our Lady of Czestochowa, the Black Madonna. It was and remains the greatest religious treasure of Poland and has been so for over six centuries. My father somehow got out of the camp and fled to Jasna Gora, remaining there for several days until he was discovered by a Ukrainian guard from the camp who had come to pray at the shrine.

Whatever punishment awaited my father was never carried out. Within a day or two of his capture, he and a number of other prisoners were transported by train to the HASAG facility at Skarżysko-Kamienna. Here my father found the worst of his many places of incarceration. At best, conditions in the spring of 1944 in Skarżysko-Kamienna (which the Jews called *Skarzisk* in Yiddish) were described as a "daily struggle for survival on two fronts: in the plant, the backbreaking labor, constantly raised quotas, and blows rained on [the prisoners] by their German and Polish masters. . . . In the camp they fought hunger, crowding, filth, disease and the officials of the internal administration."[23]

My father's situation became even more serious because he was assigned to Werk C. "It was," one author wrote, "a place outside human existence. A site of abandonment and madness." Another eyewitness wrote that "whoever passed through Werk C will be haunted for the rest of his life by memories of monstrous days and nights, when men envied the lot of the dog who could walk about freely and had food to eat."[24]

Into such a world my father came, where as he remembered it, Jews were being shot left and right. One of the worst of the perpetrators was Kurt Krause, the former head of the Werkschutz, the plant guard, a group of German and Ukrainian killers whose essential roles were to "make a small fortune while releasing one's frustrations through acts of violence."[25] My father had heard that a group of Polish partisans had threatened to kill Krause if he did not stop mistreating Polish Catholic workers. My father devised a survival strategy. He began to tell other prisoners that he had married a Polish Catholic woman in a church ceremony. Krause heard about my father's claims and questioned him. My father was able to convince Krause that he was a Catholic convert. Krause ordered that my father be sent to work with other Catholics. That meant, for my father, getting better bread and other foodstuffs.

But the worst of my father's tormentors was Paul Kühnemann, known as the "hunchback" (*der Hojker* in Yiddish). Kühnemann had become camp commandant in November 1943. He was short, heavyset, and indeed had a hunchback. He also spoke a fluent Yiddish and was aware of Jewish customs, skills he had reportedly learned as a night watchman in a Jewish factory.[26] Kühnemann was a hands-on commandant. He was everywhere, accompanied by a huge German shepherd, observing those who worked hard and murdering those he felt did not. In the few months that my father was in Skarżysko-Kamienna, he had two personal encounters with Kühnemann.

One day a prisoner from the Łódź ghetto, an older man whom my father knew slightly, came to him, terribly afraid. The Germans and Ukrainians, he told my father, were on a rampage, shooting Jews at random. Just then, Kühnemann, with his dog, approached the two of them. He had the other Jew taken away with a group and asked my father, "Do you want to go with those men. How old are you?" My father replied that he was thirty-one years old. Apparently satisfied with my father's answer about his age, Kühnemann walked away. The group of men were taken away and shot.

My father also remembered a handsome young Jewish boy who had injured his foot on a work detail. He could not stand on it. He begged my father to help him by holding him up while he walked. Before my father got the chance to do so, Kühnemann came over and with a smile of compassion asked the boy in Yiddish what was wrong. "Nothing," the boy replied. "Are you sure?" asked Kühnemann. "Please stand on one foot for me and then on the other." The boy could not, and Kühnemann took out his pistol and shot the boy in the head.

In July 1944, with Soviet troops near the edge of the Radom district, where Skarżysko-Kamienna was located, an order was issued to evacuate Jewish slave-laborers to concentration camps. At a number of other munitions plants, prisoners were sent to Auschwitz. But at Skarżysko-Kamienna things were different. A "selection" led to the murder of 500 prisoners. A few days later, on the night of July 30, 1944, in the midst of confusion, about 250 prisoners attempted to escape from Werk C. All were caught and killed. The next day a transport of 1,500 men was sent to the concentration camp at Buchenwald, near the famous city of Weimar.[27] My father was among them. He arrived on August 5, with his hands and feet bound after trying to escape from the train.

Buchenwald was the place where my father realized that the Nazi war against the Jews was paralleled by another Nazi war against human values. Buchenwald had been created in 1937 as a "reeducation" center for political foes of National Socialism, primarily communists and Social Democrats from various nations, habitual criminals, and Jehovah's Witnesses, or as they were known in Germany, *Bibelforscher.* They were soon joined by Jewish men arrested during the infamous anti-Semitic pogrom of November 9–10, 1938, known as Kristallnacht, so-called social misfits, homosexual men, and Sinti and Roma. After the Nazi invasion of the Soviet Union in June 1941, the camp also began to receive Soviet prisoners of war.

One of the first people my father met in Buchenwald was a German-

Jewish politician who had been in the camp since 1937. But it was the extraordinary array of prisoners who made up the Buchenwald concentration camp universe that made my father realize that National Socialism was an evil that had global proportions. He had had no doubt since his meeting with the SS officer in the Łódź ghetto cemetery that the destruction of Jewish life was a Nazi priority, but he also realized that the German agenda was an even larger and ultimately history-changing one.

Among the prisoners he met in the camp was Philip Auerbach, a German Jew from Hamburg, who, as a trained pharmacist, was a "big shot" because he was able to obtain and distribute whatever little medication was available. Auerbach survived the war and became a very important official in the post-war Bavarian government administration, responsible for the monetary restitution for Jewish survivors of the Holocaust. In Buchenwald he was able to provide my father with a pair of soled shoes that he needed for his work in the camps' notorious stone quarry, where he was beaten on several occasions by brutal German kapos. The work in the stone quarry was difficult, even for a younger man like my father. As my father described it, the quarry was not a work place but a place of suffering and torture. His particular work detail contained mostly French prisoners.

His stay in Buchenwald did not last very long. Two weeks later he was transferred to another HASAG camp, Schlieben, one of the many subcamps of Buchenwald, located 120 kilometers south of Berlin, in what is now the state of Brandenburg. In many respects Schlieben was his most dangerous camp. Schlieben was a work camp that specifically produced tank shells. My father was aware of this and told the camp authorities that he was a key maker, hoping not to be put in the munitions factory. But all the slave-laborers were needed to help make the anti-tank shells, the so-called *Panzerfaust*, for a war effort that seemed on the verge of collapse. My father was reunited with several friends from the Łódź ghetto who had arrived in Schlieben before him. They were starving. My father stole a number of food items from the camp kitchen but was caught. Taken before the SS Oberscharführer, my father was told he would be hanged. But a Jewish prisoner from Prague, also named Pik, who claimed he was a cousin of my father's, intervened. He was a favorite of the Oberscharführer, one of "his Jews," who provided items of value for the Nazi officer. My father was beaten, but nothing worse.

One day a tremendous explosion shook the factory in which my father worked and set off a series of dynamite explosions. He was not certain whether it was caused by an Allied bombing raid or by an act of sabotage. Of the 1,500 men in the factory, hundreds were killed or wounded. My father was among the survivors. But he had sustained several broken ribs and had lost all of his teeth. Although he could not work, he was asked to watch a group of very sick prisoners in the so-called camp hospital.

In April 1945, with the Soviet army closing in on the camp, the SS decided, as they did in many of the concentration camps, to move their "precious" cargo to a safer environment, one where they could continue the task of murdering them. A number of the camp inmates were transported to Theresienstadt in Czechoslovakia and to other camps by horse and wagon. Another group was told to march by foot to the Theresienstadt camp. My father was among the latter.[28] More dead than alive, the few Jews from the "death march" that reached Theresienstadt several days later found a scene that mirrored the chaos of the collapsing Nazi regime and the lost war effort. The Red Cross was allowed to deliver packages to the mostly Western European Jews who were left in the show camp of the Nazi concentration camp system, the place where "Hitler granted the Jews their own city."

By April 1945 there was nothing of a show place left in Theresienstadt. It was a place of the dead and dying. But the Red Cross packages were a godsend, except that the Red Cross did not provide any for the newly arrived and half-dead Jews from Schlieben. But my father survived. On May 8 the first group of Soviet soldiers entered Theresienstadt. My father had enough strength to greet them, although he weighed eighty pounds. He ran up to a Russian tank and took a machine gun from the soldier on top of the tank and pointed it at a group of German guards who immediately raised their hands.

Within days a typhus epidemic broke out in the camp. Many former prisoners were ill, and even the Soviet doctors treating them came down with typhus. But my father did not. He was able to work with the international team of doctors and nurses, former prisoners of the camp. My father remembered several doctors from Belgium, Poland, Czechoslovakia, Hungary, and one, Dr. Goldstein, who would travel with my father to the American zone of Germany.

One day in early June 1945, several weeks after the camp had been quarantined, closed to the outside and then reopened when the typhus epidemic was over, my father was sitting with two Russian military officers, one a major and the other a captain who was a Jewish doctor. Also at the table was

Rabbi Eugene Lipman, a young American-Jewish chaplain who had been transferred in June 1945 to Czechoslovakia to work with the survivors in Theresienstadt. Suddenly, a friend of my father, a cantor from Łódź who had left Theresienstadt just before the typhus outbreak to search for his family in Poland, came into the room. He walked up to my father and said, "Shalom, your wife is here."

My Mother

Standing on the ramp at the Radegast station in August 1944, waiting to board a train to somewhere, what could my mother have been thinking? Even if she had known where she was going, the name Auschwitz would have meant nothing to her. She might have known that thousands of Łódź Jews had been sent to their deaths at a place called Chelmno (*Kulmhof* in German), but she knew nothing of the killing machine, a place far from Łódź, that would come to define the evils of the twentieth century.

What she did know was that her father and three of her brothers had died in the Łódź ghetto. She also knew that she had not seen her husband, Shalom, since March of that year, and she did not know whether he was dead or alive. When my mother arrived at a train station called Auschwitz, she had no idea that nearly a million people had died in that place, victims of a plan to murder the Jewish people and many of the Sinti and Roma people as well. When she got off the train, she would have seen hundreds and hundreds of men and women being sent either to the left or to the right. Perhaps, in getting off the train onto the ramp, she might have met a prisoner in a striped uniform who would tell her that she was now in the biblical *Gehenim*—or hell—and that soon she would be drifting heavenward, just like the smoke she saw pouring from the smokestacks in the distance. She would be chosen to go to the right while others, many older or with children, would be asked to go to the left. What did it all mean? What it meant for my mother was life. It also meant that she would have her hair completely shaved off her head. Did she feel like her fellow Auschwitz inmate, Lucille Eichengreen, who wrote of her own introduction to the death camp?[29]

> As if reading my thoughts, the SS woman slapped my face hard with the back of her hand. My head reeled back, but the Kapo kept on clipping. As she shaved my armpits and all other body hair, I concentrated

on my hatred: hatred for her, hatred for the Germans who had reduced me to this sweating, naked creature, without hair, without dignity. I was no longer a human being to them, just an expendable Jew. I remembered my father and sister: had they been brought to a place like this to endure a similar degradation—or, as in the case of my father, to be murdered? Would I ever know? I wanted to scream, to kick, to scratch. Instead, I stood in silent rage.

I looked at the mountains of hair around us, hair of every conceivable color. What would they do with all this hair? For several minutes, we stood motionless, and then felt the hands of the Kapo pushing us toward the swinging doors. I was startled by a reflection in the upper glass panels—an oval, egg-shaped head with two dark eyes and large, protruding ears. Was this hideous sight me? I lifted my arms to touch my head, but revolted by the reflected image, I dropped my hands, denying for a moment the shock, the nightmare that was me.

My mother would spend no more than a month in Auschwitz, living in the women's barracks at Auschwitz II, the infamous Birkenau complex where the gas chambers and crematoria were located. She did not have a number tattooed on her arm. She would be struck under her heart by an SS soldier with the butt of a rifle—this would be her most vivid memory of Auschwitz.

From Auschwitz, my mother was shipped to a place about twenty-two miles east of Danzig (Gdansk in Polish), the infamous "free city" of Poland that had seen so much conflict between its German and Polish citizens. My mother's brother Beryl lived in Danzig, having left Zwolen to make his fortune. But my mother had no way of knowing that the place where she had been shipped from Auschwitz, called Sztutowo in Polish, was so near to her beloved brother.

The concentration camp that my mother had come to, Stutthof, was the first camp established on Polish soil in September 1939 and the last one to be liberated on May 9, 1945. During those years as many as 100,000 people were deported to the camp, many Polish non-Jews, as well as Jews from Warsaw, Bialystock, forced-labor camps in the Baltic regions, and those from Auschwitz. Of that number, as many as 60,000 died from gassings, lethal injections, and other forms of inhuman treatment. My mother was asked to work on a kitchen detail and tried, surreptitiously, to take some food for herself. But she was spotted by a Ukrainian female guard who hit my mother with an iron pot on the top of her head. Months later, even after her liberation, she had a large swelling from the blow.

On November 24, 1944, my mother and 500 other men and women were selected to travel to the German city of Dresden to work in an armaments factory. The factory was a subcamp of KZ Flossenbürg, located in Bavaria near the Czech border. My mother was number 266 on the list of those to be sent to Dresden, and her Stutthof camp number was 82 764.[30] The train arrived in Dresden on November 26, and those on the transport were immediately sent to the Bernsdorf & Co. factory at Schandauerstrasse 68, a site that belonged to the manufacturing giant Reemtsma.

My mother was in for a surprise. The civilian head of the factory was none other than Hans Biebow, the German administrator of the Łódź ghetto, who had earned huge sums of money from his activities in Łódź and who had argued against the liquidation of the ghetto because business had been so good.[31] Even before the liquidation of Łódź, Biebow, originally from Bremen, had put together a business plan to transfer his money-making operations elsewhere. Dresden became that site. What my mother did not know was that she was part of a bizarre scheme to save Biebow and his associates, Erich Czarnulla and Franz Siefert, from the possibility of military conscription and combat after the liquidation of the Łódź ghetto.

Biebow's plan was to transfer two major factories from the Łódź ghetto to Germany along with a number of the Jewish workers, numbering more than a thousand. My mother was included in a group from the second of these factories managed by the Bernsdorf & Co. concern. Upon arrival in Auschwitz, this group did not undergo a selection process, the only known group to have been spared this terrible experience in the history of the camp's existence. According to the Israeli historian, Michal Unger, "In the last stages of the war . . . this Nazi war criminal [Biebow], who participated in the annihilation of the Jews of the Łódź ghetto . . . rescued a large group of Jews as the war wound down."[32] This "Biebow's list" was not unlike the group of Jews saved by the industrialist Oscar Schindler, but with far more evil intentions.

Conditions in Dresden were far better than in Stutthof. The Jewish laborers were housed in a large building with central heating. The SS soldiers were responsible for keeping discipline but were not allowed to beat or kill those whom they were supervising. But conditions had not improved entirely.

There was still great hunger among the laborers, and many who had come from Stutthof already ill and greatly weakened did not survive.

On February 13, 1945, the American and British air forces bombed the city of Dresden, damaging the factory on Schandauerstrasse. My mother and two female friends survived in the factory shelter on the outskirts of Dresden and ran toward the river to escape the bombings. It was then that the three women sought to escape from Dresden as well. They were captured and taken to a bombed-out building and put into a cellar, where they remained for over a week.[33] But my mother was fortunate. If she had been taken back to Schandauerstrasse, she would have been taken on a "death march" in the direction of Theresienstadt, a march where many who were weak and could not keep up with the other marchers would have been taken away and shot.[34] A non-Jewish woman came by and opened the cellar, allowing my mother and her two friends to escape and make their way to Czechoslovakia where they were liberated by American troops in Bohemia.

My mother made her way to Prague, a meeting point for survivors, and immediately began inquiring about my father's whereabouts. In the large hall where survivors would gather, my mother would go from table to table, asking whether anyone had seen my father. One day she came to a table, and the man she asked said, "Yes, I just left your husband in Theresienstadt. He is alive." I cannot imagine what my mother felt at that moment. Perhaps very little. What emotions were left after her ordeal? But she and this man, a cantor from Łódź who was with my father in Theresienstadt and had left the concentration camp before the typhus epidemic closed it, found a Czech man willing to take them to Theresienstadt. But it would take three weeks before they could enter Theresienstadt. When my father saw her, he did not know who she was. Her hair was all cut off. She was thin and pale and carried a pack of rags. She walked on a pair of wooden clogs. My father remembered that he had to ask my mother a series of questions about their life in the Łódź ghetto before he was certain that she was his wife.

My mother's health was very poor. The Jewish doctor that was sitting with my father examined her, listened to her heart, and began yelling for medical equipment. He shouted that she needed immediate help. For the next three months my parents stayed in Theresienstadt. My father supervised the doctors and nurses who were caring for the survivors. My father admitted that he wore a Red Army uniform during that time. It was better than wearing the stripes of his KZ uniform. He was grateful to the Soviet army. But then he began to meet those soldiers who admitted to him that they were a part of the Soviet intelligence service, the NKVD. One of the soldiers jokingly said to my father that if he were ever charged for a crime against the Soviet state, he, the soldier, would have to take my father into custody. "But," he continued, "I doubt if we would ever bring you back."

That was enough for my father. He refused the Soviets' offer to accompany them to Vienna and become a part of the Soviet occupation forces. Instead, my father worked with Rabbi Lipman to obtain transportation out of Czechoslovakia and into the American occupation zone of Germany. With tickets from the Red Cross, my father and mother traveled on a train through the city of Pilzen, a great beer-manufacturing center. When the train stopped, my father went out to look for water for my mother. He could not find any, but he did find a beer factory, and the staff gave him as much beer as he wanted. On August 22, 1945, my father and mother, who was still seriously ill, arrived in the Bavarian city of Landsberg am Lech. They were liberated but not yet free.

6

Hitler Is Always at Our Door: From Landsberg to America

When my parents arrived in Landsberg, they knew that there was a camp for displaced persons in the town of about 10,000 people, but they knew nothing else about the town itself. They were met by American military officials and taken to the Saarburgkaserne, the former Wehrmacht installation that had housed 2,500 German soldiers during the Second World War. They had little time to examine their surroundings. My mother needed medical attention, and my father needed work. My parents also had no desire to meet the non-Jewish inhabitants of the camp, of whom there were at least 1,000 from the 6,000 persons that made up the so-called Landsberg Assembly Center. They had even less desire to have contact with the local Landsberg population, who represented for them the murderers of their families and of Polish Jewry.

But if one were a visitor to Landsberg on the River Lech and did not care about anything but its travel-guide history, then one would have seen a picturesque setting located in what is known as Swabian Upper Bavaria, which lies near the end of a two-hundred-mile stretch called the "Romantic Road." Along the Romantic Road sit a number of glorious medieval towns, some nearly 2,000 years old; they still appear as they must have looked during the Middle Ages.

Founded in the thirteenth century, Landsberg features numerous works of the rococo (eighteenth century) master architects, the brothers Johann Baptist and Dominikus Zimmerman. A number of churches and the city hall are a part of the Zimmermans' creativity, and there is a gymnasium in the town named after Dominikus. But suppose that one were a Jewish visitor to Landsberg and wanted to know about the history of Landsberg's Jewish community. Jews were not a popular topic in Landsberg, not for nearly a thousand years.

A Jewish community did exist in Landsberg from the time that Jewish life first appeared in the Rhineland region of Germany around the year 1000 until the middle of the fourteenth century. Then Jewish life in Landsberg fell victim to the great ritual-murder accusations of medieval German history. In the case of Landsberg, it was the charge that its Jews had defaced a host—the physical incarnation of Christ—that allowed a Bavarian nobleman named Rindfleisch to wipe out virtually the entire Jewish community in 1298 and take Jewish possessions for his own. The remainder of the Jewish community of Landsberg was destroyed in 1348, when another pogrom ended its existence. From the fourteenth century until the appearance of Adolf Hitler, a small number of Jews lived in Landsberg. But the community was never large enough to support a synagogue, and it traveled to Augsburg for religious services.

Yet Landsberg on the River Lech was destined for an even greater place of infamy in Jewish history. In April of 1924, a new inmate was sent to its fortress-like prison. He only spent nine months there, after having been sentenced to five years' imprisonment for his political activities, which included an attempt to overthrow the Bavarian government in November of 1923. The inmate, Adolf Hitler, managed to complete the greater part of a manuscript, which he dictated to his faithful secretary, Rudolf Hess. The manuscript was an account of his past, present, and future plans for Germany and its great enemy, world Jewry. He entitled his work *Mein Kampf.*

The Voice of the She'erith Hapletah

My father and mother would never forget their arrival into Landsberg. They were taken to the Saarburgkaserne and given a room in block number 4. Most of the rooms in the building were shared by more than one family, with a hanging bedsheet the only form of privacy. Because my mother was so ill, my parents had the luxury of having their own living quarters. The DP camp at Landsberg was opened on May 11, 1945, barely two weeks after American troops entered and occupied the town. Many of the camp's first Jewish inhabitants were survivors of the Kaufering camps, a series of eleven subcamps of Dachau in and around Landsberg.

There is no question that the Jews there sought to recapture as well as

possible their sense of Jewishness and their humanity, aspects of their identity that the Nazis had tried systematically to destroy. Despair was the greatest threat to the Jews of Landsberg and other displaced-persons camps in the
months after liberation. It was as if they were living in one vast Jewish cemetery with no hope of leaving its confines. The Landsberg camp reflected the
sense of that despair. Not only were its Jewish inhabitants surrounded by
hundreds of non-Jewish camp dwellers, many of whom in a previous life had
been their tormentors as camp guards, but they were also surrounded by
barbed wire and armed guards, as they had been in the Nazi concentration
and labor camps.

Irving Heymont, a twenty-seven-year-old American military officer from
New York, changed those conditions. He was only in Landsberg from September to December 1945, and he was a career military officer who did
things "by the book." He hid from the DPs the fact that he was a Jew because
he did not want his religion to be a factor in their relationship. But Heymont
was a compassionate and caring man, and he brought a measure of democracy and independence to Landsberg that was the envy of other DP camps in
the American zone, camps such as Föhrenwald with 5,000 Jews and Feldafing with about 3,700, and Bergen-Belsen/Hohne in the British zone with
over 11,000 Jews. My father, who did not learn that Heymont was Jewish
until many years later, spoke of him as the "gentile with a Jewish heart."
With Heymont's help Landsberg became a center of Jewish culture: an educational system, theater and musical groups, political parties, and an organized communal structure were all established. Heymont tried to describe
the conditions in the camp, both physical and emotional, in a letter to his
wife:[1]

> The camp is filthy beyond description. Sanitation is virtually
> unknown. Words fail me when I try to think of an adequate descrip-
> tion. . . . With a few exceptions, the people of the camp themselves
> appear demoralized beyond hope of rehabilitation. They appear to be
> beaten both spiritually and physically, with no hopes of incentive for
> the future.

In those early weeks in Landsberg, my parents could only think about their
families: brother, sisters, nieces, and nephews whose fates were unknown.
My father had been in the HASAG camps with members of my mother's

family from Zwolen so he had some idea of the Kolton family. Beyond that, three of my mother's brothers had died in the Łódź ghetto of starvation. But of his own family my father knew little more than anecdotal information. Ultimately my parents would learn that they had been the only survivors among their siblings: seven brothers and a sister on my mother's side, and three sisters and two brothers on my father's side.

That is what made the first event that they attended in the Landsberg camp so emotional and so difficult for them. On September 17, 1945, three weeks after my parents arrived in Landsberg, on Yom Kippur, the holiest day in the Jewish calendar, Dr. Samuel Gringauz, a survivor of the Kovno (Kaunas) ghetto and of Kaufering and the head of the camp committee led the *yiskor* service, the remembrance service for the dead. In his introductory remarks Gringauz told the assembled survivors, "For the first time I will recite *yiskor* in a free house of worship for our family members, our children and our parents, our wives and our sisters. And, in the name of the 5,000 Jewish survivors, who have been brought together here in Landsberg through this bloody tragedy, I will recite *yiskor*. I will recite it for the unknown and anonymous that have left us . . . for the six million, who rest in the bloody earth of Europe: for all of them I will recite *yiskor*."[2] Gringauz would become the intellectual architect of a revolutionary survivor ideology that saw them, the She'erith Hapletah, the surviving or saving remnant, as the bearers of a new humanism after the destructive effects of National Socialism and the Holocaust.

When the American military authorities learned that my father had worked with medical personnel in Theresienstadt and had also been an orderly in the camp hospital, he was immediately hired as an administrator. Medical conditions were far from adequate, but my father managed to work himself into a position of authority that allowed him to obtain the best possible equipment and medicines available. Much of the material that my father was able to procure for hospital use came from Germany's second economy, an economy known as the "black market." Everyone participated in the black market: survivors, local Germans, and even the American military. Even though it was illegal, it was the only way that better goods and services could be obtained. My father's experience in this system took on new meaning when he learned that my mother, despite her physical and psychological ailments, was pregnant. I have often wondered how my parents could have chosen to say yes to a Jewish future, one that included me, when they had just emerged from so dark a Jewish past. It was not until much later in my life that I learned some of the possible reasons for such a brave step.

My mother's pregnancy meant that my father would have to supplement the meager wages he earned at the camp hospital. His business background convinced him that there was money to be made as a *Hausierer*, a door-to-door peddler. He was able to negotiate the purchase of used clothing that was shipped to the DPs from America. He was able to buy watches from various Sinti/Roma and sell them to the local population. His peddling took him to small villages like Scheffelding, Windach, and Kaufbeuren and to more distant places like Schweinfurt. It was not easy dealing with Germans because the eternal question of what they had done or where they had been during the destruction of European Jewry was always on his mind. An even greater immediate concern was the local German police authorities. Once my father left the confines of the DP assembly center, he had no more legal standing. He was a stateless man, with no papers to prove his nationality or place of residence.

My father met a German who was, like him, a baker of tortes and pastries. The man needed shoes for his children, and my father had them. In exchange for the shoes, this man smoothed things with several of the local police departments so that my father would not be arrested for black marketeering. But one evening my father's luck ran out. He missed the last bus home to Landsberg from one of the nearby villages and was arrested for vagrancy by a local policeman. My father needed to find someone who could vouch for him—"Herr Steinberg," as the locals called him, although they knew his real name. He managed to find such a person, a Herr Bauer, who not only vouched for him but invited my father to stay overnight at his home. My father went to bed quite early so that he could wake up and catch the first bus back to Landsberg. That is when he heard a loud argument between Herr Bauer's two children, a son and a daughter. As the argument became louder and more heated, he heard Bauer's daughter threaten her brother by saying that she would tell my father that he, her brother, had been in the SS. That was not the only time my father had to experience the ugliness of his recent past. In many of the homes he went to on his peddling trips, framed photographs of husbands and sons in SS uniforms stood in plain view, and copies of *Mein Kampf* could be seen on the bookshelves.

In February 1946 the first birth announcements began appearing in the *Landsberg Lager-Cajtung,* the camp newspaper. On May 4, 1946, I was born in the camp hospital, delivered by Dr. Salomon Nabriski. When my father was told of my birth, and that both mother and son were fine, he fainted. By the time that I was born, much had happened to change the look and the nature of the DP camp in Landsberg. Non-Jewish DPs were gone, transferred to other camps. The Assembly Center had been renamed the Landsberg Jewish Center, its streets had been renamed for Zionist heroes and great figures in Jewish history, and a new and important dimension had been added to the camp in the person of its American military administrator, Major Irving Heymont.

We were a family now, but that meant new worries for my parents. There were health issues for my mother: she was told after my birth that she could not bear any more children. Her physical and mental condition worsened without the possibility of better care than the DP camp hospital. My father was able to move us to the camp's convalescent home (*Erholungsheim*), where we enjoyed a small apartment of one room and our own kitchen. But my father's health also suffered. In 1948, just before the possibility arose that we might be able to leave Landsberg for Israel (of the 4,176 residents of the Landsberg DP camp, my parents were among the 3,112 who responded to a questionnaire asking where they wished to emigrate with "Palestine"), a spot was detected on my father's lung, and he was forced to take treatment in the sanitarium at Gauting, a town near Landsberg, for a number of months.

After the spot cleared up, the war between Israel and the Arab states had erupted, and my father no longer wanted to take his family to Eretz Yisrael. Instead, my parents and I were put on a quota list for immigration to the United States of America, where we had no relatives or friends. But our wait was a long one. My father continued to work in the camp hospital and peddle in the towns and villages around Landsberg. He would often hire local Landsberg Germans to come into the camp and help in the hospital. Many had been former Wehrmacht soldiers or perhaps even worse.

One day, when I was a little more than two years old, I saw two German brothers, both former Wehrmacht soldiers, whom my father had hired to chop wood. I spoke German to them and told my father: "Daddy, give me a gun. These are Hitler types. I want to shoot them." Earlier that week my father had taken me to the Landsberg prison, and we were able to visit Hitler's former prison cell with the help of an American military officer. I must have remembered the name Hitler and associated the German brothers with him.

For the most part, the five years that my parents and I spent in Landsberg were years of isolation and loneliness. After I was born, my father had thought about going to Poland to search for his family and my mother's. But in July new arrivals at the DP camp, Jews from Poland, told him about a terrible pogrom that had taken place in the Polish city of Kielce, where more than forty Jews had been murdered in cold blood. They also told him about other attacks against Jews throughout the country that had killed hundreds.[3] He did not go to Poland and never received any news about the fate of his brothers and sisters except through secondhand sources.

Finally at the end of November 1949, we left Landsberg and made our way to the north German city of Bremerhaven, where countless numbers of immigrants before us, both Jewish and non-Jewish, had sailed to the "land of limitless possibilities," the United States. The Jewish aid organization HIAS (Hebrew Immigrant Aid Society) was our official sponsor. But we had no idea to which city in America we were going, or even what America would be like. This little nuclear unit, two parents with no other family to speak of and their three-and-a-half-year-old son, their miracle baby, were saying adieu to the shattered continent that had been their home for centuries and to the land "soaked in Jewish blood" that had orchestrated the destruction of their world.

7

I Discover the Holocaust and Live with Its Consequences

The End of a Journey and the Beginning of Another

Forty years after her arrival in the United States on May 8, 1945, the novelist Isabella Leitner wrote about the sea voyage that made her one of the first survivors of Auschwitz to escape from one universe into another:[1]

> Dr. Mengele, we are on our way to America and we are going to forget every brutal German word you forced us to learn. We are going to learn a new language. We are going to ask for bread and milk in Shakespeare's tongue. We will learn how to live speaking English and forget how people die speaking German.

My parents and I arrived in Boston, Massachusetts, on December 2, 1949, aboard the *USS General C. H. Muir*, named for Charles H. Muir, who served in the United States Army for forty-three years and saw service from the American Indian Wars, through the Spanish-American War, the Boxer Rebellion to World War I. The passenger lists reveal a mixture of Jewish, German, Lithuanian, and Ukrainian passenger names, most of them with families of very young children.[2] Nearly all the passengers were DPs, and for the Jewish ones it must have seemed unusual and perhaps uncomfortable to once again be housed with those nationalities who were their persecutors during the Holocaust years. What did my parents remember about the nearly two-week voyage from Bremerhaven to Boston in cold and choppy North Atlantic waters? My father fared well on the voyage. As soon as crew members of the *Muir* discovered that he was a creator of fine tortes and cakes, they asked him to prepare a special cake for the birthday of the *Muir*'s captain and to join him at the captain's table during the party.

The invitation was extended to my mother and to me, but we never came to the celebration. Instead, both of us spent the greater part of the voyage violently seasick. Because men had separate sleeping quarters from the women and children, my father could only look in on us as we lay in our bunks or stood with our heads in toilet bowls. The seasickness lasted for days, but when it was finally over, I begged my father for some soup made with flour, a staple of my diet during the Landsberg DP camp years, when fruits and vegetables were almost unobtainable. When we landed in Boston, we were taken to a hotel with other Jewish passengers, accompanied by officials from the HIAS. My parents did not like the clamor and bustle of Boston and could not wait to be sent to their final destination, which they hoped would be a smaller community. After some days of becoming acquainted with the rules and regulations of life in the care of the American Jewish communal organizations, instructed by Yiddish-speaking officials, we boarded a train in Boston and set out for our final destination—Waterbury, Connecticut.

My parents spoke no English and traveled with all their worldly goods, the worldliest being a bedspread stuffed with goose feathers. For whatever reasons, this one item seemed to have a historical identity all its own. Immigrant group after immigrant group, Jewish and non-Jewish, seemed to believe that this possession was the one necessity they could not live without in the journey from the Old World to the New. Upon our arrival in Waterbury, a city of just over 100,000 people known for its brass and watch industries, we began a constant search for a suitable place to live. Unlike the amenities provided to Jewish immigrants from the former Soviet Union in the early 1980s, Jewish communal organizations in the late 1940s were not prepared for the 100,000 or more Jewish Displaced Persons who came to America from Germany, Austria, and Italy.

We were moved around to a succession of cheap, substandard apartments, which for survivors from the DP camps seemed several steps up the comfort ladder from what we had known in Landsberg. It was not the apartments that concerned my parents but those who rented them to us. All of them were Jews, some of whom had even come from Eastern Europe at the turn of the twentieth century. But they seemed to have developed a case of amnesia when it came to dealing with three poor Jews from "the Old Country."

The term "greenhorn," a new arrival uneducated in the ways of his surroundings, was not created for the generation of Holocaust survivors that
arrived in America in the late 1940s and early 1950s. That honor belonged to
the earlier group of Jews who had come to the United States between the
years 1881 and 1924 in numbers that ultimately totaled well over two million. They came for economic opportunity and to leave the restrictiveness of
anti-Jewish legislation that symbolized the Czarist Russian attitude toward
its Jewish populations. They were the first greenhorns, *die griene* in Yiddish.
They came to America from the hundreds of villages they had left behind,
the *shtetlach* of the Old World. Most, but not all, came to and settled in New
York City.

But this group of survivors, my parents among them, came to America
with a totally different set of issues, a social and psychological baggage that
was not easy to understand, even for the sons and daughters of the earlier
griene. Elie Wiesel, who arrived in Buchenwald as my father was leaving,
wrote, "What the survivors wanted was to transmit a message to the world, a
message of which they were the sole bearers. Having gained an insight into
man that will forever remain unequaled, they tried to share knowledge with
that world."[3]

There were other survivors who tried to tell the story when they arrived in
North America. What they found, as Elie Wiesel found, was another kind of
exile, another kind of prison. People welcomed them with tears and jobs
when they stepped off the boats, then turned away. And why not? One Canadian survivors' magazine wrote, nearly two decades after the end of the war,
that "there are those people who say—forget what was—forget what went on
in Europe. This is North America. You should begin a new life."[4]

One survivor recounted her first years in America: "My cousins were
America-born Jews—kind, generous people who also shrank from me a little. You understand, the concentration camp experience is nothing that
endears you to people."[5] Shortly after her arrival in America in 1951, a survivor had the experience of being told by her American-born Jewish neighbor
in Brooklyn that she should write fiction. "You have a terrific imagination,"
the neighbor told her upon hearing a tale about selections and gas chambers.[6]

In Israel too, where survivors should have found the least resistance to
their experiences during the Holocaust years, there was a form of rejection.
Yitzhak (Antek) Zuckerman, one of the great heroes of the Warsaw ghetto

uprising, wrote that "there was something distressing in our [the survivors'] relationship with the *yishuv* (the pre–Israel Palestinian Jewish community). It was a one-way love affair on our part which was never reciprocated."[7] For my father it was easy to ask those Jews with whom he came into contact in Waterbury whether they understood what he and my mother had experienced and how my parents had waited for them, the American Jews, to save them as they had in previous tragedies that had befallen Polish and other Jews in the twentieth century.

Was that why no one wanted to listen? Was that why officials from the Jewish community were only interested in how my father had spent the money they had given our family so that we might have food and shelter?

Whatever the reason, I remember my father's anger when he was told by one of our landlords that American Jews, too, had suffered during the war years, that there were shortages of butter and milk and meat. It was then, I believe, that my father decided he had no choice but to remain silent, that no one was interested in his suffering or my mother's or that of millions of European Jews. There were no truths to be shared and no lessons to be learned to change the nature of our world. During those early years my mother's physical and mental conditions deteriorated. She would scream and cry in private or in public at the slightest provocation. Perhaps that was her way of expressing the anger of her seven murdered brothers, at the way the world was treating their beloved baby sister.

And yet there were those who *would* listen. Every apartment in which we lived, owned by Jewish landlords who lived above or below us, was situated in a predominantly African American community. One might call it the "ghetto," but it was very different from what my parents understood as a ghetto. With one exception: everyone around us was poor—but not as poor as we were, financially, linguistically, or socially. In a sense we were one more poor family in the community, although we had white skin. Indeed, our black neighbors could not believe that any Jews could be so poor. But those African Americans, themselves the victims of violence, discrimination, and hatred, did their best to help us learn what we needed in order to survive.

What was especially important was the fact that a small number of our black neighbors had been in the American military and had seen firsthand what the Nazis had done to the Jews of Europe. Some of them had been cooks in American Army units in the vicinity of camps like Buchenwald and had obeyed the order of General Dwight D. Eisenhower that American soldiers should see the bodies "stacked like cordwood" so that they would understand why this war had been fought.

My father often told me that he only felt comfortable coming home from his job with the Waterbury Companies, a manufacturer of plastics, when he entered our black neighborhood. It meant that he would not have to see any policemen, who still symbolized the threat of terror for him.

And my father also had another individual who would listen. I had no choice but to listen—and what my father described to me when I was perhaps seven or eight years old, the stories about the HASAG work camps or Buchenwald, meant that the monsters who were his tormentors became more real to me than the grandparents or uncles and aunts that I would never know and of whom hardly anything was said. When my father found me a "willing," if captive audience, he felt that maybe the innocent of the world, the children, would better understand whatever lessons he was seeking to teach them. Often, when he would come home from a 7:30–3:30 work shift, I would be playing with friends in my room. My father would come in and begin to talk of the Łódź ghetto and of Buchenwald and of what he had seen there. The images were stark and frightening. Nazi guards and suffering ghetto and concentration camp prisoners interacted with a brutality and helplessness that were all too familiar to me. But my friends would look at me with questioning eyes: why is he telling us these things, those eyes would ask? They rarely, if ever, came back to play.

The world that my parents inhabited was one that the American-Jewish educator Koppel S. Pinson noticed when he visited the Jewish DP camps in 1946–47. He described the camps as "ones of constant movement. . . . Not all the motion is purposeful motion. Very much of it is emotional restlessness that arises from the situation in which these people find themselves."[8] Part of the problem lay in the truth of another of Pinson's observations about the survivors, that "for the Jewish DPs the war has not yet ended, nor has liberation in the true sense really come as yet. Their problems still unsolved, their future not in their own hands, they still consider themselves at war with the world and the world at war with them."[9]

For my parents, I am certain, that war never ended until their final moments on earth. That was how I learned about the suffering of my family as a young boy and how my parents sought to teach me about a world that had murdered their loved ones and their history. Germany was the architect of that murder, and Poles, Ukrainians, Lithuanians, Estonians, and others had been their work crew. But if anything allowed my parents to leave that war for even a short time, it was their love and concern for me. I was the carrier of the legacy, the Second Generation, one of the "miracle babies" who would grow to make certain that the voice of the She'erith Hapletah would never cease to be heard.

Becoming American

There were always little indications that my parents came from an event and from a world that was different, even if as a young child I was only dimly aware of their meaning. Because my parents knew no English and could only communicate at the barest level, I became the parent to my mother and father. Basic things like writing and reading letters in English became my responsibility as soon as I was able to master the language. There were constant exchanges of letters with a "Dr. Otto Schutz" of the United Restitution Organization (URO) in New York. I remember writing letters that included names and places that had only the vaguest meaning for me, except that they all sounded foreign. Only later would I understand that they were the details of my parents suffering and were needed to file claims for W*iedergutmachung* (reparations) from the German authorities.

Often the process for reparations meant trips to the city of Hartford, the capital of Connecticut, where German-born doctors, some Jewish, some not, would examine my mother and father as part of the application procedure. I knew how difficult these examinations were for my parents. Not only did it mean having to recount the stories of their lives during the war years to mostly unsympathetic or unemotional German physicians, but it meant having to place their suffering in judgment: were their pain and their losses worthy enough for financial compensation? Were they physically and mentally broken enough and was it 50 percent, 60 percent, or even more? Were my parents mentally ill?[10]

There were relatively few Holocaust survivor families in Waterbury. My parents knew most of them, and of course there was a commonality of background that drew these families together. The Jewish high holidays were the times when the families gathered. They belonged to a small synagogue across the street from the main Orthodox synagogue in Waterbury. The rabbi of the larger synagogue would officiate at the Rosh Hashanah and Yom Kippur services at both congregations and preach the High Holiday sermon to both at different times and with a different emphasis. In the larger synagogue he discussed the affairs of the Jewish world, the need for Jews to live moral and ethical lives, and what the high holidays meant for the individual Jew and for the community as a whole. But in the *kleine schiel,* as it was known in Yiddish, the small synagogue, he preached about the Holocaust and the losses that his congregation had endured. Was the tragedy that befell European Jewry, he would ask, somehow a punishment from God for that Jewry's having strayed from Jewish tradition, from the mission of being a "holy community" dedicated to being a "light *unto* the nations?"

The survivors were always angry at this implication. What kind of God would or could do such a thing, they would ask the rabbi, an American-born Jew? What kind of God allows infants to be smashed against the sides of buildings or impaled on the ends of German bayonets? The tears that flowed during the *yiskor* service during Yom Kippur, the Day of Atonement, were no less than those shed by survivors on that terrible day of September 17, 1945, when Samuel Gringauz held the first Yom Kippur service in Landsberg. The tears were no less year after year that my parents and the other survivors attended the services. After Yom Kippur, they would gather to break the fast and talk about the "war" and what kinds of losses they had endured.

The tragedy of my parents' losses became my tragedy. How did I feel when my schoolteachers would invite grandparents to visit my school? I had no grandparents, nor did I even know their names. How did I feel when my Jewish classmates talked about birthday parties at which their uncles and aunts gave them gifts and their young cousins came to play with them? I had none of these things. Yet, I tried to fit into the world of America in the 1950s and early 1960s and to live as a young American Jew. But what did it mean to be an American Jew? For my parents American Jewry represented a community of Jews who had closed their eyes and their hearts, who had given up on their roots, on the Old World that had been the source of their religious and ethnic identity, who had worried about the shortages of butter and meat when their European cousins were being gassed and burned.

My mother bought most of my school clothes at a secondhand thrift shop. That was all we could afford. But that did not matter to my parents. I do not remember ever going out to dinner or to a movie with my parents. They stayed home, my mother always cooked dinner, and we would watch the small television that had been bought used. What was important to them was that I understand the world that had been created because of the war against the Jews. It was a world in which we could trust no one except ourselves. Nazism and Germany were just waiting for the opportunity to rise again, and this time they would come after me. Two young Italian brothers, Vinny and Joe, became my version of the Endeks, the anti-Semitic National Democratic Party of my father's days in Poland. They would wait for me in hiding after school and jump on me, beat me with their fists, and call me "Christ Killer." I lived in fear for a long time—until a very large and very strong African American classmate nicknamed "Shoo Shoo" offered to walk home with me after school if I would do his homework.

In the summer of 1958, just a few months before my bar mitzvah at the age of thirteen, my parents and I moved from the African American community. My parents had saved enough money to buy a three-family house. We would live on the second floor and have rent-paying tenants on the first and third floors. The street we moved to was a very nice, middle-class one. We had African American neighbors and neighbors from Quebec who had moved to America. There were Italian neighbors and Irish neighbors and some Jewish ones as well. My bar mitzvah was held at a Conservative synagogue. My parents had left the Orthodox synagogue when my father could no longer listen to the rabbi's sermon on the "sins" of the Jews of Europe in bringing on the wrath of God by straying from the Torah and Jewish law. The bar mitzvah was a small affair. My mother cooked all the food for the party that was held after the ceremony to mark the acceptance of my responsibilities as an adult Jew. My father was pleased that the cantor of the congregation told him jokingly that I had done such a wonderful job that he was afraid that I might take his position.

What should have been a joyous family occasion was marked by sadness and tears as my mother cried for her brothers and sister. How proud they and my grandparents would have been, she sobbed, to see me reach this important day in my Jewish identity. It was the first time that I heard her say that she wished she could be with her brothers. It was not a good sign. But I was more interested in dancing with the young girls, the classmates that I had invited to the bar mitzvah party.

My father worked at various jobs before finding one that would provide him with the income necessary to support his family. One of the conditions of the job at the Timex Corporation was that he improve his reading and writing skills. He had gone to night school, the first step in learning to read and write English. But the job that he was about to take, with supervisory responsibilities, demanded more. He enrolled in an advanced night-school course and there had an encounter that would leave him shaken for a very long time. Waterbury was home to a large Lithuanian and a smaller Ukrainian community, many of them DPs who had also come to American in the late 1940s and early 1950s. A number of them were in my father's class. He did not feel comfortable with them. Although my father was friendly with a Pole, Frantisek Perdol, and a Lithuanian from Poland, Pan Grabowski, both men had come to America in the 1920s. There was one Ukrainian man in the class who caught my father's attention. In casual conversation before the class, my father had asked the man what he had done during the war. "I was a farmer and then a forced laborer in Germany," the man replied. My father's instinct told him differently. "I think you have Jewish blood on your hands," my father told him. "It doesn't make a difference," the Ukrainian said to him. "We are in America and everything that happened in Europe is in the past, is not important in this country."

A few years later, this same man, Feodor Fedorenko, was accused of being a guard at the Treblinka death camp in Poland. He was stripped of his American citizenship and deported to the Soviet Union where he was executed for his crimes. These contradictions in my parents' attitudes—having Polish and Lithuanian friends, while harboring animosity against Poles, Lithuanians, and Ukrainians as a community; being critical of American Jewry and of America for not doing more to save East European Jewry, while having chosen to come to America to start new lives—always puzzled me.

But the one issue for which there was no contradiction was the role of Germans and Germany. There could be no compromise, no friendships, and no communication with the nation of Nazism. Every new generation of Germans was affected by the same bacillus of anti-Semitism. And like the name Adolf Hitler, the curse, *Yimah Sh'mo* (may his name be forever blotted out), applied to Germany and all Germans. But the contradictions continued despite these feelings about Germans. One day I came home from school to a most amazing sight. There, sitting at our kitchen table, were my mother and a white-haired, distinguished-looking man wearing a clerical collar. They were drinking coffee, eating some of my mother's freshly baked cookies, and discussing gardening.

I knew the man more from reputation than from anything else. He was Monsignor Edward Morrison, and he lived next door to us. Next door to us were St. Margaret's Church and St. Margaret's Catholic School. The priests and nuns who were our neighbors were mostly, like Monsignor Morrison, Irish Catholics, some of them immigrants to America. The monsignor was the best known of them, respected for his leading role in St. Margaret's Church and School but also feared by the neighborhood children who dared to play baseball on his school's property. He would often emerge from the church rectory, grab one of us by the ear, and tell us never to play in the school yard again or he would visit our parents.

A number of my neighborhood friends were Catholics and worshiped at St. Margaret's. But the monsignor never shouted at me or sought to bend my ear out of shape, although I was often a part of the band of baseball players. I have often wondered why he was treating me differently. Was it because he knew that my mother and father were Jews and had gone through the events that destroyed so much of European Jewry? That we lived next door to a Catholic church and that my mother drank coffee with a Catholic priest now amazes me as I reflect upon what my parents told me of their encounters with the Church in their days in Poland.

For many Jews in Poland, especially in the small villages, the local church was the focal point of the physical dangers that Jews faced on important Catholic holidays, especially Christmas and Easter. Jews knew better than to venture outside their homes on those days. Whatever message the local Polish Christians heard from the church pulpits, whatever they drank to celebrate the birth and resurrection of Christ, it always meant a time of physical danger for the Jewish community. My father would tell me on various occasions how he sought to avoid looking at the cross atop the church, because the sight of it filled him with fear. And here, in the early 1960s, my mother, whose experiences were similar to my father's, was sitting in our kitchen, drinking coffee with an important representative of that same church, less than two decades after the tragedy of European Jewish life.

Could Monsignor Morrison and my mother have been planting more than seeds in a vegetable garden? My own efforts in seeking to advance Christian-Jewish relations years later were a part of those seeds.

8

Capitalism Is to Blame for Everything: We Become the Generation of 1968

Running Away from the *Churbn*

As an adolescent I was an "exemplary" son. I could not bring myself to hurt my parents with bad or rebellious behavior. There was a reason for this that I sensed at a very young age. To bring disappointment to my parents, whether in school or activities outside of school, would have added to the pain that I knew was a large and very apparent part of who they were. That pain was reflected in the nightmares that would cause my parents to shout and awaken me on many occasions; that pain was caused by the fits of anger that my mother would have at the slightest provocation; that pain would be caused by the screams of my mother during an argument with my father, screams in which she indicated how much she wished her life would end so that she could once again be with her dead brothers; that pain would be caused by the nature of the world that my father sought to explain to me—how I could never trust another person except my parents because the world had been forever changed by the *churbn*.

The Hebrew and Yiddish word *churbn* was all there was in my adolescence to describe what my parents and much of European Jewry had endured from 1939–45. I knew it meant something terrible, an event that characterized the destruction of my parent's world. It meant that I could never believe in a world of goodness, either as a reality or an ideal. America was no different, my father would tell me, except that the Nazis who had escaped from Germany, and the Poles and the Lithuanians and the Ukrainians, who had found a home in America, were not organized. And still, there were plenty of other anti-Semites to replace them.

The presence of the *churbn*, the Yiddish word for disaster or destruction, that my parents used to describe the world they had endured between 1939 and 1945, was always a part of my daily life. It showed itself in scattered and sometimes inexplicable ways, but I knew what it was and that I must never add to its shadow by being anything but a source of pride and happiness, of *naches,* for my parents, as the only source of such feelings. The *churbn* was my competitor for the emotional state of my parents—and a very powerful one at that. Throughout my primary- and secondary-school years I tried to compete with the *churbn* the best I could. My academic record was a reasonably good one, and the extracurricular activities in which I participated always had something to do with Jewish life, whether in social organizations or organized sports activities. But the relationship with my American Jewish peers was always a superficial one. I did not really have close Jewish friends, but then I did not really have close non-Jewish friends. It would have been impossible, embarrassing even, to bring them to my home. I knew what would happen, especially if my father were present. I got along with all of them, but I was always on the periphery of activities. For me there were no parties or dates. The *churbn* always seemed to get in the way. American Jewish girls were not good enough for me, my parents would always tell me, nor were American Jewish boys trustworthy as friends. It would have been different in Europe; it would have been better in Europe—if only there had still been a Europe with Jews, if only there had not been a *churbn.* I was not particularly close with the two or three sons and daughters of survivor families in my high school. I knew that they, too, had issues with their parents, yet this commonality did not make us good friends.

Still, my parents seemed less critical of any non-Jewish friends that I might have had. Perhaps it was because my father had moved beyond the Jewish world in his years before the war. Perhaps Pan Solinski had shown him something positive about the non-Jewish world and he wanted me to have my own Pan Solinski. I still managed to create a world for myself. In high school my two favorite subjects were European history and German. I excelled in both, one year receiving the fourth-highest score in a statewide German examination. My parents, however, were concerned because my grades in mathematics and in science were not as good. The classes I attended in my public high school were large, and it was impossible to receive extra help outside the classroom. As a result they decided to send me to a private school for my final year of secondary education. I am not certain that they were even aware what a private preparatory school was, but someone had told them that my chances of receiving admission to a good university would be greatly improved if I attended one. I do not know where my parents found the money to send me to the Cheshire Academy, a preparatory school located a few miles from Waterbury, founded in the 1790s with a strong Christian tradition, but somehow they did.

I was a "day hop," a student who attended classes but did not board like the majority of the students. I entered a world totally unlike the one I had just left. Instead of a diverse student body of African American and Puerto Rican students mixed with students from immigrant Greek, Albanian, Hungarian, and many other ethnic communities among the student body, I encountered "blue-blood" types, both Jewish and non-Jewish. Even the Jewish students that I met, many from New York and from Latin America, enjoyed an urbane quality of life and demonstrated a sophistication that was entirely alien to me.

I became a "preppie," having to wear a blue sports jacket with the Cheshire Academy crest and a tie every day of the school week. I enjoyed my small classes and did well at Cheshire Academy, well enough that I was accepted to the American University's School of International Service in Washington, D.C. My father had traveled with me to visit the university. We went by bus, and the trip took seven hours. My father could not really afford to book a hotel room for us in Washington. So we rode all through the night in order to arrive in Washington in the morning, visit American University, and take a bus back in time to arrive in Waterbury well after midnight. Immediately after my graduation, my parents, to my shock and surprise, allowed me to travel across the country to California to visit cousins of my mother in Los Angeles. I drove from Connecticut to Illinois with the parents of a friend from Cheshire Academy, who had come east for his graduation, and then I boarded a bus in Chicago for the long ride west.

I had met one of my mother's nephews and his family when I was a young boy. We had traveled to New Jersey, where they lived, and stayed at their home for several days. I do not remember much about the visit, except that I had an argument with one of my cousins, a girl slightly younger than I was. We fought over sleeping arrangements, and I remember a lot of shoving and pushing, but little else.

My stay in Los Angeles, which lasted three weeks, was a beneficial one. I got to know the two sons of my mother's distant cousins and went with them to the beach and movie-star gazing. We never spoke about the *churbn,* although I knew that my mother's cousins had also spent time in the Landsberg DP camp as well as some of the HASAG labor camps. We were just young American Jewish guys enjoying a California summer. When I returned home by plane, the first time that I had flown in my life, I had to prepare to leave home for my first year at American University. My mother was beside herself with anxiety. How could she live without her "Abie" as a part of her daily life? What would happen to me in such a distant place without the words of my parents to guide me, without the shadow of the *churbn* to remind me not to take chances, not to expose myself to the dangers of the world?

But one day at the end of August 1964, I boarded a bus in Waterbury to begin the seven-hour ride to Washington. I felt sad to see my mother in tears, clinging to me as the bus approached. But I also felt a sense of freedom, the undoing of a burden that weighed so heavily on my life and on my desire to become something more than a *naches* machine.

Becoming More American at American

What were my first days like at American University? I was overwhelmed with feelings of freedom. Not feelings of freedom to drink alcohol and stay up until all hours of the morning as a way of "sowing my wild oats." No, I was overwhelmed with the feeling that I did not have to worry how each and every action of mine would affect my parents, whether I had done enough to overcome the *churbn*.

I was a first-year student at a university with many Jewish students who came from New York and New Jersey, a kind of Jew that I had never encountered. They were the sons and daughters of third- and fourth-generation American Jews who had long ago left the Polish and Lithuanian ghettos but who had entered into a new one when it came to their identities. For them, New York was the center of the earth, and everywhere else was an unsophisticated and cheap imitation.

I received a taste of that attitude during the first week at American. Not only were many of the first-year students from the mid-Atlantic states, but they all seemed to know each other from high school. The second or third evening of our student orientation, a huge outdoor dance party was held. I attended, hoping to enjoy an evening far away from the responsibilities of home. I met a young woman, from New York, began to talk to her and asked her to dance. She accepted, and we continued our conversation as we danced. I had already told her I was from Connecticut, a state close enough to New York to count as almost "ok." She was Jewish, spoke with a strong New York accent, and told me she was going to study elementary education. "What are you going to study?" she asked me "I am in the School of International Service," I told her. I could see her attitude change and her sense of interest in me disappear. There would be no second dance as she told me she had to go and find a friend of hers who was also a first-year student.

I did not find out until later that week that students in AU's School of International Service were seen by the rest of the student body as "nerds," bookworms with little or no personalities. I met those "nerds" when the SIS students attended a reception given in their honor by the dean and faculty of the school. I found them to be a warm and friendly group of young men and women, worldly and concerned about the need for American foreign policy to reflect the best of our national image and willing to be a part of that reflection as foreign service officers and other professional associations with international relations. They were very much like me in their academic interests, and I was delighted. I soon became part of a group of six or seven SIS students from various parts of America, many of them, for some reason, the only child in their family. They were Jewish and non-Jewish. But they were not my roommates. Those two were Herbie and Howie, two second-year students into whose room I had been placed and who could not have been more different from me in every possible way. Herbie and Howie were Jewish New Yorkers, genuine Manhattanites, genuine fraternity boys, whose ultimate interests focused on making their first million dollars before the age of thirty. For whatever reasons they decided to adopt me as a hardcore case of a human being who needed to undergo a complete "makeover." They began by renaming me "Benny" and taking me along on many of their adventures as fraternity brothers and as great romantic lovers. I was to observe everything and anything I could in order to understand what it meant to be "cool," what it meant to be everything I apparently was not.

I could not have asked for better teachers or for worse ones. Changing my identity was a full-time job. It held little room for a thing called academic studies, and for the first several weeks into the semester I barely had time to open a book. When my parents and I spoke on the telephone, I assured them that I was hard at work, studying hour after hour and assuring myself of excellent grades and bringing them additional *naches*. That did not happen in my first semester. My grades were average, and I felt a terrible guilt. Here I was, "Benny," the "cool" SIS student that every fraternity man on campus knew and to whom even the most beautiful and unattainable New York girls said hello. At the beginning of the second semester, I left Herbie and Howie and moved into a dormitory room with two SIS students, ironically also from New York and New Jersey, who could not have been more different from my two memorable "mentors" from the first semester of my first year at AU.

All of this new-found popularity changed when I went home for semester vacation. I reentered a world with which I was very familiar but one whose existence I had almost forgotten. The world of my Waterbury home quickly closed off "Benny's world." I was again part of the darkness that surrounded my parents' every waking hour and many of their sleeping ones as well.

For the next four years at American University, I sought to live between the tension of being "Benny" to the superficial ones at American University and "Abe" to the serious ones in the School of International Service. It was not always easy: the superficial ones never understood my interest and place in SIS, and the serious students never understood or liked Benny. My years at American University were the years of the war in Vietnam and the great student rebellions that were worldwide on many campus universities. I always had mixed emotions about the clash between the conservatives and the liberals, the defenders and the detractors of the conflict. My father, for instance, was a great defender of anything that insured the survival of the State of Israel. For some reason the conflict in Vietnam was important to that survival. Not only did my father support the idea of the "domino" theory, that a communist takeover of South Vietnam would mean many nations in Southeast Asia falling to communism, but that the State of Israel, too, would be in danger of disappearing. Perhaps he thought that the Palestine Liberation Organization was an affiliate of the North Vietnamese Army. I never quite knew for certain, but the connection between the two was, in his mind, a very firm one.

And yet, I never felt comfortable with the rhetoric of the student radicals, the ones who shouted, "Hey, Hey, LBJ, how many kids did you kill today?" I knew many of those students personally, and, outside of the drugs, the long hair and beards, and the revolutionary rhetoric they used, I knew them to be spoiled, self-indulgent "rich kids" who would "take over" an academic building during the day and then climb into their sports cars and head to their off-campus apartments for an evening of sex and drugs. I did not have a car, and I had to live in a dormitory room with two others. But I began to understand the need and the urgency to discuss publicly the state of America, both domestically and in terms of foreign policy. I was able to do this in a very public way. Somehow, my SIS friends convinced me to run for junior class president. My opponent was a member of Howie and Herbie's fraternity, and the members tried to talk me out of running against him. Remember what Howie and Herbie did for you, they pleaded. I am not certain how serious they were. The fraternities ran American University's student organization life, and an SIS "bookworm" had little chance of beating a fraternity man. But as I campaigned I discovered that many "unaffiliated" students, those who had no fraternity or sorority connections, despised the "brothers" and "sisters" of the fraternity and sorority world.

It was that resentment at the "cool" kids that led to my astounding victory in the election. When the results were announced, my friends and supporters became delirious with joy. It was not only I who had won. They too had made a statement that non-fraternity types, "nerds" and others, could overcome. What my victory meant was a place on the student senate and a place to debate publicly the issues that were most meaningful to American students in the mid-1960s. At American University those issues were the war in Vietnam and the growing Black Power movement. My interest in the efforts of young black men and women to define their own identity went back to my days in the African American community in Waterbury. I helped to lead a drive to raise money for the student council at Washington's Howard University to redefine that institution from a "negro" institution to a "black" university.

I also met an extraordinary group of leaders in the Black Power movement, among them Eldridge Cleaver—one of the founders of the Black Panther movement, a militant organization dedicated to protecting the black community from police brutalities—and Muhammad Ali, the great heavyweight champion, who was forced to give up his title because he refused to join the military and fight in Vietnam. I fell in love as many do during their university lives. One of those times led to a "puppy love" engagement to be married and a subsequent breakup that was, at the time, the most painful event of my young life. When my father heard over the telephone how heartbroken I was, he traveled from Waterbury to Washington by bus to deliver a home-cooked turkey and a number of other "goodies" that my mother thought would cure my condition. Apparently it did because by the end of my senior year, I had fallen in love again, this time permanently, with a young woman from Maine by the name of Jean Marcus. She was a second-generation Jew whose grandparents had come to America from Russia and Belarus at the beginning of the twentieth century. But she bore a Yiddish name, Genia, and was named for a relative who had died at the hands of the Nazis.

What did my parents think? I think they were pleased that I had chosen a Jewish girl. But could she be trusted? After all, she was American, and thoroughly so. That issue would never be resolved. There was always a doubt, a wish that I had found a girl from Europe, one that reflected what they believed was the ideal type of Jewish woman for me. But in June 1969, at the tender ages of twenty-one and twenty-three, Jean and I were married in Portland, Maine. My parents attended the wedding, but they were the only ones of my family to come. The small number of relatives in California and New Jersey, all on my mother's side, were unable to come, and her two Israeli nephews and their families were too far away. Ironically, the cantor at our wedding was Cantor Kurt Messerschmidt, a German-Jewish survivor of Auschwitz who had recorded performances of sacred music in Munich in the late 1940s that were broadcast to the Jewish DP camps in the American occupation zone of Germany by American Armed Forces Radio. My parents looked forward to those radio programs because Cantor Messerschmidt had a magnificent cantorial voice and brought a bit of *Yiddishkeit*, of Judaism, into their difficult lives.

Marx, Mao, and Marcuse

Very few students can remember much about the courses they took during their university days. Even fewer can remember one outstanding professor that seemed to guide them toward an understanding of the world around them or the career path they would ultimately choose. I was fortunate in having such a mentor. His name was Professor Albert Mott, and he taught courses in SIS on Western Europe. He was a brilliant lecturer, who seemed to be able to take the great and often totally obscure thinkers of the European experience and make them come alive, make them seem relevant to the world of a young undergraduate.

I took my first course with Dr. Mott in my first year at American University. I would take many courses with him and begin to understand a bit about the origins and the historical background of my great shadow and burden, the *churbn*. I learned from Albert Mott about the various ways that anti-Semitism had changed as Western Europe changed, from a Christian imperium to a system of nation-states to a genocidal society. Professor Mott was able to dissect the strands of those changes through the worlds of philosophers and poets, novelists and statesmen. I learned from him about the varying stages of human isolation that developed as the anciėn regime gave way to a dizzying array of ideologies, from the Reformation to the Enlightenment, to Romanticism and Reaction, Imperialism and Fascism. It was an extraordinary journey that he took me on. Even though his focus was not only on the ways in which anti-Semitism became the crystallization of all this upheaval, this uncertainty, this longing for the past, and ultimately this planning for a new European future devoid of Jews and Judaism, I was always seeking to find answers to the question, How could what happened to my parents and their families, and consequently to me, have happened at all?

Mott was also a keen observer of the student movements in European and American history. He sought to make his students understand the history of those movements, the revolts of the sons against the fathers, and how they related to what was happening in America and Europe in the late 1960s. For me and for other students in Professor Mott's classes, the chant of French and other European students as they proclaimed their societal idols, "Marx, Mao, and Marcuse," was more than just the rantings of a group of disaffected students. The ideologies and the ideologists of the student movements became clear. Herbert Marcuse was not just a professor in California with a famous student by the name of Angela Davis, an advocate of class revolution and of Black Power; he was a theoretician of immense importance who was able to show the limits of human freedom within established forms of democratic systems. The Frankfurt School of analysis and its shapers, Adorno, Horkheimer, and others, were more than old-fashioned German academics; rather, they were keen critics of the society in which they taught, a society that had ultimately forced them into exile because they were Jews and that became the prototype for their analysis of the authoritarian personality.

With Dr. Mott's help I applied to and was accepted into the master of arts program in the School of International Service after my undergraduate graduation. Despite the interest I had once had in pursuing a career in the American foreign service, I now became obsessed with European and German history and the rise of anti-Semitism and National Socialism. Professor Mott encouraged me in this direction and provided me with a constant source of new readings to equip me with the knowledge necessary to undertake what he considered a long and very taxing intellectual journey. But to what end? Did I want to teach at the university level? Did I want to go into some aspect of Jewish communal work? Did I want to become a rabbi? I was not concerned with any of these possibilities in the autumn of 1968 as I began my MA studies. I only knew that perhaps I had been competing with the *churbn* in an unfair way. I could never bring as much joy to my parents, as much *naches*, as the *churbn* could bring them pain and sadness. Perhaps I needed to know what the *churbn* was, how it happened, who the people were who had made it happen, and how they could have done the things they did, in order to confront my burden and my shadow directly. Perhaps I needed to understand the *churbn* in order to understand myself.

9

Into the Belly of the Beast

Difficult Choices

With my newfound interest in German and in Jewish history, I began to
catch up on all the readings that I needed to feel comfortable in preparing to
write an MA thesis. But reading was not enough. I also wanted to discuss
Germans and German history with a German. Despite having a reasonably
good command of the language, both reading and speaking, I had always
felt uncomfortable in my university classes in German language and literature. The professors were native speakers, and the course material focused
on mastering the vocabulary and grammar of the language and on reading
selections from classic German writings. None of those writings dealt with
the topic of anti-Semitism or on the period of National Socialism. What I
received from my professors was the vision of a nation of "Dichter und Den-
ker" (poets and thinkers) that shaped the destiny of European culture.

I wanted to ask about the Nazi period and the murder of millions of Jewish men, women, and children, but I did not know enough about those
events, and I hesitated to engage in a discussion about my personal family
history with those whose nation bore responsibility for what that family history had become. I felt uncomfortable around Germans because I had to
repress the desire to ask questions and that led to an intense frustration.
Then I met Petra Kelly. She was two years behind me at the School of International Service. I remember her clearly from the first time I saw her: a
young, blonde-haired woman running to some meeting or to some class. She
had dark circles under her eyes from a lack of sleep, but she always had a
smile.

Petra befriended Dr. Mott and became, like me, one of his disciples. I met
her one day in Professor Mott's office. Her English was accented, but there

were so many foreign students at AU that she could have been from a half-dozen countries in Europe or even Latin America. She was from Virginia, she told me, but had also lived in Georgia. "But where were you born, I asked?" "Germany," she replied. My stomach muscles tightened, as always, when I heard the word "Germany." I wanted to ask her about National Socialism, about the Jews, but could not. Instead, we discussed student life and civil rights. I found her to be extremely well informed and devoted to working for the rights of African Americans and the poor. I could not help but like this enthusiastic idealist who not only spoke about what she believed in with a great passion but also acted upon those beliefs through participation in political activism. She became a great friend of Senator Hubert Humphrey and worked in his office as a volunteer.

Finally, after two years of friendship with Petra, I worked up enough courage to ask her about her German identity and about National Socialism. Petra was not prepared for my questions. She knew that I was Jewish but did not know anything about the history of my parents. When she found out, she was terribly saddened. It was an individual sadness, a sadness from the heart and soul of an extraordinary humanitarian, but not sadness as a German. I do not think Petra Kelly had ever met a son of survivors. In all the years that I knew her at American University, this was the only time that she seemed confused and remained silent. I sensed shame in her silence but also a need to think about my questions.

We spoke many times after that, and Petra admitted to me that she had never spoken to her mother or grandmother about the Nazi years or about the murder of the Jews and that they had never offered any information either. "But I will speak to them," she told me. "What I do know," she said, "is that you and I believe in a world that must change, a world that must do away with injustice, oppression of the poor and the weak, and with nuclear weapons." "That includes," she continued, "any form of anti-Semitism." "You and I cannot change the past," she told me, "but we can work to make a different future."

My affection for Petra Kelly, my admiration for her beliefs and for her activism made her German background almost inconsequential, but not quite. "You should go to Germany," she told me, "and ask your questions about Germans and National Socialism and the Jews." She actually helped me receive an invitation to become part of a program sponsored by the city of Duisburg in which I would do an internship with that German city's political administration. But when I told my parents about the internship, they were adamant in their refusal to let me go. "Your life would be in danger," they told me, "and you are all we have. Please do not hurt us by going to 'Nazi Land.'" I had to turn down the invitation. But I followed Petra's career after her graduation from AU in 1970. I never saw her again but was pleased that she went back to Germany and became a founding member of the Green Party, a member of the German parliament, and a figure of international importance. Her death in 1992, at the hands of her "soulmate," retired Major General Gert Bastian, robbed the world of an important voice for social and political change.[1]

After my qualifying examinations for the MA degree, in which I received an "outstanding," I chose to do a thesis on the question of German-Jewish identity from the Napoleonic era to the Weimar Republic. I was fortunate to receive a study desk at the Library of Congress and to befriend Dr. Arnold H. Price, the bibliographer of the German history collection at the library. Price was a virtual encyclopedia of knowledge about books and articles dealing with my topic, and I spent hours with him discussing German history and Jewish identity. I was also fortunate to have as my study carrel neighbor Dr. George W. F. Hallgarten, a historian of European imperialism before 1914, whose book on the topic was a classic long before I met him.[2] Hallgarten, who came from a distinguished German-Jewish family, a part of which had immigrated to America in the nineteenth century and established a successful investment company, left Germany in 1936. When I met him in 1970, he had just published his autobiography, *Als die Schatten Fielen* [As the Shadows Fall].[3] He presented me with a copy of the book and gave me an insight into his extraordinary life, which began as the schoolmate of Heinrich Himmler. From Hallgarten I learned something about the identity of German Jewry at the time of the Nazi takeover in 1933 and how an assimilated Jew such as Hallgarten had understood the place of Jewry in its German environment.

As I was writing my thesis, I was also thinking about the future. I had married in June 1969, and my academic life at AU would be ending in the spring of 1970. What would I do after that? Dr. Mott suggested that I pursue a PhD in some aspect of my interest in Germany and the rise of anti-Semitism. But could I spend more years in classrooms and archives? What about my wife, Jean, and the possibility of starting a family? Jean was more than a wife. She was a partner and a willing participant in any adventure we might undertake. She encouraged me to apply to a doctoral program, but where?

My desire was to go to Germany, to experience for myself the people and the society, and to work with German academics on the topics that I needed to investigate. But I could not do that and bring pain and worry to my parents. Finally, after researching PhD programs, I settled on the University of East Anglia (UEA), located in Norwich, England. The University had a School of European Studies somewhat similar to SIS at American and two professors, Michael Balfour and Volker Berghahn, whose research focused on German history. England was close to Germany, but was not Germany. I hoped that my parents would accept the possibility of my going to study in England. They were less upset than when I had informed them about my going to Duisburg, but it was still a shock to them that I was thinking of going so far away. It was not an easy decision for Jean, either. She was very close to her parents and her two brothers and sister. But her parents encouraged us to go. We were young, they said, and it would be a wonderful experience for us to be on our own, with only ourselves to depend upon in a new environment.

In the spring of 1970, I received my MA and admission to the PhD program in the School of European Studies at UEA. The summer before our departure was a difficult one. My parents, especially my mother, were beside themselves with worry: how would we live without jobs? What kind of housing would we find? What kind of food would we eat? We booked passage on a grand old cruise ship, the *SS France*, so that we would have time to enjoy the journey to England.

Norwich, an old cathedral city in the rural county of Norfolk, was a delightful find. It was a small enough city that one could walk to most places but a large enough one that anything we needed was available. The prices of things were much less than in the United States, especially at a wonderful open-air market in the center of Norwich. Upon our arrival in the city we stayed at a small bed-and-breakfast, and in our first full day as residents of England, I discovered that our small hotel was almost directly across from a synagogue. We both went over and were greeted by a wonderful couple who became our surrogate parents, Hetty and Harry Levine. They, too, were new to Norwich. Harry had been a school teacher and a journalist until his retirement and was then invited by the small Jewish community of Norwich to be its lay rabbi. For Jean and me, and for our families, it was a wonderful discovery. The Levines and the Norwich Hebrew congregation became our second home away from home. When I told my parents in my first transatlantic phone call about Hetty and Harry and the synagogue, I could hear some of the worry in their voices begin to disappear. For the three years that we lived in Norwich and in England, my parents found consolation in my absence because of the wonderful Jews of Norwich.

Only after I had left Norwich and gone back to the United States did I learn about Norwich's dark past regarding its Jewish community. In March 1144, just before Easter, the Jewish community of Norwich was accused of murdering a young Christian boy, William, and using his blood for a Passover ritual. Mobs attacked Norwich's Jews, and the community, one of England's largest at the time, was forced to flee the city. That accusation was the first of the so-called blood libels, anti-Semitic myths that spread across England and Europe and led to the deaths of thousands of innocent Jews. But in 1970 all Jean and I knew was that we were in a community that cared for "our American Jews" and that my parents were able to sleep at night.

Within a few short months after my arrival at UEA, I was asked to develop a topic for my PhD thesis and to spend the rest of my days as a doctoral student researching and writing what was supposed to be a publishable work of history. Although Michael Balfour was my immediate advisor, he was nearing the end of his teaching career and close to retirement. I spent most of my time with Volker Berghahn, a young German academic who had done his PhD in England. Berghahn was already recognized as a leading scholar of Wilhelmine Germany,[4] as was Balfour, who had written an important book on Kaiser Wilhelm II and his times[5] and who was very well acquainted with scholars of German history in England, Germany, and the United States.

After much discussion I decided, with Berghahn's help, that I would research the influence of the *völkish* movement on traditional German conservative politics. I wanted to undertake this research project because it would take me directly into the history of the evolution of German anti-Semitism, into the monstrous force that lay behind the Final Solution and the plan to destroy European Jewish life. But there was one catch. I had to visit numerous archives in Germany, both in the western Federal Republic of Germany and the eastern German Democratic Republic, where no American scholar had been allowed to research since early in the Vietnam War.

Into the Belly of the Beast

Before I was ready to do original research in archival institutions, I needed to read a wide variety of secondary sources in order to gain a firm grasp of modern German history and to understand the development of the political groups with whom I would be dealing. I read relentlessly for months until the end of the first semester. By December my wife and I both felt that a trip to the continent would be a good way to relieve the stress of study and work. In addition, Jean's brother came to visit us during his semester break from his first year at university. We decided to travel to Paris, Munich, and Zurich. Travel in the Europe of the early 1970s was inexpensive, and we began by visiting Paris during a snowy late-December week. The weather was cold, but the city was a tourist's dream, both in terms of the culture and the food.

After Paris we set our sights on Germany. I was extremely nervous about the overnight train we were to take from Paris to Munich. My fear increased as we crossed the French border into Germany. Suddenly, uniformed German immigration officials came on board the train to inspect passports. I do not think any Jew who is approached by a German in uniform asking for his "pass," can feel anything but fear. We all felt it in that moment of confrontation, but after checking our passports the officials left with a polite "thank you." Here I was, in the land of my birth and of my parents' greatest fear. I had told my parents about our trip, and they were apprehensive. But then I told them about my plans to visit Landsberg, the town where I was born. My father agreed that it might be a good idea to visit Landsberg but that I would most likely find nothing there.

The trip to Landsberg was uneventful. But as the train came closer to the town, I began to see familiar names of towns and villages that my father had mentioned in his stories. Finally, I saw the swans swimming on the Lech River, a scene that my father had often described to me. I did not have much time, so I hurried to the Landsberg city hall. I told an official that I had been born in the DP camp in the town and that I wanted to see the camp and the building in which my parents and I had lived. After what seemed like an endless wait, another official came and told me that no entrance was permitted into the Saarburgkaserne because it was an active military operation, jointly staffed by American and German military personnel. Only later did I find out that the camp was also the command center for Pershing missiles in southern Germany and that nuclear warheads were stockpiled a few miles from Landsberg. But now the prospect of a lengthy research trip to Germany without my wife became a reality. Would I meet real Nazis? Would people stare at me as though I had the word "Jew" written on my forehead? Could I be tolerant enough not to assume that any man over fifty that I might meet was involved in the Final Solution?

My first large research trip took me to Koblenz in 1971, the site of the German Federal Archives. I spent a number of weeks in Koblenz, beginning the arduous task of going through *Bestand* after *Bestand, Nachlass* after *Nachlass,* archival holdings relating to my topic. In Koblenz I was able to find a small *pension* within walking distance of the Federal Archives. The owner of the pension seemed to be a very nice woman, a widow who was interested in the fact that I was attending a British university. The first weekend of my stay, she asked me if I could help her daughter, a high-school student, write a letter to her English pen pal. I agreed enthusiastically. That Sunday afternoon my landlady invited me for *Kaffee und Kuchen* (coffee and cake) and, as we made polite small talk, she asked me what I thought of Germany. "It is very beautiful here along the Rhine," I told her. "Yes," she replied, "but there is a dangerous element that threatens our nation." "What is that?" I asked "The Jews," she whispered. She must have seen my face turn various shades of color, because in the next breath, she added, "But I have nothing against them." I was gone from this pension in a matter of days, and what my parents had warned me about "Nazi Land" seemed less a part of their hysteria. I could not, however, let this interfere with the research that I had to do. Jean was back in Norwich, working as a library assistant at Norwich City College, bicycling back and forth to work and paying most of our bills. I owed her that much. Over the next two years I spent weeks in Germany visiting archives in Hamburg, Dortmund, Marburg, Mönchengladbach, as well as in London. Only once did I have an encounter that left me shaken and unable to concentrate on my research.

In September 1972 I was in Marburg on the Lahn River, working at the Staatsbibliothek Preussischer Kulturbesitz. It was also the time of the Summer Olympics in Munich, and I eagerly looked forward to finishing my daily research so that I could go back to my pension and watch the Olympic events on television. One day I was walking from the Staatsbibliothek to my pension when I saw a large crowd of people standing in front of a department-store window. I walked up and saw that they were looking at a report of a terrorist attack on the Olympic village and the taking of several Israeli athletes as hostages.

I hurried home to the pension and met the landlady, a woman in her sixties who knew that I was Jewish. "Oh, Herr Peck," she said. "What a terrible tragedy. They have taken athletes from your country hostage and are threatening to kill them!" "I'm not an Israeli," I told her, "but it is a tragedy." I stayed glued to the television as long as I could. Finally I had to go to my room to get up early for the next day of research. When I came downstairs the next morning for breakfast, the landlady was rushing around, wringing her hands and saying over and over, "They are all dead, they are all dead, the Jews are all dead." I could not believe what I was hearing, especially coming from the mouth of this German woman who had made me into an Israeli.

I could not work that day or the following one either. I wished that Jean were with me. But I had no one to talk to except the woman at the pension. It was a terrible two days, and being in Germany made it that much worse. To hear a German woman tell me that "the Jews are all dead" seemed worse than any nightmare I could imagine.

From the DDR to a Fulbright Fellowship

For more than two years, from 1971 to 1973, I had been seeking admission to the archives of the German Democratic Republic (DDR). Each time that I applied, I received the same letter informing me that because of America's actions in Vietnam, the German Democratic Republic had no choice but to deny me entry. Finally, at the beginning of 1973, with the war in Vietnam coming to a conclusion, I received the much hoped-for letter, telling me that I could now do research in the main archives of the DDR, the Zentrales Staatsarchiv, and its two locations in the cities of Potsdam and Merseburg. At the same time I received the very good news that I had been selected to receive a Fulbright fellowship for a year's study in the Federal Republic of Germany.

I decided to schedule my research trip to the DDR in June and stay until the end of August. Jean would go back to the United States and live with her parents until she could join me for my Fulbright year. The thought of being separated for nearly three months was difficult for both of us, but we both knew that because the most important archival collections for my dissertation were in the DDR archives, we had little choice. We would keep in touch by writing to each other every day and calling at least once a week.

I left London on a rainy day in June and flew to West Berlin. I had all the clothing I would need for three months in one suitcase and all of my research notes in two other suitcases and a briefcase. I was afraid to let Jean take them back to the United States for fear they might be lost. I took a taxi from the West Berlin airport to the famous Checkpoint Charlie, the border crossing between West and East Berlin and the Bundesrepublik and the DDR. The taxi driver asked me why I would want to go "over there." I told him about my research, and he wished me luck and told me to be careful. I took his advice seriously. The United States had no diplomatic relations with the DDR, and if I ran into any trouble, I would have no American diplomatic officials to help me.

I crossed over the border with no difficulties. My papers were all in order. I had made certain to be as accommodating as I could when I went to the DDR consulate in London to obtain my visa. As I sat in the waiting room of the visa section, I struck up a conversation with an older woman who was also there to obtain her entry papers. She was a Jewish woman from Berlin who had left Germany with her parents after the November pogrom of 1938 and settled in England. She had not been back to Berlin in all those years and now wanted to visit the graves of her grandparents in the Jewish cemetery of Weissensee, located in East Berlin. When she was called into the visa office, I overheard her telling the DDR official that she wanted to visit "East Berlin." He corrected her immediately, with a sense of irritation, by telling her there was no place called "East Berlin" only the *Hauptstadt* (capital) of the DDR. I knew enough not to repeat her mistake when it was my turn to see the official. Not only did I mention the *Hauptstadt der DDR*, but I told him that my parents were *Opfer des Faschismus*, victims of fascism, a term that I knew would carry weight with the "only German state with no history of Fascism," as the DDR liked to portray itself.

I had booked a hotel room in Merseburg through the DDR travel agency. The agency informed me that I would have to see the head of the Zentrales Staatsarchiv in Merseburg in order to receive information on registering at the hotel. Because of delays with the train from East Berlin to Merseburg, I did not arrive in the city until after the archive had closed. I asked the taxi driver to take me directly to the hotel. I think this hotel, the only one in Merseburg, is closed for summer vacation, the driver told me. Indeed, when we arrived at the hotel, a large sign on the hotel door informed me that it was closed for summer vacation and would not reopen until the following week. The DDR travel bureau had conveniently forgotten to inform me of this.

What was I going to do, stuck with no place to stay in a city in the middle of the DDR? I asked the taxi driver for advice, and he said he would take me to the headquarters of the VOPO, the DDR Volkspolizei. Perhaps they could help me. This advice was more alarming than it was soothing. The VOPO were the public guardians of the DDR's security. They were known for shooting DDR citizens seeking to escape over the wall that had separated the DDR from the Federal Republic since the early 1960s. But what choice did I have? I went to the VOPO headquarters, knocked on the door, and introduced myself as a researcher with permission to travel the length of the DDR. The VOPO were actually quite kind to me. They listened to my story of the closed hotel, examined all of my papers, and asked me whether I was insane to be carrying all of those suitcases. They offered me a foul-tasting bottle of cola manufactured in Bulgaria and told me to wait in an office until they could contact the head of the archives. While I was in the office, I saw a group of VOPO officers bring in two young boys and place them in the room next to mine. A few minutes later the VOPO official began questioning the boys. Apparently they had left home without the permission of their parents and were reported missing. The VOPO officer shouted at them, telling them that they were a disgrace to the DDR. Did they know that a young man from the West was sitting in the next room? What would he think of their actions? You have brought shame on our republic, the policeman shouted. Your parents are coming to get you, but there will be consequences from your actions!

Later that evening one of the policemen came in and told me to gather up my suitcases and come with him. He drove me to a school for commerce that had dormitories. I was shown into a small room with a bed. It was not elegant, but I was grateful to rest after an exhausting day. "We will pick you up tomorrow morning and take you to the archives," the policeman informed me. Indeed, the next morning a man in a suit came by in a large black automobile with no police markings. He drove me to the Zentrales Staatsarchiv where I would meet the head of the archive. I arrived with all my suitcases and went directly to the director's office. He greeted me and told me that I was expected but that he would have to make arrangements with the hotel. "Why don't you go and meet your research advisor," he told me, "and I will inform you later about your accommodations."

The advisor turned out to be an attractive woman in her late thirties. She seemed pleased with my research topic and was surprised that I was familiar with the holdings of the archives. "Yes," she told me, "we have *Findbücher*, archival finding aids, but you will not be able to examine them. We will provide you with the materials that will be important for your work." After two years of intensive archival research in the Federal Republic and in England, where I had had access to any finding aid I wished to see, this was a puzzling and upsetting development. But I was not in a position to question the procedures of the archive. I agreed, and she then asked me whether I was familiar with the publications of DDR historians who had written about the *völkisch* movement in the nineteenth and early twentieth centuries in Germany. "Yes," I told her, "I have read a number of them." "Good," she told me. "I know you will utilize Marxist interpretations of the ruling classes and their exploitation of imperial Germany's worker and agricultural communities." "I have a great respect," I told her, "for those communities and for their political activities."

She seemed satisfied with my answers and took me into the reading room. At closing time the head of the archive came to my desk with a letter that he told me to present to the hotel desk when I arrived there. "But," I asked him, "won't the hotel be closed until next week?" "Don't worry," he replied, "everything has been arranged." I arrived at the hotel in the automobile of an archive staff person. The hotel was open, with dozens of staff and guests milling busily about. I could not believe my eyes. The evening before, the hotel was dark and totally closed. Less than twenty-four hours later it was alive with guests and music. I never learned how this miraculous change had taken place, and I chose not to ask. I only wanted a place to sleep so that I could do the research necessary for my dissertation.

I had taken every precaution I could to make certain that I would not run afoul of the DDR and its totalitarian rule. I had brought no camera, tape recorder, or item that could get me in trouble—or so I thought. The first weekend that I was in Merseburg, I walked to a nearby park on a sunny and warm Sunday afternoon. I sat down on a park bench next to an elderly man and wished him a good day. I then took out a German version of Thomas Mann's *Magic Mountain* and began to read. The man next to me casually looked over to see what I was reading. What he saw must have frightened him, because he got up immediately and left without saying goodbye. It was not until after I had left the DDR that I realized that the works of Thomas

Mann were not permitted in the DDR. Apparently, neither had the customs officers who had examined my luggage at the Checkpoint Charlie crossing.

One morning, a day or two after I had checked into the hotel, the clerk at the hotel reception desk asked me how much longer I intended to stay. I told him at least another two weeks. "I hope you have enough money," he told me. "Your room is expensive." "Expensive?" I asked. "But I know how much it is in DDR marks and I have calculated the amount for my stay." "You do know, don't you," he asked, "that your room cost per day is twice the quoted amount since you are a Westerner?" I had not known and realized at once that I would only be able to stay for half the time that I needed for my research before my money would run out.

What could I do? That very morning I asked to see the head of the archive. I explained my situation and then told him that my parents were *Opfer des Faschismus* and that I hoped their experience would allow an exception to be made in my case regarding hotel charges. "This is highly unusual," the head replied, "but let me see what I can do." That evening he came over to my desk to tell me that the travel bureau in Berlin had looked favorably on my situation. I was to stay with a private family for the rest of my time in the DDR, both in Merseburg and in Potsdam. The cost would not only be less than the cost of a hotel room for Western visitors, it would be less than the charge for a visitor from a socialist nation.

I took a taxi that evening to the apartment of a widow with one son. For the final weeks of my stay in Merseburg, I had a comfortable bed and breakfast each morning prepared by this kindly woman, who cleaned my room daily and asked me no questions. Merseburg was a city with little to offer a tourist. I had no interest in seeing its "attractions," but I did go to the city center in order to see what life was like in the first "workers' paradise" in German history. The shops in Merseburg, while not bursting with consumer goods, were fairly well stocked with cheap, if passable items of food and clothing. They were of lesser quality than the goods in West Germany, but there were no long lines of shoppers, as one saw in other socialist countries.

But what I did want to see quite badly was the concentration camp of Buchenwald, where my father had been a prisoner beginning in August 1944. I took a bus from Merseburg to the historic city of Weimar, home to the German poets Goethe and Schiller and the birthplace of the Weimar Republic, and then another bus to the camp memorial. I was transfixed by my visit. I could not believe I was standing on the same ground where my father had stood nearly three decades earlier, and I looked at the bizarre words on the entrance gate to the camp: *Jedem das Seine* (to each his own). I walked the distance to the stone quarry where my father had labored daily for hours in the hot summer weather of Saxony and had struggled to survive from day to day. What surprised me most was how little the camp exhibit reflected the experience of anyone but communist prisoners, especially the last leader of German Communism, Ernst Thälmann, a communist functionary from Hamburg who was murdered in August 1944 while my father was also in the concentration camp. According to my father, the camp contained many different kinds of prisoners in addition to communists: Jews, gay men, Jehovah's Witnesses, and Russian prisoners of war.

After three weeks in Merseburg, I took the train to Potsdam and the second part of my research trip. The Potsdam section of the Zentrales Staatsarchiv was the institution's showcase. Potsdam was an old Prussian military town and also the site of the summer palace of Kaiser Frederic the Great, Sanssouci, which was surrounded by a beautiful park. In Potsdam I found living quarters in the home of a family whose ancestors had come to Germany from France as members of the persecuted Protestant Huguenot community. The husband was an agronomist whose chief duty was to make certain that Marxist agricultural theory was turned into reality. His wife and two children were delightful people, and I could not have asked for a better set of living circumstances.

In the Potsdam archive I met several other PhD candidates working on their dissertations. Among them were Geoff Eley, a British doctoral student now at the University of Michigan, whose research paralleled mine in terms of looking at the German political Right,[6] and Robert Gellately, a Canadian, now at Florida State University.[7] I had hoped to stay in touch with Jean on a regular basis through letters and telephone. I found that I could not make calls to the United States from a DDR phone, and I received very few of her letters during the whole time that I was in East Germany. Fortunately I became a part of my host family's life, especially during the weekends, where I would take a little time off to visit Sanssoucci and walk through the many parks in Potsdam. On one visit to Sanssoucci, I witnessed a shouting confrontation between a group of Soviet soldiers and several Chinese visitors from the People's Republic. I did not know what the argument was about, but clearly both sides were angry and confrontational.

On weekends I would have a chance to discuss world events with my host.

One evening he invited me into his study to show me his book collection. He poured me a glass of brandy and we drank a toast to world peace. He asked me what I thought of DDR women, and I told him that I tried to avoid too much evaluation because I was certain my wife had spies checking on my every activity. "Yes, Herr Peck," he told me, "you are not unobserved in our country." I took that to mean that not imaginary, but real people were watching my movements, and they were not working for my wife. He also offered to show me his proudest possession. When I said, "Yes, I would like to see it," he went to a book case and opened a small wall vault behind a row of books. He took out a book and told me that, although it was not allowed to be displayed by the DDR authorities, it had belonged to his parents and even the State could not make him give it up. He showed me a first edition copy of Adolf Hitler's *Mein Kampf*, a gift that all couples about to be married received from the Führer.

My host came from a distinguished Prussian family who had been prominent in German foreign and military affairs. Perhaps that is why the DDR let him privately own two houses, one for his own use and a home that had belonged to a relative but was in a state of significant disrepair. One Sunday morning as I was finishing breakfast and reading one of the several newspapers the family received, all carrying the same articles and reporting a 99.9 percent successful harvest, my host came into the dining room and asked whether I cared to accompany him to his other house, where there was a problem with a flooded basement. We got into his little East German Trabant and the two-cylinder vehicle huffed and puffed its way to a large, neglected-looking apartment building a few miles away. We entered the basement, where the water was knee high. My host decided to call a plumbing company because he could not fix the problem himself. Clearly frustrated, he asked me jokingly whether I would be willing to buy the building from him for one DDR mark. It clearly was an albatross around his neck. As we came up the basement stairs, a young woman holding an infant and a little boy by the hand asked him whether he thought there would be heat in the building that winter. "I hope so," he said, "although I cannot be certain."

After six weeks of intensive research in Potsdam, I had read through all of the important archival collections that were necessary for my dissertation. I also needed to leave for Hamburg, where I would be spending my Fulbright year writing my dissertation and where in a few short days I would be meeting Jean. On the day before my departure, my host suggested we again go into his study to discuss settling my financial obligations. He totaled up the amount that I owed him in DDR marks, a currency that had a ratio of 1:1 parity with the West German mark at home but was worth barely six DDR marks to one West German mark abroad.

"You've been to the Intershop," he said to me, referring to the chain of tourist-oriented shops located in the DDR, "and you know the quality of the goods they have in there. You also know that a citizen of 'Unser Republik' cannot use DDR currency to buy any of those goods." "Well," he told me, "there is a wonderful typewriter that my daughter wants so badly for her schoolwork. Can you please pay your housing costs in either West German marks or in English pound sterling? My daughter would be so pleased."

What was I supposed to do? Westerners were not allowed to use *Devisen*, foreign currency, in any manner in the DDR, except in exchange for the purchase of DDR currency on a 1:1 ratio. Could my very nice host be setting me up to commit an illegal activity and cause my arrest? "Is that not illegal in the DDR?" I asked him. "Look, my dear friend," he said, "I am a loyal citizen of the DDR. I think 'Unser Republik' is the most important thing to happen to German history since its unification. But no citizen of the DDR obeys all the laws. What would be the harm of making a young girl happy?"

I did not have a lot of time to think. Impulsively, I said, "Fine, I will do it," expecting DDR state security officers, the STASI, to come bursting through the door. But nothing happened. I paid my host in English pound sterling, and in return he gave me a set of the writings of Karl Marx in several volumes, a set that I had already bought earlier in my stay along with many others that were cheaply produced and even cheaper to buy. I took the set and gave it to an English PhD candidate who had arrived at the archive a few days earlier.

On the last day before I was to leave Potsdam, the head of the archive came by and told the researchers in the reading room that the building would be closing at noon. We all wondered why but were afraid to ask. He sensed our curiosity and said that the staff was going to a nearby park to demonstrate against a putsch, a coup in Chile that had overthrown President Allende, a friend of the DDR. As we left the building, we saw dozens of placards and posters lying in the hall. An English colleague and researcher suggested we follow the archive staff to the demonstration. We did, and I stood in a crowd of thousands as General Heinz Hoffmann, the minister of defense of the DDR, denounced American imperialism and the CIA for their complicity in the overthrow and murder of Salvador Allende. I am certain I was the only American in the crowd, and I sought to appear as inconspicuous as possible as speaker after speaker followed Hoffmann with similar charges. But on a sunny morning in September, I boarded a train in Potsdam along with dozens of pensioned DDR citizens who were leaving the country to either move to the West or to visit relatives. They were the only DDR citizens allowed out of the socialist "workers' paradise" except for those with government approval. Retired pensioners were useless to the DDR. They contributed nothing to the growth of Germany's first socialist state.

I felt a sense of sadness in knowing that the people I had met in the DDR could not get on a train as freely as I had. And yet I felt a certain affection for the place. Somehow, because of its claims that it was everything the Federal Republic was not, that it had eliminated any traces of fascism and anti-Semitism from its midst, I felt differently about the DDR. I had used the *Opfer des Faschismus* explanation to enter museums and exhibits without having to pay an admission charge. People respected the status of my parents and by definition my status as a son of the "Victims of Fascism." Only later would I discover that Jews were considered second-class victims and that only communists who had been persecuted by the Nazis were considered the real victims. They received higher pensions than the small community of DDR Jews who had also suffered under National Socialism. The story of Jewish suffering received little if any official attention.

I left the DDR with even more suitcases than I had taken into the country. But it was worth it. I had taken copious research notes and ordered several reels of microfilm for those materials that I could not copy by hand. The officials at the Zentrales Staatsarchiv had worked out a microfilm frame-for-frame arrangement with me. For every frame of DDR material, I was to order a frame of material from the National Archives in Washington from a list that the archive officials gave me. Within a few months my reels had arrived from Potsdam. I had gone to Hamburg with every intention of ordering the reels from the National Archives. But the National Archives had doubled the cost of copying materials, and the DDR did not know this. The order would have cost me a small fortune, and I just did not have the money. I never ordered the microfilms from the National Archives and have always carried a nagging sense of guilt about the fact.

Hamburg: A Year of Living Dangerously

Hamburg, a beautiful city in northern Germany, seemed like another world compared to the DDR. Even the tramps and the homeless in Hamburg were elegantly dressed by comparison. Jean and I moved into a small one-bedroom apartment in a building owned by the University of Hamburg, a building that contained many of the foreign faculty and students who were at the university. The apartment house was located on the Rothenbaumchaussee, a beautiful street not far from the university. Across the street from the building was the university MENSA, its central dining facility, where Jean and I took many of our meals. Close by were two research institutions that I would be using, the Hamburg Forschungsstelle für die Geschichte des Nationalsocialismus (Hamburg Research Facility for the History of National Socialism), whose director, Professor Werner Jochmann, was an acknowledged expert on the growth of racial anti-Semitism in Germany during the First World War,[8] and the Institut für die Geschichte der deutschen Juden (Institute for the History of German Jewry) whose director, Dr. Peter Freimark, was a scholar of Jewish life in Hamburg.[9]

We enjoyed Hamburg: the walks along the beautiful Alster River, the wonderful shops, and the quality of life in the city. Jean took a job as an English instructor at a foreign language school, and we made a number of friends from among her students. I was fortunate enough to accidentally land a small non-speaking role in a film directed by Otto Preminger and starring Peter O'Toole. And Jean became pregnant with our first child.

I had chosen the University of Hamburg for a very good reason. Its Historisches Facultät (history department) consisted of some of the most important historians working in the area of German conservative politics. Among them were Dirk Stegmann,[10] Peter-Christian Witt,[11] and Jens Flemming.[12] They were all students of Professor Fritz Fischer, whose books, *Griff nach der Weltmacht*,[13] published in 1961, and *Krieg der Illusionen*,[14] published in 1969, argued convincingly that Germany's aims for European domination had been a contributing, if not *the* contributing factor, to the outbreak of the First World War.

Fischer's thesis was attacked by conservative politicians, who labeled him a *Nestbeschmutzer* (literally, a soiler of his own nest, a traitor) among many other defamations of his character. What resulted in the decade after Fischer's books, beyond the "Fischer controversy," was the development of what came to be called the "Kehrite"[15] school of German social history, with its focus on the manipulative social imperialism of Germany's ruling preindustrial elites, led by the East Elbian Junkers, as well as the growing racial anti-Semitic and "prefascist" tendencies of political groups such as the Alldeutscher Verband[16] and the Deutsche Vaterlandspartei.[17]

Many of Fischer's students were adherents of a "primacy of domestic politics" understanding of German history during the Kaiserreich, as well as believing that Germany's path during this period constituted a *Sonderweg* (special path) among the European powers. Volker Berghahn was a moderate Kehrite, and his writings and our discussions influenced the direction of my dissertation research with one exception. Most of the Kehrites did not focus on the development of German anti-Semitism and the role it played during the Kaiserreich and into the Weimar Republic. I wanted to pursue a different path and try to understand how anti-Semitism contributed to the "prefascism" of imperial German social and political movements.[18]

The Fulbright year in Hamburg was an exciting one, and my research, reading, and discussions with the "Fischer students" gave me insights into German history and into the dynamics of German social and political history. The direction of Germany in the period after its unification in 1871 and its relationship to Jews and Judaism became as important a matter of inquiry as the beginnings of my comprehension about what it all meant for me and for the history of my family. Perhaps it even created an anger that I had not experienced in the nearly four years of repeated trips to Germany, both West and East. That anger had a chance to become tangible in Hamburg. It was stirred when I learned that the former Jewish Community Center had been located on Rothenbaumchaussee, just a few minutes' walk from our apartment, but no plaque or any kind of indication of its existence was evident. My anger increased when I learned that a green area across the street from the S-bahn stop Dammtor, quite near to our building, had been the site of the *Umschlagplatz* (place of shipment) where Jews from Hamburg had been rounded up and sent east to their deaths in the years after 1939.

Finally, the anger reached a boiling point when I learned that a Hamburg publishing house had unveiled a new magazine devoted to life in the Third Reich but with an emphasis on depicting that life as "normal" and focusing on the "good" side of Nazi culture and its leading personalities. Why that anger spilled over very near the end of our stay in Hamburg is a mystery to me. But spill over it did when we went to visit some friends in another part of

Hamburg, and I stepped up to the Dammtor station attendant to buy tickets for the S-bahn. I only had a pile of small coins but enough for the tickets. The ticket agent refused to take the change and insisted that I had to have paper money. I exploded in a kind of anger that I do not believe I have ever experienced since. I denounced him and I denounced Germany for its pettiness and coldhearted treatment of foreigners. I told him that what Germans had done to my family and to six million Jews was a result of the bureaucratic mindset of little Führers like him. Two elderly women standing in line behind me begged me to take their paper money to pay for the tickets. I stormed out of the station with Jean behind me.

I knew then that it was indeed time to leave Hamburg and to leave Germany. I needed to say adieu to Europe a second time to think through what I had learned about the darkness that my parents had seen when they and other survivors looked over the abyss into the face of complete evil. I needed to understand more about that evil and those who carried it out, but I could not do it by shouting at ticket agents and little old German ladies.

10

Opening the "Iron Box": The Holocaust as Burden and Hope

In September 1974 Jean and I returned to America and to Maine. With a baby due in a few short months and a dissertation to complete, I accepted the gracious invitation of my in-laws to house us until I was able to find employment. Our daughter Abby was born on January 24, 1975. I remember standing with my face pressed against the window of the maternity room that housed the newborns. I kept looking at my daughter and could not believe that I had a child. My parents were thrilled and wanted to come and see their granddaughter, who was named for my uncle and her great-uncle Asher Selig, my mother's brother, and who, like me, became an extension of our shattered family life. But my mother was not well at the time, and it would be some months before they were able to come when the snowy Maine winter finally ended.

I worked on the dissertation and was able to find a position as a substitute high-school history teacher. I also found a position, as did Jean, teaching at a local college in an evening program. The writing of the dissertation moved along, but slowly. I had accumulated so much research documentation that just sorting it out into a comprehensible set of notes took time. I sent out resumes, joining the ranks of doctoral students looking for their first university teaching position. I had finally realized that the path I had chosen gave me little alternative but to pursue an academic career. But positions teaching history at an American college or university were difficult to find. Indeed, the history profession had been in a major crisis for a number of years, with many more students receiving their PhDs than there were available jobs.

At the end of 1975, I went to Chicago to attend the annual meeting of the

American Historical Association. Not only was the annual meeting a time for scholars to present their latest research, but it was also the place of the so-called cattle market, where interviews were conducted for possible hirings in departments of history. I interviewed along with hundreds of applicants who already had their PhDs, as well as hundreds more who were still finishing their degrees. I was in the latter category and that put me at a clear disadvantage, although my academic research was much more in-depth than most doctoral candidates at American universities.

While I was in Chicago Jean had read an advertisement for an assistant director of the American Jewish Archives (AJA) located at Hebrew Union College in Cincinnati, Ohio. She did not know exactly where Cincinnati was located, except that it was the home of the Cincinnati Reds, a baseball team in the major leagues. She had decided that the criteria listed in the advertisement were those that I possessed and had sent in an application along with my curriculum vitae. She told me about it when I returned to Portland, but I heard nothing until late spring. Then I received a call from the American Jewish Archives, asking me to drive to a beautiful part of Maine called the Belgrade Lakes, about seventy-five miles from Portland. There I was to speak to a Professor Samuel Sandmel about the position.

I did not know that Samuel Sandmel (1911–79) was one of the most distinguished Jewish academics working in the area of Jewish-Christian relations, as well as in the origins of Christian anti-Judaism.[1] He was also an ordained liberal rabbi and director of graduate studies at the Hebrew Union College–Jewish Institute of Religion in Cincinnati. Every summer he and his family traveled to their summer home on the Belgrade Lakes in Maine. I drove to the Sandmel home and had a long and pleasant interview/conversation with Professor Sandmel. We discussed my research and my experience. At the end of the interview, he told me that he liked my background and would recommend that I travel to Cincinnati to be interviewed by the director of the American Jewish Archives, Dr. Jacob Rader Marcus (1896–1995). My interview with Professor Marcus the following month was extraordinary. He came to the interview from his home, a tall, dignified, elderly man in a black, three-piece suit. He asked me to sit down in his office and took out three books, one in German, one in Hebrew, and one in Yiddish. He asked me to translate a paragraph from each one and then asked me: "Are you a good Jew?" That was the interview.

I left Cincinnati with no idea whether I had done well or not. But the following week I received a call from Dr. Marcus's assistant, offering me the position of assistant director. I accepted at once, and Jean and I prepared to leave Portland, Maine, with our eighteen-month-old daughter to begin a new life in Cincinnati, whose nickname was the "Queen City of the West." I worked feverishly to finish the dissertation and did so a few days before our departure.

Hebrew Union College (it merged in 1949 with another liberal rabbinic seminary located in New York, the Jewish Institute of Religion) grew into a four-campus institution devoted to rabbinic training for Reform rabbis as well as graduate studies in various areas of Jewish studies. While New York, Los Angeles, and Jerusalem were important campuses, the campus that housed the major holdings of the Klau Library, one of the most important Jewish libraries in the world, and the American Jewish Archives, the largest institution in the world devoted to the North American Jewish experience, was in Cincinnati.

It was this institution that Dr. Jacob Rader Marcus founded in 1947. When I met him, Marcus was already eighty years old and had been a part of the life of Hebrew Union College as a rabbinic student and a professor for over sixty years. After his rabbinic ordination in 1920, Dr. Marcus spent two years as a junior faculty member at HUC before traveling to Berlin to study for his PhD. He studied at Humboldt University with Friedrich Meinecke, among other faculty, as well as with Rabbi Leo Baeck and Professor Ismar Elbogen at the Hochschule für die Wissenschaft des Judentums, Germany's liberal rabbinical seminary. After completing his dissertation at Humboldt Universtiy, Marcus spent a year in Palestine before returning to Cincinnati to assume his teaching responsibilities. He began as a historian of German Jewry, but he was able to read the handwriting on the wall for the future of German-Jewish life, and he turned to a little-known area of study, the history of American Jewry. Marcus taught the first course on the American Jewish experience in the early 1940s and founded the American Jewish Archives in 1947. The institution's first archivist was Selma Stern-Tauebler, a distinguished historian of German Jewry.

After learning about his background, I began to understand why I had been offered the position. I had worked long years in German archives, could read three languages that were heavily represented in the holdings of the archives, and was young and trainable. The first day on the job, Dr. Marcus came in to meet me. He told me, "Boy, I have a lot of books still to write. You mind the shop here at the archives. I'm going home to work. Keep in touch." That was the beginning of a twenty-year relationship with the "dean of American Jewish historians," a truly great scholar and human being, that only ended when Jacob Rader Marcus died six months short of his one hundredth birthday in November 1995. He had two books still awaiting publication at the time of his death.[2]

Assuming responsibility for administering an internationally known research institution at the tender age of thirty was a challenging and terrifying moment for me. But I found that I was equal to the task because I had an innate love for archival institutions and the scholarly research opportunities they provided. After two decades at the head of the American Jewish Archives, I was extremely proud when others wrote that no book on any aspect of the American Jewish experience could be written well without a research trip to the American Jewish Archives. I also assumed the managing editorship of *American Jewish Archives,* the scholarly journal published twice yearly by the AJA; I also directed an ambitious program of academic publications and exhibits on many aspects of the American Jewish experience.

Cincinnati was home not only to a large and distinguished group of Jews whose ancestors had emigrated to the "Queen City of the West" from various parts of Germany, primarily Bavaria and Baden-Würtemberg, but also to a large community of Holocaust survivors. I was astonished at the number of scholars and administrators who had a direct relationship to German-Jewish life. Among them were Alfred Gottschalk, the president of HUC-JIR, who came to America from Nazi Germany in 1939; the German-born Jacob Petuchowski, a distinguished scholar of Judaism and an active participant in the Christian-Jewish dialogue, whose grandfather, an Orthodox rabbi in Berlin, was one of Professor Marcus's favorite preachers; Michael A. Meyer, also German-born, who was an important scholar of the history of liberal Judaism in Germany and America, as well as the editor of a most important series on German-Jewish history; Alexander Guttmann, who was a professor at the Hochschule; Werner Weinberg, also a survivor; Mattityahu Tsevat; Israel O. Lehman, who received his rabbinic ordination from the Hochschule; and Uri Herscher.

Equally as important, I met a number of sons and daughters of Holocaust survivors and within a few months of my arrival was involved in a "therapy" group for children of survivors. For someone who had had relatively little contact with other sons and daughters of survivors, it was an eye-opening moment for me, one that many children of survivors have commented upon: the realization that you are not alone, that there are others who have gone through something similar and can immediately relate to what you thought was only possible for you to understand. Among this group were two young men from Montreal. Benny Kraut was a professor at the University of Cincinnati and a modern Orthodox Jew. Abie Ingber was the director of the University of Cincinnati's Jewish Students Association, known as Hillel. He was also an ordained rabbi from HUC-JIR. For a number of months, we met weekly and discussed a range of topics that dealt with our relationship to our parents and their experiences during World War II, our siblings, our spouses, and the Jewish and non-Jewish worlds. We sought to create a sense of what all this meant for us and how we could work together to define an identity that would allow us to share a sense of who we were.

By the spring of 1977, the Jewish community knew about our group and so did a reporter for the *Cincinnati Post,* the city's afternoon newspaper, who asked if he could attend one of our meetings. We did not feel comfortable letting someone who did not share our background into one of our sessions. "Would you write a piece then," the reporter asked, "for the *Post?*" We did not quite draw lots, but I was chosen to write the article to reveal our group to the outside world. I did not want to make us seem an oddity, a group of maladjusted members of society, but at the same time I had to describe what I had learned about the issues that seemed to be a part of all our lives. And yet, we had created, over the few months of our meetings, a kind of identity that had a shape and a form. Could I put that into words? The resulting effort was titled by the *Post* "A Jew Whose Ancient Roots Were Cut Shares His Holocaust."[3] It was not the title I would have chosen, but I did not see it until the day it appeared in the newspaper.

For the first time I used the word "Holocaust." I knew that it was a term that was being used more and more often to describe the destruction of European Jewry and the murder of six million Jewish men, women, and children. The term came from Latin, Greek, and French words meaning something that was burnt whole. It was not the word that my parents or I had ever used to describe what had happened to them, to their families, and to Polish Jewry, but it seemed to resonate with the nonsurvivor, non-Yiddish speaking world much more than did the Yiddish word *churbn.* In the article I tried to describe the worlds inhabited by survivors and their children. "For the survivors," I wrote, "liberation in 1945 was merely a physical one. From the harrowing experience of being an 'individual in the concentration camp,' the survivor found himself the victim of the 'concentration camp in the individual,' a situation where stress and suffering over a sustained period often left him an emotional cripple. The isolation of captivity in the camps also manifested itself in some survivors in an inner isolation, leaving them unable to respond 'normally' to a 'normal' post-camp experience." What happens, I asked, "to the concentration camp survivor when that person leaves the 'gates of no return'? How much of the experience has one internalized and to what degree can one adjust to 'normal' life?"

I concluded that in the postwar lives of most survivors living in America, "what emerges is a tale of triumph and sorrow, always tempered by an inability on the part of the survivors to forget or comprehend the tragedy that shaped the remainder of their years." I then wrote the following in an effort to describe what I had learned about my fellow sons and daughters of survivors in the months of our sessions:

> The children of survivors share with them this often unnatural world. Their condition is less well-known than that of the survivors. It is only within the last two or three years that some of these children have begun to come to grips with the reality of their situation. For many, nearing the age of 30, it is the first time that they have begun to question their own views of life and the effect that the Holocaust has had upon that existence. Certainly, no two survivors experienced the Holocaust in a similar manner. Neither has every child of survivors formulated his or her views of adolescent experiences in the same way. Many of us live with a great and terrible burden, apparent only to those like me, who are children of survivors. We have been called a "separate sub-community of Jews," successful like many of our parents externally. We are career-oriented and middle-class in our values, but we bear the traumas of life with the survivor, of life with the "concentration camp in the individual." I often fear that part of the syndrome we labor under is an inability to know when not to blame the Holocaust for misguided or inappropriate deeds. We cannot allow the Holocaust to become convenient as a whipping boy for our actions. Yet, despite these fears, we continue to seek each other out, enjoying a certain spontaneity we can find with no one else. Most of us, I believe, are

seeking a real liberation from our own personal Holocaust. We want to clear away the myths surrounding our parents' lives and confront what has been considered not to be confrontable.

I did not know it then, but my essay was in line with a growing sense of identity among sons and daughters of Holocaust survivors across America and beyond. Our Cincinnati group was one of the first of what is now called the Second Generation dialogue groups to form and actively seek to shape our identities.

Two years later, another child of survivors, Helen Epstein, published a book entitled *Children of the Holocaust: Conversations with Sons and Daughters of Survivors*.[4] The book would become the Bible of the Second Generation, the sons and daughters of the Holocaust. In the book Epstein wrote about her Holocaust-survivor parents who raged against the world but without making her understand why. "For years," she wrote about the need to understand that rage and its effects on her, "it lay in an iron box buried so deep inside me that I was never sure just what it was. I knew I carried slippery, combustible things more secret than sex and more dangerous than any shadow or ghost."

Epstein traveled across America interviewing a wide range of children of survivors. Many, like me, were just beginning the process of personal reflection, seeking to understand what we had experienced with our parents and with history and ready to "come out" and tell of their inherited traumas, exploring their own identity and unlocking the "iron box" of their family history. But Epstein also discovered many other sons and daughters who were not interested in examining their lives and the lives of their parents, either because they were too frightened to approach such an intimidating and potentially dangerous task or they were not interested in anything but living life like any young American Jew with family and professional responsibilities.

I could not blame the latter group for their concerns. I, too, had a family and a professional responsibility. But I had too the need to understand not only who I had become because of the Holocaust, but why the Holocaust had happened in the first place, how it had been designed and executed by Germany and Germans, with the help of many others, and how they could have done what they did. I did not yet realize that those who committed the crimes had also been individuals with families and professional responsibilities. How had their actions affected those sons and daughters?

Between the Holocaust and the American Jewish Experience

In 1978 I experienced the dream of every doctoral student. My revised dissertation was accepted for publication by the University Press of America located in Washington, D.C. Titled *Radicals and Reactionaries: The Crisis of Conservatism in Wilhelmine Germany*,[5] the book sought to trace the growth of German radical and racial anti-Semitism, especially in the war years between 1914 and 1918, and the roles played by extra-parliamentary organizations like the Pan-German League (ADL) and the Agrarian League (BDL).

I was delighted and grateful that I had been able to pursue such research. It allowed me to begin to see the rise of racial anti-Semitism within the context of German political and social change, beginning with the departure of Otto von Bismarck from the German political scene in 1890 to the creation of the "prefascist" German Fatherland Party in 1917. Finally, some of the questions were being answered: how could Germany have carried out the murder of six million Jews and what reasons lay behind these actions? The reasons did not start in 1933 with the Nazi seizure of power in Germany but had their roots in the long century of German history beginning with the post-Napoleonic era. Was this century a German *Sonderweg*, a special path to the Third Reich and to the Holocaust? The trained German historian would probably deny such a path and ask that this history be seen in the comparative framework of Europe's century as well.

Another interest of mine was able to develop in Cincinnati. I had become friendly with a number of Christian clergy who were working on PhDs in Jewish Studies at HUC-JIR. The College-Institute had instituted a Christian Fellows program in the late 1940s, a program that brought to the Cincinnati campus Catholic priests and Protestant ministers from every denomination, from the very liberal to the very theologically conservative. I always enjoyed meeting and speaking with the Christian students. I noticed that at the communal lunch hour they would usually sit by themselves at their own tables. I always made a point of asking whether I could join them for the meal, and they were always grateful to me that I did. I was often astonished to hear that outside of their classroom involvement they rarely, if ever, interacted with rabbinical students and HUC-JIR faculty. I was aware that for more than a dozen years, since 1965, the Catholic Church had been working to remove any traces of anti-Jewish writings from its liturgy and from its educational textbooks. I also knew that the impetus for such an action was directly related to a meeting between the great Catholic pope, John XXIII, and a French-Jewish survivor of the Holocaust, Jules Isaac, who presented the pope with a book Isaac had written entitled *The Teaching of Contempt*.[6] In the meeting between pope and Holocaust survivor, Isaac urged the pope to consider the fact that what had happened to European Jewry during the Holocaust years was not simply the result of the ideas of National Socialism and racial anti-Semitism but had deep roots that stretched back to the first anti-Jewish teachings of the early Church Fathers.

It was with this conversation in mind that Pope John XXIII had conceived of a statement denying Jewish complicity in the crucifixion and death of Jesus Christ and restoring Judaism as a legitimate and "sister" faith to Roman Catholicism. Pope John died before the statement could be created. But the statement, *Nostra Aetate* (In Our Time), drafted during the Second Vatican Council and ratified by the church in 1965, was an historic and far-reaching effort at a new era in interreligious dialogue and cooperation. Yet, in the lunch room at HUC-JIR, none of this was discussed among the Christian scholars and the rabbinic students and faculty more than a dozen years after *Nostra Aetate*. I resolved to change the situation. With the enthusiastic support of Dr. Alfred Gottschalk, the institution's president, I began to develop plans for a three-day conference that I called "Religion in a Post-Holocaust World." The purpose of the conference would focus on the efforts of Jews and Christians to rethink their religious values in a post-Holocaust world. The conference would be an historic one because it would bring together not only internationally renowned scholars and religious leaders but also Jewish, Protestant, and Catholic seminary students, the future leaders and representatives of American Judaism and Christianity, to discuss for the first time what the Holocaust might mean for a new direction in Jewish and Christian relations.

The three-day conference, held at HUC-JIR from November 19 to November 21, 1980, brought together some of the most important Jewish and Christian scholars working on Christian-Jewish relations and the Holocaust. Among the Jewish participants were Rabbi Irving Greenberg,[7] a towering figure in Jewish thought after the Holocaust, and Professor Yaffa Eliach,[8] a survivor of the Holocaust and the creator of one of the first Holocaust centers in the United States. Among the Christian participants were Professor Rosemary Radford Ruether,[9] the author of a scathing indictment of Christian theology as the basis for historical anti-Semitism, and Professor David Tracy, perhaps the most important American Catholic theologian of the past half-century.

As important as the presence of these scholars was the attendance by representatives of eleven Christian seminaries, Catholic and Protestant, who met for hours on end with the rabbinical students of HUC-JIR and discussed with them their thoughts on the lectures of each conference session. The conference was filmed by CBS television and produced as a half-hour documentary for the program "For Our Times," hosted by Douglas Edwards, an important American newsperson. The program was shown nationally. I was also approached by the Fortress Press of Philadelphia, which was interested in publishing the conference papers. They asked whether I could find someone of importance in the area of Holocaust scholarship to introduce the book. I immediately thought of Elie Wiesel, who by the late 1970s was already a major voice for Holocaust survivors in America and an important novelist and essayist. I wrote to Wiesel, told him about myself and the fact that my father had been a prisoner in Buchenwald shortly before he had arrived there, and asked him to write the introduction. Wiesel agreed and the book, *Jews and Christians after the Holocaust,* was published in 1982.[10] More than three decades after its publication, the book and many of its articles are constantly cited in other publications and are required reading on many Holocaust and religion curricula.

In 1979 our family was expanded by one with the birth on February 15 of Joel David Peck. He was named for another of my mother's brothers, Jankel. Again my parents were thrilled, especially because a boy had been added to the family, but they could not see Joel until several months later. After nearly thirty years living in Waterbury, Connecticut, my parents sold their home and moved to Florida. My mother's health, never good, had gotten progressively worse, and her physicians advised my father to leave the difficult winter climate of New England.

The more I spoke with my father about his experiences, the more I realized how little had been written about the period of the Jewish Displaced Persons. I began to read the issues of the *Landsberger Lager-Cajtung,* the very fine publication of the Landsberg DP camp that began publication in October 1945. To be honest, I began because I wanted to find the announcement of my birth or a mention of my parents. I did not find either one, but I began to discover something as important: the development of an idea of survival, of being more than "living corpses" at the mercy of an uncaring world.

But was this idea about how to live after the Holocaust only a Landsberg one? I had to read more. I read *Unzer Weg*, the publication of the Central Committee of Liberated Jews in the American zone of Germany, published in Munich; *D. P. Express*, also published in Munich; *A Heim* in Leipheim; *Bamidbar* in Föhrenwald; *Dos Freie Wort* in Feldafing; *Unzer Wort* in Bamberg; *Unzer Leben* in Berlin; *Unzer Mut* in Zeilsheim; *Der Neuer Moment* in Regensburg; *Unzer Hoffenung* in Eschwege; *Auf der Frei* in Stuttgart; *Der Morgn* in Bad Reichenhall; and *Unzer Sztyme*, published in the Bergen Belsen/Hohne DP camp in the British occupation zone of Germany. I read and read until I decided that there was indeed a common understanding of what it meant to be a *She'ris Hapleita Mensch*, one of the "surviving remnant" who had looked over the abyss of the Holocaust but who had not been swallowed by it.

I worked long and hard to write an article that would try to bring to life this voice of the She'erith Hapletah, one that I felt had been lost to the ages. I submitted a proposal to the Eighth World Congress of Jewish Studies, to be held in Jerusalem in August 1981. The proposed paper was entitled "An Introduction to the Social History of the Jewish Displaced Persons' Camps: The Lost Legacy of the She'erith Hapletah."[11]

What was the essence of my paper? I argued that the term *Sherith Hapletah* (in Hebrew) was the term that survivors of the Holocaust used as their identity in the years after 1945. It was, I further argued, "an identity that would ultimately give birth to a revolutionary ideology created from the inner being and experience of the She'erith Hapletah." The ideology called for the creation of a new humanism whose goals would be the social and moral perfection of humanity. The survivors, I argued, felt themselves called upon to be the vehicle of change toward such ideals, within both the Jewish world and the non-Jewish environment. Their tragedy, the destruction of six million Jewish lives, gave them the right and strength, the belief, to achieve such aims. "The voice of the She'erith Hapletah," I wrote in the paper, "was a voice that sought to change the direction of Jewish destiny and of human destiny. It was a prophetic voice, in tune with the biblical voices of the prophets in their quest for social justice. Finally, it was the voice of enduring legacy, established for the children of the She'erith Hapletah." And I was one of those children.

The day of the session when I was to read my paper was one of the most intense days I have ever experienced. The room in which our panel met was crowded with an audience that I could see was made up of many Holocaust survivors from Israel. After I read the paper, there was applause, but I could not be certain whether it was genuine or merely polite. The moderator asked for any questions, and only one man raised his hand and said, "I remember that time very well. I am so happy you have discovered it for yourself. It is your legacy." After the session ended, a tall, balding gentleman came up to the panelists' desk to see me. "I am Gideon Hausner," he said, extending his hand to me. I knew immediately who he was. Gideon Hausner (1915–1990) was the legal advisor to the Israeli government and the chief prosecutor at the war crimes trial of Adolf Eichmann in 1961. "Thank you for your paper," he told me. "It is important that our Holocaust survivors feel a sense of worth. For too long, Israel has not given them the proper credit for ideas such as those you spoke of today." I do not know whether it was due to the presentation of this paper in Israel, but suddenly I began to receive invitations to speak about the DP camp experience from various places in America and in Germany. In October 1981 I was invited to attend a two-day International Conference of Liberators held at the American State Department in Washington, D.C. There I finally met Elie Wiesel, who was the chair of the conference and who greeted me like an old friend.

I also met Major General Aleksei K. Gorlinsky, a retired Soviet Army officer who had helped liberate my father at Theresienstadt. When I told my father that I was going to the conference, he told me to thank those who had liberated him for their bravery. When I was introduced to Major General Gorlinsky, I repeated my father's thanks for his bravery. "It was not I who was the brave one," he told me through an interpreter. "Your father was the brave one."[12]

The meeting with Elie Wiesel was an important one. In 1982 I published a revised version of my Jerusalem paper in the journal *Shoah*.[13] In the article I referred to Elie Wiesel as the last remaining voice of the She'erith Hapletah. A few months later I received a telephone call from Wiesel's office at the United States Holocaust Memorial Council, inquring about my interest in receiving an appointment to the council's Board of Advisers. Elie Wiesel had been named chair of the council with the mandate to build a Holocaust memorial museum in Washington. I eagerly accepted the offer of an appointment and was named to the board in 1984 and named vice chair of its Committee on Archives and Library two years later. The appointment would begin a decade-long relationship with the council and with the United States Holocaust Memorial Museum, which opened its doors to the public in the spring of 1993. In addition, in the early 1990s, I was elected to the vice presidency of the Association of Holocaust Organizations, an institution of more than a hundred Holocaust museums and centers around the world. I was the only board member not directly associated with a Holocaust museum.

Focus: German Jewry and Jewish Life in Germany

My interest in German Jewry was nearly as strong as my desire to understand why during the Nazi period that community of Jews became a *Schicksalsgemeinschaft* (community of fate). The year 1983 gave me a perfect opportunity to explore the question through an exhibit remembering the fiftieth anniversary of the Nazi *Machtergreifung* (seizure of power) in 1933. I planned the exhibit so that it would include the memories and observations of those German-Jewish refugees from Hitler who were living in Cincinnati. The community of those German Jews was large enough to enjoy its own synagogue, New Hope Congregation.[14] I also planned the exhibit as a tribute to the courage of these German Jews and to the new lives they had created for themselves in the lands of their immigration.

But I also wanted to make the exhibit reflect the national experience of those German Jews who had come to America as refugees. I approached the Leo Baeck Institute, the major institution devoted to the history of German-speaking Jewry, as well as the *Aufbau*, the newspaper founded by German-Jewish refugees from Nazi Germany in the 1930s, for help in collecting materials for the exhibit. I also invited Dr. Kurt Silberman, the president of the Federation of Jews from Central Europe, to give the main presentation at the opening of the exhibit.

On the evening of November 9, 1983, the forty-fifth anniversary of the infamous *Novemberpogrom* of 1938 that marked the end of German-Jewish life, the exhibit opened to a large audience, many of them German-Jewish refugees to America and their families. A surprise visitor that evening was Hans Steinitz, the distinguished editor of the *Aufbau*. Two weeks later, Steinitz reported on the exhibit in the pages of his newspaper:[15]

The impetus for this exhibit came from an idea by Abraham J. Peck, the young associate director of the American Jewish Archives. An accomplished historian with Polish roots, Peck was born in Germany and grew up there, and he has spent much of his professional career studying German and Jewish history. We German Jews can be satisfied with what we have fought for and accomplished. Here in this country—as in Israel and, to a modest degree, other countries as well—we have kept alive the torch that must be passed from one generation to another.

Six months later I was asked by the Cincinnati chapter of the American Jewish Committee (AJC), a human-rights organization founded in the early part of the twentieth century, to address a group of young German professionals who were visiting various American cities to see a "living American Judaism." The program was part of an exchange that had been developed between the AJC and Germany's Konrad Adenauer Stiftung. All the German visitors were recipients of Adenauer Stiftung grants and all were Christian, except one man.

It was that one man who drew my interest. He worked as a newspaper editor and publicist in Munich. Like me, he was a son of Holocaust survivors and, like me, he was born in a German DP camp. But unlike me, his parents, Polish-born Jews, had never left Germany. There was an immediate friendship between the two of us. I asked him how he felt about coming on this trip. "My mother would kill me if she knew I was here among all these conservative Germans," he told me. "Are there groups of sons and daughters of survivors who meet to discuss their identities in Germany, as there are here in the United States?" I asked him. "You American Jews are fortunate," he told me. "You live far from the scene of the crimes against us. We Jews in Germany live with the reality that the only way to escape the past is by leaving it, by leaving Germany. I would like to leave, but my mother is elderly and not well. I am her only child."

"So how do you cope?" I asked him. "We escape inside ourselves, sometimes by falling in love with German Christian men or women, who find us fascinating and perhaps a way to soften their own sense of guilt over the actions of their parents or grandparents during the Holocaust. We don't need to discuss our identities. We know exactly who we are: a generation of

Jewish men and women who blame their parents for staying in Germany; who blame ourselves for not leaving Germany. What more do we need to know?" I was, frankly, stunned. My assumption that the "revolution" sweeping through the children of Holocaust survivors in America was also taking place in other countries was obviously a wrong one. "Why don't you come to Germany and see for yourself what we have to endure?" he asked me. "See what 'Jewish life in Germany' is all about and how Germany continues to deal with its 'Jewish problem.'"

Two years later I received the opportunity to do just that. I was invited by the German Foreign Office to be part of a group of American "experts" asked to visit Germany to observe "Jewish life in Germany today." The trip was three weeks in November and December 1986. When I arrived in Frankfurt and was met by a representative of the German Foreign Office, I learned who my fellow "experts" were: Rabbi Malcolm Sparer, from San Francisco, was the head of the Northern California Board of Rabbis; Dr. Michael Nutkiewicz, the son of a Holocaust survivor, was the executive director of the Los Angeles Jewish Federation's Holocaust Museum; Dr. Mary Felstiner was a professor of history at San Francisco State University and was writing a biography of the German-Jewish artist, Charlotte Salomon;[16] and Charles Barrack, a Germanist from the University of Washington in Seattle, an Arab-American and the only non-Jew in the group.

The trip was extraordinary. We had our own van and driver between the many cities that we visited: Frankfurt, Cologne, Bonn, Worms, Heidenheim, Hamburg, and Berlin, where we visited Jewish communities in both the eastern and western parts of the city. There were many memorable parts of the trip: meeting with and discussing Germany's attitude towards its Jewish citizens with members of the German Bundestag; an evening meeting with a member of Helmut Kohl's Christian Democratic Party (CDU), who came to our hotel to ask us specifically about the plans for the Holocaust Memorial Museum to be built in Washington. He knew that I was a member of Elie Wiesel's advisory board. Could I ask Chairman Wiesel, he inquired, if plans for the museum could include a section on the "new Germany?" The German government would look favorably upon such a development.

I remember standing in the cemetery of the Jewish community of Worms, a city in which the famous Jewish philosopher, Rashi (Reb Shlomo Yitzchaki, 1040–1105) had lived and taught, in front of the grave of the Maharam (Meir of Rothenburg, ca. 1215–May 2, 1293), one of the great teachers of Jewish law, who was buried in the cemetery in 1307. Standing next to the grave, the oldest Jewish one in Europe, in a late-afternoon sun, was one of the most extraordinary moments I have ever experienced. It seemed as if all of European Jewish history was reflected in the rays of the setting November sun.

I remember going with Rabbi Sparer to Hamburg's notorious Reeperbahn, an area of brothels and sex shows, to seek out Jewish women who may have been lured to work in the "oldest profession" of prostitution in order to save them from sin. We did not find any, but Rabbi Sparer took me to places that no Jewish scholar should ever willingly visit.

I also remember sitting in the elegant Hamburg offices of the weekly journal, *Die Zeit,* speaking with former German chancellor Helmut Schmidt, the paper's coeditor. Rabbi Sparer was the most aggressive of our group and constantly pressed Schmidt on the issue of continuing anti-Semitism in Germany and the role of Holocaust memory in the country. Schmidt denied that there was any anti-Semitism in Germany, official or otherwise; he called his dear friend Eric Warburg, the last remaining member of the famous Jewish banking family to still live in Germany, asking him to please tell us that no such thing as anti-Semitism was a part of German life in 1986. Somehow, Warburg's comments did not satisfy us and especially not Rabbi Sparer, who pressed Schmidt on the steps that Germany was taking to normalize relations with its Jewish community. "It is not up to us," replied Schmidt. "It is up to the Jews."

We flew to Berlin, where we were met by officials from the Berlin Senate and chauffeured to our hotels in a line of black Mercedes, the means of travel for our entire stay in Berlin. We were supposed to meet with Heinz Galinski, perhaps the most powerful Jewish communal leader in all of Western Europe. His office told us that he was out of the country during the entire time of our stay in Berlin, but we ran into him accidentally in the offices of the Jewish Community Center. He spoke to us for five minutes and then left.

I was somewhat nervous as we crossed the border from West to East Berlin. It had been thirteen years since I had left the DDR, and I had never ordered the microfilms for the Deutsches Zentralarchiv. Could my name have been on a most-wanted list for nonpayment of a microfilm debt? The DDR border guards checked my passport and waved all of us through.

We met Peter Kirchner, the head of East Berlin's Jewish community and his son Gernot, a medical student, at a hotel in East Berlin for coffee and discussion. Accompanying the Kirchners was a woman who introduced herself as a member of the East Berlin city administration. We all knew better. Consequently, our "discussion" centered on the religious and cultural life of Jews in the DDR, relations with Jewish communities in the West, and the weather. But Kirchner did take us on a wonderful tour of the Berlin Weissensee cemetery, the largest in Europe. It was like walking through the pages of German-Jewish history as each gravestone after another revealed a name that had significance for the German-Jewish experience.

What, ultimately, did I learn about "Jewish life in Germany" during those three weeks? Like all government-sponsored trips, we saw and were introduced to those places and people that the government wanted us to see. Perhaps the only real deviation was the X-rated buildings of the Reeperbahn. We thus only scratched the surface of issues that our group and I thought crucial for our visit. A few weeks after my return to the United States, Cincinnati's *American Israelite* newspaper, founded by Rabbi Isaac Mayer Wise in 1854, asked me to comment on my trip to Germany:[17]

> Peck has returned to the United States with a number of disturbing insights about the character of the Jewish community in Germany and the way the current government is dealing with the Holocaust. "I felt great kinship with the Jewish people we visited. I was interested in what could have been if my parents had been unable to leave Germany."
>
> "Jews undoubtedly identify through the Holocaust," Peck says, "but they live in the land of the murderers and the murdered. The Holocaust is all around them. Monuments and ceremonies take on a different meaning." And an identity as German Jews? "It is shattered, there is no tradition anymore," Peck concludes.

What disturbed me as an academic was the state of Jewish studies in Germany. We visited a number of Judaica departments at various universities and found mostly non-Jewish academics teaching non-Jewish students. One could almost feel Jews and Judaism being talked about in a museum-like atmosphere, as if there were no living Jewish culture. It reminded me of the Nazi plan to build a museum for the "disappeared Jewish race."

In November 1987 I was invited to be the keynote speaker at a "Kristallnacht" program sponsored by the Northern California Board of Rabbis and the San Francisco Jewish Community Relations Council with cooperation from the Goethe Institute and the German Consulate in San Francisco. I was reunited with Rabbi Malcolm Sparer and Professors Mary Felstiner and Charles Barrack, and I met two Jewish academics teaching in Germany. The first was Professor Julius Schoeps, the son of Hans-Joachim Schoeps, a pioneer in German Christian-Jewish relations; Professor Schoeps taught at the University of Duisburg, which I had visited on my previous trip to Germany in 1986. The second was Professor Karlheinz Schneider, who taught at the Hochschule for Jewish Studies in Heidelberg; this was the official institution for the ordination of rabbis and cantors in Germany, although in all the years of its existence it had never ordained anyone.

I chose as the topic for my lecture "The Year Zero and the Development of Jewish Life in Germany after 1945." In part I explained that the current Jewish community in Germany drew its origins from the "surviving remnant" of Jews who remained for a multitude of reasons: refugees from East and West Europe, concentration camp survivors, Jews who hid during the war years, and those who intermarried with Germans or tired after waiting years for their emigration papers. By 1955, I told the audience, some 17,000 Jews remained in Germany, "a land soaked with Jewish blood," where they lived as pariahs, shunned and unwilling to accept the hand of reconciliation from a German government that they increasingly mistrusted.

The Jews in Germany could not bear the question they heard repeated by world Jewry, but especially American Jews: "How can you live there?" Their only response was to justify their right to exist, while the *Judenfrage* continued to haunt both the oppressor and the victim. Those of us who had been on the German trip appealed to the audience: it was time to open the gates of understanding between the Jewish communities in Germany and the United States. "For too long," Rabbi Sparer added, "American Jews have disregarded and stigmatized those Jews who for one reason or another have chosen to live in West Germany."[18]

The response from many members of the audience was surprising, at least in terms of its intensity. A number of individuals decried the intellectual and spiritual poverty of the Jewish community in Germany, its unwillingness to find common ideological ground with other world Jewish communities, and the future of its continued viability. Others insisted that Jews in Germany would be better off not living in the country, and one individual suggested that communal funds to Jews in Germany should be cut off. The evening was a difficult one for those of us who had gone to Germany and met Jews who were wonderful people and deserved the right to live where they chose to live as Jews and—if they or their children ultimately decided to—as Germans. The officials from the Goethe Institute were stunned by the reactions from audience members. They did not know whether to defend first those Jews living in Germany or the German government, which they felt had made important strides in "normalizing" relations with Jews in their nation, with Israel, and with world Jewry.

A Death in the Family and a Return to Roots

On March 7, 1988, at 7 a.m. in the morning, the telephone rang at our house. It was early for the phone to ring, and I assumed it was a friend of my son or daughter calling about school. I answered the phone and heard the sad, slow words from my father: "Oh, Abe, your mother is no longer alive. She had a heart attack in her sleep this morning and I could do nothing to save her." I remember screaming, "No!" as my mind refused to accept what I was hearing on the other end of the phone. I had never known death in my family, except through the stories of my father. I was devastated as my wife and children ran to comfort me. That safe, often turbulent, warmth that was the world inhabited by the three of us, father, mother, and son, was shattered forever. The three of us, who had struggled against a world that had done so much to deprive them of a normalcy taken for granted by others, were now only two.

I do not know how I flew to Florida to help my father with the funeral arrangements. My father, normally a stoic and calm individual, the peacemaker in our family, could not function. He again became the child to my fathering as he had done when a letter needed to be written or a bill interpreted in the early years of our lives in America. When we went to the funeral home where my mother's body had been taken, I begged the funeral director to let me see her, if just for a moment. In Jewish funeral practice, such a request is not allowed by ritual law, but when the director heard the circumstances of my mother's death, he reluctantly agreed. I looked at my mother for the last time. Wrapped in a ceremonial white shroud, she looked calm, almost asleep. I noticed that her face was set in a smile, showing a happiness and a calm that I had never before seen. Perhaps, I thought, she is finally with her seven brothers, something she talked about and wished for as long as I could remember.

The funeral itself was small, with a few people from my parent's building and my wife and children. The rabbi who officiated at the funeral was a former rabbinical student at HUC-JIR, and I knew him well. He asked me if I wanted to say a few words, but I could not. My father and I sat shivah, the seven-day period of mourning, for my mother. I remember sleeping on the cold floor with my father because he could not bear to sleep in the bed in which my mother had died, and I could not bear to let him sleep there alone. For the first time in many years, my father woke up screaming during the night or swore that he saw my mother's apparition floating across the room at the first light of daybreak.

I returned to Cincinnati, worried about the well-being of my father, who had just turned seventy-five. Our many friends came over to console me, and they all commented on how sad I looked, much sadder than they had ever seen a son in mourning for a parent. How could I tell them what I felt? A world that my parents and I had created, a world that allowed almost no one else to penetrate its thick barrier, had been shaken to its foundations. Even while we lived several thousand miles apart, my parents and I were connected by a past that was always with us. Perhaps the "black box" that Helen Epstein described had a different set of contents from mine, and perhaps my mother's death had released them for the first time. But would I know what to do with those contents?

In 1988 my life would be forever altered by the death of my mother. Not only was there a hole in my being, something that is true for almost any son or daughter who loses a loved one, but a hole was placed in my world, and even the love of a wife and children could not entirely fill it. But in Judaism, after a year of mourning, life must go on. I tried to follow this teaching by occupying myself with several publishing projects. The results were reflected in two books that I published in 1989, each one as editor.[19]

I also received a telephone call from Colonel Irving Heymont, the American military commander of the Landsberg DP camp who had come there only two weeks after my parents' arrival in August 1945. Several years earlier, quite by accident, I had received, without any previous knowledge, a packet of letters written by Irving Heymont to his wife in the four months that he was in the Landsberg DP camp. I was astonished at the story, because it was my parents' story. I quickly contacted Heymont, told him who I was, and offered to publish his letters under the imprint of the American Jewish Archives. The book was published in 1982 and quickly became one of the most important primary sources on the history of the Jewish DP camps.[20]

I had kept in touch with Heymont and his wife, Joan, having dinner with them whenever I was in Washington for meetings at the Holocaust Museum. Heymont had also kept in touch with members of the Landsberg community, including its mayor, Franz Xaver Roessle. Now in 1989 Irving Heymont was undertaking a project to make certain that the events of the Landsberg DP camp would be remembered. He was financing the creation of a memorial plaque that would be placed on the front of the former DP camp, now in its last stages of use as a combined American and German military facility. The ceremony would take place on September 10, 1989. Would I be the main speaker on the program, he asked me? I had not been back to Landsberg since that cold winter day in 1971 when I could not gain access to the Saarburgkaserne to visit the place of my birth.

I told Heymont that I would come. I arrived in Landsberg two days before the dedication of the plaque. After those two days neither Heymont nor I was certain that Landsberg was ready to rediscover a chapter of its post-1945 history. Every time we had gone to dine at one of the charming old restaurants in the middle of the town, we had had to endure angry stares from the other diners. Heymont received a letter from a resident of Landsberg who claimed that she would disrupt the ceremony. Why? Because she wanted Heymont to apologize for supposedly authorizing a survivor "day of rage" in which, she claimed, the DP camp Jews beat a number of Landsberg residents, including a group of young children on their way to a church communion. Even more threatening, a right-wing revisionist from a neighboring community announced plans to pass out anti-Israel materials in front of the Saarburgkaserne. Perhaps most discouraging to Irving Heymont was the fact that a children's fair was scheduled in the center of Landsberg at the same time as our ceremony.

Before the ceremony I met with three young Germans who were certain they knew why Landsberg's reaction to our planned event had been less than enthusiastic. Edith Raim was then a twenty-four-year old student of history. In 1983 she was among a group of Landsberg high-school students who won a first-prize award in a national history competition sponsored by the president of the Federal Republic of Germany. The theme of the competition was daily life in the Third Reich. Raim and her fellow researchers decided to investigate the history of a Nazi plan called Project Ringeltaube—the creation of a jet aircraft that would turn the war in favor of Germany—and the eleven satellite camps of Dachau in the region around Landsberg and the nearby village of Kaufering.

The others I met with were Martin Paulus, an artist, and Thomas Riemerschmid, an architect. Both men were in their late twenties and had attended the same gymnasium as Edith Raim. They were the creators of a monument that stood in front of one of the remaining barracks of the Kaufering VII camp. The monument was made of wood with two holes on each side. The entire monument was supposed to represent the face of a Kaufering prisoner, tormented and in pain. The railroad tracks also represented the connection to the deportation of the Kaufering prisoners.

Paulus told me that the history of Landsberg from Hitler's incarceration to the execution of war criminals after 1945 was like a theater drama that only a mad playwright could have written: "This history has been too much for Landsberg," he told me. "It is impossible for the town to try and work through it," he said. "Let me give you an example. The hotel you're staying in was the place where the families of the war criminals stayed awaiting their loved ones' execution or their release. And across the street from the hotel, that used to be a restaurant that Hitler would visit on his free weekends from prison. It's simply too much for so small a town."

Anton Posset, who taught all three students at the Dominikus Zimmerman Gymnasium, and was the driving force behind a citizen's group in Landsberg that was determined to compel the town to face its own past, agreed with Paulus when I met with him. "There is probably no city in all of Germany that has to carry such a burden from the Nazi past," he told me. Posset had come to Landsberg in 1975 to teach history and French at the gymnasium. It was during an initial class project that he first discovered the existence of the Jewish DP camp. According to Edith Raim, very little information about the Kaufering camps existed in the city archives. Most of it was found at the Institut für Zeitgeschichte in Munich and in other German and American archives. When it came to doing oral histories, Edith Raim and her fellow researchers had an especially difficult time. "People would either not talk about the period," she told me, "or they would recount how they provided food for the prisoners."

Even though their project won a first-place award in the national history contest, there was not much joy in Landsberg. Edith Raim and other students received telephone threats and were told to stop searching for things that were none of their business. At his school Anton Posset ran into difficulties with his fellow teachers. He was accused of being a disruptive force in the life of the school and verbally abusing other teachers. Finally, much to his shock, Posset discovered that his own school's headmaster had been a guard at one of the local concentration camp sites; the headmaster told Posset and his students that he, the headmaster, had seen only "well-nourished and well-dressed prisoners." When I first met Anton Posset on the day before the dedication of the DP camp plaque, he was nervous, even agitated. He took me on a tour of the Kaufering camps. He would occasionally sweep his hand across the site of the camp where we stood and almost shout that "this is what they want to deny ever happened here!" The "they" ranged from ordinary citizens to his high-school colleagues to local and regional politicians.

The time for the dedication ceremony finally came. My speech tried to reconstruct the life of the Jewish DP camp in Landsberg. I based my words on letters that Irving Heymont had written to his wife while he was in the camp, on the Yiddish newspaper the *Landsberger Lager-Cajtung*, which was published there, and on conversations with my parents. I told the audience about the ideology of the survivors, created in Landsberg by Dr. Samuel Gringauz, perhaps the most original thinker among the Jewish DPs. "Here in Landsberg," I said, "the voice of the survivors, the one that sought to change human and Jewish destiny, was born. Here, I will not allow it to die."

After the ceremony I thought about all that had taken place. I had returned to the place of my birth. That part of my curiousity had been satisfied. But I was still curious. Could the courageous young people I met, as well as the very vocal and dynamic Anton Posset, could they have made Landsberg into the site of a new beginning for those Jews and Germans who shared the legacy and burden of its recent, terrible history? What better place, I wondered, to allow the silence of a generation to be buried than in the place where the Holocaust was born?

11

A (Mis) Step in the Direction of Reconciliation?

My research on the Jewish DP camps and my role as a consultant to the United States Holocaust Memorial Museum allowed me to meet some of the most outstanding scholars in the area of Holocaust studies. One of those meetings led to an invitation to present a paper on the ideology of the She'erith Hapletah at the 1991 conference on the Holocaust and the German Church Struggle. This conference was the oldest extant annual program on the Holocaust in the United States, created in 1970 by two distinguished academics, Franklin Littell, then at Temple University, and Hubert Locke, then at Wayne State University in Detroit.

The conference was a March meeting at the Richard Stockton College of New Jersey, not far from Atlantic City. I had never been to that part of New Jersey and looked forward to meeting both Littell and Locke. A number of familiar names were on the conference program, but one name and topic immediately caught my attention. Gottfried Wagner was to present a paper on the "Legacy of Richard Wagner and his Music." Gottfried Wagner was the great-grandson of the German composer, Richard Wagner, one of the cultural giants of German history and a known influence on the development of German anti-Semitism. Holocaust denial was very much an issue in 1991. Could this Wagner have any connection to that movement? I could not believe that a distinguished conference such as the Holocaust and Church Struggle would let someone of that persuasion present a paper.

When I arrived at Stockton, a medium-sized rural institution, the entire conference was discussing the appearance of Gottfried Wagner. A number of conference participants, as well as the large number of Holocaust survivors coming to the lecture, were concerned with what Wagner might say.

There was talk of a demonstration as well as verbal diatribes at the session in which Wagner was to speak. I had not heard of Gottfried Wagner, but I was very aware of the Wagner family legacy in German history. Yet I could not believe that the organizers of the conference would invite someone in line with such thinking. But that did not deter a state of near frenzy among the conference participants and the Holocaust survivors who were attending the evening's lecture.

The lecture was scheduled for 7:30 p.m. When I arrived at the large hall at about 7:15, there were only a few seats left. Ultimately, there would be a standing-room-only crowd to hear the great-grandson of Richard Wagner. I heard survivors sitting in seats around me talk about their concentration camp experiences: hearing Richard Wagner's music played as they marched off to their work assignments each morning and again when they came back to their barracks, sometimes fourteen hours later. How could the organizers of the conference do this to us, they asked each other? Professor Hubert Locke was the moderator of the program. Locke was one of the few African Americans working in the area of Holocaust Studies. He was a kindly, intellectual man, and I would have an excellent relationship with him over the next several years. But this evening Professor Locke took a very rigid approach to the rules of the lecture. There would be no questions taken from the audience after Gottfried Wagner's lecture. Attendants would, however, collect written questions from those in attendance, and Professor Locke would choose those questions that he felt were appropriate.

Gottfried Wagner was introduced to the audience as the son of Wolfgang Wagner, the director of the Bayreuth Wagner Festival. Gottfried was a musicologist with a PhD from the University of Vienna, where he had written his dissertation on the musical composers Kurt Weill and Bertold Brecht. He had visited Israel a few months earlier where he spoke on the controversy surrounding the banning of Wagner's music in the country, a ban that had been in place for decades. I heard the survivors whispering to each other when they heard that Gottfried Wagner had spoken in Israel. The tension in the room seemed to relax somewhat.

Gottfried presented an imposing figure. He was tall and well dressed and bore an extraordinary resemblance to his great-grandfather, especially the characteristic "Wagner nose." He began to speak and one could note immediately that he was not fluent in English. His heavy German accent made it difficult for many to understand his words, and he had great difficulty pronouncing many of them. But he spoke well enough to make clear that he was not his father's son as far as the music and legacy of Richard Wagner was concerned. Indeed, he denounced his great-grandfather for his avowed anti-Semitism and did the same for his "anti-Semitic" family that included his great-uncle, Houston Stewart Chamberlain, and his grandmother, Winifred Wagner, whom he accused of being a loyal follower of Adolf Hitler and a Holocaust denier. He appealed to the members of the audience to understand that he had broken with his family, with Germany, and with the politics of the repression of the Nazi past. He lived in Italy, was married to an Italian woman, and considered her family to be his family as well. His father had recently banned him from the Bayreuth Festival grounds. Finally, he called for reconciliation between Germans and Jews and the beginning of a dialogue that would lead to such reconciliation.

There was uproar from the audience, but it was not against Gottfried Wagner. It was for him. The survivors stood and applauded this man who had sacrificed his professional and financial success as the heir to his father and the financial empire that was the Bayreuth Wagner Festival. But still, there would be no verbal questions from the audience, only written ones. I decided to write a question and submit it to the usher. It took Hubert Locke some minutes to sort out the questions written on the notecards, and then he began by asking mine as the first one. "Dr. Wagner," he said, "I have a question from Abraham Peck. He would like to know if you are aware that in Judaism there can be no reconciliation without forgiveness and that forgiveness is only possible between a victim and his perpetrator. He states that you and he are neither victim nor perpetrator and that the victims, in this case the millions of Jewish men, women, and children murdered in the Holocaust, can hardly offer forgiveness." Gottfried Wagner did not really know how to respond except to state that he, as a Roman Catholic, was unaware of this position on reconciliation in Judaism. He only knew that it was important for Jews and Germans of his generation to begin to talk to each other honestly so that some of the shame and guilt that he felt as a "son of perpetrators," as he called himself, might be lessened.

The program that evening went on for a very long time. The audience, especially the survivors, rushed to the stage to speak with Gottfried Wagner, to applaud him for his position, and to tell him how much they admired what he had done with his life and what he had said about the music and politics of Richard Wagner. I, too, was surprised by what Gottfried Wagner had said. In all my years of living and researching in Germany, this was the first German I had met who spoke with an honesty that was extraordinary to behold. I was troubled by his call for reconciliation because that seemed to be the watchword of how Germans understood their relationship to Jews. It seemed, in my experience, that any time Germans and Jews came together, formally or otherwise, it was taken by the German side as a "step toward reconciliation." It was a phrase that bothered me each time I saw it. The position was insensitive to the feelings of the Jews to whom it was directed, because the Germans never bothered to inquire if the Jewish side also saw their meeting as a *Schritt nach Versöhnung* (a step toward reconciliation), which, of course, they did not. My great fear was that, in his anguish and his desire to reconcile, Gottfried would ask me to forgive him for the actions of his family toward Jews and Judaism for over a century. I immediately thought back to the dilemma created for the future Nazi-hunter, Simon Wiesenthal, when he was asked, during his time as a concentration camp prisoner, to forgive a dying SS man for murders the young Nazi had committed during a roundup of Jews.[1]

Wiesenthal could not and would not forgive the dying man. I could not and would not forgive Gottfried if he asked because I was not a victim and he was not a perpetrator. It was true that in Jewish tradition a direct victim could forgive a direct perpetrator. But most Holocaust survivors could never take that most agonizing of steps without incurring the stilled voices of six million Jewish men, women, and children who screamed in silence: "Do not forgive, do not forget."[2]

Much later that evening Gottfried Wagner sought me out at a reception in the hotel in which we were staying. He asked if we might talk because he wanted to know more about the Jewish understanding of *Versöhnung*. We found a table and began to talk. We spoke for hours, until early in the morning. I was fascinated by Gottfried's story, and he listened to mine. He had attended my presentation so that he knew about my birth in Landsberg. He told me that in 1924 his grandmother, Winifred, had sent Adolf Hitler, whom she greatly admired, a package of items. The package went to the prison in Landsberg where Adolf Hitler was a prisoner because of his attempt to overthrow the Bavarian government in November 1923, in cooperation with the revered World War I general, Erich Ludendorff. Hitler had asked Gottfried's grandmother for stationery, and she had sent it. Hitler would use that paper to dictate to his faithful secretary, Rudolf Hess, his vision of Germany's past, present, and future. He would call the completed work *Mein Kampf.*

The hour grew very late, and we could no longer carry on the conversation. We were exhausted. We would both be leaving the conference the next day. "Could we continue our conversation by mail," Gottfried asked. "There is much that I need to ask you about your life and the sufferings of your family. It is very important to me that we begin a dialogue without a need to discuss reconciliation." I told Gottfried about my visit to Landsberg in 1989 and my feeling that perhaps in that city, a place where his history and mine intersected in such an ironic way, a genuine dialogue between post-Holocaust Germans and Jews might begin. "Perhaps Landsberg can still be the center of our dialogue," Gottfried told me. "It means much to both of us, our lives and identities as Germans and Jews."

I agreed to continue our discussions. I needed to understand what such a dialogue would seek to accomplish. If we did not have reconciliation as a goal, what, then, was our purpose? "You spoke in your lecture," Gottfried said, "about a survivor ideology that sought to change the world and bring back a sense of humanity to a world that had lost it during the Holocaust. Might that be a purpose we could discuss?" I agreed. The spirit of the She'erith Hapletah would have wanted me to do so.

12

Holocaust, Genocide, and the Clash of Civilizations (1992–2005)

During the early 1990s I had focused more and more of my academic and professional interests on the Holocaust. For nearly seven years, from 1987 to 1993, I acted as an advisor to various directors of the United States Holocaust Memorial Council, Museum, and Research Institute. I was also appointed the vice chair of the Museum's Committee on Archives and Library, with the daunting challenge of helping to envision and then create a world-class archives and library on the Holocaust. In 1993 I organized the first international conference to honor the opening of the USHHM's Research Institute. Over one hundred scholars from four continents attended, and in 1998 I coedited and introduced an eight-hundred-page volume of papers from that event with my friend and colleague, the distinguished Holocaust scholar and the Research Institute's first director, Professor Michael Berenbaum.[1] Finally, I was elected vice president of the Association of Holocaust Organizations, an organization that represented dozens of Holocaust museums and centers around the world.

The year 1995 marked the fiftieth anniversary of the end of World War II and the Holocaust. It was a year of much excitement and activity for me. I traveled once more to Landsberg at the invitation of Lord Mayor Franz Xaver Roessle, to participate in the fiftieth-anniversary commemoration of the liberation of the Kaufering/Landsberg concentration camps. I was reunited with Colonel Irving Heymont and Anton Posset, and I also met a wonderful group of survivors of those camps who had traveled from the United States, Israel, and various European countries to be present at the series of events planned by the towns of Kaufering and Landsberg.

Among the most memorable of the survivors were Uri Chanoch, the chair of the Israeli Kaufering/Landsberg survivor group; Solly Ganor, another Israeli survivor and a well-respected author; Mark Weinberg, from Chicago, who had been the manager of the Landsberg DP boxing team; Bernard Marks, one of the youngest of the survivors; and Harry Guterman, whom I had met just a few months earlier in his adopted home town of Tulsa, Oklahoma, when Gottfried and I spoke there at a conference. Harry and his late wife, Ursula, z"l, were generous and marvelous hosts. I would form a warm friendship with Harry, as would Gottfried. Harry came from the Polish town of Konstantynów, near Łódź, and was also in the Łódź ghetto at the same time as my parents. A few years after Ursula died, Harry remarried. His second wife is a remarkable woman from Israel whom he had known in the Łódź ghetto. Her name is Frania, and she was also in Stutthof and Dresden at the same time as my mother, of blessed memory.

But the most memorable of the survivors was Fritz Schaffranek who had converted to Christianity after his liberation from Kaufering and become a Lutheran pastor. He admitted to me in a moment of reminiscence that he still enjoyed a "good piece of kugel," an East European Jewish delicacy. Pastor Schaffranek held the unenviable position of having to listen to the anti-Jewish remarks of his congregants, none of whom knew about his Jewish heritage.

I received a wonderful invitation in the beginning of 1995 from a colleague and former academic fellow at the American Jewish Archives, the Austrian historian Thomas Albrich. Thomas was one of the first scholars to research the history of Holocaust survivors in Austria.[2] A professor at the Institut für Zeitgeschichte at the University of Innsbruck, he wanted his students to have an opportunity to learn about the American Jewish experience and to enter into a dialogue with a member of the American Second Generation. The invitation was timed to coincide with the fiftieth anniversary of the end of the Second World War. Albrich had the support of the Institut's longtime director, Professor Rolf Steininger. I received an appointment as a visting lecturer/guest professor for an intensive course on American Jewish history and the Holocaust.

Although Innsbruck, and especially its old city, was beautiful, and the Austrian Alps with their snow-capped peaks that surrounded the city took my breath away as I gazed at them from my office, the image of Austria in the Jewish and international communities at this time was not a very good one. Unlike Germany, Austria had not even made a public effort to confront the Holocaust. It maintained a convenient myth, created by the Allies as early as 1943 in the so-called Moscow Declaration, that the country had been Nazi Germany's "first victim." Less than a decade before my arrival, the former secretary general of the United Nations, Kurt Waldheim, had been elected Austria's president despite the revelations that his Wehrmacht service in Yugoslavia during the Second World War may have included massacres against the civilian population and the deportation of Jews to death camps in Poland. His election provoked international outrage and ostracism and a war of words between Austria and the World Jewish Congress, an organization that was seen by many Austrians as the focus of an international "Jewish conspiracy."

It was also in 1995 that Jörg Haider, the leader of Austria's Freedom Party, a party that advocated "freedom" from Jews, freedom from Sinti and Roma, and freedom from all foreign immigration and Balkan refugees, characterized former SS officers as "men of character" who sent criminals to "punishment camps." But these students, I reckoned, were an elite group, studying at an institute renowned for its research and writing on the plight of Jews in the Austrian Tyrol and on anti-Semitism during the Nazi years and staffed by progressive academics like Thomas Albrich and Rolf Steininger.

I could not have been more mistaken. My class of some twenty students, most of them between twenty and twenty-four years of age, was interested in my lecture on the various groups of European Jews who made up the largest group of Jewish immigrants to America. They seemed proud of the fact that an Austrian-Jewish immigrant, August Bondi, rode with the famed abolitionist John Brown. They were less impressed with my discussion of East European Jewish immigration between the 1880s and the early 1920s. "We know all about the Galician Jews with their *Zoepferl* [earlocks] and their *Kaeppi* [yarmulke or skull cap]," one student told me. "Have you ever met one?" I asked her. She said, "No, but we used to have lots of them in Austria before the War."

My lecture on America and the Holocaust took a convenient detour to describe the post-1945 attitudes of both Germans and Austrians to their small Jewish communities, made up primarily of displaced East European Jewish survivors. Opinion polls in both nations found attitudes toward those Jews ranged from outright hostility (they were being given special privileges denied to non-Jewish Germans and Austrians) to a view of Jews as "black marketers" and spreaders of venereal disease.

Because of the "first victim" myth, Austria did not, as did Germany, have to adjust its attitudes toward its Jewish community as a litmus test of readmission to the community of "civilized" nations. I was very clear about the actual facts that disproved the "first victim" concept. "Do you know about Karl Lueger (1844–1910), the (moderately) anti-Semitic mayor of Vienna at the end of the nineteenth century?" I asked them. "Do you know about Georg von Schonerer (1842–1921), the nineteenth-century Austrian politician who was an early advocate of racial anti-Semitism and Pan-Germanism? Have you ever read Hugo Bettauer's futuristic and satirical novel, *Die Stadt ohne Juden. Ein Roman von Uebermorgen* [The City Without Jews: A Novel of Our Time] written in 1922 and which foreshadowed the Holocaust by postulating a scenario in which the city of Vienna passed a law making it illegal for any Jew to live in the city?" Bettauer, a Protestant Christian, wrote the book as a kind of comic fantasy, satirizing anti-Semitism as ridiculous. Two years later, in 1924, Bettauer was shot and killed by a self-proclaimed "Aryan" who saw Bettauer and his work as a menace to German *Kultur.*

"Has not Bettauer's fantasy become a near reality?" I asked them. Vienna's prewar population that numbered over 200,000 Jewish residents at its height today numbers fewer than 10,000. Finally, I told them about the long list of "illustrious" Austrians who made up a large percentage of the most heinous of the Nazi war criminals: apart from Adolf Hitler, there were Adolf Eichmann, responsible for deportations of Jews from the German Reich and most of occupied Europe; Odilo Globocnik, a gauleiter of Vienna, who supervised the death camps in Poland; Ernst Kaltenbrunner, who succeeded the assassinated Reinhard Heydrich as head of the RSHA (the Reich Head Security Office), which coordinated the bureaucratic portions of the Final Solution; and Arthur Seyss-Inquart, Reich commissioner of the Netherlands, who was responsible for the deportation of Dutch Jews. In addition, I continued, at least 40 percent of the personnel and most of the commandants of the death camps at Belzec, Sobibor, and Treblinka were Austrians as were 80 percent of Adolf Eichmann's staff.

Was this the history of National Socialism's "first victim?" Some of the students agreed with my assessment, but many others insisted that even if these statistics were true (but some were "fabricated" by Simon Wiesenthal, the Vienna-based Nazi hunter, they told me), the fact that a Jew, Bruno Kreisky, was elected chancellor in 1970 showed that anti-Semitism did not play a role in today's Austria. The same could not be said, they insisted, for the *Pifkes,* as they referred derogatorily to the Germans, especially those from the former region of Prussia.

Exasperated, I did not mention that Bruno Kreisky played down his Jewish background and tended to minimize Austrian anti-Semitism. He was a rabid anti-Zionist and appointed several ex-Nazis to his political cabinet. The students replied that America had allowed many more Nazis to enter after 1945 than Kreisky had appointed. I then sought to interest the students in the issue of *Familiengeschichte,* telling them how important it was for their generation to ask parents and grandparents about the Nazi period and describing my dialogue with Gottfried. "Many of us have," they told me, "at least of our parents' generation. Our grandparents are too old and we could not hurt them with these kinds of questions."

What did it mean for the dialogue between Second Generation Jews and Austrians? I assumed that unlike the Second and Third Generations in Germany, who seemed to have created for themselves a new direction as a "society of victims," either discarding or seeking to bring balance to their self-understanding as a perpetrator society, Austrians, at least since the late 1980s, had overthrown the myth of being the "first victim" of National Socialism and had begun to accept their role as a society that participated in monstrous expressions of anti-Semitism during the Reichspogrom of November 9–10, 1938, and in the near destruction of European Jewish life.[3]

But had Austrians really given up the effort to live a lie, a *Verdrängung,* a repression of the truth that had lasted for more than four decades? Would they be able to "mourn" for the generations of Austrians and their government who had thrived under that lie and in the process denied the legitimate claims of their victims, whether Jewish or Roma, while at the same time allowing thousands of "little" and "big" Nazis the right to return to productive and peaceful lives after 1945? How would our two Second Generations be able to find a common understanding of what needed to be understood by Austrians and by Jews?

My time in Innsbruck was revealing. I recognized that Gottfried and I had created something special in the Post-Holocaust Dialogue Group, something that was clearly a minority among minorities. The memory of the Holocaust was still a battlefield where many sat on the fences, not knowing which way to react: was it appropriate for Germans and Austrians to pursue discussions that should have been created on the day after the end of the Second World War regarding the roles played by Nazi perpetrators and the millions of bystanders who contributed to the Final Solution by doing nothing in order to benefit from the murder of millions? Which generation after 1945 was the most appropriate to establish a real dialogue between Germans, Austrians, and Jews? How was memory about the Holocaust, both individual and collective, created and toward what ends?

Holocaust and Genocide

At the end of 1996, I received a telephone call from an international recruiting firm, asking if I would be interested in discussing the possibility of becoming the director of a new Holocaust museum in Houston, Texas. The newly built museum, at the time the third largest Holocaust museum in the United States, behind Washington, D.C. and Los Angeles, was located in a city of four million people and contained a Jewish population of over 50,000; approximately 400 were Holocaust survivors.

So began a series of visits to Houston to see the facility and to meet the large board of over sixty directors. By the beginning of 1997, I had agreed to accept the position of executive director of Holocaust Museum Houston. In a letter that I addressed to the Holocaust survivors of Houston, I wrote that "when your fathers and mothers, brothers and sisters, your sons and daughters, in the last moments of their lives, beseeched you to survive, to tell the world what was done to them, you took a vow. Now you have asked the Second Generation to repeat the vow, never to stop telling the world what you endured, what you witnessed—the collapse of our civilization. In my capacity as the executive director . . . in my capacity as a son of survivors, let me tell you: I accept this awesome responsibility. This museum will share the story of the few who saved you, and it will tell the story of those who sought to destroy you or who stood by and did nothing."[4]

I held the position of executive director of Holocaust Museum Houston for the years 1997 and 1998. During that time I became more and more aware that if the Holocaust was to mean anything to those beyond the Jewish community and present its lessons to the world, it would have to share our understanding of the genocidal society, of the victim, bystander, and perpetrator in history, with other watershed events of the twentieth century. I was more and more convinced that it was Jewish victimization that had driven Jewry to maintain the idea that, through our tragedies, the world would learn about the human condition. Perhaps that was the role that we were appointed in some grand, cosmic scheme.

Four events stand out in my mind during those years, events that gave me greater insight into this consideration. The first was my encounter with Peter Balakian, a professor of English at Colgate University in New York state, whose memoir, *Black Dog of Fate: An American Son Uncovers His Armenian Past*,[5] allowed me to understand that other sons and daughters of other genocides could also experience a transformation of their identity through an understanding of their family history. I invited Professor Balakian to speak at Holocaust Museum Houston, and his lecture was given to a standing-room-only audience of Holocaust survivors and children and grandchildren of Armenian genocide survivors, the first time that this community had joined the Houston Jewish community for a public event.

The second event was a visit to my office by an Iraqi Kurd, a Muslim who came to see me and share with me photographs of a horrendous event that had taken place in the Iraqi village of Halabja where a poison gas attack authorized by Saddam Hussein killed some 5,000 Iraqi Kurdish villagers in March 1988 at the end of the bitter Iran-Iraq war. "Please help us through your museum," the Kurdish gentleman asked me, "to tell all of Houston and the world about the war of genocide that is being waged against the Iraqi Kurds by Saddam Hussein." I was shocked at the pictures of dead men, women, and children so reminiscent of photographs taken during the Holocaust. On a beautiful autumn day members of Holocaust Museum Houston and Houston's Kurdish community planted a tree on the museum grounds and installed a plaque commemorating the victims of Halabja.

The third event was my effort to create a Polish-Jewish dialogue between members of the Polish Catholic community and Holocaust survivors from Poland. The dialogue was a bitter, difficult affair highlighting the very different views of Polish Christians and Jews on their suffering and experiences during the Holocaust. The dialogue was moderated by the Catholic Bishop of Houston-Galveston and future president of the American National Conference of Catholic Bishops, Joseph Fiorenza. During a particularly difficult phase of the dialogue, when both sides were shouting accusations at each other, Bishop Fiorenza asked both sides to calm themselves and listen to him for a moment. "If you consider that it took Catholics and Jews nearly twenty centuries to create a new relationship through the promulgation of the statement *Nostra Aetate* [In Our Time] during the Second Vatican Council under Pope John XXIII, your road to a new relationship will be, I am certain, a much shorter one." And finally, I was approached by representatives of the Jehovah's Witnesses and invited to participate in a conference in Brazil on Jews and Jehovah's Witnesses during the Holocaust.

My father, of blessed memory, had told me of seeing men with a purple triangle in Buchenwald, without knowing who they were or what the triangle represented. In my research before delivering lectures in Rio de Janeiro and Sao Paulo, I came to the conclusion that Jews were without choices during the Holocaust, condemned to die under any and all circumstances. But Jehovah's Witnesses did have choices. They could sign a form renouncing their beliefs as a *Bibelforscher*—the German name for the Jehovah's Witnesses—and be freed from their concentration camp imprisonment. Hardly any did, and many were murdered through torture and beheading. They truly died *al Kiddush haShem* (for the sanctification of God's name) in ways that Jews did not because Jews had no such choices.

In the year 2000, after I had left Holocaust Museum Houston to become the director of operations and research for the American Jewish Historical Society in New York, I was privileged to participate in an historic program at the Ludwig-Maximilians University in Munich on Janurary 27, the date observed by many European nations as the day of Holocaust remembrance. At this program, in which I delivered a lecture entitled "Eine echte Stunde Null? Deutsche und Juden auf der Suche nach neuen Anfängen" [A Genuine Zero Hour? Germans and Jews in Search of New Beginnings], I shared the podium with Sinti and Roma survivors, Jehovah's Witnesses survivors, witnesses to the activities of the Weissen Rose (White Rose) anti-Nazi movement at the University of Munich, and anti-Nazi resistance fighters.

Our sense of being a *Schicksalsgemeinde,* a community of fate, even though we were from different religious and national backgrounds, gave me a new understanding of the wars waged by the National Socialists. There was a war against the Jews that the Nazis won, if not in actuality, then certainly in terms of the trauma and the losses inflicted on the Jewish people and on the survivors and the following generations. But there was also a Nazi war against human values, and there the victims included members of the gay community, Jehovah's Witnesses, Sinti and Roma, the handicapped, and Western civilization itself.

Holocaust and the Clash of Civilizations

In 1999 my wife's mother began to suffer from various illnesses that included increasing dementia. We drove from Westchester County, New York, where we had our home, to Portland, Maine, nearly every weekend so that my wife could be with her mother. At the same time the daily commute from my home to New York City, a journey of over ninety minutes each way, began to exhaust me. Such commutes are done with ease by people under fifty, but at the age of fifty-three it was becoming very difficult.

For over a year, we drove the 500 miles round-trip each weekend to see my mother-in-law as her health became more fragile. One day my wife said to me, "I have wanted to move back to Portland, Maine, for thirty years. It is the most comfortable place in the world for me. I have my mother here, as well as my brother, my aunt and uncle and cousins. My other brother and sister live within two hours' drive. This could be our last chance to move to Portland and begin new careers." She had certainly paid her dues, living in cities where I had gone for employment. Yet, she was hardly an appendage. A highly successful editor, teacher, and television producer, she had also published an acclaimed book on the history of four Holocaust survivors, from their early family histories to their suffering during the Holocaust and their ultimate success in America as respected medical professionals.[6]

I liked the beauty and easier pace of life that was Maine. But could I, used to the finest research facilities, international travel, and the amenities of the big city, adjust to a community of 65,000 people? Reluctantly, but with the understanding of how much my wife loved Portland and the state of Maine, I said I would join her in recreating ourselves for a new life. Change, I thought, is good—usually. Fortunately, we had been coming to Portland during summers and for family occasions for over thirty years. We had built up a network of family and friends, and when they heard that we had decided to move to Portland, they sprang into action.

Within weeks I had an interview with the president and provost of the University of Southern Maine to discuss the possibility of joining the university in some capacity. But what strengths did I have that would allow me to sell myself to an academic institution of over 10,000 students and three campuses? In the end, after numerous negotiations and the vision and enthusiasm of Richard Pattenaude, the president of the university, and Joseph Wood, the provost, an offer was made to me, one that I accepted at once. I would join the Univesity of Southern Maine in three capacities: as director of an institute on what we called "Post-Holocaust Christian, Jewish and Islamic Studies"; I would become a full adjunct professor in the department of history; and I would become the scholar-in-residence of the Judaica collection for the Sampson Center for Diversity in Maine, an archival and research facility located in the university's Glickman Library.

In many respects, this was an extraordinary opportunity. I would be able to utilize my interests in interreligious dialogue and study; my growing interest in the broader questions of genocide and the Holocaust; and my twenty-five years of experience directing the major archival and research institutions in the world focused on the American-Jewish experience. I joined the University of Southern Maine in January 2001. My wife found a position at the university teaching media studies and directing the media studies student intern placements. Almost immediately I made an effort to contact the major religious organizations in Portland. I met with Tom Ewell, the longtime director of the Maine Council of Churches, an organization that represented the major Protestant denominations, as well as the Roman Catholic Diocese of Portland. When I began to discuss my ideas with Ewell, he said to me: "Abe, I have been waiting for someone with your experience and vision for fifteen years. Now, you are finally here."

I was also approached by the Jewish Community Alliance of Southern Maine, the representative institution of Jewish communal life in the area and by the Holocaust and Human Rights Center of Maine, whose executive director, Sharon Nichols, had served with me on the board of the Association of Holocaust Organizations. Both groups asked me to join their respective boards, and I gratefully accepted their invitations. It would mean an enormous amount of responsibility, within both the university and the broader community. But I could not refuse. With such a limited number of people (the entire state has only slightly more than one million residents), every talent was coveted and fortunately, for me, there were few others in Portland who had my experience in the areas of interreligious dialogue, Holocaust and genocide, and archival leadership.

I also received a call from the director of the Bangor Theological Seminary, an institution affiliated with the United Church of Christ and one of the oldest religious seminaries in America, dating back to the early nineteenth century. Would I be interested in joining a discussion group on the place of Jesus Christ in Christian-Jewish relations? I was somewhat reluctant.

The place of Jesus in Jewish thought has always been a difficult one. Jesus is the great stumbling block in the relationship of Judaism and Christianity. Jews have been the great "nay-sayers" to the Christian belief in Jesus as the Messiah, and it has cost the Jewish people dearly for nearly two thousand years. But I had to establish a working relationship with Portland's Christian community. So I said yes to Dr. Andrew Grannell, the director of the Portland branch of the seminary. He and I would work closely on many projects, and his friendship and advice would prove invaluable.

At about the same time, I met a Nigerian Muslim, an attorney who was also studying for his master's degree at the Muskie School of Public Service, one of the university's most prestigious institutions. Najim Animashaun was a brilliant lawyer, educated in England and a member of the legal bar in Nigeria, England, and the United States, and extraordinarily well versed in the history and practice of Islam. I always considered him an *alim*, one who is knowledgeable and competent to represent Islam as a religion and a civilization. I suggested to Dr. Grannell that we add a Muslim to our group. Like me, Najim did not want to enter the sensitive issue of a Jesus discussion, even though Islam considers Jesus a prophet and his mother, Mary, has an entire chapter of the holy Qur'an devoted to her. We needed, he said, to focus on what united us as the children of Abraham, the three great monotheistic faiths.

We began to meet in March 2001. On September 11, 2001, the entire world witnessed the destructive passions that resulted in the tragedy of the twin towers in New York, the Pentagon in Washington, D.C., and on a field in Pennsylvania, with the loss of 3,000 innocent lives. Even though the entire nation was traumatized, Tom Ewell from the Maine Council of Churches was working in his office. He received a phone call from the office of Maine's governor, Angus King. Could Tom put together, a staff member asked, a group of Jews, Christians, and Muslims to attend a special ceremony in two days at Blaine House, the official residence of the governor, to promote interreligious understanding in this time of heightened religious tension? When Tom called me, I told him that he would have his interreligious group. I began to call the Christian, Jewish, and Muslim members of our discussion group, and we agreed to meet in Augusta, the state capital. I offered to drive Najim, who was one of our Muslim representatives, to the program in Augusta. When I met him earlier in the day, he told me that we should meet in front of one of the university buildings. At the time he was wearing a rugby shirt and slacks. When I picked him up later that day, he was dressed in a full Muslim prayer outfit. By that time, two days after the plane hijackings on September 11, national antagonism against the American Muslim community had grown to dangerous levels. Several incidents of threats and actual physical violence against Muslims had already taken place. The city of Portland was shocked to learn that two of the Muslim hijackers, including the one who had piloted the first plane into the twin towers, had stayed in a Portland motel the evening before the attacks and had flown to Boston's Logan Airport, where the planes where hijacked, from the airport in Portland the following morning. The ride to Augusta took about an hour. I was frightened each minute of the way, as I encountered the hostile stares of other motorists when they saw Najim in his Muslim prayer robes. Fortunately, nothing of any great danger took place. When we arrived at Blaine House, we were immediately taken in to see the governor, who greeted us with thanks for arranging to come as a group for the program.

The members of our group asked me to speak for them. I spoke for only a few minutes, but in that time I told the assembled audience on the front lawn of the Blaine House that the events of September 11 would not deter our interreligious dialogue and the search for peace. I also told them that, as a son of Holocaust survivors, I was shocked to see the fear and uncertainty in the faces of our Muslim participants. "I never thought," I said, "that I would witness another group of people experience the terror that my parents and other Jews experienced during the Holocaust. The attacks against our Muslim neighbors were an attack against all of us who believe that blaming all Muslims for the actions of a few was wrong."

The following year, on the first anniversary of September 11, our group was again invited to Blaine House. This time we came prepared with a proclamation that we entitled the "Blaine House Declaration on Interreligious Peace and Cooperation":

In the Name of God who is Almighty, Merciful and Compassionate, we, who have gathered as religious representatives from the Muslim, Christian and Jewish communities on this extraordinary day of remembrance, declare our commitment to ending the violence and bloodshed that denies the right to life and dignity and dishonors the name of the Creator.

According to our faith traditions, killing innocents in the name of God is a desecration of God's Holy name and defames religion in the world. We are people who worship God, yet we acknowledge and respect our differences; the Jewish people worship God and await the coming of the Messianic age; Christians worship God as revealed in their Savior, Jesus Christ; Muslims worship God and believe Muhammad to be his last prophet.

We want to send a message of reconciliation to the people of Maine and to the world. On the first anniversary of the September 11 tragedy, we join together and follow the light of peace. We invite members of all Maine's faith communities, its political leaders, its educational leaders and all of its residents to join us by signing their names to this Declaration.

We ask the people of Maine, the peace state, to discover their common humanity and to appreciate and learn to live peacefully and constructively with the profound differences that define the religious pluralism of our nation and our world. That is the very least we can do to honor the thousands who one year ago today at this very moment lost their lives to a terror and an inhumanity that we condemn.

Augusta, Maine
September 11, 2002

The Blaine House Declaration was signed by many citizens of Maine, and we took this response as a sign that our organization, now renamed Interfaith Maine, would join with the Academic Council for Post-Holocaust Jewish, Christian, and Islamic Studies to form both a community interreligious dialogue and an academic effort to understand each of the religious communities in the decades since the Holocaust. We believed that the Holocaust was a caesura that marked the end of one era and the beginning of another in the relationship between Judaism, Christianity, and Islam. We needed to speak to each other differently and with a new vision of the relationship between Jews, Christians, and Muslims. If, as the Harvard professor Samuel Huntington[7] had postulated, the end of the Cold War meant the beginning of a new international conflict, the one between civilizations, especially between the West and Islam, we, as the members of Interfaith Maine, had to do whatever we could to prevent such an occurrence in our little corner of America and the world.

Two events in the year 2005 moved that task along significantly. The first was a program in April 2005 entitled "Living in an Age of Genocide." The program commemorated 2005 as the one hundredth, ninetieth, and sixtieth anniversaries of the Herero genocide (in German Southwest Africa), the Armenian genocide, and the Holocaust. A panel of participants representing those communities who had endured cultural or physical genocide related the effects of those genocides on subsequent generations. The panel members included Native Americans, African Americans, Armenians, Second Generations of the Holocaust, Cambodians, Rwandans, Kurds, and Fur people. The program was based on an historic event that had taken place in Rwanda in November 2001. My dear friend, Dr. Yael Danieli, a pioneer in the treatment of Holocaust survivors and their families through her Group Project for Holocaust Survivors and Their Children and the IBUKA, the coalition of the Rwandese associations of genocide survivors, cosponsored an international conference of survivors from Armenia, Bosnia, Cambodia, Rwanda, and the Holocaust. The event was called "Life after Death. Rebuilding Genocide Survivors' Lives: Challenges and Opportunities."[8] One of the stated objectives of the conference was the desire to create a worldwide network of victims/survivors of genocide.

Our 2005 program took this call to heart.[9] We issued a proclamation entitled the "Declaration of the Generations of Genocide to End the Slaughter of the Innocents." The declaration read in part:

We, the survivors, families of victims, and witnesses
To gross human rights violations have suffered and seen
The slaughter and agony of individuals, family
Members, communities, especially the more vulnerable
Such as children, women and the elderly, due to
Inhumane and barbaric acts emanating from decisions
And policies of state governments.
The failure of state governments to prosecute dictators
And perpetrators of the heinous crimes of genocide,
Crimes against humanity, war crimes, and the crime of
Aggression doubly victimizes our already
Impoverished bodies and souls and puts to shame the
Memory of those martyrs who perished.
One of the profound desires of genocide survivors is
Not to see it repeated ever again. More than anyone,
Survivors and their descendants know the horrors that

Human beings can experience; how humanity can be
Denied, subjected to unspeakable suffering imposed
In most cases by those whose responsibility is to
Protect citizens. The agony and the terrible
Consequences of genocide do not end when the actual
Acts of genocide cease. Instead, their destructive
Impact on individuals, families and society live on for
Generations inflicting the younger generations of today
On the occasion of the 100th anniversary of the Herero
Genocide and the 90th anniversary of the Armenian
Genocide, the first large-scale genocide of the last
Century that has gone unpunished, paving the way for
The Holocaust, whose 60th anniversary we
Commemorate this year—we must vow as world
Citizens to stand up for justice and fair treatment of all
Peoples. As descendents of horrific crimes of
History, we, as families of survivors, have the distinct
Role to remind the world of the consequences of
Ethnic cleansing against any people, nation, race or
Religion.

The program ended with the recitation of the *El Mole Rachamim*, the Jewish prayer for the deceased, chanted for all the victims of genocide by Cantor Kurt Messerschmidt, the ninety-year-old survivor of Auschwitz who had officiated at my wedding. It was an evening of tears and understanding.

Finally in June 2005 the Academic Council for Post-Holocaust Christian, Jewish, and Islamic Studies, now grown into a cooperative arrangement between the University of Southern Maine, Bangor Theological Seminary and St. Joseph's College of Maine, a Roman Catholic college, developed a week-long symposium entitled "Religion and the Challenge of America: Judaism, Christianity, and Islam." The program featured some of the most important international scholars and religious leaders active in interreligious dialogue. It was cosponsored by the Cordoba Institute, based in New York, an Islamic project headed by Imam Feisal Abdul Rauf [10] that seeks to increase international intercultural communications and heal the relationship between Islam and America, and by Religions for Peace–USA, also based in New York, a coalition of religious communities engaged in multireligious cooperation and common action in pursuit of justice, reconciliation, and peace.

I began the opening evening by stating the following: "In 1938, the great Yiddish poet and composer, Mordechai Gebirtig, wrote a poem after a devastating pogrom destroyed the Jewish community of a small town in Poland. His poem sought to be both a warning and a call for action:

FIRE!

Fire, brothers, fire!
Our poor town's on fire!
Raging winds so full of anger
Shatter, scatter, tear asunder
Fanning the flames ever wilder
Everything is on fire!

While you stand there looking on
With folded hand
While you stand there, looking on
At the fire brand.

Fire, brothers, fire!
The dreaded moment
May soon come
When the town with us included
Will be turned to flames and ashes
As after battle a city falls,
With empty, blackened walls.

Fire, brothers, fire!
It all turns to you
If you love your town,
Take pails, put out the fire,
Quench it with your own blood too.
Show what you can do!

Don't look and stand
With folded hand
Brothers, don't stand around,
Put out the fire!
Our shtetl burns!

I then continued:

"Religion and the Challenge of America" takes place with a background of a world that is burning. Not only the terrible fires of the twin towers of the World Trade Center but the fires that burn in more than 18 nations where religious conflict between Christians, Jews, Muslims, Hindus and animists continues to destroy lives and hopes.

Over these next six days we will seek to develop a climate of interreligious understanding in the prevailing atmosphere of fear and mutual suspicion between the sons and daughters of Abraham.

Despite the genuine differences that exist among Jews, Christians, and Muslims, we all put forward visions of peace. During our sessions we will consider how the enduring virtues of these three great religions can be used to build a shared community in terms of mutual respect, openness, trust, dignity and responsibility. We need not meet as rivals. We can meet as partners and moral equals in building a shared future and a path to *tikkun olam*, a repairing of a world that needs so many repairs. We can begin now to know each other; we can give the best of our traditions and values and in turn create a lasting and important partnership to stop the fire that threatens to burn out of control.

It took fifteen years, but those words brought forth the vision that Gottfried and I had created for ourselves and for our Post-Holocaust generations of Germans and Jews.

The synagogue in Zwolen destroyed by the Nazis in 1939–1940.

Synagogue in Linshits/Łęczyca, Poland.

Three of Abraham's mother's seven brothers. From left: Yankel, Chaskel, and Asher Zelig. None of the seven brothers or her only sister survived the Holocaust.

Five documents from the Buchenwald concentration camp that relate to Abraham's father's arrival there on August 5, 1944. He appears on the documents as Szulim Pik. Courtesy of the Thüringisches Hauptstaatsarchiv Weimar, Archiv Buchenwald.

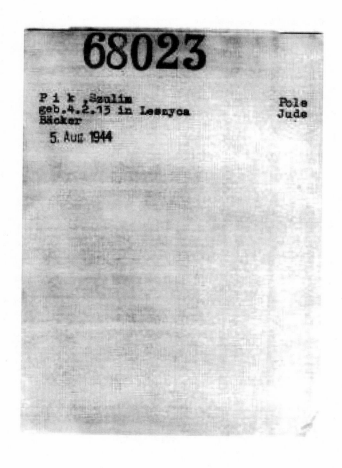

68.021	Jude Pole	5.8.44	4.1.25	Prochownik	Moszek				
2	Jude Pole	5.8.44	23.11.14	Bakmann	Josek	F			
3	Jude Pole	5.8.44	4.2.13	Pik	Szulim	56			
4	Jude Pole	5.8.44	12.11.22	Mann	Gustav	56			
5	Jude Pole	5.8.44	21.6.13	Piotrkowski	Semul				+
6	Jude Pole	5.8.44	--.23	Zajtman	Salek	56			
7	Jude Pole	5.8.44	1.11.00	Włodarski	Wolf	F		1	2834
8	Jude Pole	5.8.44	15.7.10	Lipszyc	Mordche	56			
9	Jude Pole	5.8.44	24.12.25	Rozman	Chiel	56			
30	Jude Pole	5.8.44	15.10.16	Lewkowicz	Andje				

Konzentrationslager Art der Haft: _____ Gef.-Nr. 68023

Name und Vorname: _Pik Szulim_

geb.: 4.2.1913 zu: _Leczyca Kr. dem. Warthegau_

Wohnort: _Litzmannstadt zd. Franziskanska 34 Warthegau_

Beruf: _Böcker_ Rel.: _mos_

Staatsangehörigkeit: _Pole_ Stand: _ve.h._

Name der Eltern: _Vater: Chaim P. verst. 1935 in Lodz_

Wohnort: _Mutter: Marens P. geb. Borkowicz verst. 1935 in Lodz_

Name der Ehefrau: _Shana P. geb. Kolton_ Rasse: _____

Wohnort: _Litzmannstadt ul. Franziskanska N° 34_

Kinder: _—_ Alleiniger Ernährer der Familie oder der Eltern: _____

Vorbildung: _5 Kl. Volksschule_

Militärdienstzeit: _____ von – bis _—_

Kriegsdienstzeit: _____ von – bis _—_

Grösse: _154_ Gestalt: _schw._ Gesicht: _länglg._ Augen: _braun_

Nase: _gerad_ Mund: _gew._ Ohren: _abst_ Zähne: _12 fehlen_

Haare: _schw._ Sprache: _polnisch_

Ansteckende Krankheit oder Gebrechen: _—_

Besondere Kennzeichen: _—_

Rentenempfänger: _____

Verhaftet am: 5.3.1944 wo: _Litzmannstadt_

1. Mal eingeliefert: 5.8.44 K.L. Bü 2. Mal eingeliefert: **5.8.44** Jn.1.a.Kommenno

Einweisende Dienststelle: _____

Grund: _____

Parteizugehörigkeit: _____ von – bis _____

Welche Funktionen: _____

Mitglied v. Unterorganisationen: _____

Kriminelle Vorstrafen: _____

Politische Vorstrafen: _____

v. g. u. Der Lagerkommandant

Szulim Pik

N a c h t r a g zur Veränderungsmeldung vom 5.8.1944.
Namentliche Aufstellung der -1459-Neuzugänge (Zeltlg.)

Schutzhäftlinge Juden:

67984	Schlesinger, Max
997	Bretisch, Stefan
68146	Salm, Justinus
3o2	Leipziger, Herman alias Rosenstein, Krschel
561	Pick, Rudolf
563	Langer, Hans
631	Cohen, Elias
667	Mayer, Alfred
822	Engel, Salamo
828	Hauser, Leopold

Polen Juden:

67501	Rolider, Jakub
2	Niesenbaum, Dawid
3	Milsstajn, Majleh
4	Milsstajn, Salamo
5	Milstein, Jakob
6	Neumann, Bernard
7	Goldfarb, Salamo
8	Böcker, Josef
Block 4o	9	Zweig, Stepan Jazy
1o	Zweig, Harry
11	Schotland, Chaim
12	Frydenberg, Nuchim
13	Rodsonodrsewo, Aron
14	Teichler, Dawid
15	Keil, Salo
16	Baumgold, Chaim
17	Klots, Boleslaw
18	Teichler, Samuel
19	Judenherz, Mordka
2o	Trieger, Chaim
21	Lewkowicz, Majlech
22	Saterenfeld, Mendel
23	Herzig, Markus
24	Wajsband, Ryson
25	Goldsztajn, Motek
26	Sendrowicz, Hersz
27	Hirschfeld, Usser
28	Konewka, Jedidie
29	Maagowski, Chaim
3o	Garbarski, Lejbus
31	Gyferblat, Israel
32	Abramowicz, Jakub
33	Hirschfeld, Mozes
34	Owerman, Abram
35	Milsstajn, Zanek
	+ verstorben 1o.8.1944
36	Rosental, Marian
37	Puterman, Jakob
38	Birn, Fritz
39	Katz, Aron
4o	Antmann, Hermann
41	Hirschfeld, Chaim
42	Kolbauer, Leiser
43	Reinhers, Markus
44	Kornfeld, Bernad
45	Mosskowicz, Jozef

Polen Juden:

67546	Luksenberg, Kopel
47	Marchewka, Uryn
48	Reinhers, Wolf
49	Herling, Samuel
5o	Zalcman, Azryl
51	Wasserman, Abram
52	Lustiger, Izrael
53	Wajsband, Lejbug (s)
54	Elenowajg, Jakob
55	Rosner, Abraham
56	Waldman, Predek
57	Baumgarten, Mordka
58	Grossman, Izak
59	Krischer, Mozes
6o	Kurtz, Jakob
61	Antmann, Leo
62	Finkelstein, Szaja
63	Antmann, Fiszel
64	Aizenberg, Dawid
65	Ajsenberg, Josek, Icek
66	Saubel, Eljasz
67	Laks, Chil
68	Saubel, Lejzor
69	Silberberg, Hersch
7o	Lejtman, Mieczyslaw
71	Lustiger, Samul
72	Osser, Majer
73	Weingarten, Szymcha
74	Ajzon, Chaim
75	Rozenblat, Zelik
76	Zawierucha, Hersz
77	Profesorski, Szabsa
78	Profesorski, Bernard
79	Ajsenberg, Abraham
8o	Ajsenberg, Jakeil, Moszek
81	Zingier, Kalma
83	Dombrower, Majer
82	Steif, Mendel
84	Finkielsztajn, Berek
85	Barber, Nenassa
87	Braun, Moszek
88	Salamowicz, Moniek
89	Wajublum, Jozef
	+ verstorben 9.August 1944
9o	Krajtsztajn, Chaim
91	Fridman, Pelta
92	Muzykant, Majer
93	Grynberg, Icek
94	Oudsinowski, Icek
95	Kenig, Roman
96	Lerman, Icek
97	Ingber, Izrael, Leib
98	Oudsinowski, Jurek
99	Wajnberg, Eljasz
6oo	Rotfarb, Isak
586	Kantorowicz, Szymon

/ b/5o9 auf Block 4o/

0003003

67961 Trajtel, Salomon
62 Rosenberg, Icek
63 Hochman, Abram
64 Fajgenbaum, Samuel
65 Markusfeld, Kiwa
66 Dynamon, Wiktor
67 Stal, Mosiek
68 Rajnberg, Salama(la)
69 Rotenberg, Fiszel
70 Dabrowski, Pinkus
71 Obstbaum, Szmul
72 Jurysta, Abram
73 Rosanberg, Alter
74 Binsztok, Mendel
75 Sperling, Leon
76 Ciesla, Izak
77 Chmielnicki, Berek
78 Rajzman, Hersschemja
79 Kuszmirak, Chaim
80 Frydman, Kalman
81 Granek, Szaja
82 Pommer, Beno
83 Lerman, David
85 Kochen, Zelman
86 Lerner, Israel
87 Klumstain, Moszek
88 Laznowski, Natan
89 Wajnberg, Icek
90 Rodolnik, Herszek
91 Lustgarten, Chil
92 Scheinowitz, Chaskel
93 Rosenbaum, Sigmunt
94 Zand, Chil
95 Okowita, Jankiel
96 Pinkus, Chaim
98 Holckimeer, Samuel
99 Szwarcbald, Henryk
68000 Silberberg, Jakob
1 Djament, Machel
2 Jamer, Josek
3 Rojzman, Jankiel
4 Prasskier, Szmul
5 Sturm, Moses
6 Glazman, Boruch
7 Glazman, Jakob
8 Bergman, Motek
9 Jelinowicz, Abram
10 Wandermann, Fuel
11 Goldrozen, Meilech
12 Trydberg, Majer
13 Wurcel, Szyja
14 Richter, Motek
15 Szwarcman, Chil
16 Feilschus, Stefan
17 Kestenberg, Jerzy
18 Kleinmann, Jakob
19 Grupstajn, Synay
20 Mouskowicz, Mihal
21 Prochownik, Mossek
22 Bakmann, Josek

68023 Pik, Szulim
24 Mann, Gustaw
25 Piotrkowski, Szmul
26 Zajtman, Salek
27 Wlodarski, Wolf
28 Lipszyo, Mordche
29 Rozman, Chiel
30 Lewkowicz, Anszel
31 Kac, Izrael
32 Swarcbard, Icek
33 Taub, Abram
34 Cudzynowski, Wolf
35 Zyngier, Mossek
36 Goldring, Dawid
37 Ptasznik, Chaskiel
38 Lipnicki, Suchar
39 Ptasznik, Majer
40 Ptasznik, Lipa
41 Kafel, Dawid
42 Aronowicz, Mordka
43 Blatt, Lajzor
44 Heitlinger, Noe
45 Kleidermacher, Lajb
46 MX Bukszpan, Chaim
47 Zylberberg, Fiszel
48 Zylberberg, Mordka
49 Silberberg, Alter
50 Blicher, Izrael
51 Warszawski, Icek
52 Kurst, Jakob
53 Markowicz, Herman
54 Kurz, Abraham
55 Horowitz, Szymon
56 Nisson, Zygmunt
57 Pulka, Alter
58 Bryl, Josek
59 Szpidbaum, Mordchaj
60 Strigler, Motek
61 Hartman, Mojzesz
62 Lewin, Luzer
63 Hofermann, Chaim
64 Mates, David
65 Bugajski, Dawid
66 Hornung, Maksymilian
67 Jakubowicz, Synaj
68 Drabinowski, Heinrich
69 Pinkas, Abraham
70 Pasternak, Lejbus
71 Rosenberg, Leib
72 Drabinowski, Leo
73 Reich, Naftali
74 Weldung, Josef
75 Drabinowski, Pereo
76 Turner, Szymon
77 Czajkowski, Abram
78 Kaczala, Mendel
79 Jakubowicz, Benjamin
80 Kersaner, Mendel
81 Wargon, Izak
82 Bryl, Alter

F. S. Stelle

Fernschreibstelle **K. L. Stutthof**

□ □ □	**1815**	
Fernschreibname	Laufende Nr.	

Angenommen / Aufgenommen		Befördert:	
Datum: 24. Nov. 194**4**		Datum: 25. Nov. 194**4**	
um:	Uhr	um: 06.12	Uhr
von: 21.15		an:	
durch:		durch:	
		Rolle: 55	

Vermerke:

Fernschreiben
Posttelegramm von:
Fernspruch

		An Kommandanten
Abgangstag	Abgangszeit	

Vermerke für Beförderung (vom Aufgeber auszufüllen)	K.L. Flossenbürg
	Bestimmungsort

Betr.: Häftlingsüberstellung.

Bezug: FS Nr. 14119 vom 23.11.1944 des Amtsgruppenchefs D im H-WVHA

Am 24.11.1944 Transport mit 216 männlichen und 284 weiblichen
Judenhäftlingen zum AL. Bernsdorff u. Co. Dresden nach Schnatation
Dresden-Reick abgerollt.

Erbitte Nachricht, wann Übernahme in dortige Stärke erfolgt.

gez. Hoppe

Nicht zu übermitteln:

□ □ □ □

A document ordering the transfer of prisoners from the Stutthof concentration camp to Dresden. Courtesy of Eva Unterman, Tulsa, Oklahoma.

```
233. Salomon        El....eth   1.4.25    Sch...pol.  Ung.    39 406
234. Isikowitsch     Basia      5.6.17       "         "      48 435
235. Ringermacher    Schine     88 5.08      "        Lit.    48 436
236. Dawidowitsch    Rebekka    19.2.26      "         "      57 349
237. Kozlowski       Eechama    31.12.23     "        poln.   57 416
238. Kozlowski       Rosa       15.5.25      "         "      57 417
239. Kulas           Charne     15.7.20      "         "      59 005
240. Aes             P....a     15.8.20      "        Lit.    6a 813
241. Swiraka         Ba.ča      5.3.19       "        poln.   60 843
242. Curmanski       Kocha      24.9.22      "        Lit.    60 845
243. Tronowska       Fania      28.11.21     "        poln.   60 867
244. Holzer          Elsa       24.12.27     "        RD.     60 989
245. Hirschanhauser  2.4.27     Bruc         "         "      61 050
246. Steinweg        Ruth       25.3.24      "         "      61 782
247. Pukacz          Erika      14.12.23     "         "      61 808
248. Zamoscik        Haja       8.5.26       "        pol.    69 788
249. Joffe           Ella       25.12.19     "        Lit.    70 2o4
250. Korpelowska     Ella       20.6.25      "        Polen.  70 653
251. Feiertag        Regeina    25.6.25      "         "      74 824
252. Kalman          Ella       2.5.22       "         "      75 507
253. Katz            Rosa       20.12.12     "         "      75 531
254. Krępitzke       Irka       5.9.22       "         "      75 608
255. Krzepicki       Janka      23.9.18      "         "      75 609
257. Lipschitz       Mocha      17.10.23     "         "      75 636
258. Lipschitz       Cimia      25.5.22      "         "      75 637
259. Aronson         Alina      5.6.23       "         "      81 331
260. Drechsler       Lena       3.3.24       "         "      81 495
261. Brendzel        Pole       5.5.19       "         "      82 016
262. Minke           Freida     20.3.21      "         "      82 053
263. Judenherz       Chenna     25.1.4.11    "         "      82 237
264. Krell           Sara       13.11.19     "         "      82 242
265. Petersmann      Lola       21.3.21      "         "      82 471
266. Pick            Andza      19.3.15      "         "      82 764
267. Lilienberg      Saca       28.6.15      "         "      82 907
268. Gutgold         Gina       25.2.23      "         "      83 010
269. Kozlowska       Bela       22.9.15      "         "      83 121
270. Lessmann        Pela       19.3.23      "         "      83 175
271. Kedrzycka       Adela      22.3.25      "         "      83 231
272. Federmann       Chaja      20.8.22      "         "      83 755
273. Wisniak         Nina       4.11.26      "         "      85 170
274. Flink           Seda       8.9.22       "         "      85 330
275. Forgasch        Berta      11.5.18      "         "      85 554
276. Gendel          Helene     21.10.21     "         "      85 560
277. Krakauer        Margod     3.2.24       "         "      85 439
278. Spritzer        Felicia    5.6.24       "         "      85 633
279. Novak           Musa       10.12.20     "         "      884114
280. Novak           Dora       10.7.21      "         "      884118
281. Nowak           Anka       15.10.22     "         "      88 116
282. Klein           Golen      17.3.27      "        Ung.    51 917
283. Steiner         Sari       19.9.28      "         "      51 979
284. Stein           Zseni      23.1.24      "         "      52 274
285. Stein           Piroska    16.6.27      "         "      52 275
286. Wiss            Dora       22.1 1.25    "         "      52 339
287. Precel          Anita      8.12.18      "        Tsch.   82 772
288. Jakubowitsch    Luba       12.2.14      "        Poln.   88 525
289. Aizen           Leah       3.4.09       "         "      87 815
290. Puttermann      Malka      6.3.15       "         "      87 812
291. Schwimmer       Bett_      19.4.22      "         "      76 377
292. Lefkowitz       Hinda      1.1.21       "         "      82 575
293. Bloch           Rifka      23.12.12     "         "      82 014
     Vermerk: Gestrichen lfd. Nr. 16, 19, 75, 135, 136, 143, 201, 204
```

A list of prisoners being transported from Stutthof to Dresden. Abraham's mother is listed as number 266. Courtesy of Eva Unterman, Tulsa, Oklahoma.

In Abraham's father's arms at the Landsberg Jewish DP camp (1947).

The USS General C. H. Muir, *the troop ship that brought the Pecks from Bremer-haven to Boston (November–December, 1949).*

A Jewish New Year's card: Abraham, his mother, and his father shortly before leaving Germany for the United States (1949).

MUSYKANT, Mayer

MEIER, Samuel, Jacheta, Salomon (3 yrs.)

NIEDZIELA, Wolf

PAKUS, Benjamin

PANITZ, Mark

PERNER, Pinkus, Regina, Klara (2 yrs.)

PERL, Moses

PERL, Michael, Sara

PERLMUTTER, Josef, Elle

PIK, Salomon, Anna, Abraham (3 yrs.)

POLANSKI, Josef

POLLAK, Leopold, Mary, Edith, Abraham (1 yr.)

PUDLIKOWSKA, Dora

RAFALOWICZ, Heres, Chaja, Chana (3 yrs.) with Mala

REDLICH, Eugeniusz, Stanislawa, Eva (2 yrs.)

RIMLER, Abraham, Irena

RODZICKI, Lazur, Franka, Chasia (1 yr.)

ROSENBERG, Kurt

ROSENBERG, Josef, Agatha, Helena

RUBINSTEIN, Moses, Dora

RUBINSTEIN, Frieda

SAKOWSKI, Abram, Regina

SALZBERG, Leib, Malka

SAMULEWICZ, Josef, Sofie

SCHUSTER, Hirsch

SCHWARTZ, Deezoe, Maria, Willi (1 yr.)

SINGER, Filip, Zonia, Ruwen (1 yr.)

SINGER, Markus, Cyla

Another part of the USS General Muir *passenger list including Abraham and his parents under the name "Pik." Courtesy of American Jewish Historical Society, New York.*

Appointments aboard General Muir
December 2, 1949

DP Boat # 123

Names follow:

ARBEITMAN, Chaim

BALLHORN, David

BARAN, Isak, Henia, Dodek-Pepa (9 yrs.)

BEDER, Gerszon

BERGER, Oskar, Rosa, Heinrich (2 yrs.)

BIALAGLOWA, Chaim

BINSZTOK, Israel, Pesa, Ichhok (2 yrs.)

BLASER, Josef

BLOBSTEIN, Lewy, Anna, with Stepchild BLOBSTEIN-GLATZER, Peta

BOBIK, Nina

BORENSZTAJN, Israel, Luba, Abram (2 yrs.)

BORCWER, Heres

BOROSCHEK, Auin, Dorothea, Gerry (2 yrs.)

BRAND, Abram, Estar, Chaja (8 mos.)

CELNIK, Jakob

CHOJNACKI, Leo-Leib

CIGELMAN, Jankel

DEUTSCH, Miklos

DUEM, Marton, Olga, Erika (3 yrs.) with Aniko (2 yrs.) with Herman (10 mos.)

EISENBERG, Genia

ELIZEROWICZ, Izaak, Henia

EMER, Pinkas

-2-

A partial list of immigrants to the United States sailing on the USS General Muir.
Courtesy of American Jewish Historical Society, New York.

Abraham in conversation with a man in Linshits/Łęczyca who remembered his father's family while Eugenio and Alberto watch (August 2005).

56 Franciszkanska Street, renamed Franzstrasse by the Germans, the first building in which Abraham's father lived in the Litzmannstadt (Łódź) ghetto (August 2005).

The plaque commemorating the April 1945 death march "Todesmarsch" of Jewish prisoners from the Landsberg/Kaufering camps in the direction of Dachau (Landsberg, 2005).

Ulica Zydowksa (Jews' Street), Linshits. Ghetto began at this spot in 1939 (Łęczyca, 2005).

Abraham sitting with Stephan Kwapisiencz, who remembered his mother's family in Zwolen (August 2005).

Father Zbigniew Luczak, the Łęczyca priest who tried to help Abraham find his family records, with Eugenio and Alberto (August 2005).

The site of the Jewish cemetery in Zwolen before the Nazis destroyed it. Now nothing remains (August 2005).

The stone quarry (Steinbruch) where Abraham's father worked in the Buchenwald concentration camp (August 2005).

Schander Strasse 68, the cigarette factory in Dresden where Abraham's mother worked as a slave laborer from November 1944 to February 1945 (August 2005).

Hans Biebrow, the German administrator of the Łodz ghetto and the head of the Dresden factory in which Abraham's mother was a slave laborer.

The plaque commemorating the Jewish slave laborers who suffered and died in the factory at Schandauer Strasse 68 in Dresden (August 2005).

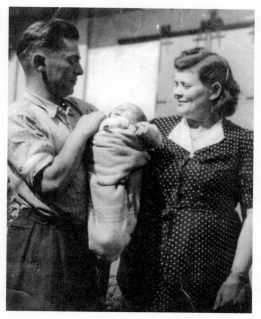

Abraham and his proud parents shortly after his birth (1946).

Abraham's adorable children, Abby and Joel.

Abraham and his wife, Jean, on a visit to the University of Cincinnati.

(Top photo) Major Irving Heymont (left) speaks to Jewish displaced persons at the Landsberg DP camp as Rabbi Abraham Rosenberg of the Joint Distribution Committee translates into Yiddish. (Bottom photo) Dr. Samuel Gringauz (wearing a cap) in discussion with American General Onslow Rolfe during Rolfe's visit to the Landsberg DP camp, 1945. Courtesy of American Jewish Archives, Cincinnati, Ohio.

III

Post-Holocaust Germans and Jews

Abraham J. Peck

13

What Do They Have to Say to Each Other? Post-Holocaust Germans and Jews in Dialogue

"Memorial Candles" and the Search for Meaning[1]

In their search for meaning, many children of Holocaust survivors, the Second Generation, have come to a dead end. Gone are the halcyon days of the 1970s and 1980s when the sons and daughters of survivors took an oath in the shadow of Jerusalem's Temple Wall in 1981 and declared *mir szeinen doh* (we are here), mirroring their parents' affirmation of life in the weeks and months after the Liberation.[2]

It was a heady slide into the abyss of inactivity or worse, this decades-long preoccupation with identity by a diverse group of adults, long beyond their childhood years, who gratefully became "children" once again. When they first started to come together, the children of survivors understood only that, as different as they were from everyone else, among their own kind there was a sameness that gave them a warmth and understanding that they had never known. And it was important that they reformulate their identities because the same thing was happening to their parents. Beginning in the early 1980s, survivors and their children began to occupy a unique role in the evolution of the Jewish presence in history. The Holocaust and its observance became in its rites and rituals an American concern. Indeed, the 1980s emerged as the "decade of the survivors," as they were asked to speak in the classroom and in front of the video camera.

The 1980s was also the decade of the Second Generation. For the better part of that decade, the American children of survivors sought to implement a number of aims and ideas that connected them, perhaps without their knowing it, to the idealism of Holocaust survivors who immediately after the Liberation had formulated a kind of neo-humanistic response to the tragedy that had befallen European Jewry during the 1930s and 1940s.[3] They did so at the individual level, through their own involvement in the helping professions; they did so collectively, moving to a kind of political engagement that saw them demonstrate against unjust governments and ultimately take a "leap of faith" to conduct a dialogue with Yasser Arafat and the PLO in pursuit of peace in the Middle East.[4] The Second Generation was also active in helping to create Holocaust centers and museums across America.

In a sense the writer and editor Eva Hoffman is correct: the Second Generation is the "hinge generation," through which either "the meanings of awful events can remain arrested and fixed at the point of trauma; or in which they can be transformed into new sets of relations with the world and new understanding."[5] We considered this at the very time that we were beginning our dialogue. We assumed that every other member of the Second Generation, Germans and Jews with whom we spoke, would see that these were our two choices and would join with us in an ever-expanding dialogue between members of the Second Generation of post-Holocaust Germans and Jews.

We were wrong. We found much more resistance to the idea than any form of acceptance. And if there was acceptance, it was framed against the backdrop of still-living survivor parents who, as one Second Generation member told us, "would have a heart attack if they ever thought I would sit and dialogue with a German." Such a feeling is understandable. The hatred and unforgiving attitudes of many survivor parents toward Germans and Germany was one of the easy, nonreflective beliefs passed on to their children.

In 1991 we were among a very few organized or occasional encounters between Second Generation Jews and Germans. The encounters were difficult to say the least. Often, they would begin with terrible accusations by the Jewish side toward the Germans, allowing long-held emotions to finally be uttered toward a place that would have some direct impact. But was it the right place? In our encounters one of us often wanted to say to the other— no, shout at the other— "Do you know what your parents' and grandparents' generation did to mine? Do you realize that I have lost a family, a civilization, a culture, and a language, and it was Germans and Germany that were the cause of all of these losses?"

The German dialogue partner, Gottfried, understood those words perhaps even better than the Jewish one. He understood them against the backdrop of his own family history and the "conspiracy of silence" that formed the German world into which he was born in 1947. It was difficult and painful to enter a dialogue with a Wagner who so rejected and hated the family and the country that were his. In our times together, both formally and informally, the Jewish partner was shocked and hard-pressed to understand the depth of the German partner's animosity toward his family, especially his father. He could not picture himself in such a family relationship, and he worried that Gottfried's consuming hatred would block the path toward a meaningful dialogue.

And what of my father? He was aware from the beginning that Gottfried and I were engaged in a dialogue to understand our legacies and how we could move beyond them to a point where words could change into meaningful action. In 1997, in the fifth year of our dialogue, Gottfried and I again discussed our work under the meaningful direction of Professor Hubert Locke. I spoke of our dialogue, my father, and my hopes for the next generation:[6]

We want to forge a kind of symbiosis that goes beyond what Professor Dan Diner talked about as a negative symbiosis, a victim and victimizer, into a joint effort to overcome this awful burden, this awful legacy that, as I have already mentioned, twisted the psyches of my parents and their generation and poisoned, I think, both Gottfried's humanity and mine.

My father is eighty-three years old. My mother died in 1988. . . . What I do will never be enough for him. Indeed, no amount of museums or memorials will ever change the fact that he has to go to bed at night and deal with his nightmares and his memories. But I will tell my children the stories that I heard from my father . . . of how ordinary men and women became possessed by an evil that poisoned their very souls. Doctors, engineers, military leaders all devoted to cleansing the earth of "lives unworthy of life."

And, I think I will pass on to my children the lessons that my father asked me to draw from his sufferings—the place of Jews in the world, the role of Christian anti-Semitism and the Holocaust, those few who sought to help Jews, and the many more who did not. What can justify the suffering of my parents? The loss of my family? The "Other" status among my own community? So, Hubert, my father doesn't approve of my dialogue. He thinks it is too little and too late. But, I know that in his own life he has sought to carry forward a message not unlike the one that Gottfried and I seek to share with all of you. He was quickly disillusioned, I think, by a world unwilling to listen. And, I guess, my prayer for myself and my children is that we do not share his fate.

Gottfried was not alone in those hatreds that, at the time, consumed so much of him. In dialogue group after dialogue group, the German Second Generation's animosity toward the First Generation was apparent, often beyond the understanding of the sons and daughters of Holocaust survivors.[7] Despite this large divide between dialogue groups, numerous efforts have been made to develop a meaningful encounter between the post-Holocaust generations.[8] There is a sense of "touchy-feely" camaraderie among many of the groups, a dialogue that ends in tears and a hug of forgiveness.[9] But more is needed.

Post-Holocaust Germans and Jews have begun to emerge from the shadows that darkened the lives of both groups. In encounters across America, in Israel and in Europe, more and more of us have begun to sit down, one with the other, and ask what it is that has separated us for so long and what might ultimately bring us together. Yet no encounter has been quite like ours. No other set of post-Holocaust Germans and Jews have asked as much from ourselves and from each other in terms of family and national histories. We have approached the relationship of Germans and Jews from history, from family history, from philosophy, and from religion. We have examined the encounter from the time of Jewish emancipation in Germany to the present and concluded that if First Generation Germans are indeed responsible for a first and second guilt—murdering millions and then failing to face the tragedy and its consequences[10]—then Second Generation Germans and Jews may, if they do not enter into a full-fledged encounter, be guilty of a third, namely the inability to remove from ourselves the comfortable ghettos of fear, mistrust, hatred, and hostility that we have built since 1945.

But that is a goal that is still far in the future. In the meantime Germans must still face themselves and their family histories before they can face the sons and daughters of survivors. Gottfried has already done this and has written a book about the encounter.[11] He has also found it easier to look at his generation of Germans from a distance, happy in his now-not-so-new

Italian surroundings but also aware that he cannot go home again—that for him Germany can never be equated with *Heimat*.

The Second Generation of sons and daughters of survivors has traveled far from our first inklings of who we were. We have gotten up from the therapist's couch, looked around for a very long time, and sought to define for ourselves a place in our no longer "children of survivors" middle age. We now talk to each other in Internet discussion lists, rediscover our beginnings in the Displaced Persons Camps of Germany, Austria, and Italy and the work camps of Siberia and Central Asia,[12] and worry about a world without the moral authority of our parents. Second Generation American Jews are at the head of the pack. The Israeli Second Generation, at one time skeptical of our aims and inspirations, is now fully with us. They have learned just how similar in attitude, if not in manner, was the destructive reaction of native Israelis to the survivors who came to build a Jewish state in 1948.[13] The European Second Generation is now coming into its own and beginning to ask some interesting questions, as a conference on the Dutch Second Generation members made clear: "Are we the second generation of war 'victims?'" "Is it a blessing or a curse to be born a Jew after World War II?" "How do we handle the fact that we are both Second Generation and Jewish?" And finally, "Do the Dutch differ in this regard from Israelis, other Europeans, and Americans?" So we, like our German counterparts, continue to seek self-definitions. As do Gottfried and I.

The Burden of the "Other"

As the son of Holocaust survivors who did not quite fit into American-Jewish life and society and as the "black sheep" of a family that was very much on the inside of Germany's social and cultural elites, we understand and have taken on with enthusiasm the role of being the "other" in our respective societies. We have accepted the burdens of our legacy, and they have made us travel different paths from many of our contemporaries. Perhaps we see the uglier side of the human condition a bit more readily, understand the fragility of sacred icons of society, their ability to crack in the face of overwhelming evil in order to save themselves or profit from the situation.

Being a part of the minority immediately allows us to understand the plight of other minorities, to listen to their cries for compassion and justice. That is why we both believe that we must understand what the Holocaust has done to our Second Generation of both Germans and Jews and what effect that has had on the third and subsequent generations, a fact that I will discuss in the next chapter. Breaking the silence that has been a part of Germany's encounter with itself for nearly seven decades is a commitment that we both share. And we need to have every member of the German-Jewish dialogue confront the question: do Germans understand what they have done—not a deed carried out by some small group of fanatics acting "in the name of the [Greater] German people," a phrase that eased the burden of conscience of millions of participants, *Mitlaufer*, but by the ordinary men and women at the front and in the ghettos and camps who joined for pleasure or for conviction in the murder of millions?

What we understand about being a minority is that the majority of Germans and Jews do not want to go beyond a certain level in the confrontation, in the dialogue between Germans and Jews. Teach the Holocaust in Germany and America, build museums to describe the event, but never sit down as German and Jew and say what you really feel—the pain, the guilt, the shame, the anger, the confusion. We both want to know—why does it have to be this way? What united the first generation of Jews and Germans—beyond the intimate knowledge of Paul Celan's immortal phrase "death is a master from Germany"—was silence. For many first-generation German parents it was the silence of self-protection from the indictment of crimes against humanity—as a perpetrator or as bystander. That burden of silence is what many of us share as Second Generation Germans and Jews. The need to protect our Holocaust-survivor parents kept the silence long into our adult years—until our parents felt the need to bear witness before their voices were forever stilled. But many second-generation Germans never understood what the silence of their parents meant. Their politicians, their educators, even their left-wing student heroes did not mention the unmentionable, did not discuss the depth of Germany's crimes against humanity. That silence drove many of us into each other's arms, as it were. And perhaps it was a kind of warm bathwater for many young Germans, this dialogue with those who dared sit with them as Jews and as sons and daughters of Holocaust survivors. The results of those early dialogues were mistrust, then realization, then emotional catharsis and a kind of intense joining of souls. And the majority of those dialogues occurred beyond German soil, primarily in the United States.

In the more than twenty years since we have led our dialogue group, we have spoken to thousands upon thousands of individuals. Many have been Germans and Jews, some from the Second Generation. But not all. And from those non-Germans and Jews has come a torrent of support for what we do. Non-Germans and Jews have expressed passionate agreement with our objectives, wanting to be a part of our greater vision, even though we have, for the most part, focused on our relationship between post-Holocaust Germans and Jews and somewhat less on post-Holocaust Austrians and Jews. For Americans, we believe, this need to be a part of our efforts to cut through the wall of hatred, shame, guilt, and fear that separates most Germans and Jews is due to their need to create a way of remembering the Holocaust as a part of their American future.

Why does this need for "memory" now seem to play a larger role in political and civic life, not only in America but in many parts of the world? It may be that in a postmodern, posthistorical world, the negative side of Western civilization and its less than positive history toward other civilizations has led us to a state of gloom and exhaustion. In that exhaustion we need to find something good to salvage from our history. The Holocaust has become, in the opinion of some, an instrument for teaching the professed values of American society. This "Americanization of the Holocaust" has drawn criticism from European observers, who see the phenomenon as an "American Disneyland"[14] version of a non-American event at best, and a new instrument of American foreign policy at worst, in which America reaches a new moral high ground where any nation that does not involve itself in Holocaust education remains without a "most favored nation" status, antidemocratic and un-American. Certain scholars have objected to a "surfeit" of Jewish Holocaust memory at the expense of other genocides.

That is a cynicism that does not surprise us, coming from the continent that produced two world wars and the Holocaust. Perhaps that is why Germans and Jews speak best together in the shadow of the so-called American century, which defined for many the direction of the past twentieth century. Yet we are not certain that many have still drawn the connection between the consequences of the Holocaust on European soil and the loss of faith in the future. But the connections are there because some of us understand just how much the events between 1933 and 1945 shattered our belief in the progress of humanity. When we seek to break down the barriers that hold down our separate but binding legacies to address the issues of tribalism, intolerance, injustice, and suffering, it is a vision of the future shared by former victims and victimizers. As the number of those in our world who see themselves as victims grows, either as victims of a tyranny of "dead, white, European males," or of continued ethnic subjugation, or of sexual and gender violence, or of religious violence, the notion that victims and victimizers can break through all that separated them must have meaning and relevance to an entire world of those who suffer and those who are responsible for that suffering.

What we have learned from our encounters in Europe is that there is still great reluctance and inability for that dialogue to emerge with the same force and success that it has in its North American setting. Perhaps too many Jews in Germany continue to follow the maxim that "in the house of the hangman, one does not discuss the noose," even though more than 100,000 Jews in Germany now make up the fastest-growing and most vibrant Jewish community in Europe. Yet, the shadows of that noose continue to cast their darkness and their burdens on much of the European continent.

But there is something else we have learned. There are those worthy individuals in places such as London and Berlin, among others, to whom the evolution of the "New Europe" will not mean the dissolution of those issues at the heart of the "Old Europe," including the burdens of the Holocaust. What we have learned as well from our encounters with members of the Sinti and Roma communities, whom the world disparagingly calls Gypsies and whose parents, too, were prisoners in Auschwitz and would not speak to their children about their suffering, and our encounters with the offspring of Dutch collaborators and with the sons and daughters of German military personnel who fathered children with Dutch women and then left, often before the children were born, is the amount of pain that still needs to be experienced and the number of tears that still need to be shed in a dialogue format.

Our Second Generation dialogue has an enormous territory that it has not yet even begun to approach with groups that we could have never envisioned two decades ago. In all the weeks, days, and hours of our dialogue, we have always wondered what, in the nearly seven decades since the end of the Holocaust, Germans and Jews wanted, one from the other. Do Jews want Germans to get on their knees and ask for collective forgiveness? Do Germans want Jews to finally forgive them and announce a reconciliation of sorts? What have we post-Holocaust Germans and Jews done to each other that we need to ask for forgiveness and reconciliation? Why, then, do we meet and talk to one another? If the truth be told, being a member of a German-Jewish dialogue group is not an entrée into either German or Jewish star status. The sons and daughters of survivors know full well that soon the burden of the Holocaust and its legacies will fall upon their shoulders. Will they be able to understand those legacies and the manner in which they must be carried out? How many of them at the age of sixty or more are in a position to continue the task of bearing witness, albeit in a secondhand manner? What advantage does such an encounter hold for post-Holocaust sons and daughters of German perpetrators or bystanders? Does it bring an easier sleep? Does it grant a certain victim status to the individual, knowing that he or she has been the victim of a national repression of the Holocaust and the attitudes of "ordinary Germans?"

We have left one of the most murderous centuries in recorded history. Despite the dialogues, despite the revelations and the hugs and tears, the question in the twenty-first century of the future of the German-Jewish encounter and the post-Holocaust generations' dialogue is one that has found no easy answers. But one thing we know for certain as we move into the generation that will bear responsibility for Holocaust and post-Holocaust memory: until Germans and Jews fully appreciate the depths of their human and moral losses, until we have all been able to sit down with the remaining groups of our parents and grandparents and take the risk of breaking the silence of the First Generation Germans and Jews, and until we consider what we shall do with the results of our many dialogues, we do not and cannot hope for a better world or a less murderous century.

14

Holocaust Memory: In the Shadow and Light of Family History

On Collective Memory

Nearly seventy years after the last Jew was murdered and the last concentration camp inmate found freedom but was not yet free, Holocaust memory has given survivors and their offspring a sense that their suffering was not in vain. Survivors feel vindicated. Their children feel a sense of relief that they live in a different time than their parents. In those years no one cared; no one condemned the fact that there was an active effort to destroy the Jewish world.

For the Jewish people as well as for Judaism, the twentieth century was a time of death but also a time of promise, the promise and flowering of a two-thousand-year-old hope of a return to a promised land. But what Jews also understand is that the Holocaust was an event projecting the utmost of human cruelty and the diabolical potential of the human being. Germany was the executioner, while the crime was in general accepted by the rest of Europe. The hunt for the criminals of the Holocaust has moved from the individual, to the corporation, to the nation-state. Jews, and especially survivors, now understand just how utterly alone and abandoned their fellow Jews were during the Holocaust years. Allies and Axis nations both profited from their destruction.

Sons and daughters of survivors continue to marvel at the ability of their parents to say yes to a Jewish future, to say yes to their children's futures as they saw the results of the darkness and despair that had surrounded them for so many years before the Liberation. But we must ask: if those parents had known then, at the moment of their liberation, the extent of the conspiracy to murder them and the greed that gripped both supposed friends and definite enemies during the years of fire and flames, would they have said yes so willingly?

Yet, they did say yes. After nearly three decades of being peripheral to the growth of American Jewish life, survivors and their children entered that life in a dramatic fashion. They became part of a willingness to remember the Holocaust and its "lessons," which reflected a kind of collective memory that transcended national boundaries and the guilt or innocence of those who were active participants in the slaughter of millions. Survivors and their families are no longer told to forget the past.

It was not only that the day of Holocaust remembrance, Yom Hashoah, was commemorated by every state in America; it was not only that nearly every American state had at least one Holocaust museum or center; it was not only that an entire museum devoted to the history of the Holocaust stood in the midst of American sacred space and memory; it was not only that the United Nations designated January 27, the anniversary of the liberation of Auschwitz, as International Holocaust Remembrance Day. It was more. The traditional discourse about the Holocaust has become part of an international collective memory. Nation-states whose hands and history were bloodied between the years 1933 and 1945 now became active participants in the call for a collective political action and mobilization. In January 2000, dozens of national delegations attended an unprecedented meeting in Stockholm that issued an unprecedented statement:[1]

Declaration of the Stockholm International Forum on the Holocaust:

We, High Representatives of Governments at the Stockholm International Forum on the Holocaust, declare that

1. The Holocaust (Shoah) fundamentally challenged the foundations of civilization. The unprecedented character of the Holocaust will always hold universal meaning. After half a century, it remains an event close enough in time that survivors can still bear witness to the horrors that engulfed the Jewish people. The terrible suffering of the many millions of other victims of the Nazis has left an indelible scar across Europe as well.

2. The magnitude of the Holocaust, planned and carried out by the Nazis, must be forever seared in our collective memory. The selfless sacrifices of those who defied the Nazis, and sometimes gave their own lives to protect or rescue the Holocaust's victims, must also be inscribed in our hearts. The depths of that horror, and the heights of their heroism, can be touchstones in our understanding of the human capacity for evil and for good.

3. With humanity still scarred by genocide, ethnic cleansing, racism, anti-Semitism and xenophobia, the international community shares a solemn responsibility to fight those evils. Together we must uphold the terrible truth of the Holocaust against those who deny it. We must strengthen the moral commitment of our peoples, and the political commitment of our governments, to ensure that future generations can understand the causes of the Holocaust and reflect upon its consequences.

4. We pledge to strengthen our efforts to promote education, remembrance and research about the Holocaust, both in those of our countries that have already done much and those that choose to join this effort.

5. We share a commitment to encourage the study of the Holocaust in all its dimensions. We will promote education about the Holocaust in our schools and universities, in our communities and encourage it in other institutions.

6. We share a commitment to commemorate the victims of the Holocaust and to honour those who stood against it. We will encourage appropriate forms of Holocaust remembrance, including an annual Day of Holocaust Remembrance, in our countries.

7. We share a commitment to throw light on the still-obscured shadows of the Holocaust. We will take all necessary steps to facilitate the opening of archives in order to ensure that all documents bearing on the Holocaust are available to researchers.

8. It is appropriate that this, the first major international conference of the new millennium, declares its commitment to

plant the seeds of a better future amidst the soil of a bitter past. We empathize with the victims' suffering and draw inspiration from their struggle. Our commitment must be to remember the victims who perished, respect the survivors still with us, and reaffirm humanity's common aspiration for mutual understanding and justice.

The late Professor Tony Judt was surely correct when he wrote that the "centrality of the Holocaust in Western European identity and memory seemed secure" by the end of the twentieth century.[2] But in that same troubling article, in which he argues that only history and the historian can protect our memory of the "truth" of National Socialism's evil, he also believes that a certain "measure of neglect and even forgetting" are part of the necessity of Europe's civic health. But Judt also admits that "a nation has first to have remembered something before it can begin to forget it."[3] Can we really have it both ways?[4] What have Europe's primary Holocaust players—and here one must count Germany and Austria as those in the first rank—remembered and what and how are they seeking to forget? And does this sense of remembering and forgetting apply to Holocaust memory in the United States?

When the French Catholic sociologist, Maurice Halbwachs, who arrived in the Buchenwald concentration camp at the same time as my father, lay dying of typhus there in March 1945,[5] he could never have imagined that one day he would be mentioned in the same reverential way as his teachers, Emil Durkheim and Henri Bergson. He could never have imagined that his theory of collective memory would allow society to remember, understand, and even change the past. Since Halbwach's death in 1945, we have learned that there are various ways in which our memory and our understanding of the past are reflected. We understand that human memory does not behave like a computer's hard drive, in which stored memory can be recalled in almost perfect form. Pierre Nora has argued that "sites of memory" replace the "real" living memory that was with us for millennia but has now ceased to exist. For Nora, constructed history has replaced true memory.[6] Sites of memory can vary. They may be places such as archives, museums, cathedrals, cemeteries, and memorials; they may be concepts and practices such as generations, mottos, rituals, and commemorations; and they may be objects such as commemorative monuments, manuals, texts, and symbols. What is important is our realization that such sites are artificial and have been deliberately fabricated. They help us recall the past and give that past a collective meaning. They act as identity markers for nations, regions, and social groups and in so doing help those institutions achieve certain goals such as nation building and identity formation.

In a sense the two primary vehicles of collective memory—history and commemoration—have become intense rivals. It is no longer necessary or important to write history "as it was." In a world that struggles with enormous issues of national innocence and guilt, the moral significance of an historic event has become far more important than the causes and consequences of events as they occurred, one after the other. As Halbwachs wrote, "There are no recollections which can be said to be purely interior, that is, which can be preserved only within individual memory. Indeed, from the moment that a recollection reproduces a collective perception, it can itself only be collective."[7]

No area of memory has felt the influence of collective memory more than the Holocaust. The French political scientist, Pierre Nora, describes it thusly: "Whoever says memory, says Shoah."[8] The late Dagmar Barnouw called it "a gigantic construct of memory stories of singular Jewish suffering,"[9] that reflects a growing annoyance with the "semi-religious" status of the Holocaust in America and American Jewish memory and the politicization of the memory of World War II.[10]

Could Barnouw's piece, written by a prominent *Germanisten,* be the opening salvo in an external attack on the "uses and abuses" of Holocaust memory in the United States? Perhaps Professor Barnouw was unhappy that the Holocaust has come to play such an important role in the life of the German Studies Association's annual meeting, where for the past several years issues that dealt with Holocaust themes were prominent among the GSA's numerous sessions. At the 2005 annual meeting, for example, one could find, beyond topics dealing with Jews and with the Holocaust, interesting new issues on "Germany and Transnationalism," but also several sessions on the "Luftkriegsdebatte (The Debate over the Air War)," "Die Besatzungspolitik der Siegermächte (The Politics of Occupation and the Victorious Powers)," "Diplomacy and Memory in Postwar West Germany," "Representations of the RAF," "Günter Grass: Issues of Time and Memory," "Victims and Perpetrators: (Re)Presenting the Past in Post-Unification Culture," and "The Power of Guilt and the Difficulty of Forgivness: Responses to a Tradition." And it continues to this day.[11]

Of course, the internal attack on "Holocaust memory" and its "instrumentalization" was already evident in the late 1990s and the beginning of 2000 when Peter Novick,[12] in a scholarly manner, and Norman Finkelstein,[13] in a polemical, sad, and pathetic presentation, sought to portray the growing awareness of the Holocaust in American life and memory as an "industry" and a "business" that was used by American Jewish organizations to achieve certain aims, including fund-raising and identity politics of the "super-victim" in American society. In Finkelstein and Barnouw's views, "With mounting international criticism of Israel's occupation strategies, Jewish leaders found it increasingly useful to draw on the authority of 'the Holocaust' to support belief in the unique claims of a 'chosen' people's unique victim status—claims that were echoed in the Germans' increasing preoccupation with their unique collective guilt and 'inability to mourn' their victims."[14] Perhaps the Jewish journalist and author Henryk Broder was correct when he quoted a supposed Israeli psychoanalyst named Zvi Rex, who wrote that "the Germans will never forgive the Jews for Auschwitz."[15]

In an American age that Charles Maier has characterized as plagued with "a surfeit of memory," it pays to remember suffering.[16] The meaning of the Holocaust has never found a consensus. Was it a policy devoted to the destruction of all Jewish life or was it an attack against Roma and Sinti, Soviet POWs, Jehovah's Witnesses, etc.? Who has the right to be called a Holocaust survivor, and must we include the word "Jewish" when we identify such a survivor, as though there were other Holocausts against other peoples? But American popular culture, in an effort to salvage or indeed to find common values in the diversity of American multiculturalism and to "recoup the nation's founding fathers' lost ideals of liberty and human rights," has found it rather easy to utilize the Holocaust as part of an American identity. Now anyone can feel like a survivor of "a Holocaust" and can change the past "from remembrance of time to memorialization in sites of memory."[17] And who is to argue that for African Americans a visit to sites of slave deportations in Africa or that for Native Americans a visit to the site of the Wounded Knee massacre does not play as positive a role in remembering the past and the suffering as does a visit to Auschwitz?

As the survivor generation dies, their children draw more and more on "postmemory," the phenomenon that Marianne Hirsch describes as "the experience of those who grow up dominated by narratives that preceded their birth, whose own belated stories are evacuated by the stories of the previous generation shaped by traumatic events that can be neither understood nor recreated."[18] Or, as James Young understands it, a vicarious past "which the post-Holocaust generation can access only through memory."[19] It is "postmemory," then, a kind of secondary witnessing, that will shape the direction that the sons and daughters of survivors must travel in order to give credence to the "voice of the She'erith Hapletah." But only if they choose to do so.[20]

Is that how the Jewish Second Generation is to face a future without the moral authority of their parents? And is that the opening that those committed to reshaping Holocaust memory and the memory of those nations who continue to bear the burden of an individual and national "inability to mourn" await as the last survivor dies?

Efraim Sicher has challenged the Second Generation—the "hinge generation"—to consider what will happen when "there will soon be few left with the personal experience of the Holocaust. . . . What kind of memory is being handed down and what kind of post-Holocaust Jewish identity is it helping to create?"[21] The Polish sociologist and leading postmodernist Zygmunt Bauman has even challenged the right of the Second Generation in the manner that it remembers and seeks to transmit memory of the Holocaust. It is the six million Jewish dead and the survivor generation, Bauman reminds us, who are the real victims, not those who became their sons and daughters and who now develop a corpus of self-witnessing about their own suffering.[22] One must ask, as has Efraim Sicher, what will happen to the future of Holocaust thought and representation in the hands of the Second Generation, its writers and its artists: "There is both awesome responsibility and ironic ambivalence in imagining the past in order to remember the future. There can be no future without the past, but, when remembrance relies on imagination to give it meaning, one must be aware of the risks that are involved."[23]

Remembering and Forgetting

Gottfried and I made our first joint presentation on March 3, 1992, at the twenty-second annual Conference on the Holocaust and the Church Struggle at the University of Washington in Seattle. The title of our session was "Sharing the Burden: Post-Holocaust Germans and Jews and the Search for a New Beginning." In the question-and-answer period, a young woman, obviously German, began to tell us how grateful she was for our presentation. It gave her the courage, she told us tearfully, to admit a family secret that she had not spoken of before in public. During a family event, at the age of thirteen, Katharina von Kellenbach learned that a great-uncle of hers, Alfred Ebner, had not only been an SS officer but was the deputy commissioner of the Belarus town of Pinsk, a town with a large Jewish community. Ebner was accused of overseeing and participating in the murder of at least 30,000 Jews. His trial was discontinued because of his health problems, and he was never convicted of the allegations.[24]

Family discussions about the Nazi past were rare in the post-Holocaust era. Indeed, even Katharina von Kellenbach's father responded to the questions about her great-uncle with silence.[25] German silence about the Holocaust and the crimes of Germany has been the great accusation over the past decades since 1945. It was a silence that was very much related to the component of collective memory that dealt with family history. This component, tied to the notion of affective family bonds, may be termed a compromise or reconciliatory state, in which different generational consciences coexist between the generations. The older generation has its grounding in the past, the working adults are set in the present, and the youngest group is oriented toward the future.

It is clear from the studies of researchers such as Dan Bar-On that in order to protect the unity of the German family in the immediate postwar period, a kind of "affection of conciliation," (read silence) operated in many family situations and was used to avoid familial conflict. When Bar-On began interviewing the children of Nazi perpetrators, he discovered that, despite the participation of thousands of Germans in the process of genocide, hardly any German he interviewed was able to recall anyone whose parents had actually participated in crimes against humanity—despite the fact that they were aware that their own parents were identified as perpetrators.

Family silence and the affection of conciliation were subsets of what Harold Marcuse identifies as three founding myths related to memory in postwar Germany.[26] The first of these was a long-lasting one he called "the myth of victimhood." If anything, it was this myth that was discussed around family tables in the early decades after 1945. It was a myth that saw the German people as victims of National Socialist crimes, crimes committed "in the name of the German people." The vast majority of Germans, therefore, were victims of totalitarianism on an equal level with Jews, Sinti and Roma peoples, and Slavs. This despite the fact that Jewish victims of National Socialism, among others, were not recognized as such in the public commemorations of the Federal Republic of Germany until the end of the twentieth century. The second myth was the "myth of ignorance," a view that most Germans had been totally ignorant of any crimes committed by friends, neighbors, or relatives. Finally, the third myth was the "myth of resistance," which saw most Germans as active resisters to the Nazi regime.

Sitting around the German family table in the early years after Germany's surrender "and around the *Stammtisch,* memories of wartime bombings, horror stories of rapes, and heroic tales of life among the rubble were traded, elaborated, and passed on to children and grandchildren. The experiences of those Germans expelled from the east, far from being shrouded in silence, were discussed by politicians, studied in detail by sociologists and historians, mobilized by visible and vociferous expellee organizations, and publicly recognized on such occasions as the *Volkstrauertag,* or Day of Mourning reinstated in 1952, which commemorated the expellees as well as the civilian and military war dead."[27]

A lack of *Vergangenheitsbewältigung* (overcoming the past), was clearly not the problem, as many critics of German society maintained. The German past-as-victim was very much a living issue. But the German past-as-perpetrator was much more problematic. Other social critics, such as Theodor Adorno[28] and Margarete and Alexander Mitscherlich,[29] recognized this shortcoming as a serious inability to come to terms with a past that included genocide. Adorno accused most Germans after 1945 of the inability to begin "a serious working through of the past, the breaking of its spell through an act of clear consciousness." Instead, most Germans sought to "turn the page" and eliminate it from their memory.[30]

The Mitscherlichs were more wide ranging in their analysis. They began their study of Germany's inability to mourn with Sigmund Freud's famous work *Mourning and Melancholia* (1917). Melancholy is an arrested process that forces the depressed and traumatized self to remain narcissistically identified with a lost object of great affection. But mourning, a step beyond melancholy, allows an engagement with trauma and depression and an overcoming of the earlier state by accepting the pastness of the past and the ability to leave it.[31]

According to the Mitscherlichs, Germany's identification with Adolf Hitler as father figure and national savior, and his subsequent suicide, could only be worked out by accepting this loss and confronting it—and by confronting the fact that reliance on Hitler and his policies had led the nation to see in acts of murder, robbery, and violence the carrying out of "national ideals," ideals that had ended in the genocide of the Jews.

The Mitscherlichs argued that in not recognizing these realities, and in not mourning for the lost father figure of Adolf Hitler, Germany should have fallen into a state of melancholy after 1945. That it did not was due to the nation's intense focus on its economic rebirth, a focus that allowed Germans to live "happy lives" devoid of melancholic misery and "immoral lives" devoid of mourning. Indeed, one needs to ask exactly who, besides the lost figure of Hitler, Germans should have mourned after 1945? Was it the murdered Jews of Europe, a group that, as Anthony Kauders has pointed out, had been vilified as parasites in their own nation and branded as the great enemy of the German *volk*?[32]

Perhaps melancholia was not a necessary component of German society after 1945. Kauders argues that melancholia never was a major part of the German state of mind: "Either they (Germans) had abandoned Hitler in the dying years of the regime or they had, at a somewhat later stage, embarked on a path of economic recovery that forestalled melancholic gloom."[33] Or perhaps mourning did take place: not for "such abstractions as Hitler as *Übervater* or to the mass murder of Jews, Sinti and Roma and mentally ill human beings," but for missing relatives, fallen soldiers, and destroyed cities.[34] It also meant the "propensity of so many postwar Germans to regard themselves as the primary victims of the war."[35]

Not only were they the primary victims of the war, but they had played no role in the terrible crimes committed against the Jews and other peoples. The American Jewish military investigator, Saul Padover, born in Vienna in 1905, undertook an investigation into the "German character and the German mentality." The kinds of attitudes he discovered would shape the attitudes of Germans for more than three decades after the Second World War:

> We have been busy here for two months. We have talked to many people and asked all of them a number of questions, and we have not found a single Nazi. Everyone is an anti-Nazi. All the people are against Hitler. In fact, they have always been against Hitler. What does that mean? That means that Hitler did what he did completely alone, without the help or support of a single German.[36]

Even though Chancellor Konrad Adenauer admitted in 1951 that "unspeakable crimes have been committed in the name of the German people, calling for moral and material indemnity," and found that such an action opened the door for Germany's readmission into Western civilization, the bombing war against hundreds of German cities, the expulsion of German ethnic groups from eastern Europe and Czechoslovakia, mass rapes, death, loss, and suffering "was something that people—especially women—always possessed."[37]

What did the number of nearly six million murdered Jews mean, when one's own figures numbered fourteen million German expellees, of whom anywhere between 500,000 and a million died during the expulsions and flight, or the 500,000 to 600,000 who died as a result of the Allied air war, the majority of them women and one-fifth of them children? Those were German numbers that could only be thought of as victim numbers, and they belonged to Germany.[38]

But not all Germans felt compelled to accept a victim status. The philosopher Karl Jaspers, writing in 1946, acknowledged that "virtually everyone had lost close relatives and friends, but how he lost them—in front line combat, in bombings, in concentration camps or in the mass murders of the regime—results in greatly divergent inner attitudes." "Suffering differs in kind," he added, "Most people have a sense only for their own kind." Jaspers dismissed the notion that one could call "all equally innocent. On the whole, the fact remains that we Germans—however much we may now have come into the greatest distress among the nations—also bear the greatest responsibility for the course of events until 1945. Therefore we, as individuals, should not be so quick to feel innocent, should not pity ourselves as victims of an evil fate, should not expect to be praised for suffering."[39] Even earlier, in April 1942, as he reacted to a British bombing raid on his hometown of Lübeck a month earlier, Thomas Mann, in exile and broadcasting for the BBC, told his "German listeners" that

The time is coming—in fact it has already arrived—when Germany will weep over what she has suffered, and this time of emotion will get out of hand. In the recent bombing raid of Hitler's country, the old city of Lübeck had to suffer. That affects me. That is my home city. The attacks were aimed at the port and the military installations, but there were fires in the city, and I wish that it were not so. . . . Yet perhaps from these ashes, a Germany will awake that wins the people's love instead of their mortal hatred.[40]

But nothing, it seems, could shake Germany from its founding myths of victimhood, ignorance, and resistance. Yes, the Cold War brought a certain relief from the closely held microscope of scrutiny that was applied by the Allies in the immediate days and months after Germany's surrender. And yes, the generation of 1968 began to ask difficult questions of their parents, refusing to "empathize any longer with their parents' tales of flight, rape and bomb trauma," instead seeking to ask what their parents had done to aid the Nazi state and the murder of European Jewry.[41] And, finally, in the 1980s, a phased-in insistence by public intellectuals, scholars, and exhibit designers that Germany accept the primacy of Auschwitz, German guilt and responsibility, and the suffering of Jews and others, forced a kind of "revolution from above" in German public discourse and memory.[42]

The question in the 1990s was how much more Germans could take. In earlier decades calls for "getting over the past" toward a normalizing discourse, in which a final line—a *Schlusstrich*—could be drawn under the guilt column in German postwar history, was seen at best as the nationalist rantings of old or neo-Nazis. But the best-selling book by Daniel Goldhagen[43] that found an entire nation guilty of an "eliminationist anti-Semitism"—a display that highlighted the war crimes of Germany's "last" refuge of national honor, the *Wehrmacht*[44]—and the introduction of numerous Holocaust museums and memorials in cities across the globe—including Berlin at the beginning of the twenty-first century—none of which put little or any emphasis on Germany's postwar democratic society, but highlighted only the crimes of the National Socialist state, may have been enough. Apparently, the moral cudgel (*Moralischerkeule*) of Auschwitz that Martin Walzer mentioned in his 1998 Frankfurt Book Fair speech was the opening shot in a reaction to the expanding knowledge of German crimes that proved more and more troubling to many Germans: "German suffering was claiming more space in public debate and personal memory."[45]

Three important German authors have figured prominently in the new emphasis on German victimization. W. S. Sebald (1944–2001) argued in various essays and in his book *Luftkrieg und Literatur* (Airwar and Literature, 1999) that the Allied bombing of German cities was a "destruction, on a scale without precedent. . . . It seems to have left scarcely a trace of pain behind in the collective consciousness."[46] The novel *Im Krebsgang* [Crab-walk] (2002)[47] by Günter Grass (born 1927) pivots around the sinking of the *Wilhelm Gustloff*, a ship named for an assassinated Nazi leader (shot by a German Jew, David Frankfurter), that was sunk in the Baltic Sea by a Soviet submarine in January, 1945. Many of the estimated 9,000 dead in the greatest of all maritime disasters were refugees from East Prussia, either expelled from their homes or fleeing ahead of the Soviet advance. In 2000, Grass foreshadowed his book by commenting at a conference in Vilnius how "curiously disturbing" it was that "we remember only belatedly and with hesitation the suffering that came to Germans during the war." It was only in a marginal way that one could read about the "death of hundreds of thousands of civilians, [killed] by saturation bombing, and the expulsion and misery of some twelve to fourteen million East German refugees," who needed a voice to speak up for the "silence of the victims."[48] Finally, in 2002, the historian Jörg Friedrich (born 1944) also asked for a new understanding of German suffering at the war's end. In a large, nearly 600-page tome entitled *Der Brand: Deutschland im Bombenkrieg* [The Fire: Germany in the Bombing War][49] he sought to show the consequences of the Allied bombing campaign against Germany through photographs chosen to highlight the suffering of the German population.

All three authors are men of the political left who have asked for Holocaust remembrance and a confrontation with the German past. That they should have chosen themes that for decades had been the poster tragedies of the political right is part of the phenomenon of victimization that has "exploded" into German popular consciousness. Why?

What would drive Friedrich to appropriate Holocaust terminology and describe the air war against Germany as a "massacre," the intentions of the Allies as "extermination," and burning buildings as "crematoria," usage that the New York University historian Mary Nolan has characterized as "particularly inappropriate and inflammatory"?[50]

Do we stand before a "sea change, when it comes to the politics of remembrance" in Germany, as the historian Norbert Frei sees the new emphasis on Germans as victims in World War II?[51] Is part of the issue the fact that, like the Holocaust survivor generation, the generation of Germans who experienced the Allied air war and the expulsion of ethnic Germans from the east is quickly disappearing? Like the Second Generation of sons and daughters of survivors, they too need to make a decision on how they will shape the

German discourse about the past. Will they choose a focus on Germans as victims?

We are already seeing an interesting discourse between the generations, those that continue to sit around the German family table. The sociologist Harald Welzer has described the formation of a German "victim culture" that threatens to obliterate the question of historical and personal responsibility.[52] It may be, according to Welzer and others, that a reconciliation between the generation of 1968 and its aging parents as well as Germany's entrance into the "age of competing victimhoods" will play roles in the new German understanding of itself. Certainly, the third and fourth generations after World War II have already begun to reinterpret the roles of their grandparents during the Third Reich. Welzer's study of forty families from West and East Germany has shown that grandchildren and great-grandchildren have reinterpreted their grandparents' slight or nonexistent efforts to help Jews during the Third Reich as acts of heroism. Indeed, two-thirds of all the stories told by grandparents and great-grandparents were interpreted by the younger generations as stories of victimization during the Nazi past and/or of heroes of everyday resistance.[53] The grandchildren and great-grandchildren who made these statements were well schooled in the history of the Holocaust. Yet their educational achievements and their personal family histories were two entirely different phenomena.[54] It is instructive to cite from Welzer's conclusions about the potential consequences of his study:[55]

> Our study's findings, like the popularity of books focused on German suffering, indicate that this culture [the German postwar commemorative culture's focus that Auschwitz should not happen again] may be undergoing a restructuring. This ominous development reveals that the real effect, in terms of lived history, of the twelve-year period between 1933 and 1945 is becoming more visible with growing temporal distance. . . . It has become clear that the lasting distortion of family and individual biographies by the twelve years of Nazi power was much more pervasive than any involved in dealing with the past had ever dared believe. What does the creation of a German culture of victimization mean for the German-Jewish dialogue? And what of the importance of family history, clearly a history that is being revised according to the new German understanding of itself as a society of victims?[56]

Interestingly, it is the considered opinion of many in the Jewish Second Generation that we cannot consider ourselves victims—that such a standing belongs to our parents. Yet the view of many in Germany's Second Generation seems to be that German victimization is the way of the future. How do we understand phrases such as the "inability to mourn" or "overcoming the past?" What relevance do they now have to the dialogue between Second Generation Germans and Jews? Is it important for Germans to understand themselves as victims? Is it important for Jews to understand Germans as victims?[57] Can Germans and Jews continue to engage in a dialogue that includes a narrative of suffering on both sides?

But not all Germans agree with the need for victimization. Joschka Fischer, Germany's former foreign minister and a German whose family was expelled from Hungary in 1945, explained the need to understand what happened before 1945 and the fact that German aggression and crimes against humanity had led to the death of millions and millions of Germans by the war's end, not all of them innocent victims of Allied retribution. "The real issue," Fischer stated, "was what we have done to ourselves not what others have done to us. The cause of our pain is what we have done to ourselves not what others have done to us."[58] To a generation of sons and daughters of Holocaust survivors, who understand the pain of what was done to their parents and their own lives, but do not fully know why, the need for Germans to understand Fischer's words is appropriate and even crucial—not only for them but for the future of our common dialogue.

15

Facing the Past

Shadows of the Past:
A Trip through Time and Trauma (2005)

Since 1992 Gottfried and I had been talking about traveling together to Auschwitz. After we attended several events together in Dallas in March 2005, Gottfried's son Eugenio wrote a letter to me:

Dear Abraham,

I wanted to tell you about my desire to visit the Auschwitz concentration camp with you—I know of the sorrow you carry deep in your heart, and the many injustices that have been committed against you. My heart is close to those who have suffered. My eyes have seen the suffering on television, but that is not enough. I want to see it myself, so that I might be able to contemplate more deeply what happened. It would be a great honor for me to meet you, free from the burden of moral judgments.

Yours sincerely, Eugenio.[1]

I replied,

Dear Eugenio,

I was very moved by your beautiful letter. I know from your father the story of your early life and, of course, the story of your years in Cerro Maggiore and the wonderful life you now have. I hope very much that we will be able to meet and to visit those places of darkness that have so affected our lives. In the meantime, I wish you much success with your studies and with your reflections on the life you are creating for yourself.[2]

277

My father died on July 5, 2005, at the age of ninety-two. That terrible event heightened the anxiety surrounding our trip, and it also triggered a profound identity crisis for me. I explained this crisis in an email to the director of the Böhlau publishing house in Vienna:

> My father's illness and death not only robbed me of the last member of my immediate family, they also took away the heart of my Holocaust memory, which permitted me unusual access to those events that define who and what I am.[3]

Originally, the trip we were planning was to take place with our sons. Unfortunately, my son Joel could not come. This trip would be a way of allowing Gottfried and me the opportunity to revisit the sites of our parents and our early youth. But it was primarily taken because of my need to visit the sites of my parents' joys and sorrows, when their families were intact and when they were destroyed forever. It was because of the chance for me and for both of us to stand together in the shadows of a past and a legacy that shaped who we were and who we have become that this trip held so much meaning and so much importance. And so, with Gottfried's encouragement, it is for me to record the sites and emotions of that trip.

A Painful Decision

As August 2005 approached, I was exhausted. I had organized two major academic conferences, cared for my father in the final weeks of his illness, watched him die, arranged his funeral, and sat shivah for him, all in the space of four months. It was Thomas Wolfe who reminded us that "you can't go home again." But I knew that on August 8 I would be leaving from Boston's Logan Airport for a journey to the closest thing I had to an historic home: the places where my ancestral roots were located and where I was born.

Gottfried and I had planned this trip for months, finding the funding for expenses and preparing for what would be the last chapter of our book and a final, upfront confrontation with our *Familiengeschichte,* our family history. What neither of us had prepared for was the illness and death of my father. The shock of it was devastating. The foundations of my identity crumbled. I was no longer the son of survivors but an orphaned adult. I no longer had my father's memory and mine in the first person. I was now the lead plane preparing for takeoff to the *olam haba*—the world to come.

When I first told my father that I was going to Poland to visit the places of his and my mother's life, he seemed interested. Such a conversation had never before taken place between us. It was just assumed that Poland was "off limits," a country that both my parents had placed in *herem,* a country from which I was banned, unlike Germany, from which my parents had lifted the *herem.* Perhaps it was his illness and the dementia that affected many of his final days, perhaps it was a change of heart, but my father seemed pleased that I was planning the trip to Łęczyca, Zwolen, and Łódź. And I could not wait to tell him what I had seen of those places that were names to me, but without any shape or form, very much like Landsberg had been to many of us who were born there but had never returned: a place that was and wasn't. But in the final days of his life, my father's attitude toward my planned Poland trip changed. Among the last things he said to me when I told him again that I was going to Poland was, "Don't go." My father had always reacted that way to any indication from me that I might be putting myself in harm's way. But he and my mother had accepted and learned to live with my going off to a university hundreds of miles from home, had accepted and learned to live with my leaving America for England and then Germany.

In the weeks of observing *shloshim,* the thirty-day period of intense mourning that would last until just a few days before I was to depart, I thought long and hard about my decision to go. I decided that I had to go, if only because this might be my only opportunity to visit the roots of my identity and to utilize the book that Gottfried and I were writing to justify the trip. Armed with a letter of introduction from Marek Lesniewski-Laas, the honorary consul of the Republic of Poland for New England, I boarded a Swiss International Airlines flight to Milan.

From Landsberg to Bayreuth

Gottfried picked me up on the morning of August 9 at Milan's Malpensa airport. It was my first time in Italy and my first opportunity to meet Gottfried's family. The short drive to Cerro Maggiore, the small town where Gottfried lived, was a pleasant one. Gottfried took me to a small hotel where I would stay for two nights before our departure. I was able to shower and shave before he picked me up for lunch. Lunch with an Italian family is not a typical American "sandwich" affair. It is a long, rather drawn-out affair if possible, and the pasta and wine are plentiful. Lunch with Gottfried was no exception. During lunch I finally met Mama Antonietta, Gottfried's legendary mother-in-law, whose belief in Gottfried's work and whose basic humanity encouraged her to visit Auschwitz and Israel when she was already in her seventies. Cerro Maggiore had been a center for the local Gestapo, and Mama Antonietta had seen a friend of hers arrested and sent to a concentration camp for suspected resistance activities.

I also met Eugenio, Gottfried's twenty-year-old son, a survivor of the Ceaușescu-era Romanian orphanages, who has been adopted by Gottfried and Teresina at the age of five and a half. Eugenio was a sensitive young man, well aware of what he had suffered in the years before his adoption. His quiet, assured manner belied his youth. I would find in him a wisdom and understanding that was extraordinary. I also met Alberto, "Albi," a twenty-year-old university student, who was Eugenio's best friend. They had grown up together and, although different in temperament and career interests, were as close as two first cousins could be. Indeed, when Eugenio had first come to live in Cerro Maggiore and began to attend school, it was Cousin Alberto who defended him against the taunts and bullying of other students. Albi would be joining us on our trip. He replaced my son Joel, who could not go at the last minute. Joel had accepted a position with an institution devoted to Jewish life in the southern part of the United States, an opportunity that he could not refuse.

After two lovely days of water outings at Lago Maggiore and Lago Como, the time had come to begin our journey on August 12. After an eight-hour ride in Gottfried's twelve-year-old Audi 4, we arrived in Landsberg and the Hotel Goggl. In a sense, coming back to Landsberg was like visiting an old friend with whom you are comfortable, if not entirely at ease. When I checked in at the Hotel Goggl, the manager behind the desk noted that I had been a guest of the hotel before and that it was a pleasure to welcome me once again. Our friend, former Lord Mayor Franz Xaver Roessle, came to the hotel to take us on a tour of Landsberg's Holocaust history. Our first stop was the former Jewish DP camp, the place of my birth. I had last visited Landsberg in the winter of 2000. Even since then, the former DP camp had undergone great changes. The memorial plaque dedicated in 1989 by Irving Heymont had been moved to a new site. It was now attached to the side of a public school on the grounds of the old *Kaserne*. New construction was also under way, and the plan was to convert the old army barracks, including Block 4, where my parents and I had lived for several months, into condominiums.

Now, in August 2005, the building project was complete. All the former DP camp dwellings were condos with outside terraces. Children played in front of the buildings and on nearby playgrounds. Certain buildings, the former communal dining hall, the movie theater, and the former headquarters of the American Jewish Joint Distribution Committee, were still identifiable, but little else reminded me of "home." As we stood looking at the buildings, a woman who knew Roessle came over to say hello. He introduced us, and especially me, whom he described as a *geburtiger Landsberger*, a native of Landsberg. The woman made certain to tell us that her grandmother had helped to get the few Jewish parents and their children out of Landsberg after 1938. Roessle then told us that in a few weeks he would be going to visit one of those former Landsberg Jewish families, the Willstaedters, who now lived in Oregon.

What was I to believe? I had lived in Germany long enough and had read enough studies[4] to know that if a parent or grandparent had even looked at a Jew with sympathy during the Nazi period, this often constituted and was translated into, for the child or grandchild, an act of rescue. What I did know was that Roessle's mother had taken in our friend Harry Guterman after his liberation from the Kaufering camps and had formed a fast friendship with him until Harry left for the northern German city of Bremen.

Franz Roessle, his wife, and children had become good friends of the Gutermans in 1980 and had visited Harry in America on numerous occasions. We also visited the many sites of suffering that were the result of the Kaufering/Landsberg concentration camps. We could not enter the huge underground bunker where thousands had lost their lives in 1944 and 1945, but we stood on the site of one of the many Jewish cemeteries that contained the remains of those who died in those camps. I said *kaddish* for them and for my mother and father and their families. We took Eugenio and Albi to the fortress-like prison where Adolf Hitler had composed large parts of *Mein Kampf* in 1923 and 1924. Entrance into the prison itself, still actively holding prisoners, was normally not allowed, but the former Lord Mayor, judge, and attorney, all in the person of Franz Roessle, not only got us into the prison but to the gate that separated guards from prison cells. Here we could clearly see the cell window that had been part of Adolf Hitler's home.

We had two more places to visit. One was the site of a memorial plaque dedicated in 1995 at the site where a "death march" of Jewish prisoners had made its way at the end of April 1945 toward Dachau. The site had been chosen on the recommendation of a Landsberg citizen who had stepped forward to testify that, as a young boy, he had seen the long line of emaciated men marching in formation in April 1945 with SS guards at their side. Then there was only one more site to visit. That was the "Spöttinger Cemetery," the place where some of the most notorious war criminals of the Nazi era were buried. Controversy had always surrounded this cemetery because, in addition to the leaders of at least two *Einsatzgruppen*, one responsible for the massacre at Babi Yar, and heads of concentration camps, two "unknown Jews" were also buried in this unholy site.

For years Irving Heymont and I had tried to have the bodies of the two Jews removed from the cemetery with no luck. Now in 2005 the Landsberg City Council had decided to end the controversy once and for all by removing all the identification plaques from each grave. Each of the dead, war criminal and unknown Jew, would lie forever in equal anonymity. The two young cousins, Eugenio and Albi, were fascinated with Landsberg and my part in its history. Albi was a gifted linguist, who spoke excellent English and was learning German. Eugenio did not speak either language well. Our dinner with the Roessles that evening was a mixture of German, English, and Italian, but it constituted a very warm conclusion to a day of terrible history.

From Landsberg we drove to Nürnberg, the showplace of National Socialism. It was in this medieval town that National Socialism put itself on display in all its "glory" through the camera lens of the German filmmaker Leni Riefenstahl. Her 1935 film, *Triumph of the Will*, is acclaimed as one of the greatest film documentaries of all time, but it marked Riefenstahl as a Nazi sympathizer and an ambitious, immoral human being. With the help of two of Gottfried's friends, Heide and Albert Grossman, he a retired dentist and she a teacher of English, who lived in Nürnberg, we drove to the site of the 1935 Nazi display and took turns standing on the spot where Adolf Hitler had addressed the thousands of adoring Germans who had come to see the Führer and the "new" Germany. Albert told us that Nürnberg was intent on changing its image as the Nazi showplace by becoming a city focused on human rights, with conferences, international awards, and other ways of repudiating its past and creating its new future.

We said goodbye to Nürnberg and drove the fairly short distance to Bayreuth, Gottfried's birthplace. Until now, our journey had been interesting, and we had enjoyed each other's company during the long ride from Milan. But now we drove in silence. We were approaching the city that was the source of so much of Gottfried's hatred and bitterness. Gottfried had booked us into a hotel on the outskirts of Bayreuth so that we would not have to endure the crowds of Wagner fans who had come for that summer's opera festival. But being on the outskirts of Bayreuth did not help. As we entered the hotel to check in, numerous men in elegant tuxedos accompanied by glamorous women in designer gowns passed by us on the way to numerous pre-performance parties. I could sense the tension in Gottfried and the helplessness of his son and nephew as they watched their father and uncle change from a warm and funny man into a cold, defensive "son" of Bayreuth.

We drove to the ancestral home of the Wagners, Villa Wahnfried, where Richard Wagner and his wife Cosima are buried. I was surprised at how small the house appeared, although I realized that it was actually three houses joined by a wall. Gottfried and his family had lived in one of the houses and his Uncle Wieland and family in another, called the Siegfried Wagner house. Gottfried's grandmother, Winifred, had a small apartment built for Adolf Hitler that was attached to the Siegfried Wagner House. Just a few steps from Villa Wahnfried stood the house where Gottfried's great-great-grandfather, the composer Franz Liszt, lived and died.

We then drove some minutes to the site of the Wagner opera festival. The "house on the green hill" as it is known, is an impressive building surrounded by beautiful flowers. Gottfried was not allowed to enter the building since a dispute with his father, but nothing prevented him or us from walking around the beautifully manicured grounds as the performance of a Wagner opera was taking place. Gottfried showed us the bust of Richard Wagner, done by Hitler's favorite sculptor, Arno Brecker. Gottfried had hated the bust from childhood and told us that once, as a young boy, he had defaced it. Indeed, as we walked around the grounds, Gottfried regaled us with a number of *Losbubengeschichten,* bad-boy stories, about the mischief he had caused in the opera house. As we walked, numerous people seemed to recognize Gottfried and stared at him and us. One elderly woman walked past Gottfried and said, in German, "Good evening, Gottfried." He never acknowledged her existence. Finally, as we left the grounds, Gottfried

284 | Post-Holocaust Germans and Jews

pointed to a window on the second floor of the opera house. "Here," he said, "was where Hitler would wave to the adoring masses while attending one of the Wagner operas."

Gottfried also showed us the beautiful villa that belonged to his father and his father's second wife and daughter. The house was separated from the Wagner Festspielhaus by a few hundred meters and a long chain-link fence. I understood, as did Gottfried, that if his life had turned out differently, the directorship of the Wagner Festival would have been his, as would most probably the handsome home that stood next to it. Instead, Gottfried and his son had to remain anonymous and essentially entered the family "business" as total strangers. Eugenio walked over to a souvenir stand to buy some postcards for his mother and grandmother. I rushed over to pay for them. At least I could spare him the discomfort of acting like a typical tourist in his grandfather's home.

As we left the grounds of the Wagner opera house, we noticed a memorial to the memory of Ottilie Metzger and Henriette Gottlieb, two Jewish singers of the Bayreuth Wagner Festival who had been murdered by the National Socialists. Gottfried dismissed this gesture as another effort to "kosher" the Wagner history of anti-Semitism and pro-Nazism. As we left Bayreuth, I noted that Gottfried again resumed a sense of cheerfulness and was much less tense. We were headed for Poland, and it was now my turn to encounter a nervousness and fear of the unknown that were quite unlike anything I had ever felt before.

Ghosts—But They Are My Ghosts!

Wroclaw/Breslau

We were nearly to the Polish border. I had been dreading this event and anticipating it at the same time. At the border crossing of the former German city of Görlitz, Gottfried and the two boys, with passports from European Union member states, had no difficulties. I was asked to wait, and my passport was taken by the German border police. After a few minutes it was returned to me, and we were waved through into Poland. It was August 14, in Hebrew *Tish b'Av*, the ninth day of the month of *Av*, a fast day and a day of mourning that commemorated the destruction of the first and second Jerusalem Temples and all of the great tragedies that had befallen the Jewish people. It was appropriate, I thought, that I should be in Poland on this date. Poland was the place where the greatest tragedy in terms of Jewish deaths by murder had taken place.

I felt an excitement and an anxiety that stayed with me during the entire six-hour ride to Wroclaw, our first Polish stop. Along the way, the Silesian countryside still bore the look of Germany in the construction and colors of the farmhouses that were clearly left over from the time when this part of Silesia was German. But it was a much poorer German look than even that of the former East German areas we had seen on the way to Poland. All of the area we passed through on the way to Wroclaw had been German until 1945. Then, with Nazi Germany's defeat, a mass expulsion of Germans began from this region's villages and towns. Thousands of people, families and individuals from other parts of Poland, were brought in to take over the abandoned farms, villages, and towns of once-German Silesia. Until 1945 Wroclaw was called Breslau, the capital city of Silesia. It was for centuries a multicultural community, predominantly German from the Middle Ages onward, but with substantial Polish, Czech, Ukrainian, and Jewish minorities.

With the establishment of an independent Poland at the end of the First World War, Breslau's Jewish community was the sole survivor of the city's multicultural period. Breslau Jewry was an important Jewry. It boasted Nobel Prize winners (Fritz Haber and Max Born), important political leaders (Ferdinand Lasalle), and a rabbinical seminary, the Jüdisch-Theologische Seminar, founded in 1854 and closed by the Nazis in 1939. Among its faculty and students were such important figures in Jewish thought as Zacharias Frankel (1801–1875), Heinrich Graetz (1817–1891), and Hermann Cohen (1842–1918). One could argue that it was in Breslau rather than Berlin where the Wissenschaft des Judentums (the academic study of Judaism) was born. It was to this rabbinical seminary, which understood itself as the "positive and historical" branch of Judaism, that America's Conservative Jewish movement looked for its understanding of ritual and belief. Yet nothing remained of the great institution that had stood at 1B Wallstrasse.[5] And here I stood in a place called Wroclaw, in the second-largest Jewish community in all of Poland, a community that numbered just under 300, "down" from a pre-1933 figure of 30,000. They were not part of the 1945 German expellees. The last Jewish funeral in Breslau had taken place in August 1942. A year later the Nazis declared Silesia to be *Judenrein*. Breslau's Jewish community had ceased to exist. I could not bring myself to visit the city's only synagogue, *Zum weissen Storch*, named for the pub that had occupied the spot where the Jewish house of worship was built.[6] We were in Breslau for only twelve hours. I said *kaddish* for my father in my hotel room.

The four of us walked along the streets of Breslau, and for the first ten or fifteen minutes we saw the kind of ugly socialist realism that had symbolized communist architecture. We also saw one instance of graffiti after another, some of them anti-Semitic. It was only when we entered Breslau's old city that we found a major surprise. The city square was beautiful. This is what German Breslau had looked like before 1939. Brightly colored buildings surrounded a huge square, free of automobiles and full of music and life. We decided to eat in a restaurant that advertised itself as possessing an *echt deutsches* (genuine German) cuisine. The food was plentiful and quite tasty. I could not help but notice that the people at the table next to us were speaking a strongly accented German. We struck up a conversation, and it turned out that they were expellees, born in the town of Opeln when it was still German Silesia but expelled by the new Polish government in 1945. Now they had come back to visit their roots. How did it feel being back, I asked? Great, they told me, "after all, we're all Europeans now." That may have been true in a psychological sense. But it was not true in terms of most of the Polish roads. We moved out of Breslau the next morning at a snail's pace, stymied by horse-drawn carriages, 1950s-style tractors, and road construction that would symbolize both the new and old Poland.

Łęczyca / Linshits

We drove on toward Łęczyca, my father's birthplace. We had good maps, but good maps didn't always help in Poland. Three important Polish words that I am certain none of us will ever forget were *prosto*, "straight ahead," *lewo*, "left," and *prawo* "right." My limited Polish got us to most locations, but hearing those three words was always a pleasure. As we neared Łęczyca, I felt faint. I could not believe I was heading for the place that was half of my family history. I was excited yet apprehensive.

Even after the end of the Holocaust, at a time when the small remnants of Polish Jewry faced the hostility of its surroundings just two months after a horrific pogrom in the city of Kielce had left more than forty Jews dead and hundreds wounded, a blood libel circulated in Łęczyca and was reported to the Polish government officials.[7] The *yizkor* (memorial) book of the community was published in 1953 in Israel by Rabbi J. Frenkel. Called *Sefer Linshits* (the Book of Linshits), it is printed entirely in Hebrew with no Yiddish entries. Among *yizkor* books this is somewhat unusual. Either Linshits was one of the most religiously observant towns in all of Eastern Europe or Rabbi Frenkel demonstrated a decided bias toward the world of rabbinic life and activities. Practically all of the photographs in the main part of the volume are of revered rabbis or their synagogues. But not all. There are also photographs of various school classes, and nearly six decades after he left Linshits for the great city of Łódź, my father was able to point out pictures of several boys and remember their last names and whether he had gone to school with them or even served in the Polish military with one of them.

Until 2005 I had never visited Linshits. But I saw it first through the eyes of the Polish Jewish filmmaker, Marian Marzynski, who was born in Linshits and survived the Holocaust years in Poland hidden by Catholic nuns. I met Marzynski in the early 1980s at the screening of his documentary film *Shtetl*. By coincidence, his mother was with him. She was born in Linshits, the only person besides my father that I had known from the town. She remembered my father's family and the family business (they owned several teams of horses used to transport goods and people). Marzynkski's film showed him walking through the streets of Linshits. It looked like any small East European town during the days of the Iron Curtain: inelegant groups of men in various stages of intoxication. But Marzynski made it clear just how empty Linshits was of the vibrancy that had defined pre-Holocaust Jewish life, not only in Linshits but in all of Poland, the "hole in the heart" of a nation devoid of a large and missing part of its history.

Oh yes, the Polish Christians he interviewed on the street remembered the Jews. How terrible it was, they said, what the Germans had done to them. Yet the Poles in Linshits did not seem so sad. Perhaps it was the liquor they had consumed and continued to consume. It was terrible, they said again, what the Germans had done to the Jews. But what had Poland done? Often, when I spoke to my father about his identity as a Pole and as a Jew, I received conflicting messages. Like many Holocaust survivors born in Poland who had not returned in 1945, he suffered from a deeply embedded feeling of wrong suffered during the prewar years, during the Nazi occupation, and during the postwar period. But he also suffered from the trauma of unrequited love. Many Jews of my father's generation, nearing its close, could not erase from their hearts this country where they were born and grew up, where, as the great Jewish poet, the Łódź-born Julian Tuwim wrote of them, "in Polish they confessed the disquiet of their first love and in Polish they stammered of its rapture and tempests, where they loved the landscape, the language, the poetry, where they were ready to shed their blood for Poland and be her true sons."

I kept thinking of Marzynski's words: "I returned only once to Łęczyca in 1969. But when I started asking questions about those in my family who were killed, and those who betrayed them, I couldn't take it. I decided never to return to my shtetl."[8] What was it that Marzynski could not take? Was it the drunken figures in the town square that I saw in his film *Shtetl*? Was it the description of the hanging of ten Jewish men on March 17, 1942, in the renamed Adolf Hitler Platz, a day when "Christian teachers brought their Polish pupils to watch the gallows and preached morals to the children?"[9] My father's Linshits, even though it was more than the imagined small village where the streets were covered in mud, was like a ghost town. Few people were on the streets in the late morning, and no shops seemed to be open. The main square was deserted. No drunken louts staggered about. But I did get excited when I saw a street sign that read *Ulica Ozorkowska*. Ozorkowska Street, I knew from my father's stories, was one of the main entrances to the town.

We parked and began to walk. As we passed one house, an old man came out of the gate with a bicycle. I asked him if he knew where the Jewish cemetery was. There is no Jewish cemetery, he replied. The Germans took all of the headstones and used them to pave the streets. I explained who I was and asked if he remembered my family, the Piks. He said he did. "What can you tell me about them?" I asked. "Well, they were Jews, God's people." He then began a long theological discourse on God Jehovah and punishments. I knew at once that he was a Jehovah's Witness and that, if we did not excuse ourselves, he would bear witness for an extended period. I told him that I was very familiar with the suffering and bravery of the Jehovah's Witnesses during the Holocaust. We parted with a handshake. But did he really remember my family?

We continued to walk until we came to another familiar sign: *Ulica Zydowska*, Jews' Street. Again, I knew this name from my father. The Pik family had lived around the corner at No. 19 Wiezienna, now renamed Grodzkiej Street. Ulica Zydowska had contained many of the Jewish businesses in Linshits. But I had to know more. I could not understand why so few people were on the streets. We came to the city hall and found it closed, as were all the other shops around the town square. Only later did we learn that this particular day was a Catholic holiday. We decided to find a church and see whether we could speak to a priest to get more information. We found a church not far from the town square, one that had been completed in 1916, the year my father turned three. We knocked on the rectory door, and a tall, young priest opened it. When I explained who I was and my connection to Linshits, he invited us in for coffee and biscuits. Albi and Eugenio were pleased. Both boys were practicing Catholics, as was Gottfried after his marriage to Teresina. They felt at home. But Father Zbigniew Luczak could not really help us. He did not know anything about a Jewish presence in Linshits. He offered to look in the rectory archives in the basement for any information on the family Pik. What he brought upstairs was promising. It was a thick volume that looked old. But it turned out to be late nineteenth-century records of all Catholic weddings in Linshits. As far as I knew, I had no Catholic members in my immediate family.

We spoke a bit longer about Catholic-Jewish relations and about the work of John Paul II. Finally, Father Luczak took a volume from his bookshelf and handed it to me as a gift. It was a history of Łęczyca until the year 1990, a year after the fall of communism in Eastern Europe. We went through the index looking for the name Pik, but there was no listing. When I looked through the historic photographs in the book, I found only one that had any relation to Jewish life in Linshits. It was a 1940 photograph of Jews' Street with a barbed-wire enclosure. It was the starting point of the Linshits ghetto. But I also learned something else in the book that moved me tremendously: how right my father had been about Ignacy Solinski, his mentor in the bakery business. In May 1940 Solinski was one of the non-Jews in Linshits arrested by the Nazis for acts of resistance and deported to a concentration camp, most likely Auschwitz.[10]

I left Linshits without much in the way of *Familiengeschichte*. Yet I had walked on the ground that my father and my unknown uncles, aunts, and cousins had called home. That ground was sacred because it helped to ground me in time and history.

Łódź

Łódź was the city of my parents' greatest joy and their longest period of suffering. They had both come to Łódź as young people in their twenties. They had left the world of the shtetl to experience the fullness of Poland's second-largest city and second-largest Jewish community, only to experience the misery and destruction of that community during five years of ghettoization. My maternal grandfather had been shot to death in this ghetto, and three of my maternal uncles had died of starvation as my mother cradled their heads.

Yet my parents had married in Łódź and had hoped against hope for a chance to live a normal existence in some unknowable future. It might have been fate that we booked rooms in a hotel that sat around the corner from the confectionary shop in which my father had been a partner. It might have been fate that the woman at the reception desk of the hotel, a lovely Polish Catholic woman, Mazgorzata Chrzanowska, whom we called Margaret, was also a guide for things Jewish in Łódź and gave me an opportunity to see aspects of my parents' lives in that city that I might otherwise have missed. Margaret took us to Jewish Łódź past and present. Its present was the offices of the Jewish community where we met the chairman of the *Gmina Wyznaniowa Zydowska W Łódźi* (the Jewish Community in Łódź).

Simcha Keller was an energetic man, born in Poland but with a clearly good Jewish background, including the Hebrew language. He was optimistic about the future of Łódź Jewry although it numbered fewer than 400 people. The community was active in researching the history of Łódź Jewry including the Nazi period. But when I asked Keller whether there were any survivors of the Łódź ghetto in the community, he said no. All the residents of the Łódź Jewish Home for the Aged were from other parts of Poland. I was delighted to see some signs of Jewish life. Keller's phone rang constantly. His offices were full of documents on the history of Jewish life in Łódź, and he had the keys to the only functioning synagogue in the community. When I entered the synagogue, I imagine that I felt like Gottfried, Eugenio, and Albi in Father Luczak's office. It was a comfort to be in surroundings that spoke of Jewish existence, however slight. I was also interested to speak to the man responsible for the care of the synagogue. A Catholic, he was converting to Judaism. I reminded him that a *ger,* a convert, held a special place of importance in Jewish life.

From Jewish life we went to the places of Jewish death. Our first stop was the site where my father had first lived in the ghetto. I stood across the street and tried to imagine him coming home every evening from a day of burying Łódź's Jewish dead. Ultimately, he would be part of a group that buried over

43,000 men, women, and children, Jews, Sinti, and Roma. We then drove to the Łódź city archives. I hoped that I might be able to find some information on my parents and relatives because many of the original Łódź ghetto records were part of the millions of documents housed at this large and impressive building. If there is one place in which I can speak the language of the house, it is an archive. Within minutes, while Gottfried took Margaret on an errand, I had several microfilm reels to examine. I spent nearly an hour going through those reels but found nothing about my parents. I did find a death certificate made out for Golda Guterman, age sixty-six, from Konstantynow. She was Harry Guterman's grandmother. We also drove to the Radegast railroad station. My parents had been deported from there in March and August 1944. It was such a small station for a place that sent thousands of Jews to their deaths in the Chelmno camp. The boys noticed railroad cars on the tracks. They were two of the original cars that had taken Jews from this station. Eugenio and Albi clamored on board. I could not, just as I could not enter the original Deutsche Reichsbahn car at the United States Holocaust Memorial Museum. I was afraid of what I would feel and what I would hear—the voices of the dead.

Our final stop was at the entrance to the New Jewish Cemetery, perhaps the largest in Europe. It was in a portion of this cemetery, known as the Ghetto Fields, where my father had worked on the burial detail. There are no gravestones here, except for ones placed by families long after the end of the Holocaust. It is just a vast field of the unmarked dead. I stood there and said *kaddish* for them as had my father over sixty years earlier. Before we left Łódź we did a bit of sightseeing and shopping along the city's "Fifth Avenue," Ulica Piotorkowska. We managed to visit a bookshop owned by two young Polish Catholics that had an impressive display of books on Polish Jewry and on Judaism. I asked them whether they had many customers for these books and they said, "Yes, there is a great interest." "Do you know any Jews?" I asked them. "A few," they replied. "There are not many Jews in Łódź or in Poland."

On the way back to the hotel, I noticed a restaurant with a sign that displayed a fiddler playing on a roof. Naturally, the restaurant, called the "Anatevka," promised a genuine Jewish kitchen. I was skeptical. I knew what a genuine Jewish kitchen was, and here in this less-than-genuine Jewish environment, I doubted that such a kitchen could be found. I could not have been more wrong. The food was my mother's cooking, and I did not want it to stop. Gottfried and the boys had never seen a menu such as this, and I delighted in guiding them through the culinary pleasures of Polish Jewish cooking. As we ate, a young woman, not Jewish, played klezmer songs, beautifully, on a violin.

This was the beginning of an experience that I had read about. Polish Jewry had an almost unnatural grip on modern Poland through books, music, and food, and would not let go. The ghosts were all around—and they were my ghosts.

Zwolen/Zvolin and Skarżysko-Kamienna

We drove to Radom, the largest city near Zwolen, my mother's birthplace. After checking into a hotel and eating dinner there, we went to bed at a reasonably early hour. At least Gottfried and I did. The boys were twenty-year-olds, and although they had been extraordinarily attentive throughout the trip—observing, asking questions, and carrying my suitcases, they were still boys. Their nocturnal activities and their ability to get up for early departures were controlled by Gottfried, not always successfully.

But we did get an early start toward Zwolen. When we arrived, on a beautiful summer day, I was surprised at how lovely a place it was. It was not at all like Linshits, crumbling buildings surrounded by a desolate town square, but a modern, Western European–looking community that could have easily been an English small town. We immediately went to the city hall and found to our delight that not only was it open, but we were treated as honored guests. The Zwolen city administration was eager to try to help me, although they were not certain that they could find someone who would remember my mother's family. A city hall staff member walked with us a short distance to a row of older homes. He stopped at one, a rather dismal-looking structure, and said, "If anyone can remember your mother's family, it is the gentleman who lives here." A barking dog greeted us as we walked around to the back of the house. An elderly man opened the door and peered at us. "Come in," he said. "How can I help you?"

We sat around a simple table as our city hall guide explained what I needed to know. Did he remember a Jewish family called Kolton? At first he could not. But after a few minutes, Stephan Kwapisiencz changed his mind: "Yes, I remember the family. Some of them lived very near here." I cannot describe how grateful I was to him for this information. I walked with our city hall host to take photographs while Gottfried and the boys remained inside to continue speaking with the elderly gentleman. When Gottfried joined us, he told me that Kwapisiencz had begun to cry as he described the roundup and deportation of Jews from Zwolen. But we were not yet done with Zwolen. Our host asked if we would be interested in seeing the city archives and museum. Perhaps they had information for me.

The museum/archives was a busy place. Computer terminals, fax machines, and documents were stuffed into the office in such numbers that there was little room for anything else. Posters hung on every inch of wall space. The staff, led by its director, Elszbieta Nowakowska, was friendly. They made room for us at a small conference table, and we began to discuss the reason for my visit. My Polish was technically not good enough to explain details. We tried a little Italian and English, but German seemed to be the best source of communication. There was good reason for all this activity. The six-hundredth anniversary of Zwolen's founding would take place in 2006, and among the events planned was an exhibit on the history of Zwolen Jewry. There was an intense search for information on Zwolen's Jews. "Did you know," I asked, "that a history of the community exists in the form of a *yiskor* book?" They had heard of such a book but did not have a copy.

We then began to discuss some archival cooperation. I would make the *yiskor* book available to them if they would, in turn, provide me with materials from the exhibit, especially any that dealt with my mother's family. The most enthusiastic member of the staff was Piotr Wajs. He spoke reasonably good German and offered to take me to the site of the Jewish cemetery. But, he warned me, I must tell you that there is nothing there that would tell you that it was a cemetery. The Nazis destroyed all the *mazteivas,* the headstones, except for three that we keep in the basement of the museum. I was surprised that he knew the Yiddish word for headstone. Hardly any non-Jew in America would, but perhaps this indicated the level of small-town closeness that was an often overlooked aspect of Polish-Jewish relations.

We drove to the place of the former cemetery. It was simply a field, lush with vegetation, but devoid of anything that would have told us what had once been sacred Jewish ground. I said *kaddish* for all those who were buried there, including members of my family. "We want to restore this cemetery," Piotr Wajs told me. "A number of smaller villages have done this with the help of their former Jewish residents. We are a poor town. We need the help of our former Zwolen Jews."

Months later, I received an email from Piotr Wajs. He wrote to me in German that he had found a copy of a Polish history of Jewish life in Zwolen and the surrounding area. "I read the book during the night," he wrote, "and I was moved to tears by the terrible fate of this town's Jews."

From Zwolen we drove to the town of Skarżysko-Kamienna. It was in this camp that my father had experienced his most intense period of suffering in the concentration and labor camps. We saw a sign on the highway into Skarżysko-Kamienna that described a concentration camp museum. When we came to the museum, we discovered that it focused on the history of military weaponry in Poland and included a few display cases on the history of the concentration camp in which thousands had died. I asked an attendant where the former KZ was located. "No," she said, "there is no camp. Nothing exists from that time."

Cracow

We should have scheduled more time in Cracow. Here is where Polish-Jewish fantasy and reality stand at a crossroads. For a number of reasons, Cracow has emerged as the Jewish cultural center of Poland. Nowhere else have so many synagogues survived fires and bombings; nowhere else does Jewish klezmer music dominate an entire section of the city; and nowhere else does the serious study of Polish Jewry and the Holocaust have such a secure place among academics.

The city itself is beautiful. We walked along the old-city walls, where castles and beautiful old buildings were everywhere. The apartment that we rented was adjacent to Cracow's main square, a place where a tourist could enjoy shops, restaurants, and churches. Churches were an important part of Cracow's history, as were its synagogues. Many of those synagogues were located in the district known as Kazimierz. But unlike Łódź, where the district of Baluty contained much of the city's Jewish community, most of them poor, Kazimierz contained only 10 percent of Cracow's Jews, the poorest and most religious. When one considers that before 1939 at least 25 percent, or about 65,000 inhabitants of Cracow were Jewish, a visit to Kazimierz does not tell the whole story of the city's Jewish history.

But Kazimierz is all there was, and we had only a few hours and even less daylight to see what was Poland's premier Jewish spectacle. We only had time to see the outside of the several synagogues that had survived World

War II in Cracow for various reasons. The walk took us past the so-called High Synagogue, the Old Synagogue, the Wolf Popper Synagogue, the Isak Synagogue, and the New or Remu Synagogue, named for the famous Rabbi Moses Isserles, with a Jewish cemetery in back. Yet there were only about 200 Jews in Cracow, hardly enough to support one or two congregations, much less five or six. The Remu Synagogue was the only one active.

If it was activity that we sought, we did not have to go far. Across from the Remu Synagogue were two famous "Jewish" restaurants, the Café Ariel and the Klezmer Hois, a converted *mikveh* (ritual bathhouse). The noise inside both places was deafening, with voices and with klezmer music, and sickening with clouds of cigarette smoke. We decided not to have dinner in either place, but we did stand inside each restaurant for a few minutes to listen to the music. It was wonderful and represented only a small sampling of the annual summer klezmer festival that brought bands to Cracow from all over the world. I walked from restaurant to restaurant, asking hosts and serving staff whether they were Jewish or spoke Yiddish. No one was and no one did. I picked up a flyer that advertised a restaurant called "Once upon a Time in Kazimierz." At Ulica Szeroka 1, one could find memories of a time when "two communities, Polish and Jewish, once lived side by side. They differed in just about everything: language, customs, creed and culture. . . . They patronized the same workshops and bought their food from the same little grocery stores. And this is what kept them so close to each other. All barriers between them appeared to just disappear and melt away."

You could, if you wished, visit the sites of Chajim Kohan's general store, Szymon Kac's tailorshop, Benjamin Holcer's carpentry workshop, and Stanislaw Nowak's grocery store. And in this restaurant all these shops are "separated from each other only by imaginary partition walls, turning the adjacent premises into a single cosy and inviting space, symbolizing integration between two peoples and their religions and culture." What history of Polish-Jewish relations in the twentieth century had the author of these words read? Had anyone decided to ask the two hundred Jews of Cracow whether they and their Polish-Catholic neighbors were integrated religiously and culturally? Would the thousands of Cracow Jews who had been murdered during the Holocaust agree that an "integration between two peoples and their religions and culture" had taken place before their brutal deaths?

Cracow was also the city of Oskar Schindler and of Amon Goeth, the notorious Austrian commander of the Płaszów labor camp. The city is a symbol of the little good and the great evil that marked the Holocaust. It was thus only fitting and quite daring that in 1986, when Poland was still under communist rule, the 600-year-old Jagiellonian University, one of Europe's finest, opened a Research Center on the History and Culture of Jews in Poland under the direction of Professor Jozef Gierowski. It was the first of its kind in Poland. This was followed in 1998 by the creation of a Centre for Holocaust Studies, and two years later by the inauguration of the Postgraduate Holocaust Studies Program, the first time that the Holocaust was taught to Polish university students.

Before we left Cracow we had one more task to accomplish—a visit to a church on the main square that had been home to Cracow's Archbishop Karol Josef Wojtyla who would become Pope John Paul II. The boys wanted a chance to pray and spend some time reflecting on what they had seen on our journey. I could think of no place more appropriate than the church of the man who had done so much to change the history of Catholic-Jewish relations.

Auschwitz / Oświęcim

I never took the words of the German-Jewish sociologist and philosopher Theodor Adorno seriously. Adorno argued that "writing poetry after Auschwitz is barbaric." Especially after discovering the "voice of the She'erith Hapletah," the redeeming voice of survivors in the Jewish DP camps of Central Europe, I had come to believe that one can depict life optimistically, even in the shadow of the Holocaust and the ultimate evil of Auschwitz. But I was afraid of Auschwitz in a way that did not compare with the unknown that awaited me in Linshits, Skarżysko-Kamienna, Łódź, or Zwolen. I was afraid that I could not stand up to the face of pure evil and that I would crumble before all it symbolized.

We arrived at Auschwitz on the morning of August 18. Even at that early time of the day, the memorial site was filled with people from all over the world—Japanese, Israelis, Italians, Spaniards, English, and Canadians. What did they feel when they walked through the gate that told them "Arbeit macht frei," work makes you free? I had been to Dachau, Buchenwald, and Neuengamme, outside of Hamburg. Those camps had saddened me and brought home the reality of the Holocaust as a killing machine. But Auschwitz was different. It did more than sadden me and make me realize what my mother had endured and what fate she escaped even in the short time that she was a prisoner here. It frightened me and disoriented me. I could feel evil all around me.

We all wanted a guide. We needed more than just ourselves to explain the history of each building and exhibit. But guides for a group of four were not available that day, or so a staff member told us when we inquired. I would not take no for an answer. I decided to see whether my colleague, Dr. Franciszek Pieper, a member of the Department of Historical Research at the Auschwitz-Birkenau State Museum, could help. Pieper was the world authority on the number of prisoners killed at Auschwitz. His estimate of just over one million victims, over 90 percent of them Jewish, was the universally accepted standard. I had worked with him during the 1993 United States Holocaust Memorial Museum international scholars' conference and published his essay in *The Holocaust and History*.[11] It turned out that Dr. Pieper was on vacation. But the fact that my name was known to the staff at the Department of Historical Research got us our guide. He was a young, well-trained historian with an encyclopedic knowledge of Auschwitz-Birkenau, the Camps I and II of this place of infamy. After I told him about my background and the fact that my mother had been a prisoner at Auschwitz-Birkenau, he began the tour by telling me that most Jews did not realize that the first prisoners in Auschwitz were Polish Catholics. That did not shock me. Indeed, as director of Holocaust Museum Houston, I had mounted an exhibit of the paintings of Jan Komski (1915–2000), Auschwitz prisoner #564, who arrived in Auschwitz on June 14, 1940, among the first transport of 727 prisoners. There were some Polish Jews among the group, but they came to Auschwitz as political and not as racial detainees.

The fact that I had met Komski, who had come to Houston for the opening of his exhibit, and that I was aware of Polish-Catholic Auschwitz prisoners, gave us a mutual respect that lasted for perhaps ten minutes. From that point on we disagreed about almost everything he had to say, not about Auschwitz and its history, but about the thousand-year relationship between Polish Jews and non-Jews. Auschwitz had never been a German town, he assured me, disputing the findings of Deborah Dwork and Robert Jan Van Pelt in their acclaimed book on the town's history.[12] He also alluded to the "otherness" of Polish Jewry, of its inability or unwillingness to become a part of Poland, rather than simply living in the country. Finally, he was certain that after World War II, Polish Jews had been the leading force in a Judeo-communistic takeover of Poland. I tried to make him see my points of view on these issues, but the enormity of Auschwitz seemed to make our differences unimportant.

When we entered one of the buildings in Auschwitz I, the original part of the camp, the so-called *Stammlager,* we found a room in total darkness, except for a circle of lighted candles. Benches surrounded the burning candles, and we all sat down. Suddenly, a deeply melodic voice began to chant the *El Moleh Rachamim,* (O God, full of compassion). Whatever I had kept inside, the visits to the places of my parent's birth and to the places of their suffering now came out. I burst into sobs, and I could not stop. I cried for my parents and for all the family that neither I nor my wife and children would ever know. At some point during the tour of Auschwitz I, Eugenio also began to be more open with me. He and I had finally begun to speak about his memories of Romania and the hell of the orphanage in which he had lived for several years. Albi's sensitivity was demonstrated in another way. He had suffered from a nervous stomach and its consequences from the very beginning of our trip to Poland and Germany, and it only increased as we began the Polish part of the journey.

When we drove the few miles to the site of Birkenau, the real killing fields of gas chambers and crematoria, I could not believe the enormity of the camp. It stretched for as far as the eye could see, and what I saw was almost beyond human comprehension: the platform from which newly arrived prisoners were sent to life or to their deaths; the gas chambers; the grounds and pond filled with human ashes and bones. Our guide guessed, based upon the arrival of my mother's transport from the Łódź Radegast station to Auschwitz, that she had lived in section BIa or BIb of the women's camp in Birkenau. Although the barracks were no longer standing, I tried to visualize what they had looked like and what Birkenau must have been like for her.

We had booked rooms in a hotel in the town of Oświęcim, but when we arrived there after leaving Auschwitz-Birkenau, we discovered that it was situated in front of railroad tracks. Gottfried, who had been to Auschwitz on several occasions, remembered that he had stayed in this hotel one of those times and that he heard the sound of trains passing his window the entire night. We drove to another hotel far from those tracks and never cancelled our first reservation. Perhaps Adorno was not entirely wrong in what he had written about Auschwitz. That evening I felt a sense of despair and gloom that did not allow me to write about what I had just experienced. On the other hand I wrote the following: "I cannot believe how grounded I feel in my family identity. This was always missing in my life. Linshits, Zwolen, Łódź, Skarżysko-Kamienna, and now Auschwitz. I've been there and the shadows have become realities. But it is too late to talk to my beloved parents, z"l, about all they have told me and what I have experienced for myself."

Dresden

Our next stop was the former East German city of Dresden. Known before the Second World War as the "Florence of the Elbe," Dresden was one of Europe's most beautiful cities. All of that changed on the night of February 13, 1945. For two days American and British bombers devastated the city in an extraordinary firestorm. The most reliable figures estimated that at least 30,000 people were killed during the bombing. But my mother survived, and I had an address that she never forgot: 68 Schandauerstrasse. That was the place in which she worked as a slave laborer from November 1944 to February 13, 1945. I wanted desperately to see that place. But did Schandauerstrasse still exist? What stood on the place of my mother's imprisonment?

A friend of Gottfried's had arranged for a tour guide. Matthias Bräutigam was a cellist in the Dresden City Philharmonic, and he was prepared to take us on an extended tour. When he arrived, I was only interested in seeing 68 Schandauerstrasse. Did such a street still exist? "Yes," he replied. That was what I wanted to hear. As we drove toward Schandauerstrasse, we passed an ugly building with absolutely no windows. This is our new synagogue, the cellist told us. I remembered, from conversations with Dresden-born Henry Meyer, a friend of mine and of Gottfried's, a world-class violinist and a survivor of the Auschwitz men's orchestra, that former Dresden Jews were interested in helping to finance the rebuilding of one of the city's most beautiful Jewish houses of worship. But if this was the result of that interest, I was keenly disappointed. The fact that no one could see in or out spoke volumes about how secure Dresden's small Jewish community felt in 2005.

We came to a street with a sign that said "Schandauerstrasse." As we drove slowly, I counted each building and each number. Then I saw it. A large building that was a cigarette factory, as it had been until World War II. A large plaque was placed on a brick column next to the building's gate. It read:

Between November 1944 and April 1945 there stood in this spot at 68 Schandauer Street an external camp of the Flossenbürg concentration camp. Approximately 500 inmates, mostly Jews from Poland, had to perform forced labor for the German armaments industry. They suffered the brutalities of the SS camp leadership and only a few Germans came forward to provide a semblance of living necessities for the prisoners. Many of the inmates were driven to their deaths through forced labor or on death marches at the end of the Second World War.

The plaque was dedicated in 2002. It had taken nearly fifty years for the city of Dresden to realize that there were other victims besides those who died in the firebombing of February 13–15, 1945.

Buchenwald

Even though I had visited it twice, once when it was a part of the DDR and again when it was a part of the reunited Germany, the visit to Buchenwald was important for me and for Gottfried and the boys. Buchenwald symbolized the two wars that the Nazis waged: one against the Jews and the second against human values. My father had been incarcerated in Buchenwald with Soviet soldiers, gay men, communists, and Jehovah's Witnesses. There could be no clearer example of the second of those wars and the groups, among others, against whom the Nazis waged that war.

As we walked among the buildings of Buchenwald and looked at the excellent exhibit that the post-communist administration of the former concentration camp had mounted, I felt grateful that I had been able to make this two-week journey into my parents' past. I stood with Gottfried, Eugenio, and Alberto, staring down at the granite quarry that had been the most brutal of my father's experiences in Buchenwald. I realized then that, like the mythical story of Sisyphus, the prisoners in that quarry had carried massive stones in tiny wheelbarrows up and down the hill that took them to the area where they unloaded the granite, only to have to go back down again day after day as though the stones had fallen back to the places from which they had been gathered.

Knowing what I knew about a world that screamed "Never again" after the Holocaust but saw genocide repeated time and time again, I realized that our civilization was like Sisyphus. We could never reach the top without the stones falling back to earth. The gods had condemned Sisyphus to a fate that forced him to roll a boulder to the top of a mountain, only to have the stone fall back down because of its weight. But who had condemned humanity to commit genocide repeatedly?

The journalist Jonathan Kaufman wrote a book about his travels documenting the efforts of Jews in Eastern and Central Europe to rise from the ashes of destruction after the Holocaust. What that destruction meant for Europe after 1945 was made clear by the title of Kaufman's book, which he called *A Hole in the Heart of the World*.[13] On the long ride back to Italy, I realized something. The journey through the time and trauma of my parents' world before 1945 had also exposed a hole—one that was in my heart and in my world and would never be filled.

IV

Viewing the Past but Looking to the Future

Gottfried Wagner

16

Reflections on the Trip to Auschwitz in August 2005

Eugenio Wagner[1] summed up his experiences of the trip to Auschwitz after half a year:

When I was thirteen and asked my father about the Shoah, he answered me with sensitivity, but this topic remained threatening for me, in a way I couldn't express in words. The sense of threat derived from the excess of destruction, violence and death.

The official days of remembrance depicted in the media, like the liberation of Auschwitz commemorated on January 27th throughout Europe, the liberation from Fascism and National Socialism on April 25th celebrated in Italy, and the "Night of the Pogrom in the Third Reich" (also called "The Night of Broken Glass") on November 9th in Germany actually increased my fear and didn't help me at all to handle the overwhelming images and information about the death camps and the shocking events of the Second World War. I therefore sought further discussion with my father, who tried to help me understand that history, especially regarding the Shoah, consists not only of abstract figures and terms but also of personal human persecution, death and pain. He told me about his first trip to Auschwitz in 1995. It was during my time in middle school in 1999 that I undertook reading the report from Auschwitz entitled *Survival in Auschwitz—the Nazi Assault on Humanity*, written by the famous Italian Jewish writer Primo Levi. While reading the book, I learned from my parents of Levi's fate. During the discussion, my father told me openly about the close contact of the Wagner family with Hitler, and said:

"Unfortunately, the German part of our Wagner family, especially your great-grandmother Winifred, your great-uncle Wieland and your grandfather Wolfgang, left us with the burden of their admiration and active support of Hitler. For that reason you and I have a special responsibility to learn from family and German and European history. Don't remain silent when you can prevent injustice." I began to understand the dark sides of German history and my family's history, and the reasons for my father's commitments and his work with Abraham Peck in the Post-Shoah Dialogue Group, always in conjunction with Polish, Jewish, and the painful Peck family history. My realizations became a personal life experience when father, my cousin Alberto, and I traveled with Abraham to Landsberg, Nuremberg, Bayreuth, Wroclaw, Łęczyca, Lodz, Zwolen, Cracow, Auschwitz, Dresden, and Buchenwald in August 2005. I was confronted on all sides with German, Polish, Jewish, and family history, interpreted by Abraham and my father in explicit discussions with Alberto and me as we travelled to the above-named cities. This trip was a turning point in my life regarding my own moral position, and even made it possible for me to express my fear, as a first step toward overcoming it, living my life more consciously with joy, and being aware that Auschwitz reflects the suffering of human beings of every sort of European and family background. For me, learning from history means making room for empathy in daily life.

17

Viewing the Past but Looking to the Future

It was difficult to present topics relating to the problems of the post-Shoah generations—and thus to Abraham and me—in European countries that had once been under communist control such as Romania, Poland, and the Czech Republic. In East Germany, too, I encountered a great deal of ignorance and repression as well as a general refusal to address anti-Semitism or the Shoah, topics that have not only psychological but also ethical and human-rights ramifications.

As I discussed these topics, I always emphasized individual responsibility and personal willingness to be critical of oneself. In so doing, I was reacting against the widespread deprivation of individual rights under the totalitarian systems of the twentieth century, as well as against those systems' psychological manipulations. Because of the media these problems are getting even worse this century: "The opiate of the masses—today that is the mass media." [1]

As I think about my ethical positions—which are largely expressed in Abraham's and my statutes for the Post-Shoah/Holocaust dialogue—I often think about a statement by the Italian-Jewish writer and chemist Primo Levi. In 1961 he wrote to Heinz Riedts, the translator of the German edition of his autobiographical account *If This Is a Man*, "I don't understand and cannot tolerate when a man is judged not according to who he is, but according to the group to which he accidentally belongs." [2] This is Levi's central statement about the year he survived in Auschwitz. It is timeless, rejecting the classification of an individual by his national, religious, or familial affiliations, and that statement was significant in the development of my own ethical opinions. It applies to the Shoah, to September 11, 2001, and to the Iranian theocracy's murderous propaganda against Israel calling for a second Shoah. I fundamentally regard with skepticism any promises of salvation and a "better world in the future." Usually such promises merely conceal new forms of totalitarian claims for global power and, as such, are threats to world peace. Above all, I am referring to the lethal coalition of "religion and terror."[3]

A quotation from the chapter "History of Ten Days" in Levi's autobiography describes the constant threat to the individual. The words make one think of the Shoah, but they remain timeless:

> Above us naked, powerless, and defenseless people, men of our time were trying to kill one another with the most sophisticated instruments possible. A movement of their finger could have ... exterminated thousands of people. All of our energy and desire would not have been enough to extend for a single minute the life of just one of us.[4]

Levi warns of the dark side of man, saying: "It is a man who kills. It is a man who causes or suffers injustice. But that being who has lost all restraint and shares his bed with a corpse, that is not a man."[5] This radical judgment caused me to reevaluate my own ethical positions and consider how those positions were reflected in my work as a journalist, and how they were reflected in my everyday interactions with people. Even when I was an opera director, I did not want to be fashionable or to conform to the Zeitgeist to make friends; I wanted to work on projects that reflected what I thought, believed, and felt. For that reason I became especially involved in developing the composer Janice Hamer's opera *Lost Childhood*, which covers two generations' difficulties in dealing with the Shoah.[6]

Also relevant to my discussion with Abraham was what the historian Dan Diner wrote about the relationship between Germans and Jews after the Shoah:

> After Auschwitz, we can speak of a negative German-Jewish symbiosis. For both of them—for Germans and for Jews—the mass extermination has resulted in a new starting point for understanding themselves, a kind of contradictory common ground—whether they want it or not. Because of this event, Germans and Jews are connected to one another again. Such a negative symbiosis, established by the Nazis, will affect the relationship of both groups to themselves but above all to each other for generations to come.[7]

But can one free Germans and Jews from the history of the Shoah and the genocide of the twentieth and twenty-first centuries? What about the other groups who currently find themselves in conflict? There will always be many. What can the individual do against prejudice and hatred, which remain omnipresent, like dark shadows from an unresolved past? Is it possible or even conceivable that the sides might be able to work *together* in the future to process the mourning? I believe in such a possibility without illusions; such a belief necessarily follows from my experiences.

When we began our dialogue in 1992, neither Abraham nor I knew where our path would lead us, but we have been—and are—traveling it together. Even in the most difficult moments, I have always believed in the possibility and significance of a German-Jewish dialogue, but I also believe that it must be expanded into a trialogue to include moderate Muslims and other groups in conflict—always conscious of the Shoah, September 11, and the current danger posed to Israel by the Iranian government!

One personal question remains: how do such convictions affect my relationship to Germany? Given my choice of lecture topics and my work against all forms of historical misrepresentation, traveling to Germany in the future will be difficult for me, but also necessary. I return there to see people who respect my work, my friends, and my relatives on my mother's side. For me the following is fundamental: generalizations are one of the most powerful evils in the history of mankind. The need to return to Germany was reinforced by the death of my mother in April 2002. She died from the effects of a stroke and cancer, and she is buried in the cemetery in Cerro Maggiore. Remembering the moment of that painful goodbye makes me realize that the feeling of mourning remains—I mourn that as her son I did not receive the answers to many questions in her life, a life suffered beneath the shadow of German history and the Wagner family. I would have liked to have heard her reflection about such topics as guilt, shame, and mourning. Because of my father's closeness to Uncle Wolf—that is, Hitler—and his constant work since 1951 to preserve his limitless power over the festival, my father was never honest with me about such topics.[8] That damaging father-son relationship had at least one positive result—I promised that I would never feed my son Eugenio the Bayreuth-Wagner lies, and that I would make certain that our relationship was better than the one I had with my father.

The next Wagner generation decided to take a different path. They refused to examine honestly their family history or German history. I am referring above all to those who hide behind the idealized *Gesamtkunstwerk* facade, trying to obtain their own power in Bayreuth as part of the family legacy. They do so with full support from the powers that be, including the media, which still treat the Bayreuth Festival as a place of worship, a model of German identity and self-enhancement, even an ersatz religion. All this despite Wagner, Hitler, and the consequences of their thoughts and actions! This way was not for me. No one will ever be able to classify me as a "typical German," even worse, a "typical Wagner." I retain my German passport but only because I don't believe in altering the past. Sometimes during my trips through the eastern and western parts of Germany, I think about the passage from Lea Fleischmann's book *Dies Ist Nicht Mein Land. Eine Jüdin Verlässt die Bundesrepublik* [This Is Not My Country: A Jewish Woman Leaves the Federal Republic of Germany]:

> Germans treat each other even worse. They're even more obstinate, less understanding . . . and more merciless. I am repeatedly struck by the thoughtlessness and ease with which people in this country are pushed away, ignored, and left on their own.[9]

I do not agree with such generalizations, for Fleischmann forgets the minority of Germans who actively and responsibly fight for a different Germany after Hitler. Despite my cosmopolitan life, I have had a home for nearly thirty years with my Italian family in Cerro Maggiore near Milan. Unfortunately my work in Italy is not sufficient to pay the far-too-high Italian taxes. Since I have worked more and more with Italian history on topics such as the Shoah, National Socialism, and Italian fascism, I requested an Italian passport at the end of August 2005, and so I have that in addition to my German one. That does not mean, however, that I will behave like an Italian patriot. I am well aware of how dishonestly the Italian political right and left handle their own fascism—even today. So no "*patria mia*"—I am not going to howl with the wolves there, in Israel, in the United States, or anywhere else. I agree with Primo Levi's demand wholeheartedly and without exception: all men should be judged by who they are as individuals. With my Italian family I find the necessary peace and my joy for life. Between airplane flights and Internet searches, I develop thoughts for new books and directing projects, and, as a result of living with my wife Teresina and our son Eugenio, I believe in the future of the coming generations.

V

The Final Chapter?
Repairing the World

Abraham J. Peck

18

The Path to Tikkun Olam

Gottfried Wagner and I did not ask to be born into a post-Holocaust world that would label us as the sons of perpetrators and victims. Neither did my children ask to be born into what is now called the Third Generation. It would have been a much different life for me if I had only been part of another kind of generation, the one that is simply called the "Baby Boomer" generation, those post–World War II sons and daughters who were born between 1946 and 1964 and whose oldest representatives are ready to enter the world of retirement and leisure. And it would have been easier for my children. But my daughter, Abby Suzanne, reminds me that "this is my legacy and I can't change that." That is true. Both of my children are American-born Jews. They are both graduates of very fine schools of American higher education. Both have their MAs, and my daughter has hers from the University of London. Now both in their thirties, my daughter and son Joel David have left the proverbial home nest and taken flight to find their own lives and their own self-identities.

Nearly thirty years ago I read an essay by the psychologist Steven Luel who is the son of Holocaust survivors. It was an essay that challenged my notions of how I would try to teach my children about the Holocaust and what it would mean for them:

> We of the second generation are rearing or about to rear the third post-Holocaust generation. How do we wish to present the Holocaust to them? To what extent do we wish to share our anxieties, rages, and hurts? On the one hand, we want to remind them through remembrance and transmission of the horrific truth. On the other hand, the second generation will be best equipped to rear the third if, in

preparation, they extract themselves from a self-injurious attachment to the Holocaust.[1]

I thought about Luel's words for a time and even made a timeline of how I would gradually expose my children to the lives lived by their grandparents during the years of the Holocaust, the reasons why they had no immediate family members, and why their father was so involved in scholarly and public activities that focused on the tragedy of European Jewish life.

But, as is often said, life interferes and the best-laid plans fall by the wayside. I never pursued the timeline or the strategy. Instead, I sought both to shield my children from the graphic horrors of the Final Solution and to expose them to what its consequences meant for them as young Jews and as young Americans. As I neared the completion of my part of the manuscript that ultimately became this book, I asked both Abby and Joel to reflect on what it meant to be a part of the Third Generation and part of a family directly affected by the Holocaust. Here are portions of what they wrote:

Abby Suzanne Peck Wrote:

On the one hand, I'm proud to be the grandchild of survivors. On the other hand, it's been a miserable burden at times. Growing up, it was like having ranks upon ranks of ghosts walking through our lives. I feel like I knew too much about the Holocaust at such a young age. The pictures I would see of people in the camps haunted me. As a little girl, I would lay awake at night and hear the sounds of crickets or some kind of insects outside and I thought it was Nazis marching down the block to come get me.

I couldn't understand why my American grandparents were so relaxed and not overprotective while my European grandparents wouldn't let me swim with my head underwater, or walk anywhere by myself, and couldn't speak English properly. Grandma and Grandpa Peck's apartment always felt so closed-in and dark and sad. No family coming to visit. Again, it always felt haunted by ghosts.

I inherited your anger and that anger is so frightening to me sometimes. I felt growing up that you were shut down emotionally in many ways because of how you, Dad, grew up; yet, you couldn't have grown up any other way. Like I said, Grandma and Grandpa's story is amazing and people are always so overwhelmed when I tell them that my grandparents were Holocaust survivors. But it also makes me feel guilty—guilty for not following in your footsteps and making my life's work about the Holocaust, guilty for never going to Germany or Poland, and guilty for being too American.

But I also have anger that I didn't get to have "normal" grandparents, that there was no family to help you cope with the death of your parents, and that you grew up in some unhealthy ways and that perhaps you transferred some of that to Joel and to me. And then I feel guilty all over again for blaming my grandparents and you for having to endure such a horrible tragedy.

This is my legacy and I can't change that. My children and Joel's children are going to know who they are and what happened to their great-grandparents and how their grandfather was born in a DP camp. But I think for them it's going to just be something they read about in history books—I think there are current tragedies that will haunt them more (like my seeing one of the planes that hit the World Trade Center on 9/11 from my apartment window). I think the idea of Nazis and of Jews being rounded up and of death camps is going to seem as distant as slavery in America some day—something terrible that happened in the past, but not something that they ever need to worry about again. Just a relic from a time best forgotten.

Joel David Peck Wrote:

I know that much of my identity has been shaped by tragedy. As far back as I can remember, I was aware of an evil that existed in the world that caused so much pain to many people. My grandparents had an unspeakable pain that permeated every childhood visit to see them. This pain was different than the usual associations children have of their grandma, grandpa, and even their father.

As much as I could sense their love, I could equally sense their loss. I did not know what caused this pain for me inside, and I hoped to understand it by understanding where it originated. But no one wanted to answer the questions I felt needed answering. It was too painful for my grandparents to provide names and faces and accounts of what happened. They so desperately wanted to bring me their love, yet they couldn't help bringing their misery with it. Why did they transfer this misery to me and not explain it? It was a burden I carried throughout childhood—not knowing why I felt this way and having no starting point or direction to deal with it. As I came to understand later, my grandparents' questions had gone unanswered, too. They knew what happened—it was forever burned into their memory. Their tragedy lay in not knowing why it happened.

In public school and Hebrew school, we learned about the Holocaust. We were exposed to the gruesome images and realities of the Shoah year after year. I saw my Christian friends and classmates react with such sadness and emotion to what they learned had happened to the Jewish people. I saw my Jewish peers and teachers identify their Judaism through the events that occurred—though none of them had the direct connection that I did. I was alone in both crowds and I didn't know enough to have a connection. So why could everyone else?

When I was eighteen, I went to Israel with a national Jewish youth group. Before we embarked, we spent three days in the Czech Republic. One day, all four hundred people on the trip, including me, went to the concentration camp Theresienstadt. It was the same camp I had heard my grandfather speak of—where terrible things happened to him that he couldn't describe. I only learned what went on in Theresienstadt and the other concentration camps in books I read in school. Even then, they were just words on a page and pages in a book. So when I walked around the camp by myself, I didn't feel pain or sadness. It felt like a visit to a museum. We were taken to the crematoria and the lights were turned off and candles were lit. We sang prayers and everyone around me was sobbing uncontrollably. I kept wondering why I wasn't crying. Here it was, the actual details and tangible images of where the pain originated in my grandparents, my father, and me! None of the people around me had such a link, but it seemed they knew how to react. It was just a building to me. I couldn't feel that inner pain in a terrible place where my family may have perished. There just wasn't that sadness permeating the air like at my grandparents' apartment in Florida. I felt it there. It wasn't in these walls and bunkers and pathways. It was in my grandparents' eyes when they were looking at me. It was in their arms when they hugged me. It was in their voice when they told me they loved me. They transferred a love of equal intensity and I never once questioned that. I think that pain has shaped the love that is so much part of my identity, too.

That ill-defined pain and loss inside has enabled me to recognize it in various forms not limited to my own experience. It's always been the case that I can sense and relate to the damage in people—of all races and ethnicities. I seem to relate to others who have what I call "soul wounds." That's why I feel connected to people most times, especially in intimate settings. It's also why I feel so alone at times, especially in a crowded room.

I have never felt as proud of my children and as sad that I was unable to stop the *churbn* from becoming a part of their beings as when I read what they wrote from their hearts. But what their words have taught me is that it is possible to move beyond the Holocaust and yet never lose what it means for the Jewish people and for the world. That is certainly true for the grandsons and granddaughters of Holocaust survivors, the so-called Third Generation.[2] They are most likely the last generation who will personally know Holocaust survivors and their stories. They, too, are interested in the issue of the intergenerational transmission of trauma, albeit from a much further distance than their parents. Theirs is a different kind of "post-memory." They, too, still face the transgenerational effects of the Holocaust.[3] But they are also interested in the history and suffering of other groups who have faced genocide and its consequences. That is why they have invited young Rwandans and Darfuris who experienced the horrors of genocide and its consequences to share their stories with Third Generation groups in cities such as New York, London, and Melbourne, Australia.

Paul Rusesabagina, the real-life hero of the film *Hotel Rwanda*, who saved over 1,200 lives during the horror of the Rwandan genocide in 1994, has written, "Never again. We all know these words. But we never seem to hear them. . . . Hitler's Final Solution was supposed to have been the last expression of this monstrous idea—the final time the world would tolerate a deliberate attempt to exterminate an entire race. But genocide remains the most pressing human rights question of the twenty-first century."[4] "Never again." How often I have listened and watched as the slogan was shouted and the signs containing the phrase were carried across the cities and countries of the world. How could we not hear those words? They were shouted with such certainty, such finality.

But I also realize that "Never again" was shouted long before it was fashionable as a way for the Jewish community to tell the world that it would never allow itself to undergo another Holocaust. "Never again" was shouted from the squalor of Europe's postwar Jewish DP camps in Germany, Austria, and Italy. It was shouted in the words of the same Dr. Samuel Gringauz who recited *yizkor* with my parents for the six million during the first Yom Kippur after the Liberation. In 1946 Gringauz wrote that "our tragedy must become the starting point of a new humanism," one that would seek to close the gap between the technological advances of the twentieth century, which had built the ovens of Auschwitz, and its moral development, which has suffered terribly in the era of Nazism.[5]

Paul Rusesabagina is correct. No one seemed to hear Samuel Gringauz or the voice of the She'erith Hapletah. Nearly five decades after Gringauz wrote those words, Gottfried and I heard them. We heard them because we were the products of the ovens of Auschwitz and the failure of Western civilization and what passed as its humanity. So the words became the starting point of our "Never again." We shouted them in the six points that became the official mission statement of our dialogue, first presented in 1992.

For twenty years Gottfried and I have sought to apply these points to our lives and to our work. It has not always been easy. As a freelancer, Gottfried has had to depend on the vagaries of the lecture invitation and the occasional chance at stage direction. He has had to endure the insults of Wagner Society–inspired demonstrations against his appearances in various communities throughout Europe and North America. But he has persevered because he hears the words "Never again" so much more clearly than his German contemporaries. He knows how the phrase arose and why it has directly affected his family and his life. So he speaks in front of the European Parliament, organizations of German industrialists, and any other groups that have the power to bring about social change in a Europe that faces new challenges on a daily basis—whether it is the continuing plight of Sinti and Roma or the growing conflict between Islam and the West.

I watch his work from an ocean away and marvel at how adversity cannot defeat him. It gives me the strength to pursue the hectic lifestyle that I do. I, too, hear the words "Never again," and know that it means a dialogue between the monotheistic faiths that will bring about a new understanding of the "Children of Abraham." I know it means a creative unity between the generations of genocide, wherever this evil has created mass murder and brought cultural and linguistic destruction to peoples on many continents.

Gottfried and I refuse to perpetuate that which has traumatized and damaged Germans and Jews for the past seven decades. We refuse to allow the fires of hate that now threaten to bring about a confrontation between civilizations. But we cannot do it alone. We need those of our generation, Jews and Germans, to join with us. We need the next generation to do the same. We need them to pledge to carry on what we have begun but with a new understanding that the task is no longer to acknowledge simply who they and we, their parents, have become because of this monstrous time we call the Holocaust. The task is much larger. It can be no less than a repair of the world, *a tikkun olam* as is written in Jewish prayer and commentary.

We do not know what the future will hold, but we both know we cannot allow a recreation of the past. We are committed to our *Stunde Null*, our zero hour of new beginnings that never began in 1945. But it cannot be for us alone. The clock of conflict is ticking toward midnight, the time of Armageddon. The world, too, needs its own *Stunde Null*, its own new beginning.

VI

Beyond the Shadow of German and Family Myths

Gottfried Wagner

19

April 2012. Beyond Reconciliation with the Wagner Clan—Be Yourself

On Abraham

"We share a common desire to understand each other's burden as a result of who we are and the consequences of our family history."

> *Twilight of the Wagners: The Unveiling of a Family's Legacy,* 6.

Reflecting today on what has happened since 1991, when Abraham and I started our discussions, and sometimes moments of intensive dialogue, I read once again the following parts of his courageous foreword to the U.S. edition of my autobiography:

What Gottfried and I have found is that we both carry a kind of black box within us. And although over the years we have opened it slowly, our discussions have allowed us to really open this black box to a much greater degree than we could have ever imagined. Like Pandora's Box, it is uncertain what ultimately will emerge from this. But we continue to focus on the most important thing that separates Jews and Germans; namely the question of family history, what Germans call "Familiengeschichte." When it comes to talking about the family histories of Germans and Jews, especially during the Holocaust years, and listening to them and understanding them, every step is difficult and painful, especially for the German side. I believe that for Gottfried and me, that part of the black box has been opened fully and honestly. It is a step in a direction—not necessarily toward reconciliation because we both reject this term. Yet, we seek to understand that we have separate, but nonetheless related, legacies that have been left to us by the event we call the Holocaust; which in many respects has poisoned the psyches of our parents and certainly affected our humanity. What we seek is the opportunity to prevent some of that poison from being passed on to our children; to Eugenio, . . . Abby and Joel.

Family history is a special problem for the sons and daughters of Holocaust survivors. They have often grown up in the eye of a hurricane, surrounded by the shadows of the Holocaust. But many have asked next to nothing about the suffering of their parents or the absence of grandparents, uncles, and aunts. They fear the trauma inherent in their parents' reply.

I am one of those sons. But unlike many, I did ask. I learned as a young boy that there was a reason for the absence of my uncles, aunts, and cousins. Indeed, because I had a father who was obsessed with his own experiences during the Holocaust years, from his time in the ghetto in Łodz, Poland, from 1940 to 1944, to his imprisonment at Buchenwald and Theresienstadt, I developed an unusual knowledge, at a very early age, of my fathers' tormentors. In a way, this macabre cast of Nazi guards, commandants, and physicians became more real to me than the shadowy figures who had been the murdered members of my family. All told, there were thirteen uncles and aunts, five on my father's side and eight on my mother's. But for most of my life they have remained only names. l cannot identify them by facial features, idiosyncrasies, or any other characteristics that make up the pleasures of the extended family. . . .

It has become painfully clear to Gottfried and me on many occasions that we have not come as far as we had imagined at the beginning of our encounter. Yet we feel it is necessary to go on. Is it a coincidence that Gottfried was born in Bayreuth as the great-grandson of Richard Wagner and I was born in Landsberg am Lech as the son of Holocaust survivors—Landsberg, the place where his grandmother Winfred Wagner delivered to her intimate friend Hitler the paper to write *Mein Kampf*? Whatever the circumstances, we have been drawn together because we share a common desire to understand each other's burden as a result of who we are and the consequences of our family history.

Is the possibility for dialogue worth the encounter? I was never certain of this until I met Gottfried. He represents for me the beginning of Germany's efforts to recapture its sense of a "humane orientation" as it is understood by Ralph Giordano. Gottfried Wagner did not have to write his autobiography or lead the life he has led. But he has written it. It reflects the pain, the torment, the honesty and the hope that has made him who he is. Gottfried has assumed his responsibility.[1]

Those who want to understand what Abraham said about our efforts to share a common desire to understand each other's burden as a result of who we are and the consequences of our family history will understand. Thanks to our public discussions, I met those of the Jewish Second Generation who helped me, like Abraham, to understand how to develop visions of a meaningful life.

Remembering Dan Bar-On in 2011

The late Dan Bar-On's six questions about the aftereffects of the Holocaust on our lives remain valid until today and anyone, German, Austrian, or Jew, who wants to talk about the post-Holocaust experience has to confront him/herself with them:

When and how were we confronted with the Holocaust?
How do we cope with our rootlessness?
How do we combat our social estrangement and "otherness"?
Can we relate to the roles of victim and perpetrator?
Do we live our lives without the shadow of the Holocaust?
Through our knowledge of the Holocaust, have we found a middle path between the desire to die and to live?

Still of great importance is Dan's valuation of the "microcosm of the German-Jewish dialogue," that I would like to repeat once again. Dan Bar-On wrote:

Gottfried Wagner and Abraham Peck are brave people. Their parents would never have been able to talk with each other. Only fifty years have passed since the ancestors of one were deeply involved in the extremely atrocious act of attempting to annihilate the ancestors of the other. The survivors gave the solemn commandment to their descendants, never to forget and never to forgive. Why does Abraham try to break this commandment? Why does Gottfried try to break through the silence which came over the German people after the atrocities became public: a silence of a mixture of shame, the wish to shrink from the responsibility for the murder, to forget and to be forgiven? . . . For their own sakes they are looking for a dialogue which, though breaking their fathers' commandments, will help them address their internal quest for hope.

For me it was, first of all, the chance to meet personally between 1991 and 2006. There were these unforgettable moments of strong solidarity when we were considered as black sheep and even attacked by Holocaust survivors who recommended that I resolve my problems as a German in a psychiatric clinic and leave the Jews alone. Abraham defended me strongly as the son of survivors by pointing out that there is no other way than discussion and dialogue in the future of Germans and Jews. We also attracted other groups in conflict, like African Americans, Native Americans, and recent European and Asian immigrants, who accepted our vision of daring to confront the uncomfortable. But we had and still have to confront the problems indicated by Dan Bar-On. We had to be careful not to confront each other with monologues but work hard on our forms of dialogue, understood as the capacity to listen to each other without offending or provoking each other in order to change our opinions, and to be open for a real dialogue in the future. We knew that we were only at the beginning of a stony path, and we felt also the limits of our efforts because the shadows of our family histories were and are still present. Even the common points of our post-Holocaust statutes like the Declaration of Human Rights remained to be examined critically and self-critically to avoid lip service, especially after the publication of the German version of our joint book *Unsere Stunde Null* and especially after our journey together to Germany and Poland and our visit to Auschwitz in 2005. In the German book I wrote a detailed report of which I want to quote only the events of August 18, 2005:

Seventh Day of the Trip—August 18: From Krakow to Auschwitz

We woke up restless because we knew what the day would bring. Abraham scrutinized the map and helped me find highway 44, the road that led to Auschwitz. We hardly spoke otherwise, trying to think about something other than what awaited us, gazing at the hilly landscape and the various small towns on the seemingly endless trip to that place. But our suppression did not help: the reality of Auschwitz took us in. The enormous parking area in Auschwitz I was completely filled, which irritated me for a moment because it meant the chaos and noise of mass tourism. I noted Abraham's great anxiety as we looked at the main doors and the twenty-eight blocks of houses behind barbed wire and walls. I thought about how his anxiety compared to my feeling of unease, a mixture of guilt, shame, and mourning that came from an entirely different place.

Today, after eight years, I especially remember Block 7, Room 6 on the ground floor, which documented the living conditions, especially the sleeping area where people were piled on top of one another without sanitation or privacy and slowly died. I looked over to Eugenio and Alberto, who stood in shock. The three of us looked anxiously at Abraham, who had completely closed up and could no longer communicate. In a darkened room of Block 11, displays reminded visitors of the other National Socialist extermination camps. We sat down on a bench and listened to the *El Moleh Rachamim*, which commemorated the Jewish victims of National Socialism.[2] The music connected us to Abraham and provided a measure of comfort.

Auschwitz-Birkenau

We were deeply disturbed when we walked around Auschwitz-Birkenau to the remnants of Crematoria II and III, and past the international memorial erected in April 1967 to the victims of National Socialism. Abraham and I took photos, though we were unable to exchange any thoughts, and Eugenio and Alberto stood awkwardly in shock. Thinking of Abraham's mother, Anna, we walked slowly and quietly past the women's camp of Birkenau. We wanted to document these difficult hours. For almost fifteen years, we had been talking about visiting Auschwitz together with our children. We said goodbye quickly to our Polish guide. Our many questions—Abraham as a Jew and I as a German—had not made it easy for him. Thank God the *ragazzi* (children) were there. Even on the brink of exhaustion, as they were, they spent those hours in Auschwitz I and II with great sensitivity.

For the moment it didn't seem possible for Alberto, Eugenio, and me to ask Abraham any further questions. And we certainly didn't need to ask Abraham what he was going through. Feeling somewhat guilty, we went to an elegant restaurant in the fancy Hotel Galicia, and there we discussed whether it was appropriate to enjoy ourselves after the dark hours we had just encountered. Abraham said: "We have thought about those who were murdered and those who survived, and they would both want us to lead a 'normal' life." We smiled at each other and enjoyed the delicious Polish specialties. Back in the hotel we went straight to our rooms, exhausted. This time I could only manage to write down a few notes, which I expanded later with the rest of my notes.

But in the years after our common trip we did have difficulty in giving our discussions a new dimension for the future. We needed time to reflect on the future aims of our cooperation. This was one of the central questions: was there, after fifteen years of our encounters, still something to say to each other? We were aware that the end of our exchange of thoughts would have destroyed all our previous efforts. Thinking of Abraham today, I am grateful that his first step in March 1991 toward me and our encounters meant we could each open up new ways and forms of discussion with different groups and individuals. But there were also fortunately many joyful moments when we joked about being different Bavarians. We told each other Jewish jokes, which helped to see our situation from another angle. We both enjoyed talking about our children and were convinced that for them—and so for us— we were doing the right thing.

Janice Hamer and the Second-Generation Opera, *Lost Childhood*

My dialogue with composer Janice Hamer was quite different. Our first contact actually took place with Abraham Peck's assistance; he gave her my address in the autumn of 1992. Jan wrote the following to me on November 17. "I happened to turn on my radio last weekend and was delighted to hear you speaking about Wagner and anti-Semitism. I am a composer and choral conductor, Jewish, and born like you in 1947. . . . I found your openness and fair-mindedness heartening, given the usual polarization on the matter. Hearing you gave me a new sense of hope and understanding."

Jan went on to report about an album of Wagner recordings she had inherited from her uncle, a gift at the end of the war from a soldier friend who had looted them from the Berghof, Hitler's residence near Berchtesgaden. Stickers on the record with the word "Berghof" helped Hitler's former secretary, Traudl Junge, authenticate the album as part of Hitler's private collection of Wagner recordings. Jan's mention of these records evoked its dismal counterpart in my garage: a heavy leather suitcase that was a wedding present to my parents from "Uncle Wolf Hitler" on April 11, 1943, passed on to me by my mother.

From the beginning my exchange of ideas with Jan was intense and open. We addressed the philosophical foundation of dialogue: the dual perception of the self as fragmentary and tribal and as inclusive and universal; the demonizing of the "other"; the parallels and differences in the way second-generation Germans and Jews respond to the Holocaust; the elements in both populations of guilt, revenge, forgiveness, silence, denial, responsibility; the ways in which the Holocaust has been used and abused in subsequent generations. She made it easy for us to find common ground. Our first face-to-face meeting occurred during an international conference with Abraham Peck at Rider University in New Jersey in March 1994. The child psychiatrist Dr. Yehuda Nir, whom I had not previously met, also appeared at the meeting, presenting us with his memoir *The Lost Childhood*. That meeting and our reading of Nir's memoir were to have lasting consequences.

Several years later, after Dr. Nir and I had become friends and had undertaken several joint public discussions, Jan conceived the idea of composing an opera from Nir's memoir with the poet Mary Azrael, her cousin, as the librettist. To the wartime story of the child–Holocaust survivor Julek and his family, Mary suggested adding a fictitious dialogue taking place in 1993, nearly fifty years after the Holocaust, between Julek and a German man born after the war to an unnamed Nazi-sympathizing family. That addition would shift the emphasis to the Second Generation and our own time. Given my own parallel commitment to dialogue, I was delighted to be included from the beginning as a consultant to this project. The many years of development of the work included numerous well-received workshops, under the auspices of American Opera Projects in New York, the New York City Opera Orchestra in its VOX-Showcasing American Composers program, and the International Vocal Arts Institute in Tel Aviv. Mary provided the following synopsis of the opera for these events:

Lost Childhood is based on Dr. Yehuda Nir's memoir of his childhood in hiding from the Nazis in Poland during World War II. When Nir's father was arrested in 1941, Yehuda (Julek) was eleven years old. He, his mother, and his teenaged sister Lala were forced to enter the brutal game of survival as the Jewish family moved from place to place disguised as Polish Catholics. Their story, played out against a background of terror and loss, is often darkly humorous and ultimately triumphant as they evade the monstrous power of the Third Reich. In the opera Julie's memory of his "lost childhood" emerges from a fictitious conversation that takes place fifty years later between Judah Gruenfeld (the adult Julek) and Manfred Geyer, a German. Manfred was born after World War II, the son of a prominent family of Nazi sympathizers. Burdened with shame and anger because of his family's close ties and continued loyalty to Hitler, he has changed his name and left Germany. He insists that he is not like other Germans, and he urges Judah to confide in him about his experiences as a Jew during the war.

For fifty years, Judah has kept silent about this period of his life, and he is reluctant to talk about it, especially with a German. Full of bravado and self-mockery, he gives a brief picture of his family at the start of the war. Then, after a harrowing account of his father's arrest, afraid of his own grief and rage, he refuses to tell Manfred more. Nevertheless, Manfred's questioning has opened the floodgates, and Judah's memories come rushing back, carrying him deeper and deeper into his past. Over a period of several days, the two men confront each other and wrestle in private with their own painful memories; and a powerful bond develops between them as they face the past and their complex, unexpected feelings about each other. The characters of Judah and Manfred, though fictitious, were inspired by the friendship of Dr. Nir and Dr. Gottfried Wagner, a passionate proponent of dialogue between second-generation non-Jewish Germans and Jews born after Hitler.

The painful confrontation between Judah and Manfred in the second scene of act one particularly touched me. My discussions with Jan and Mary helped to shape Manfred's feelings in this scene (shame and guilt by family association, the desire for absolution) to match those of many children of Nazi perpetrators, but at the same time the passage reminded me of Abraham's nightmares.

Here is Manfred's and Judah's crucial interchange:

Judah:
    (bitter) All that spring I asked myself

Why we didn't run
And suddenly it was too late.
My father was a broken man.
He let us down.
(This is difficult and he wants to change the subject.) And your *father?*
Manfred: *(stiffly, defensive)*
He played his part.
Judah: *(challenging)*
What about your *family?*
Manfred:
I was born after the war, Judah,
born into silence
and blinding denials.
But I saw, I will always see
what I wasn't supposed to see.
As a child, I hadn't learned to deny my eyes.
The Devil's face at the night window—
the grownups said it wasn't there,
but I knew.
Judah: *(persists)*
Tell me about your father.
Manfred: *(uncomfortably)*
You know about my family.
Everyone knows.
(almost pleading)
But I am not my father.
Every morning when I awake, I tell myself—
I am not my father.
I have no father, Judah.
Judah:
You have *no father, Manfred?*
Your father *is alive. . . .*

The opera's ending is not a traditional, happily-ever-after conclusion, but at least it offers the possibility of Judah's and Manfred's evolving beyond stereotypes to listening to and accepting each other and the hope of a general transformation beyond their individual destinies. This spirit is diametrically opposed to the quotation from Beckett's *Malone Dies* that served as the epigraph to Yehuda Nir's memoir:

Let me say before I go any further that I forgive nobody. I wish them all an atrocious life and then the fires and ice of hell and in the exerable generations to come.

Only at the end of the opera do Judah and Manfred manage to reach a genuine dialogue:

The world is still dark with burning. But our children must know we are listening. Nothing is forgiven. / Nothing can be undone. The world is still dark with smoke. It must not end with this. Tell me, Manfred. Tell me, Judah. Tell me how it was, how it is.

It is not they, however, but the child survivor Julek, hopeful of better times in a threatened world, who utters the last word. The opera does not attempt to replicate Yehuda Nir's memoir in music and poetry but rather uses some of its material for a different purpose—a work of art and a plea for dialogue between non-Jewish Germans and Jews living since the Holocaust, and by extension for resolution through dialogue of current conflicts, human rights violations, and genocides, an aim with which I deeply concur. I look forward to *Lost Childhood*'s soon finding its world premiere.

Peter Pogany Wnendt and Intergenerational Post-Shoa Discussions

The publication of the German edition of the book that was a joint project by Abraham and me led to Peter Pogany Wnendt, a psychotherapist in Cologne and leader of the Düsseldorf-Cologne committee working on intergenerational effects of the Holocaust. Peter openly supported the constructive possibilities of discussion between Abraham and myself and studied the book intensively; he also examined my autobiography from the point of view of a psychotherapist. He considered the basically constructive power of human aggressiveness, which primarily serves the process of adjustment to life. Unfavorable circumstances in a child's development, such as lack of love and abuse by the parents or enforcement of obedience, can lead to a deformation of the development into destructive energy.

These thoughts were influenced by the theories of the psychoanalyst Arno Gruen, whose work we both value and which to a great extent became the starting point for our discussion. Gruen's emphasis on the importance of empathy and compassion as the basis of human coexistence became the red thread throughout our dialogue.

After very positive cooperation in a book presentation with Ralph Giordano at the Heinrich-Heine-Institut in December 2008, Peter and I further developed the theme of the effects of the Holocaust based on the example of our families over three generations. Thus we cooperated in three presentations on this theme in Cologne, Bundy, and Bielefeld with a presentation entitled "Beyond Silence and Mistrust." By means of a text selection from the revised version of my autobiography (2010), I illustrated the break from my family legacy due to the refusal of the Bayreuth Festival leadership, from Hitler's dictatorship until today, to face up to and honestly deal with the philosophical legacy of Richard Wagner and its consequences for German society and politics.

Far removed from the "philo-Semitic" falsifications of history practiced by the mighty neo-Bayreuth business, in the second part of this presentation I read texts explaining and illustrating my commitment to an open dialogue between the generations after Hitler. We connected this with Peter's autobiographical *Stolperstein Experiences*.[3] We read and discussed, dealing with our own family histories and also our attempts to overcome a paralyzing moralizing attitude to the past in order to achieve a common, creative culture of compassion and empathy. A precondition for this, however, according to Peter, is that one's own situation must be clearly defined, as he wrote to me in an email dated on July 23, 2008:

Gottfried comes from a family which was deeply involved in National Socialism, a so-called family of perpetrators. His grandmother was an intimate friend of Hitler, his father and his uncle were his protégés. The "Fuehrer" was a frequent welcome visitor of the Wagners. I come from a Jewish family who became victims of the National Socialist mania which Gottfried's family actively supported. Both my parents survived the Holocaust in Hungary as young people. Whereas my father lost both parents, my mother and her closest relatives survived the war. She lost one grandfather and three uncles.

Gottfried and I met in 2008. I had read "Our Zero Hour," the book about dialogue in the second generation co-written by him and Abraham Peck and was very impressed by it. After this book had impelled a very lively discussion in our literary circle we wrote to Gottfried Wagner. Thus we both embarked on an e-mail discussion which became more and more intense and more and more personal. I soon gained respect for the honest way he had confronted and dealt with his difficult family history from his childhood days onward. A common starting-point was the admiration we shared for the books by the psychoanalyst Arno Gruen. They deal with love and compassion or rather the lack of them being the causes of violence and motives for the development of perpetrators. We also exchanged thoughts on the problems of dialogue among people of the second generation.

For example I wrote the following thoughts to Gottfried on 23 July 2008:

I believe that one of the most difficult problems in the dialogue of the Second Generation is how to deal with the hate which we have taken over from our parents and which slumbers on hidden inside us, and indeed this is the case on both sides. In the case of the children of survivors it is the parents' hatred of the perpetrators; in the case of the children of the perpetrators it is the racist hatred which the parents never overcame and which is carried on subconsciously by their children, without their noticing. That was one of the problems of the youth of the 1968 generation who rebelled understandably against the deeds and the silence of their parents, but without noticing that they also identified with the ideology they were struggling against. Under the cloak of left-wing ideologies the youth of '68 frequently represented potentially fascist and authoritarian ideas without noticing it. I do not wish to discredit the youth of the 60s or compare them to the Nazis, I only wish to point out how the destructiveness of fascism can continue to exist unnoticed. Perhaps the most striking example of this is the former RAF-member Horst Mahler [Red Army Faction also known as the Baader-Meinhof

Gang] who is today a self-declared Nazi. In an interview initiated by the magazine *Vanity Fair* Mahler greeted his discussion partner Michel Friedman with the words "Heil Hitler." He went on to deny Auschwitz . . . I firmly believe that the success or failure of a dialogue between members of the Second Generation depends decisively on how the theme of hate is dealt with.

In order to clarify his own situation, Peter went on to tell the painful story of his grandparents:

I never knew Miklós und Erzsébet Pogány, my grandparents on my father's side. They were murdered before I was born, probably in December 1944. The Red Army had already reached the gates of Budapest. Nobody knows how they died. It is very likely that they, like countless other Jews, were shot on the banks of the Danube. Perhaps at the hands of the German Nazis, or perhaps at the hands of the Hungarian Arrow Cross Party, who were no less brutal in their actions after the invasion of the German army and the SS on March 19, 1944. The story my father told me was that on that morning, against the advice of a friend, they went to their work in a military hospital as usual. My grandfather did not want to leave his patients in the lurch. They never returned. Were my grandparents heroes because they paid the price of loyalty with their lives? Or did my father fabricate a heroic story to embroider their tragic and brutal death so that he could soothe his own ineradicable pain which he was not to overcome for the rest of his life? The painful story of my grandparents had a decisive effect on my childhood and my later life. As a child I only knew a father who was almost always sad and suffered in silence. As a child I sensed his sorrow and instinctively wanted to help him and ease his sorrow. I wanted to turn my father into a happy person. But I could not succeed in this. Instead of this I "took over" his sorrow, supposedly in an attempt to take over his burden in my childlike way. I was never able to speak with him about this. In August my brother and I had two *Stolpersteine* laid for our grandparents at their house on Rakoczi ut. 68 in Budapest. This was also the house where I was born on November 15, 1954. I spent the first two years of my life there, till we left Hungary in November 1956 at the time of the Hungarian Uprising to emigrate to

Chile. It was not until the process of the laying of the Stumbling Blocks that I realized that I had suffered a deep loss before my birth. For the first time I was able to feel my own pain. This pain was different from the empathic pain I had felt as a child on behalf of my father and turned into my pain. Up to this point I had felt the pain inside me as a heavy oppressive burden, which I could not throw off. Being able to differentiate made it possible for me to mourn my own pain and at the same time to "give my" father "back" his own pain and thus instead of taking on his pain, for the first time feeling real pity for his suffering.

At the end of our lecture tour in July 2010, Peter came to the conclusion that:

We told our stories so that you could gain a lively impression of our personal past. Neither of us knows what the "beyond" of silence and distrust might turn out like and how we will be able to get there. The Holocaust did not only cause the physical destruction of the victims; above all it was an attack by the perpetrators on humanity. The psychoanalyst Arno Gruen writes: "The monstrosity of the Holocaust was the revenge of all that was alive in people. Their revenge was directed against individuality, which had been taken away from them; this was the reason they felt they had the right to eliminate others" (*The Loss of Compassion*, 2005, 223). Therefore we believe that it is the duty of those who have the Holocaust as their legacy to work together to ensure that a "culture of compassion" can be recreated. We understand the term compassion, according to what is meant by Gruen, as being "our built-in barrier against inhumanity." Along this troublesome path the bright moments of enlightenment are relatively few. This does not, however, discourage us from continuing. That is why we hope to have a stimulating and constructive discussion with our listeners, so that we do not only transmit something, but take something away with us from the discussions, so that our ongoing path of dialogue and the struggle for compassion can be continued in a less burdensome way and with continuing positive results.

Having had many discussions with Peter that had to do with the takeover of the Bayreuth Festival by my sisters Eva and Katharina, I hoped our friendship would last well into the future, but later we disagreed too much about the importance of family neurosis on our own lives. I am fully aware of the guilt of the Wagner clan in Bayreuth, but I am not responsible for it. I have made my choices in my professional and private life, fighting for privacy and not to be put into any box. My autobiography and this book make it evident for those who want to understand.

The Death of My Father and the Search for a Path from Hatred

After the death of Gudrun Wagner, my father's second wife, in November 2007, I tried to reestablish contact with my sisters Katharina and Eva. In my first exchange of emails with Katharina in May 2008, I refrained from discussing painful episodes from our past and instead wrote about our first highly enjoyable but, sadly, solitary meeting when I met her as a child in my father's house on Festival Hill. After various abortive attempts to arrange a personal meeting, I sought to show an interest in the difficult situation of Katharina and Eva as the daughters of Wolfgang Wagner and my predicament as his son. Although I did not receive an answer from either of them, I planned to travel with Teresina and Eugenio to the Bayreuth Festival. But things turned out differently because I needed two eye operations in June 2008 due to a detached retina and hence was unable to work or travel for months on end.

My father died on March 21, 2010. Since then there have been far too many uninformed comments in public and in the media that have nothing to do with my wish for a candid and private dialogue with my sisters. I expressed my pain about the loss of our personal communication in a poem for my son:

Lament of the Ostracized Sons on their way to my father's grave
For Eugen, the grandson in memory of his unknown grandfather
You daughters did not see our pain about what you had left behind
  for us, the ostracized.
You continued on the path against which the wise Spinoza had
  warned:
"Hate increases as a result of returning hate with hate."
We, the ostracized, discover behind the mask of "the final spoken will
  of the father"

Your will to limitless power with willing "witnesses."
We were frightened and found his and your hatred against those who
   went along the path of the philosopher out of hate: "Hate increases
   as a result of returning hate with hate.
Love is the only remedy."[4]
We the ostracized will one day visit the grave of my father in absolute
   peace to bring him what he and you had lost: Love

My attempt to generate a discussion with my uncle Wieland's children after my father's death about the role of our fathers in the Third Reich—including our relatives living at Lake Constance[5]—and their neo-Bayreuth ideology of suppression failed. This was because, like my sisters, they could not face up to the pain of our joint confrontation with the involvement of our fathers in the Third Reich,[6] the indispensable prerequisite for a dialogue. How can one escape from this vicious circle? Arno Gruen provides an important indicator: "Hate can only be ended by admitting sadness about the insufficient love of the parents."

Both Katharina, Eva, and I, as well as my cousins, have all experienced a lack of love. Each and every one of us must decide whether he/she wants to admit this sadness, which involves pain. If we are unwilling to understand through self-criticism the fatal split into perpetrator and victim and thus overcome it, we will remain victims and perpetrators because we do not recognize that our own "perpetrator side" stems from our entanglement in our family history that can only be overcome by dialogue with and empathy for the other side. Hence, you have to start with yourself if you want to change your life. I am ready and willing to overcome my "perpetrator side" by developing empathy and dialogue with my sisters and other relatives of my generation. My proposal is that we stop squabbling about who was chiefly responsible for the breakdown in communication in the Wagner family. I am prepared to scrutinize my position in the light of the truth and sift through the facts. I shall not refuse to maintain communication with my generation and the next Wagner generation, particularly when we try to end the split in our family since the founding of the Bayreuth Festival and Wagner's ideology. But I cannot do this on my own. If things turn out differently, my sadness will remain.

20

From Tel Aviv to Bayreuth and Back Again to Teresina, Eugenio, and Stella: A Journey with Ella, Noam, Peter, and Simon into the Past and into the Future

In the light of the events I have described, I decided to travel to Bayreuth in the middle of August 2011 with those who were prepared for an open dialogue. Peter Pogany Wnendt, the Israeli composer Ella Milch-Sheriff and her husband Noam Sheriff, the Israeli conductor and composer, along with the multimedia artist Simon Goritschnig, were my understanding companions on the difficult return to Bayreuth.

Background History

Prior to March 2011 a visit to Bayreuth seemed to me to be quite impossible, given the strained relations between me and my sisters. My attitude changed after meeting Ella Milch-Sheriff and her husband Noam Sheriff at the end of March 2011, at the final event of the concert series in Bochum entitled "The Wound of Wagner." During this performance Wagner's concept of the total art work, his ideology and his influence, were contrasted in provocative compilations of his dramas and compositions with the works of Jewish composers. A series of fringe events helped to enhance the debate. I participated in a discussion in a lecture hall next to the Bochum Concert Hall with Noam Sheriff, the Israeli diplomat Shimon Stein, and Norbert Abels, the head dramaturge of the Frankfurt Opera House and organizer of the program, prior to the final concert on March 24, in which excerpts from *Lohengrin* and *Die Meistersinger von Nürnberg* were performed together with Leonard Bernstein's *Kaddisch*. The interdependence of ideology, the plays, and the controversies over playing Wagner in Israel right up to the present formed the focus of our candid discussion. Shimon Stein and Noam Sheriff shared my position that Wagner's concept of the total art work cannot be divorced from his life and his racist ideology, while recognizing his importance for the history of music. The audience remained silent, which hardly surprised me given the tradition of the Wagner myth cultivated in Germany and particularly influenced by academics and media close to the Bayreuth establishment. Noam, Ella, and I continued our discussion about Wagner after the concert by the Bochum Symphony Orchestra under its Israeli conductor Steven Sloan.

But Ella's family history became more important for me. Her father, the gynecologist and Holocaust survivor Dr. Baruch Milch, had lived in Bayreuth from 1946–1948 with his second wife Lusia and their daughter Shosh, Ella's older sister. Baruch had built up an outpatient clinic in a house on Lisztstrasse 16, in which he had treated Jewish Displaced Persons in particular. Baruch's apartment, in which he had lived with Lusia, baby Shosh, who had been born in Passau in 1946, as well as some other relatives, had been located in an impressive house. Just a couple of houses further down, at Lisztstrasse 7, stood the house that had been the practice of Dr. med. Helmut Treuter, my grandfather Siegfried's doctor and the occasional personal physician to Adolf Hitler whenever he visited Bayreuth.[1] Treuter was deeply implicated in the Nazi euthanasia program of the late 1930s and early 1940s.

The Milchs had lived close to the gardener's house on the estate of Villa Wahnfried, where I had lived to the age of seven with my parents and my sister Eva. Ella and I were extremely moved about the overlaps in our lives. Shosh had visited Bayreuth while researching the history of the Milch family, but Ella and Noam had never been there. On parting in Bochum, we had decided to make a journey to Bayreuth together. How difficult this decision was for Ella can be ascertained from the appalling background history of her parents as Holocaust survivors and of Shosh and Ella as members of the Second Generation. When we said good-bye on March 24, 2011, in Bochum, Ella gave me a copy of a TV production by Radio and TV Berlin-Brandenburg dealing with her life and work as a composer. On reading the brief information on the DVD cover, I guessed what Ella had been through:

"My heaven is full of music": Ella Milch-Sheriff grew up in Israel with the silence of her father. Only when she read his diary did she discover his appalling mystery. "Heaven is empty," Baruch Milch had written in Poland in 1942. She translated his story into her language: "music."

The day after I got back home I let her know how deeply the TV documentary had moved me and asked her for further references to her other operas and books. Her reaction was open and friendly, emphasizing how touched she too was about our Bayreuth family histories. From this point in time we began exchanging details about Lisztstrasse 16, and she sent me her father's autobiography, *Can Heaven be Empty?* and her own autobiography, *Ein Lied für meinen Vater* [A Song for my Father], which she had published with Ingeborg Prior in 2008. Equally important for my coming to terms with Ella were the libretto of the cantata *Can Heaven be Empty?* (2005) and her operas *And the Rat Laughed* (2005) and *Baruchs Schweigen* [Baruch's Silence] (2010).

Ella had produced the libretto together with Shosh, assimilating central parts of her father's autobiography published in 2003 with extracts from Paul Celan's poem "Engführung" [The Straightening]. The libretto of the cantata expresses the never-to-be-overcome pain of Baruch for the loss of his beloved first family. He remembers his murdered son Eliash-Lunek and his wife Peppa, Lunek's mother. The pain made a lasting impression on me listening to the words of the narrator and of the singer in the cantata:

July 1943:
   Can heaven be empty?
Narrator:
   July 1943.
   I am hiding in the loft over a stable, in a village, and with good people.
   The risk of death is ever present, and any lack of vigilance on my part
      may cost me my life.
   I do not know whether I shall live to finish writing.
   And these are my 10 commandments:
   Thou shalt have no other god save thyself.
   Do only that which shall serve thyself and do not sacrifice thyself for
      another.
   Live life to the full and enjoy every moment.
   Love thyself above all.
   Do not do unto others that which pleases you.

Do not uselessly burden thy mind.
Harden thy heart and listen not to it.
Do not get close to others and do not allow them to get close to thee.
Rely on nobody.
Do not believe—heaven is empty.
(His voice is fading out slowly as a background to the singer's words)
I was born in 1907 in Podhadjce, a small district capital in eastern
  Galicia most of whose inhabitants were Jews. The countryside
  around Podhajce is beautiful. To the East, there is a high mountain
  crowned with a virgin forest of conifers. The River, which flowed
  among the foothills of the mountain, expanded into a fine bathing
  beach on the outskirts of town. The river's waters were cold with yel-
  low and white water lilies and other river flowers floating on its sur-
  face.
Singer: *(spoken)*
  On Friday, September 1st, 1939 his real life ended.
  It was first when I read father's manuscript that I understood.
  I grew up in the house of a dead man.
  Strong and wise, but dead.
  He taught me not to need any emotional support,
  Not to cry in public,
  Any sign of emotion considered to be a weakness,
  Only the strong ones survive,
  He thus moulded me in his image.
  I kept my promise.
  I have finished your book, Father.
  From your book I learned to forgive you, to miss you.
  Now you may finally rest.
  Rest in Peace.

I read the sad stories of the lives of Baruch, Luisa, Ella, and Shosh slowly and intermittently; first Baruch's autobiography, then Ella's. I met with many other painful episodes, such as the suffocation of their nephew Eliah by a brother-in-law, a further insurmountable trauma causing pain, guilt, and the desire for revenge, as well as the longing to forgive and forget.

Only afterward did I view and listen to Ella's operas *And the Rat Laughed* and *Baruchs Schweigen* on DVD and made a lot of notes. After working on them thoroughly, my contact with Ella via email and Skype intensified as August 11 drew closer. Ella read my autobiography in the meantime. The individual study of each other's family history prior to our meeting was the basic reason for our decision to travel to Bayreuth together. Shortly before I flew to Cologne, I wrote to her: "Your music reaches deep levels of my soul." Ella answered me immediately: "I hope that our new experience will lead us to something worthwhile that we will both be proud of. . . . Concentrate on the positive in our lives because we will gain nothing from doing the opposite." Ella's gentle gesture was very helpful in soothing my nerves and helping me to take the flight to Cologne in a much more relaxed frame of mind, particularly as I knew that Peter, Noam, and Simon were aware of the predicament that Ella and I were in.

The day before our departure to Bayreuth, I looked up Ralph Giordano in his Cologne flat and informed him about my travel plans. Very few people in Germany understood as Ralph Giordano does—we have been friends since 1988—that the following days in Bayreuth would be a logical continuation of my biography. His gentle encouragement was a great boost.

Searching for Clues in Bayreuth: August 11–August 13, 2011

August 11—The First Search for Clues

How fortunate I was in being able to discuss with Peter on our train journey from Cologne to Bayreuth the psychological problems affecting the Second Generation as a result of the family histories of the Milchs and the Wagners. When I came with Peter and Simon to collect Ella and Noam for our first walk in Bayreuth, it seemed to us that we had known each other for a long time. What we experienced during the days together is difficult to put into words, but I would like to try to record some impressions.

Our first walk took us across the Bahnhofstrasse to the Luitpoldplatz, from there to the synagogue in the Münzgasse, then into the Opernstrasse and past the Margrave's Opera House and the Golden Anchor Hotel leading up to the Sternplatz. We had a stop at the Capri ice cream parlor, run by a lady who had been a friend of my mother's and whose daughter lives as an orthodox Jew in Israel. We proceeded on into Richard Wagner Strasse, the Villa Winifred, the Siegfried Wagner House with the Hitler annex, the gardener's house, and on to Wagner's grave, finally reaching Lisztstrasse 16, our destination. There is no such thing as normality! The density of my family history that is embodied in all the individuals: each and every meter and stone resembles a surreal variant from the Inferno and the Purgatorio of Dante's *Divine Comedy*. For me this often meant too much Richard Wagner, too much Hitler, and too many Wagner family stories. Yet the presence of Ella, Noam, Peter, and Simon made this necessary and tolerable, just as did the moments outside the synagogue. It is difficult for me to explain, but having an experience that we had been through together proved to be meaningful and liberating. And yet I can convey happy moments of my childhood that took place in the overwhelming solitude of the Wagner family, from which I could escape as a small boy through my cheerful daydreams. Ella's words were about her family's time in Lisztstrasse 16—from autumn 1946 to spring 1948—after the persecution and loss of beloved relatives, two years of outside existential peace and safety, their last abode before emigrating to Israel and Ella's birth in Tel Aviv.

And in the end Ella too remains hopeful and prepared for dialogue.

August 12—A Second Search for Clues

Accompanied by a friend, Eberhard Wagner, the five of us proceeded to the Bayreuth real-estate registry and were informed in a friendly fashion how we could gather more details about the Milch family during its stay in Bayreuth. I promised Ella that I would follow up these issues in the autumn at the registration office and the municipal archives. We walked past the municipal hall and the ruins of the backstage of the last production of *Götterdämmerung* in front of the Jean Paul monument. This was where the concert of the Israel Chamber Orchestra conducted by Roberto Paternosto had been staged on July 26. I found the program, which ranged from Hatikva via Mendelssohn to Wagner's "Siegfried Idyll," extremely discomforting. Ella and Noam had similar feelings of discomfort.

There is no such thing as normality, and something had changed in Bayreuth. The people of Bayreuth could no longer repress Wagner's anti-Semitism after July 26, 2011, and will have to live with it forever. We walked through the court garden to the Richard Wagner Archive in the Siegfried Wagner House next to Villa Wahnfried. We were received very kindly by the deputy director, Dr. Föttinger, who had prepared the documents on the prelude to *Tristan* that Noam and Ella had asked to see. There could not be a greater contrast than to explain to them the exact details of Hitler's visits and of the rooms in the Führer annex and then to hear Noam's splendid theory of musical colors in interpreting the epoch-making composition sketches. And all this in the former second music room, where the safe in which my grandmother Winifred had lovingly preserved the correspondence of the Wagner family with Hitler had been located. The safe was disposed of—a further example of how the Wagner family dealt with major historical documents. I could not repress my anger at this thought.

We spent our lunch break at the Bayerischer Hof hotel. Our host was Peter Deeg, who had a great interest in Ella's family history. There came another difficult matter. We traveled up to the performance of *Die Meistersinger von Nürnberg* on Festival Hill. I pointed out the wretched statues of Wagner, Liszt, and Cosima by Arno Breker. Another look at the family window in the king's annex: too much Hitler once again. Our breathing was heavy. I tried to ignore the people gossiping behind my back about my return after twenty-one years of absence. Those who tried to reinterpret my presence as a public reconciliation ceremony got short shrift from me.

I was worried when I saw Noam and Ella heading to their box for the first act. I was in the Festival House restaurant, relieved that I would be sitting in the narrow auditorium for the first act. During the first interval I was relieved to see Ella and Noam return in one piece, yet they were not enthusiastic. We understood each other without the need for many words and agreed to meet up for a discussion afterward. The conclusion of Katharina's production of *Die Meistersinger von Nürnberg* horrified Noam and Ella. Things know no bounds. We bid each other a cordial, silent farewell. That evening I slept badly.

August 13—The Third Search for Clues

We marvelled at the Margrave's Opera House. In the afternoon we went to the graves of the Wagner family in the municipal cemetery. Here are Ella's salutary words (spoken after the journey) about what happened at my father's grave:

> Arriving at the Wagners' grave we see a big but simple stone. The names of Siegfried (Richard Wagner's son), Winifred and then chronologically

according to the dates of death (without any dates mentioned) all the other names were engraved on it. The last one is Wolfgang, Gottfried's father. We stood there in silence. Gottfried, at first, told us more about the family and then he took out a piece of paper, a certificate of "Keren Kayemet" (Jewish National Fund) saying that he had planted a tree in Israel in the name of Wolfgang, Eugenio (Gottfried's son) and Gottfried in Israel. The certificate is in Hebrew and English. He puts it on his father's grave and cries. What a moment! A certificate in Hebrew of a tree planted in Israel on Wolfgang's grave—he who refused any contact with his son after his visit to Israel. Both Noam and I felt privileged to be with Gottfried in such an intimate moment of his life. We know, and he told us, that he would not have done it without us and the blessing of his wife and son. We were happy we could be there for him. On our way back, Gottfried and I fantasized an imaginary meeting between Baruch (my father) and Wolfgang (his father). We both agreed that it would have been a disaster which could have led to real physical violence.

But Baruch and Wolfgang are no longer alive and I feel the words of Ella and Shosh to their father as a source of consolation:

In front of your book I have learned to forgive and miss you
Peace at last.
Peace on your ashes.

Tears of sorrow and the thought: What would have happened if my father, Eva, and Katharina had gone through the family history of the Wagners with me?

Ella and I can only come so far in our dialogue because we have faced up to our pain and both of us have come to terms with our individual family history. There followed a final discussion with Ella, Noam, Peter, and Simon, our young friend and companion who did not merely document the whole journey with dedication on video but enhanced our discussions. A cordial and melancholy farewell. This journey to Bayreuth fulfilled for me its purposes: Ella knows that Bayreuth is part of her father, mother, and sister but not of her life between 1945 and 1947 because she was born in Israel much later. I was glad to help her with this recognition. I mourned naturally at the grave of my father as a son who has lost his father and put a copy of the tree of life given to my Eugenio on his grave as a peaceful gesture of the son and grandson. I recognized then that I was relieved and that the past must not block my life here and now with my Italian family, which has nothing to do any longer with the past of the Wagner clan in Bayreuth.

VII

New Allies: Holocaust, Genocide, and Human-Rights Studies

Abraham J. Peck

21

From Holocaust to Genocide

Twenty years ago Gottfried and I saw only a mere possibility. We saw a possibility to approach areas of dialogue and discussion that would have been impossible for our fathers and mothers. We saw an opportunity to create an honest, if painful examination of the historic relationship between Germans and Jews in Germany and beyond in order to understand why neither community had spoken to the other except in ways that had led to death and destruction.

Twenty years ago, the First Generation of Germans and Jews was still a factor; it guarded the gates of noncommunication, of shame, guilt, hatred, and every other emotion that would not and could not allow any aspect of compassion, understanding, and hope to enter. The First Generation is nearly gone. Now Germans and Jews in their sixties are the generation of record. Gottfried and I approach an age when state pensions and medical benefits should top the list of our present and our future concerns. But that is not for us. We still cherish the possibilities of our Stockton meeting and still work to make it a reality.

In 2008 I met an extraordinary group of women, all affiliated with the University of Maine at Augusta (UMA). The campus, one of seven in the University of Maine system, is situated in an attractive rural setting, very unlike the University of Southern Maine's urban environment. About five thousand students attend UMA, located in Maine's capital city. Peggy Danielson was the dean of the College of Arts and Sciences at UMA; Jill Rubinson was a professor of English with a specialty in Shakespeare; and Wendy Hazard was an historian of world civilizations. They formed the nucleus of a group of faculty who were intent on creating an academic program in Holocaust, genocide, and human-rights studies. One of the most important factors in their enthusiasm for such a program was the realization that the

Holocaust and Human Rights Center of Maine (HHRC), founded in 1985, was finally moving into its own facility, a beautiful building named for Michael Klahr, a French Jew who had survived the Holocaust as a hidden child, emigrated to the United States, and ultimately married a Maine native, Phyllis Jalbert. That building would be located on the UMA campus. After Michael Klahr's death, Phyllis Jalbert sought some way to honor the memory of her husband and the terrible ordeal that he and millions of other European Jews had endured during the Holocaust. The answer was simple: she would provide a major part of the funding necessary to create a Holocaust center in his name.

I had served on the HHRC board for eight years and understood the importance of the Michael Klahr Center. For the first time in its history, the HHRC would have a permanent place to tell the story of Maine's Holocaust survivors and liberators and to become a force in the struggle for human rights in Maine and in the nation. My colleague Sharon Nichols retired as the longtime executive director of the HHRC and the center's new director, Robert Bernheim, was a Holocaust scholar with a vision and an enthusiasm to create both an academic and a public center for Holocaust remembrance and issues surrounding human rights.

I had taught a course on genocide at the University of Southern Maine since 2001, a course that Wendy Hazard was interested in bringing to UMA. Peggy Danielson, Jill Rubinson, and Wendy Hazard were very persuasive: they asked if I would teach the course at UMA beginning in the fall semester of 2008 and hinted that, if things worked out, that course could become part of a minor in Holocaust, genocide, and human-rights studies, a program that would be unique in Maine and in New England. That was all I needed to hear, and I immediately accepted. It was an opportunity to enter an exciting new venture: a university campus that would house a Holocaust and human rights center dedicated to the education of middle- and high-school students and an academic minor for university students.

The three academic powerhouses, Peggy, Jill, and Wendy made it happen. In the fall semester of 2009, I was appointed visiting professor and director of a brand-new minor on Holocaust, genocide, and human-rights studies (HGHRS) at UMA. An interdisciplinary faculty of twenty, from both the Augusta and Bangor campuses of UMA, teaches in the minor. A number of the courses are distance-learning offerings, allowing those who are place bound and students outside of UMA to take advantage of courses offered by faculty from the disciplines of history, philosophy, English, mental health and human services studies, sociology, women's studies, humanities, American studies, justice studies, and art. Our students also spend a semester at various internship venues, including the Holocaust and Human Rights Center of Maine, the Assistant Attorney General of Maine's Office of Civil Rights Education and Enforcement, the Center for Grieving Children, the Maine Civil Liberties Union, the Maine State Office for Refugee and Immigrant Affairs, and the Portland Office of Multilingual and Multicultural Affairs. A lecture series, begun in 2009, has brought a diverse group of speakers to the campus on a variety of topics, including Native American issues, the Armenian genocide, Hitler's African victims, Holocaust memory in Germany and Israel, the Cambodian killing fields, reconciliation efforts in postgenocide Rwanda, political violence in Zimbabwe, the ongoing genocide in Darfur, the Israeli-Palestinian conflict, and Islam in America.[1]

Together with the work of the Holocaust and Human Rights Center of Maine, the University of Maine at Augusta is able to reach students at nearly every level of their education. There is nothing else like it in the United States. Imagine: the HHRC sponsors programs that allow middle- and high-school students to understand that the issue of human rights begins in their own classrooms, where instances of bullying, homophobia, and racial and religious slurs have been on the increase, not only in Maine but throughout the United States. The hope is that by the time these students arrive at UMA, they will have begun to understand that there is no such thing as a just world, that the need to heal that world begins in their homes, their classrooms, and their communities. And then UMA will introduce them to the terrible history of human injustices that marked the twentieth century and now the early part of the twenty-first. They will understand racism, sexism, colonialism, homophobia, and the terrible role of the "outsider" in society, a role that has resulted in the murders of over 170 million men, women, and children by their own governments. They will learn about the "crime without a name," as Winston Churchill called it before the Jewish scholar and Holocaust survivor, Rafael Lemkin, gave it a name—genocide. They will learn how little humanity has learned afer 1945; how meaningless the "Never agains" have become in the face of continuing genocides and the ongoing abuses of human rights. They will learn that in one week in December 1948, the United Nations created two pieces of legislation that would forever, on paper, change our world: the Universal Declaration of Human Rights and the Convention on the Prevention and Punishment of the Crime of Genocide. But they will also learn how many nations and how many political leaders act as though they had never heard of these two historic declarations and how little they seem to matter.

If those students take with them not only the intellectual capital that will allow them to find meaningful professions but the moral and ethical capital to become "upstanders" to the injustices of our and their world, to leave behind the bystander mentality that defines most of those who are never victims or perpetrators, then perhaps I, too, will find meaning. Perhaps I will find meaning in the suffering of my mother and father. Perhaps I will find meaning in the murders of my grandfather, uncles, aunts, and their families. Perhaps I will find a hope that I can pass on to my children and that they can pass on to their children. Perhaps I can give them a legacy that they will want and accept as their own.

VIII

Afterwords

22

Discourses on Holocaust and Genocide: Have We Learned Anything from History?

Gottfried Wagner

> When I despair, I remember that all through history the way of truth and love has always won. There have been tyrants and murderers and for a time they seem invincible, but at the end, they always fall—think of it, always.
>
> *Mahatma Gandhi*

At the beginning of my dialogue with Abraham Peck, in March of 1991, it was his desire to discuss the Holocaust/Shoah, the genocide of the European Jews as the unique event in human history. Our first talk, in the presence of compassionate Rabbi Steven Jacobs, consisted of alternating monologues on our very different family histories under the shadow of the Third Reich. Even then I felt uneasy being classified as a "son of perpetrators." Already, by the end of the 1970s, I had developed an aversion to false identities and ambiguous attributes ascribed to Germans in general, German Jews, and all other Jews born after 1945. Aspects of my family history omitted in my part of this book, as well as recent events in my life, may clarify why I no longer accept stereotyped generalizations about my own or future generations in non-Jewish German families. Therefore, I now feel I must speak about other members of my parents' families.

On the Drexels, My Mother's Family

Without any preparation I, a child of ten years, was introduced[1] to the connection between the Third Reich and the Wagner clan through a documentary film that aroused my lasting interest in this topic. My mother, Ellen Drexel, became a central figure for me because of her own painful experiences with the Wagner clan from 1942 onward and the war trauma and the tragedies in her Drexel family. She constantly repeated a phrase that I did not fully understand until much later: *"Choose your own way of life."* She accompanied these words with stories about her uncle, Hans Drexel, who was prevented by the Nazi ban from working as a painter (*Berufsverbot*),[2] his art being labeled as degenerate (*entartet*). She suffered all her life from the loss of her younger brother, Ernst Drexel, who had vanished as a twenty-year-old soldier of the German army in Russia. There was no contact between the snobbish Wagner clan and the Drexels, the latter being regarded as socially of "lower" rank, something I did not accept. Ignoring the rules of the Wagners in Bayreuth that prohibited me from finding out facts about the family history, I learned that my grandmother, Thora Drexel, had taken her own life because of the death of her son, Ernst, and my father's insistence that she sever contact with her daughter, my mother.

The Drexel family, however, did not abandon my mother. Their warm behavior drew me strongly to them. There are also other attributes that made me identify easily with the Drexels: their sincere interest in my educational work and in my Italian family, attitudes never shown by the Wagner family. Therefore, I was especially happy when Friederike Albert, the daughter of my cousin, Renate Albert-Drexel, invited me to her wedding with Bismark Oppong from Ghana in May 2012. I could speak openly with Bismark and Friederike on the connection between European colonialism and the Nuremberg racial laws. It is extraordinary that we are able today to confront such painful topics together sensitively and respectfully!

On Other Wagner–Liszt Relatives

It would be unfair to relegate all my relatives of the Liszt and Wagner families to the evils of a Nazi corner. My anti-Nazi aunt, Friedelind Wagner, and my great-uncle, Franz Wilhelm Beidler, were both persecuted for their divergent and courageous choices in life. Friedelind wrote her extraordinary autobiography, *Heritage of Fire*, in the United States in 1944. A German-language version, titled *Night over Bayreuth*, was published in Switzerland in 1945.[3] Her book made her persona non grata and not only in Bayreuth.

This pariah status evoked empathy for her in me. The other direct grandson of Richard Wagner, Franz Wilhelm Beidler, worked as a leftist cultural manager in Berlin during the Weimar Republic and married Ellen Gottschalk of the assimilated Jewish Gottschalk family in Berlin. After his persecution and escape from Nazi Germany in June 1933, the couple settled in Zurich, where he worked as a musicologist. Ellen and Franz Wilhelm had a daughter, my cousin, Dagny Richarda Beidler. In addition to my German relatives, there was also my French family. I discovered them during my preparations for the final high-school exam, when studying the speeches of the Nazi propaganda minister, Joseph Goebbels, and works of the Jewish communist writer Arnold Zweig.

My open revolt against the Nazi Wagner clan began at the end of the 1960s, though not as a part of the '68 movement, which I considered too radical and rigid. It was just then that I met my beloved French cousin, Blandine Jeanson, who like me is directly related to and even resembles Franz Liszt. She was part of the circle around the French philosopher Jean-Paul Sartre, the feminist Simone de Beauvoir, the '68-revolutionary Daniel Cohn Bendit, and other French leftists. As a journalist, Blandine worked courageously for human rights and was a cofounder of the French leftist daily newspaper *Libération*. We both wanted to change the world, but later life made us much more realistic. Blandine told me the story of her grandfather, Jacques Count Trolley de Prévaux, an admiral in the French navy, whose second marriage was to the beautiful Polish Jewish fashion model, Lotka Leitner. Both were resistance fighters against the Nazi occupation in France and were murdered by Klaus Barbie, the Nazi hangman of Lyons. No help came from the Wagner Nazi clan in Bayreuth for this French relative! Thanks to Blandine, I met their daughter Aude, who also works as a journalist for *Libération*. Aude learned of her parents' tragedy when she was twenty-three. Her very moving book about her parents, *Jacques and Lotka. A Love in the Time of the Resistance*, was published in several languages.

On Fundamental Decisions about My Own Life

Of course, all these family stories impacted my future life. My decision to write my thesis on Kurt Weill and Bertold Brecht was an act of emancipation from the Bayreuth Wagner clan. This thesis, published with a preface by Weill's widow, Lotte Lenya, in 1977, opened the door for me to work for the Kurt Weill Foundation in New York. Not surprisingly, I was not welcomed by all Jews in New York. There were Holocaust survivors who avoided me as the great-grandson of the racist and anti-Semite Richard Wagner and grandson, nephew, and son of Hitler's intimate friends Winifred, Wieland, and Wolfgang Wagner.

After my autobiography was published, this very group of New York Jews now welcomed me, expecting that I would confirm their own views of philo-Semitism as well as play the role of the token German, both attributes unacceptable because of my aversion to being manipulated by any interest group. It was difficult to make this clear without being accused of being anti-Semitic, but there were also other Jews in New York, especially Jewish Wagnerites, who wanted me to play the role of an uncritically admiring great-grandson of the Wagner cult, inviting me to be an exhibit in their "Wagner museum," and expecting me to keep quiet about Wagner's *Weltanschauung* (worldview). This role was even more unacceptable to me.

So I was looking for friends who would not categorize me, and luckily I found Hannah Busoni. She had fled from Berlin because of the Nuremberg racial laws. As the daughter of assimilated, non-religious Jews, she had not been permitted to complete her studies as a lawyer in Germany. Thus, in New York she had to earn her living by making and selling picture frames. Her husband was the artist and painter Raffaele Busoni, son of the famous composer and pianist Ferruccio Busoni, who was also the teacher of Kurt Weill. Staying in Hannah's little *Hansel and Gretel*–house beside Carnegie Hall was a wonderful experience for me. I remember her repeating this advice: "*Don't let any Jew full of resentments against all Germans persuade you that you are guilty of the Nazi crimes.*" Being accepted for what I was, and even being cared for in difficult times by Jewish friends, was an experience that happened to me again later with Janice Hamer and Mary Azrael during our cooperation on the opera *Lost Childhood.* For Janice and Mary I have never been reduced to being just a Wagner descendant or the "German," blamed for Nazi crimes of the past.

All these incidents took place before I met Abraham Peck in 1991 and after my journey to Israel with my wife Teresina, a turning point in my life. Yet, in retrospect, I must say my life from 1981 onward was even more influenced by my Italian Rossetti-Galli-Malacrida relatives, who became an important resource in the development of my self-determination.

My Italian Family

My wife and her family always supported my critical confrontation with National Socialism, Italian Fascism, and European colonialism without any reservations concerning their own family history. Their open-minded worldview also allowed them to embrace the adoption and joint upbringing of our son Eugenio in our family. Mamma Antonietta Malacrida, Teresina's mother, became one of the most important human beings for me because of her courageous life and loving dedication to all family members throughout our twenty-five years of living together. I am also close to her brother, Luigi Malacrida, who inspired me with his vast knowledge of both music and the history of World War II. What occurred with the marriage of Bismark Oppong into my German Drexel family happened also in my Italian family through the adoption of three Afro-Brazilian sons, Giovanni, Matteo, and Wellington, by Franco Malacrida, the son of Luigi. Together we constitute a global village.

Departure from the Wagner Clan, But Not from Germany

My Italian family is the center of my life, not at all a temporary berth where I live in tears, yearning for the loss of my "fatherland," suffering from the rejections of the Wagner clan. The less my life has to do with them, the better it is for me. Psychological classification that tries to reduce my work and my social behavior to being the result of the Wagner genes is a harsh manipulation of my very own life and work and my insistence on self-determination. As far as reconciliation with the Wagner clan in and around Bayreuth is concerned, there is no chance for that! There has never been willingness on their side for an honest and sincere confrontation with the historical role and individual responsibility of the family. Accurate historical research is blocked by manipulations, falsifications, and abuse of power in order to uphold the Wagners' prominent and lucrative role in the world of music.

Solely the principle of power, never the principle of empathy, has characterized the behavior of the Wagner clan. It remains disturbing that parts of the powerful, political, and cultural strata of German society can continue to celebrate and support this family despite its obvious self-idolatry. This is, after all, part of the heritage of Richard Wagner, founder of the "family business selling redemption," as I call it, a heritage based on racism, sexism, and xenophobia. The dispersal of the Wagner clan after 1945 would have been the only proper way to stop the continuation of the Wagner cult. The Wagner festival remains one of the last remaining poisoned relicts of the German past. Exhibitions had and still have an alibi character created to save the Wagner tourist industry in Bayreuth. The principle "everybody against everybody else" is still valid for the Wagner clan, both on stage and in reality. In our time, however, the secret of the success is becoming more and more evident: it is nothing but a cheap soap opera.

Self-determination and Active Cooperation

My self-determined life, far away from the Bayreuth family business, is manifested by the choice of and dedication to my own family of all generations, friends, and professional activities. The Italian and German families I have described have learned from the past and are not blocked by it from having active, passionate, and compassionate lives. I enjoy observing the development of my son as a young man, full of empathy for others, determining his own active life. His experience during adolescence and in realizing his professional goal taught him that self-pity can only be an impediment in his personal development. He also knows that he can always count on us, his parents.

Teresina, my wife, vice-mayor and cultural councilor of Cerro Maggiore, is supported by me out of deep love, respect, and gratitude for all she has done for me so discreetly and in full solidarity. For years we have both been active supporting the commemoration of all European persecuted groups. My commitment to promote the knowledge about so-called "banned degenerate music" (*entartete Musik*) is exemplified by my multimedia lectures on the work of the Italian Jewish composer, Aldo Finzi. This work is enriched by my friendship with his son Bruno and his family, who accept me as I am. My German and Italian families of this generation and hopefully the next will pursue the goal of a world free of hostile projections on others.

We cannot ignore in our various countries the ever-present reality of racism in all its shades. It does require daily confrontation, and it is the reason for rejecting stereotypes of Germans, Italians, Jews, Africans, Americans, and every other people. This conviction has increasingly influenced my discussions with Abraham Peck.

Questioning the Claim of Uniqueness of the Genocide of the European Jews

What have the reflections on the different branches of my German, French, and Italian families to do with post-1945 generations in connection with the new title of this book with Abraham Peck? Here I dare to deal with some critical remarks on opinions of second generation Jewish spokesmen, including Abraham. They still cling to many generalizing clichés and prejudices, for example, their insistence on the terms "second and third generations of Holocaust survivors and perpetrators." This is no longer consistent with a general and personal analysis of non-Jewish Germans and Jews after 1945. Even in the period of Nazi Germany and Nazi occupation in Europe, not only murderous perpetrators existed but also honest German resistance, though by a minority. Not all the Wagner clan members were archetypal Nazi perpetrators in the era of the Third Reich, though they did include fanatically adoring supporters of Hitler, like my grandmother, Winifred Wagner, her son-in-law, Bodo Lafferentz, and her daughter, Verena Wagner-Lafferentz. Likewise, there were also opportunistic bystanders and profiteers like my uncle, Wieland Wagner, who was in fact much more involved in this sordid history than my father, who unlike Wieland was not exempted from military service in World War II.[4] I have already given examples of Nazi opponents among the Wagner and Liszt relatives by referring to Friedelind, Franz Wilhelm Beidler, Jacques and Lotka Trolley de Prévaux. This applies also to other German families.

As to the situation of Germans born after 1945 in a country with such a heavy historical burden, they did not choose Germany as their place of birth! They could, for whatever reason, remain in their country or leave it, although it was more difficult to leave totalitarian communist East Germany than West Germany. Admittedly, there is no general German family tradition of dealing openly with family responsibility during the Third Reich. Yet, it would be false to claim, as some of the second and third Jewish generations do, that *only* silence and repression prevailed in both postwar German states. There are overwhelming documents that prove the contrary, as the many memorial sites in all parts of Germany testify, not least of all the Memorial for the German Resistance in Berlin. This institution, however, is mostly ignored by Jewish tourists on Shoah tours in Germany. A simplistic black-and-white picture of Germans as "eternal perpetrators" and Jews as the "exclusive victims" of the Nazis is counterproductive. A non-Jewish German opposing this distortion becomes open to accusations of anti-Semitism. Even worse, this attitude can reinforce resentment.

That anti-Semitism still exists in the Germany of today is not to be denied. Often, however, the label is too quickly misapplied, for example in the recent international debates about Günter Grass's criticism of the policy of the Israeli government. Activities of neo-Nazi and hate groups in Germany, although existing all over Europe and the United States, are notoriously interpreted in the media as proof that exclusively Germany, and especially its youth, has not learned anything from the Nazi past. Finally, the present heated debate about the circumcision of Jewish or Moslem minors and its possible prevention based on the human right of freedom from bodily harm, equally valid for children, is assailed by accusations of anti-Semitism and intolerance toward religious traditions.

Such generalizations must be confronted. One has to be in Germany from time to time to gain a more informed knowledge of Germany's pluralistic society. Present-day Germany should also not be blamed as the nation exclusively responsible for the worst atrocities in the history of mankind. This prejudice towards *all* Germans derives from the ethnocentric hierarchical valuing of suffering combined with the claim of uniqueness of the Jewish tragedy in comparison with all other genocides. Today it should be possible also for post-Holocaust Jews, in addition to their own perspective, to acknowledge other victims of genocide in modern history as equal fellow sufferers.

Cooperation is possible between Jews and non-Jews free of continuous mistrust, prejudice, and the banning of crucial issues such as Holocaust politics or violations of human rights of Palestinians under Israeli occupation. In academic historical research a process of questioning dogmas like that of the "uniqueness of the Holocaust"[5] is developing, even in Israel. Also political groups of Jews and non-Jews in Israel, Europe, and the United States, though still not mainstream, dismiss such political dogmas and champion human rights, thus cooperating truly to promote *tikkun olam* (healing of the world).

Here in this book and in my recently published book on Wagner entitled *Thou Shalt Not Have any Gods before Me—Richard Wagner, a Mine Field*, I will bring my educational work on Wagner, anti-Semitism, Jews, Hitler, the Third Reich, and all the insoluble problems in my life span to an end.

Inspired by my new family member from Africa, Bismark Oppong, I will turn to other equally important topics, present-day genocides and neo-colonialism. On the other hand, I also feel a strong desire to devote myself to music therapy. I, too, believe that music can have healing effects on both body and soul, while doubting that music of late romanticism can serve that purpose.

It is my impression that mankind has not learned from its history; thus, only individual love and empathy in daily behavior toward others can provide hope for the future. The introductory motto of Gandhi remains valid for me despite the daily tragedies in our world. December 10, the day of the UN Declaration of Human Rights, is central for me, in remembrance of all victims of past and present genocides and violations of human rights caused by various despots and rulers in power—past and present.

23

Our Dialogue Today: What Has Changed and Who Have We Become?

Abraham J. Peck

We were two damaged souls in search of some emotional repair. We were two question marks in search of an answer. We were the inheritors of legacies that neither of us wished for but had no choice except to confront. A son of survivors and a son of perpetrators—that is what we called ourselves. We were not, of course, alone. There were others like us, some willing to risk the emotional turmoil that came with the physical and verbal confrontation between the Jewish and German Second Generations. Some of us chose to shout and scream at the other—"Your parents and grandparents killed my grandparents, uncles and aunts, cousins and their families." Often we received no replies—just tears, guilt, and shame from those whom we confronted. Was that what we, the sons and daughters of the Shoah, were looking for? And was it enough for our German counterparts to collapse in front of our eyes? To heap scorn and hatred on the generation of their parents and grandparents and to do the same for themselves?

Most of us could not move beyond the emotional ghettos that we had created. The Jewish Second Generation had to live with the damaged families that could focus on nothing else but the memories of lives and families shattered after 1939, reconstructed after 1945 but with losses so great that to say one was "reborn" meant exactly that: to enter the world after the Holocaust alone, forced to relearn how to be human and how to be Jewish. The German Second Generation also lived with families that suffered the damage of knowing that for the rest of their lives they would be seen as the nation that carried out the worst atrocities in modern human history—that was the legacy that they would give to their children—that and a legacy of silence.

Neither Gottfried nor I believed that was enough to carry us through our life's journey. We had too many whys and too many of our friends and neighbors who warned, "Don't go there, don't approach the other because it will only bring pain and suffering to you and those around you." We did not listen. In 1991 we found each other at the place where we both had gone to understand some of the whys—a conference on the Holocaust.

We were not afraid to sit across from each other. We had already, in our personal and academic lives, faced those who were the accursed other: the Germans who represented the Nazi bacillus that some of us thought was a genetic certainty from generation to generation and the Jews who reminded some of us that we were the sons and daughters of murderers and citizens of a nation that would never allow itself or be allowed to forget the crimes that were committed in the name of and by the German people.

No, we were not afraid to sit and talk. We were not afraid to say to each other that we understood that we were both damaged goods living in a damaged world. As political and cultural historians we both had to look to the past, to our national and our family histories for some of the answers to our inherited legacies. But we also understood that we needed to look to the future to see whether we could do something about those individual and collective damages. For nearly two decades we probed and dissected our pasts and sought to envision a different future for our children and our world. We spoke to audiences across Europe, Israel, and North America. We wrote articles alone and together and encouraged our German and Jewish brothers and sisters to do the same. But life did not allow us to simply focus on the issues that mattered most to us. We were husbands, fathers, and professionals who lived in an increasingly complex and dangerous world that threatened and indeed did create new generations of sons and daughters who were the inheritors of genocide and mass murder. So we reached out to them as well and asked them to join us in being in the vanguard of those who sought to end this evil thing we call genocide. We also reached a point where we needed to do more than talk about our pasts. We needed to visit those pasts to confront the shadows that represented our inherited legacies, our family and national histories. The shadows of Bayreuth and Auschwitz awaited us.

In 2005 we took that physical and emotional journey. Gottfried took his son and nephew, and they too shared in all we saw and felt. Then something strange took place. Our desire to sit together and share our past and plan for our futures seemed to lose its intensity. Could it be that the journey of a life-time answered more than we realized? Perhaps there were no more questions to ask, no more whys to overcome. We began to act alone, to undertake other quests that dealt with other interests and other ways to repair the world. Distance, too, became an issue. It was more difficult to fly across the ocean and to spend days and nights on a constant rollercoaster of interviews, lectures, and challenges to our message.

In 2013 we have both reached the age of sixty-five and more, and with it the accompanying issues of health and financial security. We have also seen other issues move to the forefront of our world's concerns. The Holocaust has moved to a new place in our efforts to shape its memory. Other genocides, other perpetrators and victims, claim a legitimate place at the table of historical memory. Jews worry more about the rebirth of an anti-Semitism that has found a renewed sense of energy and purpose and threatens the very existence of the State of Israel. Germans are more and more concerned with their own national sense of pride and their predominance in an increasingly struggling European economic environment.

But we will be, I think, forever grateful that we met and created our dialogue. It was genuine and never timid, never unfaithful to our desires to reach out to the other, even when the accumulated fears of our parents' generation threatened to pull us back from the brink of discovery. Germans must continue to talk to Jews and vice versa. But it must also be more than talk. It must be an action of the kind that brings true meaning to the phrase "Never again"—to any people, anywhere, and at any time. If what we have said to each other and written about each other can add to that vision of a new future for our children and our world, then we can continue to hope.

Notes

Introduction by Gottfried Wagner

1. See also Gordon A. Craig, *Über die Deutschen* (Munich, 1992), 165–66.
2. Christoph Schulte, *Deutschtum und Judentum—Ein Disput unter Juden aus Deutschland* (Stuttgart 1992), 18.
3. Ibid., 21–22.
4. Eckart Conze and Gabrielle Metzler, eds., *Deutschland nach 1945—Ein Lesebuch zur deutschen Geschichte von 1945 bis zur Gegenwart* (Munich 1997), 277.
5. See Craig, *Über die Deutschen*, 166.
6. See Schulte, *Deutschtum und Judentum*, 10.
7. Ibid., 8.
8. Ibid., 10–12.
9. Jörg von Uthmann, *Doppelgänger, du bleicher Gemelle. Zur Pathologie des deutsch-jüdischen Verhältnisses* (Munich, 1976), 37.
10. Ibid., 53–54.
11. Ibid., 85.
12. Ibid., 52.
13. Ibid., 51.
14. Ibid., 49.
15. Throughout his text, the author uses the Hebrew word, "Shoah," with the meaning of "extermination, catastrophe." Today the term is particularly used to describe the genocide of the European Jews carried out by the Nazis during World War II. See also Bruno Segre, *La Shoah, Il Genocidio degli Ebrei d'Europa* (Milano, 1998), 119.

Introduction by Abraham J. Peck

1. Larry Kazdan, "Raphael Lemkin Labels War Crime," http://www.orato.com/world-affairs/raphael-lemkin-labels-war-crime/. For an informative sketch of the life and accomplishments of Raphael Lemkin, see Samuel Totten and Steven Leonard Jacobs, eds., *Pioneers of Genocide Studies* (New Brunswick, 2002).
2. Sabine Reichel, *What Did You Do in the War, Daddy? Growing Up German* (New York, 1989), 144.

3. Dan Diner,"Negative Symbiose: Deutsche und Juden nach Auschwitz," *Babylon* 1 (1986): 9–20.

4. Sandor L. Gilman, "Negative Symbiosis. The Reemergence of Jewish Culture in Germany after the Fall of the Wall," in *The German-Jewish Dialogue Reconsidered. A Symposium in Honor of George L. Mosse*, ed. Klaus L. Berghahn (New York, 1996), 209.

5. Paul Mendes-Flohr, *German Jews: A Dual Identity* (New Haven, 1999). Mendes-Flohr calls the first chapter of his book "The Bifurcated Soul of the German Jew."

6. Quoted in Jeffrey K. Olick, *In the House of the Hangman: The Agonies of German Defeat, 1943–1949* (Chicago, 2005), 207–8.

7. For a discussion of *Stunde Null*, see Abraham J. Peck, "Zero Hour and the Development of Jewish Life in Germany after 1945," in *A Pariah People? Jewish Life in Germany after 1945*, ed. Abraham J. Peck, 1–11 (Cincinnati, 1988); Geoffrey J. Giles, ed., *Stunde Null: The End and the Beginning Fifty Years Ago* (Washington, D.C., 1997).

8. Michael Brenner, "Wider den Mythos der Stunde Null. Kontinuitaeten im innnerjuedischen Bewusstsein und deutsch-juedischen Verhaeltnis nach 1945," in *Menora. Jahrbuch für deutsch-jüdische Geschichte* (1992): 155.

9. Quoted in Leonard Baker, *Days of Sorrow and Pain: Leo Baeck and the Berlin Jews* (New York, 1978), 145.

10. For a first-rate analysis of this transformation, see David Sorkin, *The Transformation of German Jewry, 1780–1840* (New York, 1987).

11. George Mosse, "Jewish Emancipation: Between *Bildung* and Respectability," in *The Jewish Response to German Culture*, ed. Jehuda Reinharz and Walter Schatzberg (Hanover, NH, 1985), 14ff.

12. Sorkin, *Transformation of German Jewry*, 6ff.

13. George Mosse, *German Jews Beyond Judaism* (Bloomington, 1985), 12ff. Mosse, "Jewish Emancipation," 13.

14. Klaus von See, *Die Ideen von 1789 und die Ideen von 1914. Völkisches Denken in Deutschland zwischen Französischer Revolution und Erstem Weltkrieg* (Frankfurt am Main, 1975).

15. Quoted in Abraham J. Peck, *Radicals and Reactionaries: The Crisis of Conservatism in Wilhelmine Germany* (Washington, D.C., 1978), 134.

16. Steffen Bruendel, *Volksgemeinschaft oder Volksstaat: Die Ideen von 1914 und die Neuordnung Deutschlands im Ersten Weltkrieg* (Berlin, 2003).

17. Jefferson S. Chase, "Bildung and Breakdown," *American Scholar* 72 (Winter 2003): 146.

18. Peter Gay, *Weimar Culture: The Insider as Outsider* (New York, 2001).

19. Mosse, *German Jews Beyond Judaism*, 71ff.

20. Quoted in *Jüdische Rundschau*, September 16, 1938. Tom Reiss described the end of any German-Jewish symbiosis in the following manner: "The Germans have inherited their language, but they have been denied the spark that once lit the minds of those who spoke it—created by German rubbing against Jew, Jew against German—that ultimately left one group to inherit history's greatest shame, the other its greatest accomplishment. They have inherited the library, but the books went to cousins across

the sea." Quoted in Todd Herzog, "A German-Jewish-American Dialogue?: Literary Encounters between German Jews and Americans in the 1990s," in *Rebirth of a Culture: Jewish Identity and Jewish Writing in Germany and Austria Today*, ed. Hillary Hope Herzog, Todd Herzog, and Benjamin Lapp (New York, 2008), 148.

21. Abraham J. Peck, ed., *The German-Jewish Legacy in America, 1938–1988: From Bildung to the Bill of Rights* (Detroit, 1990).

22. Wolfgang Jacobmeyer, *Von Zwangsarbeiter zum Hiematlosen Ausländer* (Göttingen, 1985). See also Mark Wyman, *DPs: Europe's Displaced Persons, 1945–1951* (Philadelphia, 1989).

23. "Homecoming," in *The Root and the Bough*, ed. Leo W. Schwarz (New York, 1949), 310.

24. Yehuda Bauer, *Flight and Rescue: Brichah* (New York, 1970); Michael Checinski, "The Kielce Pogrom: Some Unanswered Questions," *Soviet Jewish Affairs* 5 no. 2 (1975): 57–72. Jan T. Gross, *Fear: Anti-Semitism in Poland after Auschwitz* (New York, 2006).

25. Phillip Auerbach, in *Zwischen den Zeiten* (April 1948).

26. Daniel Jeremy Goldhagen, *Hitler's Willing Executioners: Ordinary Germans and the Holocaust* (New York, 1997). The distinguished German journalist and historian Götz Aly has added a new dimension to the sources of Germany's attempt to destroy Jewish life. In a new book entitled *Warum die Deutschen? Warum die Juden? Gleichheit, Neid, und Rassenhass, 1800 bis 1933* (Frankfurt am Main, 2011), he argues that anti-Semitism in Germany arose not out of an eliminationist hatred, as Goldhagen contends, but out of social insecurity and an envy of Jewish wealth and accomplishments.

27. For a book that presents such a fear, that popular culture has negatively influenced Holocaust memory and awareness, unfairly expanding that memory to include mass murder and trauma that have nothing to do with the destruction of European Jewish life, see Alvin Rosenfeld, *The End of the Holocaust* (Bloomington, 2011).

28. Steven L. Jacobs, "Holocaust *and* Genocide Studies: The Future is Now," paper read at the Second Bi-Annual Holocaust Conference at Middle Tennessee State University, Murfreesboro, Tennessee, April 2–4, 1998.

29. The turning points for both institutions seem to have come with the beginning of the crisis in Darfur. See Courtney C. Radsch, "Holocaust Museum Calls Crisis in Sudan 'Genocide Emergency'": "This is the first time in the museum's 11-year history that it has made such a declaration, which is intended to draw world attention to the situation and to apply pressure for a response from Sudan's government." (*New York Times*, August 1, 2004). In 2005 Yad Vashem, long opposed to focusing on any other genocide except the Holocaust, held a special seminar dealing with the Rwandan genocide of 1994. Dr. Motti Shalem, the head of Yad Vashem's International School for Holocaust Studies, conceded that the seminar was a "shift" in the institution's longstanding policy and that "as a center that teaches about the Holocaust, it was imperative to actively speak out against genocide and mass murder whenever it happens while still maintaining the uniqueness of the Holocaust." "Yad Vashem holds Rawanda Genocide Seminar," http://skyscrapercity.com/showthread.php?t=276532/.

Chapter 1

1. Richard Wagner, "Erkenne Dich Selbst," in *Sämtliche Schriften und Dichtungen*, vol. 10 (Leipzig, 1911), 274.

2. Ulrich Drüner, *Schöpfer und Zerstörer, Richard Wagner als Künslter* (Wien, 2003), 307.

3. Ibid., 307–8.

4. Cosima Wagner, Brief vom 29. April 1889, in *Das zweite Leben, Briefe und Aufzeichnungen, 1883–1930, an Hans Richter* (Munich, 1980), 176. See also Cosima Wagner, *Die Tagebücher*, vols. 1 and 2 (Munich, 1976/1977).

5. Karl Müssel, *Bayreuth in Acht Jahrhunderten—Geschichte der Stadt* (Bayreuth, 1993), 193–94.

6. The fiftieth anniversary of Richard Wagner's death in 1883.

7. From the author's conversation with Winifred Wagner in the Siegfried Wagner house in the middle of April, 1975.

8. See also Hans Jürgen Syberberg's 1975 portrait of Winfred Wagner, titled *Winifred Wagner und die Geschichte des Hauses Wahnfried von 1914-1975*.

9. Müssel, *Bayreuth in Acht Jahrhunderten*, 191–92.

10. Sebastian Haffner, *Germany: Jekell & Hyde, 1939—Deutschland von Innen Betrachtet* (Munich, 1998), 28.

11. Also relevant in this context are Hermann Rauschning's and Henry Pickers' notes from their conversations with Hitler between 1940 and 1942. Both authors asked Hitler about Wagner. Henry Picker, *Hitlers Tischgespräche im Führerhauptquartier* [Hitler's Table Conversations] (Wiesbaden, 1983); Hermann Rauschning, Gespräche mit Hitler (Zurich, 1940). See also August Kubizek's 1953 autobiography, *Adolf Hitler, Mein Jugendfreund* (Graz), and the Wagner studies by Paul Lawrence Rose, Marc Weiner, Joachim Köhler, Ulrich Drüner, Annette Hein, and Hartmut Zelinsky.

12. Winifred Wagner to Gottfried Wagner, Bayreuth, mid-April, 1975.

13. Franz Stassen, *Erinnerungen an Siegfried Wagner*, 1942, Richard Wagner Nationalarchiv, Bayreuth.

14. See also Chamberlain's letter of October 7, 1923, or the New Year's card of January 1, 1924 in Harmut Zelinsky, *Richard Wagner, Ein deutsches Thema* (Vienna, 1983), 169–70.

15. Michael Karbaum, *Studien zur Geschichte der Bayreuther Festspiele (1876–1976)*, part 2. *Dokumente und Anmerkungen* (Regensburg, 1976), 65.

16. See also Brigitte Hamann, *Winifred Wagner oder Hitlers Bayreuth* (Munich, 2003), 119–20 without exact reference. Hamann is not a reliable souce with regard to the Wagner family history for the following reasons: She is not an expert on the impact of Richard Wagner's total work of art, stageworks, and the festival in Bayreuth. She uncritically took over the statements of Winifred Wagner and Wolfgang Wagner, based on documents and interviews. For example, she declared in the long version of Tony Palmer's BBC documentary on the Wagner family (March 2011): "Winifred was a blessing for the Bayreuth festival." She is a historical novelist, often speculating when

reliable sources are not available (as, for example, the complete correspondence of Hitler with the Wagner family). She also has a preference for picturing intimate stories or gossip (for example, in her passages on Siegfried Wagner, Gudrun Wagner, and Gertrud Wagner) and makes uncritical use of Wolfgang Wagner's autobiography for her book. The author specifically disagrees with her version of Wieland Wagner's and Bodo Lafferentz's activities in the period between September 1944 and April 1945. Hamann rejected any serious discussion with the author about questionable sources.

17. Zelinsky, *Richard Wagner*, 169.

18. Winifred Wagner to Helena Boy on December 6, 1923.

19. Winifred Wagner to Hermann Ernst on November 2, 1971.

20. Kubizek, *Adolf Hitler*, 117–18.

21. Robert Wistrich, *Wer war Wer im Dritten Reich, Ein biographisches Lexikon* (Frankfurt am Main, 1989), 370–71.

22. Picker, *Hitlers Tischgespräche*, 116.

23. Winifred Wagner to Gottfried Wagner, mid-April, 1975.

24. Liselotte Schmidt (nanny of the Wagner children and lover of Hans Frank, general governor of Nazi-occupied Poland), January 14, 1932. Letters to her parents in the Richard Wagner Nationalarchiv, Bayreuth.

25. Winifred Wagner to Helene Roesner on October 10, 1934.

26. Winifred Wagner to the author, Gottfried Wagner, mid-April, 1975. Hans Schemm (1891–1935) was the victim of a plane crash at the beginning of March 1935, and the Wagner family was present at his burial, at which he was accorded all the honors of the Nazi Party.

27. Wolfgang Wagner, *Lebens-Akte* (Munich 1994), 442–45.

28. Brigitte Hamann, *Winifred Wagner*, see note 16, without exact reference. Winifred Wagner confirmed this encounter to me in April 1975.

29. See also the letter from Winifred Wagner to Weckherlin on June 9, 1976.

30. Winifred Wagner to Helene Roesner on September 11, 1937.

31. Adolf Hitler, *Monologe im Führerhauptquartier 1941–1944*, ed. Werner Jochmann (Hamburg, 1980), 225n., January 24 and 25, 1942.

32. See Hamann, *Winifred Wagner*, 357, who calls this illegal money-trafficking a "certainty."

33. Ibid., 358.

34. Winifred Wagner quotes from Richard Wagner's 1881 regeneration essay *Erkenne Dich Selbst*.

35. Karbaum, *Geschichte der Bayreuther Festspiele*, 119–20.

36. Ibid.

37. From Winifred Wagner to Gottfried Wagner, April 1975.

38. Helmut Paulus, "Die Reichskristallnacht," *Archiv für die Geschichte von Oberfranken* (1998): 430–31.

39. Hamann, *Winifred Wagner*, 382.

40. Wieland Wagner to Ulrich Roller, after the Nazi occupation of Czechoslovakia, Theatermuseum Vienna.

41. Compilation done by Otto Strobel, director of the Richard Wagner Memorial, on October 1, 1951.

42. Institut für Zeitgeschichte, Munich, ZS 2238, Schirach. Wolfgang Wagner, *Lebens-Akte*, 442–45. Hamann, *Winifred Wagner*, see note 16, without exact reference. Winifred Wagner confirmed this encounter to me in April 1975. See also the letter from Winifred Wagner to Weckherlin on June 9, 1976. Winifred Wagner to Helene Roesner on September 11, 1937. Adolf Hitler, *Monologe*, 225n., January 24 and 25, 1942. See Hamann, *Winifred Wagner*, 357, who calls this illegal money-trafficking a "certainty"; ibid, 358. Winifred Wagner quotes from Richard Wagner's 1881 regeneration essay *Erkenne Dich selbst*. Karbaum, *Geschichte der Bayreuther Festspiele*, 119–20. From Winifred Wagner to Gottfried Wagner in April 1975. Helmut Paulus, "Die Reichskristallnacht, in *Archiv für die Geschichte von Oberfranken*, 1998, 430–31. Hamann, *Winifred Wagner*, 382. Wieland Wagner to Ulrich Roller, after the Nazi occupation of Czechoslovakia, Theatermuseum Vienna. Compilation done by Otto Strobel, director of the Richard Wagner memorial, on October 1, 1951. Institut für Zeitgeschichte, Munich, ZS, 2238.

43. *Völkischer Beobachter*, August 3, 1939.

44. Winifred Wagner in a conversation with the author, mid-April 1975, in the context of shooting the film, *Winifred Wagner und die Geschichte des Hauses Wahnfried von 1914–1975*.

45. Meta Kropf, *Bayreuther Festspielsommer* (Munich 1978), 42–43.

46. Bayerisches Hauptstaatsarchiv München, CIC Verhör from September 14, 1946.

47. *Völkischer Beobachter*, August 26, 1939.

48. Winifred Wagner to Friedelind Wagner on September 10, 1939, in Neill Thornborrow Archiv.

49. Ibid.

50. Hamann, *Winifred Wagner*, 401.

51. From a conversation between Gottfried Wagner and Winifred Wagner, April 1975.

52. Bayerisches Hauptstaatsarchiv München, Spruchkammerakten, Verhör Winifred Wagner, 90–91.

53. Friedelind Wagner, *Nacht über Bayreuth* (Cologne, 1997), 333.

54. Ibid.

55. See also Syberberg's 1975 Winifred Wagner documentary, *Winifred Wagner und die Geschichte des Hauses Wahnfried von 1914-1975*.

56. Picker, *Hitlers Tischgespräche*, 372, Absatz 149.

57. Gertrud Strobel's unpublished diary, entry from August 25, 1942, in the Richard Wagner Nationalarchiv. Ibid., 446.

58. Renate W. Schostack, *Hinter Wahnfrieds Mauern* (Hamburg, 1998), 256.

59. Zdenko von Kraft, *Der Sohn. Siegfried Wagners Leben und Umwelt* (Graz, 1969), 256.

60. Gertrud Strobel's diary entry, October 20, 1942, Richard Wagner Nationalarchiv.

61. Hamann, *Winifred Wagner*, 448.

62. Ibid., 449.

63. Ibid.

64. Winifred Wagner to Adolf Hitler, March 8, 1943, private Wagner archive.

65. Geoffrey Skelton, *Wieland Wagner: The Positive Sceptic* (New York, 1971), 71.

66. The documents and references in this chapter on the history of my mother's family, the Drexels, are from her unpublished diaries and notes, private archive Gottfried Wagner, Cerro Maggiore, Italy.

67. Bayerisches Hauptstaatsarchiv München, Spruchkammerakten, Verhör Winifred Wagner, 90–91.

68. F. Wagner, *Nacht über Bayreuth*, 333.

69. Richard Wilhelm Stock, *Richard Wagner und seine Meistersinger* (Nuremberg, 1943), foreword.

70. Hamann, *Winifred Wagner*, 468–69.

71. Akte (Bodo) Lafferentz, formerly the Berlin Document Center, now Bundesarchiv Berlin.

72. See also the letter from Winifred Wagner to Fritz Kempfler on February 12, 1944, Richard Wagner Frauenverband und Bayreuther Bund (private archive).

73. See also Aude Yung-de Prévaux, *Jacques und Lotka—Eine Liebe in den Zeiten der Résistance* (Cologne, 2001), and Winifred's statements in conversations with Blandine Jeanson and Gottfried Wagner in August 1967 in Bayreuth.

74. Hamann, *Winifred Wagner*, 474.

75. Otto Daube, "Begegnungen eines Neuzigjährigen," unpublished typescript, 450, Deutsche Richard Wagner Gesellschaft, Bayreuth.

76. *Bayreuther Kurier*, July 21, 1944.

77. From the author's conversation with Wolfgang Wagner, December 1975.

78. Winifred Wagner to Gerdy Troost, March 3, 1963.

79. Winifred Wagner, concept draft from October 16, 1944, see Haman, *Winifred Wagner*, 485n143.

80. Hamann, *Winifred Wagner*, 482.

81. Gertrud Strobel, diary entry, December 3, 1944.

82. Gertrud Strobel diary entry, November 6, 1944.

83. Albrecht Bald and Jörg Skriebeleit, *Das Außenlager Bayreuth des KZ-Flossenbürg, Wieland Wagner und Bodo Lafferentz im Institut für physische Forschung* (Bayreuth, 2003), 124. The foreword of this book was written by Brigitte Hamann. Skiebeleit, director of the memorial concentration camp in Flossenbürg today, and Hamann, historian of the Wagner family, later disagreed on Wieland Wagner and Bodo Lafferentz's roles and activities during the period from September 1944 until April 1945. Precise documents concerning Wieland Wagner and his brother–in–law, Bodo Lafferentz, are missing for that period, see ibid., 47. Further historical research for clarification seems to have been prevented until today because private archival material is being held back by different Wagner family members. Tony Palmer's film documentary of March 2011 (the long version), concerning Wieland Wagner's concentration camp role is pure

speculation. Palmer relies only on Hamann's version, which the author unequivocally calls into question.

84. Bald and Skriebeleit, *Das Außenlager Bayreuth*, 84n20.

85. Hamann, *Winifred Wagner*, 486; Gertrud Strobel diary entry, November 6, 1944.

86. Hamann, *Winifred Wagner*, 486.

87. Ibid.

88. Ibid., 487. Hamann's footnote reference: notes from her conversation with Verena Wagner-Lafferentz.

89. Ibid., 487.

90. Winifred Wagner, March 13, 1971, Institut für Zeitgeschichte München.

91. Wieland Wagner to Winifred Wagner, December 22, 1944, New York Public Library.

92. Heinz Tietjen to Winifred Wagner, December 17, 1944, in Richard Wagner Nationalarchiv, Bayreuth.

93. Diary entry, Gertrud Strobel, December 22, 1944.

94. Wieland Wagner to Winifred Wagner, January 5, 1945, New York Public Library.

95. Ibid.

96. Ibid.

97. Gertrud Strobel diary entry, January 8, 1945.

98. Hamann, *Winifred Wagner*, 490, refers to a conversation with Wolfgang Wagner without giving a date.

99. Expert report by Wilhelm Hieber on December 2, 1948, Bayerisches Staatsarchiv München, trial documents.

100. Gertrud Strobel diary entry, June 4, 1943.

101. Ibid., diary entry, January 12, 1945.

102. Ibid., diary entry, January 4, 1945.

103. Ibid., diary entry, January 18, 1945.

104. Statement by Verena Lafferentz to Brigitte Hamann in July, 2000. See also Hamann, *Winifred Wagner*, 496.

105. The author in a discussion in the Syberberg Winifred Wagner feature with the journalist Werner Meyer in April 1975. Meyer referred to a meeting with Winifred Wagner; see also Werner Meyer, *Götterdämmerung, April 1945 in Bayreuth*, Verlag R. S. Schulz Percha, 1975.

106. Hamann, *Winifred Wagner*, 498.

107. Ibid., Winfred Wagner to unknown, March 30, 1945, 499.

108. Gertrud Strobel diary entry, April 5, 1945.

109. On April 5, 1945, according to Hamann, *Winifred Wagner*, 501.

110. Ibid., 502.

111. Ellen Drexel-Wagner on May 1, 1997, in a conversation with the author.

112. Hamann, *Winifred Wagner*, 502.

113. Otto Strobel's list from October, 1951. Strobel was the chief archivist of the Wagner archive.

114. Wolfgang Wagner, *Lebens-Akte*, 118.

115. Hamann, *Winifred Wagner*, 504.

116. Ellen Drexel-Wagner to Gottfried Wagner, May 1, 1997.

117. Hamann, *Winifred Wagner*, 503.

118. Winifred Wagner to Friedelind Wagner, June 13, 1947, Friedelind Wagner unpublished papers, in the possession of Neill Thornborrow.

119. According to a report by Wolfgang Wagner on the examination of Winifred Wagner by the CIC on September 14, 1946.

120. Hamann, *Winifred Wagner*, 516; the author believes this unverifiable version by Wolfgang Wagner, 506.

121. Gertrud Strobel diary entry, April 13, 1946.

122. Statement made by Winifred Wagner in the 1975 Syberberg documentary about her, *Winifred Wagner und die Geschichte des Hauses Wahnfried von 1914-1975*.

Chapter 2

1. Hamann, *Winifred Wagner*, 564.

2. Bayerisches Hauptstaatsarchiv, Spruchkammerakten, judgment of July 2, 1947.

3. See also Elsa Bernstein, *Das Leben als Drama, Erinnerungen an Theresienstadt* (Hamburg, 2005), commentary, Rita Bake/Birgit Kiupel, 14: "Richard Wagner's world of myth and his religious cosmos influenced and inspired Elsa early. Through hours of crying, she got her way and was permitted to go to the premiere of the Ring Cycle. She said, 'I was permitted to attend the last cycle and was introduced to Richard Wagner as the youngest Festival guest.'"

4. Winifred Wagner to the author, April 1975.

5. In 1989 research carried out by Karin Osiander, a student at the Christian-Ernestinum-Gymnasium Bayreuth, revealed details about the Bayreuth subcamp of Flossenbürg and the Institut für Physikalische Forschung. "This institution carried out experiments for the development of the V2 rocket, the so called miracle weapon for the 'Final Victory' (*Endsieg*)." Eighty-five camp inmates had to participate in these experiments as forced laborers. Osiander's research was the precondition for Bald and Skiebeleit's investigations into the Flossenbürg camp and subcamps, research that was later used by Hamann. Yet, a plaque officially commemorating the camp and its inmates was placed in Bayreuth only in December 2000, cf. review of the Bald and Skriebeleit volume, *Frankfurter Allgemeine Zeitung*, no. 208 (August 9, 2003), 37.

6. See also Bayerisches Hauptarchiv München, testimony by witnesses Spitzer and Kröninger.

7. See also *Fränkische Presse*, December 2, 1948.

8. Wolfgang Wagner to Wieland Wagner, June 15, 1948, in Wolfgang Wagner, *Lebens-Akte*.

9. Wolfgang Wagner in conversation with the author.

10. Winifred Wagner to Helena Roesener, August 22, 1948 in private archive, Verena Lafferentz Wagner.

11. Quoted in Hamann, *Winifred Wagner,* 517.

12. Wieland Wagner to Kurt Overhoff on May 6, 1946, Kurt Overhoff, Neu-Bayreuth in *Staatsbriefe* 6–7 (Munich, 1991).

13. Schostack, *Hinter Wahnfrieds Mauern,* 225.

14. Wolfgang Wagner, *Lebens-Akte,* 145–46.

15. Ibid., 74–75.

16. Syberberg, *Winifred Wagner und die Geschichte des Hauses Wahnfried von 1914–1975.*

17. Winfred Wagner to Gerdy Troost, June 6, 1949, private archive, Verena Wagner-Lafferentz.

18. Wolfgang Wagner to Winifred Wagner, January 22, 1949.

19. Hamann, *Winifred Wagner,* 569, without citation.

20. Emil Praetorius to Heinz Tietjen, May 15, 1949, Akademie der Künste Berlin Archives.

21. Hamann, *Winifred Wagner,* 571.

22. Rainer Trübsbach, *Geschichte der Stadt Bayern* (Bayreuth, 1993), 354.

23. Zdenko von Kraft, "Bayreuth Festival Guide, 1951," 15–18.

24. See Syberberg's film, *Winifred Wagner und die Geschichte des Hauses Wahnfried von 1914–1975.*

25. Winifred Wagner to Hans Grimm, July 8, 1950.

26. Overhoff, Neu-Bayreuth, in *Staatsbriefe* 6–7, 16.

27. Winifred Wagner to Gerdy Troost, June 11, 1973, private archives Verena Wagner-Lafferentz.

28. Winifred Wagner to Gerdy Troost, February 18, 1963, ibid.

29. Excerpt of the letter of Wieland Wagner to H. S. Ziegler, in Ziegler's book on Hitler in 1965 (Hans Severus Ziegler, *Adolf Hitler aus dem Leben Dargestellt*) (Göttingen), part of the library of the Richard Wagner Archive, Bayreuth. Ziegler was the curator of the infamous exhibition, *Entartete Musik* (Degenerate Music), in Düsseldorf in June 1938. Winifred Wagner bought 200 copies of Ziegler's Hitler book and sent them as presents to her old Nazi friends.

30. Winifred Wagner to Ilse Ernst, August 25, 1965, private archives of Verena Wagner-Lafferentz.

31. Winifred Wagner to Gerdy Troost, November 23, 1966, ibid.

32. Winifred Wagner to Gerdy Troost, November 11, 1968, ibid.

33. Winifred Wagner's interview with David Irving on March 13, 1971, Institut für Zeitgeschichte Archiv, Munich.

34. Winifred Wagner to Gerdy Troost, June 11, 1973, private archives Verena Wagner-Lafferentz.

35. Winifred Wagner, *Zeit Magazin,* no. 19, April 30, 1976.

36. Ibid.

Chapter 3

1. See Gottfried Wagner, *Wer nicht mit dem Wolf heult* (Cologne, 1977).
2. Bettina Fehr, *Erinnerungen,* Bonn, 2005 (privately published edition).
3. Günther Anders, "Vergangenheitsbewältigung im Fernsehen: Der Holocaust Film," in *Deutschland nach 1945. Ein Lesebuch zur deutschen Geschichte von 1945 bis zur Gegenwart,* ed. Eckart Conze and Gabrielle Metzler (Munich, 1997), 271.

Chapter 4

1. See also his significant volume, G. Jan Colijn and Izaal Colijn, *Ruin's Wheel: A Father on War, a Son on Genocide* (Comteq, 2006).
2. Helen Epstein, *Kinder des Holocaust. Gespräche mit Söhnen und Töchtern von Überlebenden,* Munich, 1990 (Children of the Holocaust: Conversations with Sons and Daughters of Survivors), 9, 11.
3. Dan Bar-On, *The Legacy of Silence: Encounters with Children of the Third Reich* (Cambridge, MA, 1989); in German under the title *Die Last des Schweigens: Gespräche mit Kindern von Nazi-Tätern* (Frankfurt, 1993).
4. Dan Bar-On, introduction to the text by Abraham Peck and Gottfried Wagner on the topic "Germans and Jews, a Generation after the Shoah" during the twenty-third annual conference on the "Holocaust and the Struggle in the German Church" on March 8, 1993, University of Tulsa, Oklahoma, published in *The Uses and Abuses of Knowledge, Studies in the Shoah,* ed. Henry F. Knight and Marcia Littell, 17: 428–30 (New York, 1997). Professor Bar-On was born in Hamburg, Germany, emigrated to Israel, and taught for many years at the University of the Negev in Beer Sheva. He dedicated his life to fostering dialogue, not only between children of Holocaust perpetrators and victims but also between Israelis and Palestinians. His death in 2008 was a great loss.
5. Abraham Peck, Introduction, in *Twilight of the Wagners: The Unveiling of a Family's Legacy,* by Gottfried Wagner (New York, 1999), 3ff.

Chapter 5

1. This section of the chapter is based on the following publications: Eva Hoffman, *Shtetl: The Life and Death of a Small Town and the World of Polish Jews* (Boston, 1997); Gershon David Hundert and Gershon C. Bacon, *The Jews in Poland and Russia: Biographical Essays* (Bloomington, 1984); Joseph Marcus, *Social and Political History of the Jews in Poland, 1919–1939* (Berlin, 1983); Iwona Irwin-Zarecka, *Neutralizing Memory: The Jew in Contemporary Poland* (New Brunswick, 1989); Magdalena Oplalski and Israel Bartal, *Poles and Jews: A Failed Brotherhood* (Hanover, NH, 1992); *Polin: A Journal of Polish-Jewish Studies* (Oxford: Institute for Polish-Jewish Studies); Michael Riff, *The Face of Survival: Jewish Life in Eastern Europe Past and Present* (London, 1992); Byron L. Sherwin, *Sparks Amidst the Ashes: The Spiritual Legacy of Polish Jewry* (New York, 1997); Michael C. Steinlauf, *Bondage to the Dead: Poland and the Memory*

of the Holocaust (Syracuse, NY, 1997); Theodore R. Weeks, From Assimilation to Anti-semitism: The Jewish Question in Poland, 1850–1914 (DeKalb, IL, 2006).

2. Simon Dubnow, History of the Jews in Russia and Poland, vol. 1 (Philadelphia, 1916), 100.

3. Isaiah Taub, Australia Jewish News, April 14, 1989.

4. On the the kinnui, see Benzion C. Kaganoff, A Dictionary of Jewish Names and Their History (New York, 1977), 127, 185.

5. Berl Kahn, "Jews in Zvolin," in Yizkor Book Zvolin, ed. Berl Kahn (New York, 1982), 8.

6. For a description of the Alexander Chasidim by a member of the community, see Isaac Goodfriend, By Fate or by Faith: The Saga of a Survivor (Atlanta, 2001), chap. 1, "Hasidim."

7. J. Karsh, Yiddish Lodz (Melbourne, 1974), 7.

8. Karsh, Yiddish Lodz, 11.

9. Marcus, Jews in Poland, 113. Marcus estimates that on the eve of World War II, the Jewish share of the textile industry in Poland was at least 70 percent.

10. Rabbi Leiserowski would survive the Holocaust and play an important role in the rabbinate that oversaw Jewish life in Munich and the Jewish Displaced Persons camps. He then served for many years as the chief Orthodox rabbi of Philadelphia.

11. For a vivid description of life in prewar Balut, see Israel Rabon, Balut (Warsaw, 1934) (in Yiddish).

12. Lucjan Dobroszycki, ed., The Chronicle of the Lodz Ghetto, 1941–1944 (New Haven, CT, 1984), xxxiii.

13. Israel Tabaksblat, Hurbn Lodz (Buenos Aires, 1946) (in Yiddish), 31. For a study that presents several new insights into life in the Łódź ghetto, see Andrea Löw's superb study Juden im Getto Litzmannstadt: Lebensbedingungen, Selbstwahrnehmung, Verhalten (Göttingen, 2006).

14. Julian Baranowski, The Lodz Ghetto, 1940–1944. Vademecum (Lodz, 2003), 6.

15. Chronicle of the Łódź ghetto, April 22, 1944.

16. Quoted in Leonard Tushnet, The Pavement of Hell (New York, 1972), 185.

17. Chronicle of the Łódź ghetto, June 22, 1944.

18. Tushnet, Pavement of Hell, 194 ff.

19. Felicja Karay, Death Comes in Yellow: Skarżysko-Kamienna Slave Labor Camp (Amsterdam, 1996), xvi. See also Mordecai Strigler, In Di Fabrikn fun Toyt [In the Factories of Death] (Buenos Aires, Argentina, 1948).

20. Tushnet, Pavement of Hell, 164.

21. Quoted in Solomon Bloom, "Dictator of the Lodz Ghetto," Commentary 7 (1949): 120.

22. Karay, Death Comes in Yellow, 67ff.

23. Felicja Karay, "Teaching the Holocaust through Music and Camps Literature Written in Camps," presentation at the International School for Holocaust Studies, n.d., Yad Vashem, 2.

24. Karay, Death Comes in Yellow, 162ff.

25. Ibid., 82.

26. Ibid., 122.

27. Ibid., 72.

28. "Der erfüllte Schwur," *Inforiot. Alternative News und Termine Für Brandenburg*, April 21, 2005, 4.

29. Lucille Eichengreen, *From Ashes to Life: My Memories of the Holocaust* (San Francisco, 1975).

30. I am grateful to Eva Unterman of Tulsa, Oklahoma, for making copies of the transportation lists available to me. Ms. Unterman was on the same trajectory as my mother—the Łódź ghetto, Stuthoff, and Dresden.

31. For an excellent study on the administration of the Ghetto under Hans Biebow, see Peter Klein, *Die "Gettoverwaltung Litzmannstadt" 1940-1944: Eine Dienststelle im Spannungsfeld von Kommunalbürokratie und staatlicher Verfolgungspolitik* (Hamburg, 2009).

32. Michal Unger, "After an Alibi: Hans Biebow and the Rescue of Three Jewish Groups from the Lodz Ghetto (1944-1945)," paper presented at the conference "Holocaust as Local History. Past and Present of a Complex Relation" (University of Macedonia, Thessaloniki, Greece, June 6, 2008).

33. Werebejczyk, Miriam, "Zeugenaussage über das Arbeitslager 'Bernsdorf & Co.,'" (n.p., n.d.), 4.

34. Roman Halter, "Holocaust Memorial Day" (Genealogy Channel, Great Britain, 2005). See also the interesting testimony of Nancy Fordonski, who like my mother, was in Auschwitz, Stutthof, and then was transported to Dresden to work in the Schandauerstrasse ammunition factory and was on the death march to Theresienstadt. See her testimony in Voice/Vision Holocaust Survivor Oral History Archive, May 29, 1982, holocaust.umd. michigan.edu/interview.php?D=furdonski&section=28.

Chapter 6

1. Irving Heymont to Joan Heymont, September 19, 1945, in Jacob R. Marcus and Abraham J. Peck, eds., *Among the Survivors of the Holocaust—1945. The Landsberg DP Camp Letters of Major Irving Heymont, United States Army* (Cincinnati, 1982), 5.

2. Samuel Gringauz, "Jizker," *Landsberger Lager-Cajtung*, October 8, 1945, no. 1 (in Yiddish).

3. On the postwar violence against Jews in Poland, see Engel, David, "Patterns of Anti-Jewish Violence in Poland, 1944-1946," *Yad Vashem Studies* 26: 43–85, and Gross, *Fear*.

Chapter 7

1. Isabella Leitner, *Saving the Fragments: From Auschwitz to New York* (New York, 1986), 77ff.

2. Some of the passenger lists may be viewed at http://www.angelfire.com/zine2/muir/shipshistory.html/.

3. Elie Wiesel, *A Jew Today* (New York, 1978), 185–208.

4. *Die Sztyme der Sheris Hapleita* (Montreal, 1963), 29.

5. Dorothy Rabinowitz, *New Lives: Survivors of the Holocaust Living in America* (New York, 1976), 43.

6. Rabinowitz, *New Lives*, 196. See also Beth B. Cohen, *Case Closed: Holocaust Survivors in Postwar America* (Piscataway, NJ, 2007).

7. Quoted in Anita Shapira, "The *Yishuv* and the Survivors of the Holocaust," *Studies in Zionism* 7, no. 2 (Autumn 1986): 301.

8. Koppel S. Pinson, "Jewish Life in Liberated Germany. A Study of the Jewish DPs," *Jewish Social Studies* 9, no. 2 (1947): 110.

9. Pinson, "Jewish Life," 114.

10. For an understanding of the development of the *Wiedergutmachung* process and what it meant for survivors, see Christian Pross, *Wiedergutmachung: Der Kleinkrieg gegen die Opfer* (Bodenheim, 2001).

Chapter 9

1. For more on the life and work of Petra Kelly, see, above all, Sara Parkin, *The Life and Death of Petra Kelly* (New York, 1995), and Alice Schwarzer, *Eine Tödliche Liebe: Petra Kelly und Gert Bastian* (Cologne, 1993).

2. George W. F. Hallgarten, *Imperialismus vor 1914. Die soziologischen Grundlagen der Aussenpolitik europaeischer Grossmächte vor dem Ersten Weltkrieg*, 2 vols. (Munich, 1963).

3. George W. F. Hallgarten, *Als die Schatten Fielen.Erinnerungen vom Jahrhundertbeginn zur Jahrtausendwende* (Frankfurt am Main, 1969).

4. Volker R. Berghahn, *Germany and the Approach of War in 1914* (New York, 1973).

5. Michael Balfour, *The Kaiser and His Times* (New York, 1964).

6. Geoff Eley, *Reshaping the German Right: Radical Nationalism and Political Change after Bismarck* (New Haven, CT, 1980).

7. See among his publications especially Robert Gellately, *The Gestapo and German Society: Enforcing Racial Policy, 1933–1945* (Oxford, 1990).

8. His best-known publication on this topic is Werner Jochmann, "Die Ausbreitung des Antisemitusmus, in *Deutsches Judentum in Krieg und Revolution 1916–1923*, ed. Werner Mosse and Arnold Paucker, 27–65 (Tübingen, 1971).

9. Peter Freimark and Arno Herzig, eds., *Die Hamburger Juden in der Emanzipationsphase 1780–1870* (Hamburg, 1989).

10. Dirk Stegmann, *Die Erben Bismarcks. Parteien und Verbände in der Spaetphase des Wilhelminischen Deutschlands, Sammlungspolitik 1897–1918* (Cologne, 1970).

11. Peter-Christian Witt, *Die Finanzpolitik des Deutschen Reiches von 1903 bis 1913. Eine Studie zur Innenpolitik des Wilhelminischen Deutschland* (Lübeck, 1970).

12. Jens Flemming, *Landwirtschaftliche Interessen und Demokratie. Ländliche Gesellschaft, Agrarverbände und Staat 1890-1925* (Bonn, 1978).

13. Fritz Fischer, *Griff Nach der Weltmacht. Die Kriegszielpolitik des kaiserlichen Deutschlands 1914–1918* (Duesseldorf, 1961).

14. Fritz Fischer, *Krieg der Illusionen. Die Deutsche Politik von 1911 bis 1914* (Duesseldorf, 1969).

15. The school was named for Eckart Kehr (1902–1933), a German historian who argued that imperial Germany's foreign policy initiatives were directed almost exclusively to satisfy the demands of domestic and economic policies. His best-known work, the dissertation that he wrote in 1927 under Friedrich Meinecke, was entitled *Schlachtflottenbau and Parteipolitik, 1894–1901* (Berlin, 1930). Also important is the volume edited by Hans-Ulrich Wehler of Kehr's writings, *Der Primat der Innenpolitik* (Berlin, 1965).

16. Roger Chickering, *We Men Who Feel Most German: A Cultural Study of the Pan-German League, 1886–1914* (Boston, 1984).

17. Heinz Hagenlücke, *Deutsche Vaterlandspartei. Die nationale Rechte am Ende des Kaiserreiches* (Duesseldorf, 1997).

18. My Potsdam research colleague Geoff Eley, along with another British historian, David Blackbourn, mounted a serious challenge to the Kehrites and to the Sonderweg theory in an important book, *The Peculiarities of German History: Bourgeois Society and Politics in Nineteenth-Century Germany* (New York, 1984).

Chapter 10

1. Among his most important books are Samuel Sandmel, *We Jews and Jesus* (New York, 1965); *The Genius of Paul: a Study in History* (New York, 1958), and *Anti-Semitism in the New Testament* (Philadelphia, 1978).

2. On the life of Jacob Rader Marcus and his massive scholarly productivity, see Randall M. Falk, *Bright Eminence: The Life and Thought of Jacob Rader Marcus: Scholar, Mentor, Counselor for Three Generations of Rabbis and Lay Leaders of America* (Malibu, CA, 1994).

3. Abraham J. Peck, "A Jew, Whose Ancient Roots Were Cut, Shares His Holocaust," *Cincinnati Post*, April 11, 1977. For more on the psychological effects of the Holocaust on survivors and their children, see the pioneering work of Aaron Hass, *The Aftermath: Living With the Holocaust* (Cambridge, 1995) and Hass, *In the Shadow of the Holocaust: The Second Generation* (Cambridge, 1996).

4. Epstein, *Children of the Holocaust.*

5. Peck, *Radicals and Reactionaries.*

6. Jules Isaac, *The Teaching of Contempt: Theological Roots of Anti-Semitism* (New York, 1964).

7. A collection of Greenberg's most important essays may be found in Irving Greenberg, *For the Sake of Heaven and Earth: The New Encounter between Judaism and Christianity* (Philadelphia, 2004).

8. Among her most important works are Yaffa Eliach, *Hasidic Tales of the Holocaust*

(New York, 1982), and Eliach, *There Once Was a World: A 900-Year Chronicle of the Shtetl of Eishyshok* (Boston, 1998).

9. Rosemary Radford Reuther, *Faith and Fratricide: The Theological Roots of Anti-Semitism* (New York, 1974).

10. Abraham J. Peck, ed., *Jews and Christians after the Holocaust* (Philadelphia, 1982).

11. Published in the *Proceedings of the Eighth World Congress of Jewish Studies* (Jerusalem, 1982), 187–96.

12. "Hitler Victims Meet Liberators Again," *New York Times*, October 12, 1981.

13. Abraham J. Peck, "The Lost Legacy of Holocaust Survivors," *Shoah. A Journal of Resources on the Holocaust* 3, no. 2–3 (1982): 33–37.

14. My colleague and fellow son of survivors, the late Professor Benny Kraut, z"l, wrote a history of the congregation: Benny Kraut, *German-Jewish Orthodoxy in an Immigrant Synagogue: Cincinnati's New Hope Congregation and the Ambiguities of Ethnic Religion* (New York, 1988).

15. Hans Steinitz, "Fünfzigster Geburstag in Cincinnati," *Aufbau*, November 25, 1983.

16. Mary Lowenthal Felstiner, *To Paint Her Life: Charlotte Salomon in the Nazi Era* (New York, 1994).

17. "Peck Examines Jewish Life in Germany," *American Israelite*, February 5, 1987.

18. "Forum Confronts Viability of Jewish Life in Germany," *Northern California Jewish Bulletin* (November 13, 1987): 3.

19. Peck, *German-Jewish Legacy*; Abraham J. Peck and Uri D. Herscher, eds., *Queen City Refuge: An Oral History of Cincinnati's Jewish Refugees from Nazi Germany* (West Orange, NJ, 1989).

20. Marcus, Peck, *Among the Survivors*.

Chapter 11

1. Simon Wiesenthal, *The Sunflower* (New York, 1976).

2. See, for example, Anita Epstein, "Why I Cannot Forgive Germany, "*Forward*," June 9, 2010. To my knowledge, only one survivor, Eva Kor, one of the infamous "Mengele twins," has granted a form of forgiveness, what she calls "amnesty," in a 1995 declaration: "I . . . Eva Mozes Kor, in my name only and as a twin who survived Josef Mengele's experiments at Auschwitz fifty years ago, hereby give amnesty to all the Nazis who participated directly or indirectly in the murder of my family and millions of others." Quoted in *Jewish Virtual Library*, "Hans Münch," http://www.jewishvirtuallibrary.org/jsource/Holocaust/Münch.html/.

Chapter 12

1. Michael Berenbaum and Abraham J. Peck, eds., *The Holocaust and History: The Known, the Unknown, the Disputed and the Reexamined* (Bloomington, 1998).

2. Thomas Albrich, *Exodus durch Österreich. Die jüdischen Flüchtlinge 1945–1948* (Innsbruck, 1987); Thomas Albrich, ed., *Flucht nach Eretz Israel. Die Bricha und der jüdische Exodus durch Österreich nach 1945* (Innsbruck, 1998).

3. For another experience of an American academic's encounter with Austrian students, see Sondra Perl, *On Austrian Soil: Teaching Those I Was Taught To Hate* (Albany, 2005). For more on Austrians as "first victims" and memory, see, among others, Eva Kuttenberg, "Austria's Topography of Memory: Heldenplatz, Albertinaplatz, Judenplatz and Beyond," *German Quarterly* (Fall 2007): 468–91. See also Margit Reiter, *Die Generation danach: Der Nationalsozialismus im Familiengedächtnis* (Innsbruck, 2006). Reiter's book, a study of the relationship of members of the Austrian Second Generation to their Nazi parents and the familial approach to National Socialism, is similar to a study done by Harald Welzer on East and West German families, discussed in a later chapter.

4. Joan Porat, "Peck to Head New Holocaust Museum Houston," *American Israelite* (February 20, 1997).

5. Peter Balakian, *Black Dog of Fate: An American Son Uncovers His Armenian Past* (New York, 1998).

6. Jean M. Peck, *At the Fire's Center: A Story of Love and Holocaust Survival* (Champaign, IL, 1998).

7. Samuel Huntington, *The Clash of Civilizations and the Remaking of World Order* (New York, 1998).

8. For a full schedule of conference events, see http://www.preventgenocide.org /action/after/rwanbrpr.html./

9. Such a call has been repeated by the German-born American scholar, Gabriele Schwab: "To take issue with the thesis of German exceptionalism does not mean giving license to turn away from Germany's responsibility for the Holocaust. Rather, it allows one to establish a link between the Holocaust and other histories of violence and genocide. Linking these violent histories is, I think, crucial in order to begin serious thinking about a politics of alliance against oppression, genocide, ethnic cleansing and imperialist invasions of other countries. Moreover, it may finally prepare some ground for a political dialogue of such oppression between people and nations that have emerged from or still belong to the victims of such oppression and those who resist the oppression of others from within colonial or imperial nations." Gabriele Schwab, *Haunting Legacies: Violent Histories and Transgenerational Trauma* (New York, 2010), 72.

10. Feisal Abdul Rauf, *What's Right with Islam: A New Vision for Muslims and the West* (San Francisco, 2004). Imam Rauf and his wife, Daisy Khan, were at the center of the so-called "Ground Zero Mosque" controversy in 2010. Both are extraordinary people with a clear vision for the establishment of an American expression of Islam as a significant addition to the prevailing Judeo-Christian ethic that guides American social and political behavior.

Chapter 13

1. The term "memorial candles" is taken from the title of a book by Dina Wardi, *Memorial Candles: Children of the Holocaust* (New York, 1992).

2. Among the members of the Second Generation to participate in the oath-swearing ceremony was Menachem Rosensaft, a son of two prominent Holocaust survivors, Joseph (Yossel) and Hadassah Rosensaft, z"l, who was born in the Bergen-Belsen/Hohne DP camp in 1948. Menachem Rosensaft is a founder of the International Network of Children of Jewish Holocaust Survivors and a member of the United States Holocaust Memorial Museum Council.

3. See Part II

4. In December 1988, Menachem Rosensaft was a member of a five-person delegation of American Jews who met with Chairman Yasser Arafat of the PLO in Copenhagen as a way to jump-start serious talks between Israel and the Palestinian Authority. Heavily criticized by much of the American Jewish community, Rosensaft, chair of the International Network of Children of Jewish Survivors, changed his views about Arafat and dialogue and accused the PLO chair of "bad faith" in March 1990. See "Rosensaft Calls Arafat Shamir's 'Mirror Image,'" *Washington Report on Middle East Affairs*, March 1990, 42.

5. Eva Hoffman, *After Such Knowledge: Where Memory of the Holocaust Ends and History Begins* (New York, 2003) 103.

6. Quoted in G. Jan Colijn and Marcia Sachs Littell, eds., *Confronting the Holocaust: A Mandate for the 21st Century* (Lanham, MD, 1997), 142–43.

7. For example, the books and articles of the Israeli scholar Dan Bar-On, including "Holocaust Perpetrators and Their Children: A Paradoxical Morality," *Journal of Humanistic Psychology* 29, no. 4 (Fall 1989): 424–43; Bar-On, "Children of Perpetrators of the Holocaust: Working Through One's Own Moral Self," *Psychiatry* 53 (August 1990): 229–45; and Bar-On, *Legacy of Silence*. See also, among others, Doette Von Westernhagen, *Die Kinder der Täter: Das Dritte Reich und die Generation Danach* (Munich, 1987); Peter Sichrovsky, *Born Guilty: Children of Nazi Families*, trans. Jean Steinberg (New York, 1985); Niklas Frank (son of the Nazi governor of Poland, Hans Frank), *Der Vater* (Munich, 1987); Stephan Lebert and Norbert Lebert, *My Father's Keeper: Children of Nazi Leaders—An Intimate History of Damage and Denial*, trans. Julian Evans (Boston, 2001); and most recently Jens-Jürgen Ventzki (son of the Nazi mayor of Litzmannstadt/Łódź, Werner Ventzki), *Seine Schatten, Meine Bilder: Eine Spurensuche* (Vienna, 2011). For an article that suggests that if potential perpetrators knew how terribly their actions would affect their children and grandchildren they might not commit acts of genocide, see Henri Parens, "Aftermath of Genocide—The Fate of Children of Perpetrators," *International Journal of Applied Psychoanalytic Studies* 6, no. 1 (2009): 25–42.

8. Among the most important Second Generation Dialogue groups are the Austrian Encounter, the Harvard Encounter Group facilitated by Mona Weissmark, Compassionate Listening Project, the International Summer Program on the Holocaust, To Reflect and Trust, the Foundation Trust, One by One, and Second Generation Trust.

9. A notable example is the article by Mary H. Rothschild, a veteran member of the German-Jewish dialogue, who ended her piece on a week-long encounter in Berlin with the following words: "Gottfried, the former Hitler youth, was sitting next to me,

and so was Inge, who is the daughter of an SS. I thanked them for their courage to go against their culture's 'legacy of silence' and even some relatives and friends. Tears started running and I didn't try to stop them. Inge and Gottfried both grabbed my hand. I felt our connection and their love, and at that moment gratitude infused me like a prayer: 'Though I walk through the valley of the shadow of death, I shall fear no evil for thou art with me,' my fellow Germans, the second-generation righteous gentiles who walk with us and who carry their burden of the Holocaust. *It is at moments like this that I know, in a way that nothing else can tell me, God exists* (italics mine)." Quoted from Mary H. Rothschild, "Transforming Our Legacies: Heroic Journeys for Children of Holocaust Survivors and Nazi Perpetrators," *Journal of Humanistic Psychology* 40, no. 3 (Summer 2000): 55.

10. Ralph Giordano, *Die zweite Schuld oder Von der Last Deutscher zu Sein* (Munich, 1990).

11. Gottfried Wagner, *Twilight of the Wagners: The Unveiling of a Family's Legacy,* trans. Della Couling (New York, 1997).

12. A conference held in Washington, D.C. from January 14–17, 2000, entitled "Life Reborn. Jewish Displaced Persons 1945–1951," addressed this theme.

13. See Hannah Yablonka, *Survivors of the Holocaust: Israel After the War* (London, 1998).

14. Hannah Betts has described it as "a spectacle, an industry—a European event brought to us by American production values," Hannah Betts, "The Testament of Ghosts," *Times* (London), May 30, 2000. See also the discussion about a preponderance of Holocaust memory and how that has distracted from the specific historical meaning of the event in Carolyn J. Dean, *Aversion and Erasure: The Fate of the Victim after the Holocaust* (Ithaca, NY, 2010), 1–60.

Chapter 14

1. http://www.holocaustforum.gov.se/conference/official_documents/declaration/index.html/.

2. Tony Judt, "From the House of the Dead: On Modern European Memory," *New York Review of Books* 52, no. 15 (October 6, 2005).

3. Judt, "House of the Dead."

4. For an impassioned, if not entirely convincing plea that the forgetting of collective memory is the best solution to ensuring a peaceful world, see David Rieff, *Against Remembrance* (Melbourne, 2011).

5. See the moving description of Halbwach's last days by a Buchenwald survivor, Jorge Semprun, *Literature or Life* (New York, 1997), 22–23.

6. Pierre Nora, "Between History and Memory: Les Lieux de Memoire," *Representations*, no. 26 (Spring 1989), 7.

7. Maurice Halbwachs, *On Collective Memory* (Chicago, 1992), 169.

8. Quoted in Jay Winter, "The Generation of Memory: Reflections on the 'Memory

Boom,'" "Contemporary Historical Studies," *German Historical Institute Bulletin* 27 (Fall 2000): 1.

9. Dagmar Barnouw, "The Certainties of Evil and the Politics of Not-Forgetting," http://hnn.us/articles/19093.html/, History News Network, December 26, 2005. See also Barnouw's 2005 book, *The War in the Empty Air: Victims, Perpetrators and Post-War Germans* (Bloomington).

10. Barnouw, "Certainties of Evil."

11. German Studies Association Annual Meeting, 2005, https://www.g-s-g /conferences/2005/program_sessions.asp/.

12. Peter Novick, *The Holocaust in American Life* (New York, 1999).

13. Norman G. Finkelstein, *The Holocaust Industry: Reflections on the Exploitation of Jewish Suffering* (London, 2000).

14. Barnouw, "Certainties of Evil."

15. Henryk Broder, *Der Ewige Antisemit: Über Sinn und Funktion eines Beständigen Gefühls* (Frankfurt am Main, 1998).

16. Charles S. Maier, "A Surfeit of Memory? Reflections on History, Melancholy and Denial," *History and Memory* 5, no. 2 (Fall/Winter 1993): 136–51.

17. Efraim Sicher, "The Future of the Past: Countermemory and Postmemory in Contemporary American Post-Holocaust Narratives," *History and Memory* (Spring, 2000): 59.

18. Marianne Hirsch, *Family Frames: Photography, Narrative and Postmemory* (Cambridge, 1997), 22. Hirsch sees postmemory as "a structure of inter- and trans-generational transmission of traumatic knowledge and experience. It is a consequence of traumatic recall . . . but at a generational remove." Marianne Hirsch, "The Generation of Postmemory," *Poetics Today* (Spring 2008): 106. See also Esther Jilovsky, "Recreating Postmemory? Children of Holocaust Survivors and the Journey to Auschwitz," *Colloquy: Text Theory Critique* 15 (2008): 145–62.

19. James E. Young, *At Memory's Edge: After Images of the Holocaust in Contemporary Art and Architechture* (New Haven, CT, 2000), 2.

20. This is the view of Menachem Rosensaft who states that the "preservation and transfer of memory is the most critical mission that children and grandchildren of survivors must undertake so as to ensure meaningful and authentic Holocaust remembrance in future generations." He also asks that "each of us and our children and our children's children, must also see ourselves as if we had emerged from Auschwitz, Belsen, and all the other camps and ghettos, the forests and secret hiding places of Nazi Europe." He is, in effect, asking that each of the post-Holocaust generations assume a role similar to each generation of Jews who followed the generation present at the giving of the written and oral laws at Sinai—that each future generation understand and believe that it too was present at the event or the notion that during the Passover Seder contemporary Jews should feel as if they had been slaves in Egypt and celebrate their freedom. Menachem Rosensaft, "Transferring Memory: The Task of Children and Grandchildren of Holocaust Survivors," *Midstream Magazine* (Spring, 2011), http://www.midstreamthf.com/2011spring/feature.html/. What is

somewhat troubling about this statement is its proximity to the approach that is criticized by the writer and critic Ruth Franklin in her recently published book, *A Thousand Darknesses: Lies and Truths in Holocaust Fiction:* "And so it is no wonder that a common feature among second generation and other recent texts about the Holocaust is a desire, either repressed or explicit to somehow witness the Holocaust as if one had been there." She is especially critical of two well-known Second Generation literary figures, Melvin Jules Bukiet and Thane Rosenbaum and, less so, Marianne Hirsch. Ruth Franklin, *A Thousand Darknesses: Lies and Truths in Holocaust Fiction* (New York, 2010), chap. 11.

21. Sicher, "Future of the Past," 57.

22. Zygmunt Bauman, "The Holocaust's Life as a Ghost," *Tikkun* 13, no.4 (1998): 33–38.

23. Sicher, "Future of the Past," 84.

24. Katharina von Kellenbach, "Vanishing Acts: Perpetrators in Post-War Germany," *Holocaust and Genocide Studies* 17, no. 2 (2003): 305–29; Bjorn Krondorfer, *Remembrance and Reconciliation: Encounters between Young Jews and Germans* (New Haven, CT, 1995), 120–21.

25. Krondorfer, *Remembrance and Reconciliation*, 121.

26. Harold Marcuse, *Legacies of Dachau: The Uses and Abuses of a Concentration Camp, 1933–2001* (Cambridge, 2001).

27. Mary Nolan, "Germans as Victims During the Second World War. Air Wars, Memory Wars," *Central European History* 38, no.1 (2005): 15.

28. Theodor W. Adorno, "What Does Coming to Terms with the Past Mean?" in *Bitburg in Moral and Political Perspective*, ed. Geoffrey H. Hartman (Bloomington, 1986).

29. Margarete Mitscherlich and Alexander Mitscherlich, *Die Unfähigkeit zu Trauern* (Munich, 1968).

30. Quoted in Anthony D. Kauders, "History as Censure. 'Repression' and 'Philo-Semitism' in Postwar Germany," *History & Memory* 15, no. 1 (Spring/Summer 2003): 99.

31. Ibid., 98.

32. Ibid., 105.

33. Ibid.

34. Ibid., 105.

35. Dorothee Wierling, "The Changing Legacy of 1945 in Germany: A Round-Table Discussion between Doris Bergen, Volker Berghahn, Robert Moeller, Dirk Moses, and Dorothee Wierling," *German History* 23, no. 4 (2005): 530.

36. Quoted in Aleida Assmann, "Persönliche Errinerung und kollektives Gedächtnis in Deutschland nach 1945, " in *Erinnern und Verstehen. Der Völkermord an den Juden im Politischen Gedächtnis der Deutschen*, ed. Hans Erler (Frankfurt: Campus Verlag, 2003), 128.

37. Robert Moeller, "Changing Legacy," 536.

38. Nolan, "Germans as Victims," 8.

39. Quoted in Robert G. Moeller, "Germans as Victims? Thoughts on a Post–Cold War History of World War II's Legacies," *History & Memory* 17, nos. 1 and 2 (2005): 160–61.

40. Hans Erler, "Einleitung: Erinnerung und politisches Gedächtnis in Deutschland," in *Erinnern und Verstehen*, ed. Hans Erler (Frankfurt am Main, 2003), 9–10.

41. Nolan, "Germans as Victims," 19.

42. Nolan, "Germans as Victims," 19.

43. Goldhagen, *Hitler's Willing Executioners*.

44. *War of Annihilation: Crimes of the Wehrmacht 1941–1944*, created by the Hamburg-based Institut für Socialforschung.

45. Nolan, "Germans as Victims," 14.

46. Quoted in Moeller, "Germans as Victims?," 148.

47. Günter Grass, *Im Krebsgang* (Göttingen, 2002).

48. Quoted in Moeller, "Germans as Victims?" 148–49.

49. Jörg Friedrich, *Der Brand: Deutschland im Bombenkrieg* (Berlin, 2002). See also the critical review of *Der Brand* by Erica Burgauer, "Endlich am Ziel: Deutsche sind Opfer," *Risse* no. 6 (n.d.), 28–32.

50. Nolan, "Germans as Victims," 30–31.

51. Norbert Frei in *Die Zeit*, October 21, 2004.

52. Harald Welzer, "Von der Täter-zur Opfergesellschaft: Zum Umbau der deutschen Erinnerungskultur," in *Erinnern und Verstehen*, ed. Hans Erler (Frankfurt am Main, 2003), 104.

53. Harald Welzer, *Grandpa Wasn't a Nazi: The Holocaust in German Family Remembrance* (New York, 2005), 9. See also the German study published by Harald Welzer, Sabine Moller, and Karoline Tschuggnall, *Opa war kein Nazi. Nationalsozialismus und Holocaust im Familiengedächtnis* (Frankfurt am Main, 2002), and Harald Welzer, "Collateral Damage of Historical Education: National Socialism and the Holocaust in German Family Memory," *Social Research* 75, no.1 (2008): 287–314.

54. See the study commissioned by the American Jewish Committee, Tom W. Smith, *The Holocaust and Its Implications: A Seven-Nation Comparative Study* (New York, 2005), that shows knowledge of the Holocaust to be relatively high but not as high as one might expect. For further evidence that there is a major generational disconnect between children of the German war generation and their grandchildren, see the recently published volume by Moritz Pfeiffer, *Mein Großvater im Krieg 1939–1945: Erinnerung und Fakten im Vergleich* (Bremen, 2012).

55. Welzer, *Grandpa Wasn't a Nazi*, 29.

56. See, for example, two edited collections on this issue: Bill Niven, ed., *Germans as Victims: Remembering the Past in Contemporary Germany* (London, 2006), and Helmut Schmitz, ed., *A Nation of Victims? Representations of German Wartime Suffering from 1945 to the Present* (Amsterdam, 2007). The German jurist and novelist Bernhard Schlink suggests that victims, perpetrators, and their descendents, in order to recover from their mutual truamas, should enter into a process of being able to both remember and forget: "It is leaving the past in the past, in a way that embraces remem-

brance as well as forgetting." Bernhard Schlink, *Guilt about the Past* (Toronto, 2009), 36.

57. An example of an effort to cast Germans as victims took place in a Yom Hashoah lecture by Professor Atina Grossman of Cooper Union in New York before an audience of survivors and Second Generation sons and daughters in Tenafly, New Jersey in 1997. Professor Grossman, herself a Jew, spoke of her research into the suffering of Germans in postwar Berlin. Grossman spoke of the fact that "Germans present themselves as victims as Jews present themselves as survivors." The "bitter experience" of German women provided justification for them to consider themselves victims, she stated. Members of the audience supposedly voiced their "shock and disgust." Further interruptions ensued: "We are not interested." "We don't care!!" Miryam Z. Wahrman, Ph.D., "Six Candles But No Englightenment. A Holocaust Commemoration Marred," http://www.jcn18.com/newstand/wahrman/6candle2.html/. See also Atina Grossmann, *Jews, Germans, and Allies: Close Encounters in Occupied Germany* (Princeton, NJ, 2007). The issue of Second Generation Germans as victims was highlighted in a panel session at the 2007 annual conference of the German Studies Association held in San Diego, California. See http://www.thegsa.org/conferences/2007/GSA2007Prog. pdf/ for panel session 231 "The Discursive Position of Jews and the Holocaust in the Current German Opferdebatte." "Since the Germans who became individual victims at the end of World War II are also fast disappearing, the debate entails bequeathing victim status to the next generation as well as securing it for the group as a whole," quoted in call for papers issued by Anne Rothe, Wayne State University, January 7, 2007.

58. Joschka Fischer in *Die Zeit*, August 28, 2003. Bernhard Schlink expresses a similar view when he writes that "it is not for us Germans to raise objections or feel indignation [as to how victims and their descendents choose to free themselves from a traumatic past]. Instead, we owe respect to the other side's difficult struggle with a past that we made traumatic for them." Schlink, *Guilt about the Past*, 37.

Chapter 15

1. Eugenio Wagner to Abraham Peck, email from April 10, 2005 (translated by Ivan Fehrenbach).

2. Abraham Peck to Eugenio Wagner, email from April 18, 2005.

3. Abraham Peck to Dr. Eva Reinhold-Weisz, excerpt from an email of September 15, 2005.

4. See Part 11.

5. Thomas Meyer, "Rabbis für alle," in *Die Zeit*, no. 34 (December 8, 2004).

6. Julia Gogol, Lutz Henke, Izabela Kazejak, "Eine grosse Tradition ohne Kontinuität. Die Jüdische Gemeinde in Breslau seit 1945." http://oralstory.euv.ffo.de/html /jüdischeGemeinde.html/.

7. Engel, "Anti-Jewish Violence," 21n33. Again, for a comprehensive account of postwar Polish anti-Semitism and violence toward returning survivors of the Holocaust, see Gross, *Fear*.

8. Quoted in script of "Shtetl," http:/www.logtv.com/films/shtetl/scriptmenu .html/.

9. Danuta Dabrowska and Abraham Wein, eds., *The Communities of Lodz and its Region* (Jerusalem, 1976), 154.

10. Ryszard Rosin, ed., *Łęczyca. Dzieje Miasta* (Łęczyca, 2001), 468.

11. Franciszek Pieper, "Auschwitz Concentration Camp: How It Was Used in the Nazi System of Terror and Genocide and the Economy of the Third Reich," in *The Holocaust and History: The Known, the Unknown, the Disputed and the Reexamined*, ed. Michael Berenbaum and Abraham J. Peck (Bloomington, 1998), 371–86.

12. Deborah Dwork and Robert Jan van Pelt, *Auschwitz: 1270 to the Present* (New York, 1996).

13. Jonathan Kaufman, *A Hole in the Heart of the World: Being Jewish in Eastern Europe* (New York, 1997).

Chapter 16

1. Translated from the Italian and German by Eugenio Wagner with the help of Gottfried Wagner and Janice Hamer.

Chapter 17

1. See also Peter Hahne, *Die Macht der Manipulation* (Holzgerlingen, 2005), 18.

2. Primo Levi, *Ist das ein Mensch? Ein autobiographischer Bericht*, trans. into German by Heinz Riedt (Munich, 1992), 7.

3. See also Hubertus Lutterbach and Jürgen Manemann, eds., *Religion und Terror, Stimmen zum 11. September, 2001 aus Christentum, Islam und Judentum* (Münster, 2002).

4. See also Levi, *Ist das ein Mensch?*, 206 (translated from the Italian by Ivan Fehrenbach).

5. Ibid., 206.

6. *New York Times*, May 18, 2005.

7. Micha Brumlik, Doron Kiesel, et al., *Jüdisches Leben in Deutschland seit 1945* (Frankfurt am Main, 1988), 243ff.

8. Wolfgang Wagner, *Leben-Akte*.

9. Lea Fleischmann, *Dies ist nicht mein Land, Eine Jüdin verlässt die Bundesrepublik* (Hamburg, 1980), 261.

Chapter 18

1. Steven A. Luel and Paul Marcus, eds., *Psychoanalytic Reflections on the Holocaust: Selected Essays* (New York, 1984), 172ff.

2. Chloe Safier, "Inheriting the Holocaust: Survivors' Grandchildren Connect Worldwide," (*Presentense*, October 11, 2009), http://presentense.org/magazine/inheriting -the-holocaust-survivors-grandchildren-connect-worldwide/. For a comprehensive

bibliography on Third Generation sources, see Eva Fogelman, "Third Generation Holocaust Survivors Bibliography," http://www.drevafogelman.com/newsletter.html/.

3. Zahava Solomon, "Transgenerational Effects of the Holocaust: The Israeli Research Perspective," in *International Handbook of Multigenerational Legacies of Trauma*, ed. Yael Danieli, 69–84 (Berlin, 1998); Irit Felsen, "Transgenerational Transmission of Effects of the Holocaust: The North American Research Perspective," in *International Handbook of Multigenerational Legacies of Trauma*, ed. Yael Danieli, 43–68 (Berlin, 1998). See also Elise Kayfetz, "The Emotional Domino Effect of the Holocaust: Are the Relationships between Holocaust Survivors and Their Adult Grandchildren Distinct from 'Normal' Grandparent Adult Grandchildren," *If Not Now e-Journal* 7, 2007, http://www.baycrest.org/If_Not_Now/Volume7/default_11223.asp/. For an eloquent discussion of Third Generation issues, see Natalie J. Friedman, "Inherited Trauma: A Member of the Third Generation Speaks," *Connecticut Review*, 28, no. 1 (Spring, 2006): 115–30.

For an analysis of the generational impact of mass trauma on later generations of Armenian survivor families, see Dr. Anie Kalayjian and Marian Weisberg, "Generational Impact of Mass Trauma: The Post-Ottoman Turkish Genocide of the Armenians," http://www.humiliationstudies.org/documents/KalayjianGenerationalTransmission Chapter.pdf/.

4. Paul Rusesabagina (with Tom Zoellner), *An Ordinary Man: An Autobiography* (New York, 2006), 192–93.

5. Quoted in Abraham J. Peck, "'Our Eyes Have Seen Eternity': Memory and Self-Identity among the She'erith Hapletah," *Modern Judaism* 17, no. 1 (February 1997): 69.

Chapter 19

1. Abraham J. Peck, "Introduction," 3ff.

2. Note by Abraham Peck in an email to Gottfried Wagner on April 7, 2006.

3. *Stolpersteine* (Stumbling Blocks) is a national project by Gunter Demnig, a Cologne artist. Cement blocks (10 x 10 x 10 cm.) with brass plaques attached on top commemorating individual victims are set into the ground in front of their former German homes. It has also become a national project in Austria.

4. Baruch Spinoza, Ethik, Lehrsatz 43.

5. My aunt Verena Wagner-Lafferentz, her husband Dr. Bodo Lafferentz, and their children, primarily Amelie Lafferentz-Homann, who refuse to allow any access to the correspondence between Hitler and the Wagner family.

6. With regard to a dispute about historical facts as presented in the long version of the BBC documentary "The Wagner Family" in March 2011, directed by the British filmmaker Tony Palmer.

Chapter 20

1. My grandmother Winifred gave me this information, which can be checked in the land registry at Bayreuth.

Chapter 21

1. For a full listing of courses, faculty, and lectures see http://www.uma.edu/hhrs .html/.

Chapter 22

1. 1956; see my autobiography *Twilight of the Wagners*, with an introduction by Abraham J. Peck.

2. Nazi defamation of modern art as "degenerate" had already begun before 1933, culminating in 1937 in a public exhibition "Entartete Kunst" in Munich. Official bans prevented many artists from pursuing their profession throughout the Nazi era.

3. The new edition with comments by Eva Weissweiler was republished in Cologne in 1994.

4. There was a rumor that he shot himself in his left arm to avoid remaining in Poland after the German Nazi invasion—something for which conclusive evidence has not been found.

5. Cf. Research Forum on Holocaust and Genocide, a debate among six scholars from Israel, the United Kingdom, the United States, and Germany, in *DAPIM Studies on the Shoah*, Journal of the David and Fela Shapell Family Foundation (English ed.), 25 (2011): 301–369; see also Timothy Snyder, *Bloodlands—Europe between Hitler and Stalin* (New York, 2010), and Jörg Baberowski, *Verbrannte Erde. Stalins Herrschaft der Gewalt* (Munich, 2012).

Index

About the Authors

Gottfried Wagner studied musicology, philosophy, and German philology in Germany and Austria. He works internationally as a music historian and multimedia director. He has lived in Italy since 1983.

Abraham J. Peck is the executive director of the Center for Catholic-Jewish Studies and professor in the department of history at Saint Leo University outside Tampa, Florida.